THE MARITIME HISTORY OF
MASSACHUSETTS

The Maritime History of Massachusetts

1783 – 1860

BY

SAMUEL ELIOT MORISON

WITH A FOREWORD BY
BENJAMIN WOODS LABAREE

A Classics Edition
NORTHEASTERN UNIVERSITY PRESS
Boston

IN MEMORIAM

NATHANIEL G. HORTON, 1875–1907
THADDEUS C. DE FRIEZ, 1885–1918
QUINCY SHAW GREENE, 1891–1918

Dear friends and shipmates who died so young—
Nate lost at sea; Ted and Quincy in World War I
After these many years,

"They come transfigured back,
Secure from change in their high-hearted ways,
Beautiful evermore, and with the rays
Of morn on their white shields of expectation."

© 1921, 1941, 1949, 1961 by Samuel Eliot Morison
1979 by Northeastern University Press
Reprinted by special arrangements with Houghton Mifflin Company

Library of Congress Catalog Number 79-5422
ISBN 0-930350-06-5 (cloth)
ISBN 0-930350-04-9 (paper)
MANUFACTURED IN THE UNITED STATES OF AMERICA

90 89 88 87 86 85   5 4

CONTENTS

FOREWORD

Like many of the vessels he so dearly loved, one of Samuel Eliot Morison's best books now returns to sea duty after a brief lay-up for refitting. Laymen and scholars, landsmen and sailors, all will welcome this reappearance of The Maritime History of Massachusetts, 1783-1860.

Morison came to the subject of maritime history, as have most other scholars in the field, from other interests, in his case the Confederation and Federalist periods in Massachusetts. Political history continued to dominate his early writings, and service with the American delegation at Versailles even led to several publications in current foreign affairs. As a native of Boston and a summer resident of the Maine coast, however, Morison never wandered for long from salt water, and he was an accomplished sailor. Inevitably, his love of the sea combined with his knowledge of Massachusetts to produce the first edition of the present volume, published in 1921 by the Houghton Mifflin Company in a Riverside Press edition. Increasingly thereafter, Morison's scholarly writings concerned the sea. His two-volume biography of Christopher Columbus, Admiral of the Ocean Sea *(1942) is in my view his best work, though naval buffs would probably counter with his 15-volume* History of United States Naval Operations in World War II *(1947-62). Nor should we overlook his biographies of* John Paul Jones *(1959) and of* "Old Bruin:" Commodore Matthew Calbraith Perry, 1794-1858 *(1967). And his two volumes on* The European Discovery of America *(1971-74), researched in the field and written after the author had turned eighty, are books that no American historian of any age could have done so well. Over a span of sixty years*

VII

*Morison published nearly fifty books, the majority of which
dealt directly with some aspect of maritime or naval history.*

Why publish a new edition of The Maritime History of
Massachusetts *more than half a century after its initial appearance? To be sure, it has had steady use in history courses at
Harvard, Yale, Williams, and Trinity among other leading col-
leges, an important factor in any publisher's sales plans. But
beyond its commercial value lies the fact that the book has
become, in the general sense of the term, a classic.*

The Maritime History of Massachusetts *is of enduring value,
in the first place, because it clearly and accurately tells us what
we need to know about the subject. Strong chapters based on
solid research illuminate such familiar topics as the China trade,
whaling, and the clippership era along with lesser-known subjects like commerce in the Mediterranean Sea or the fisheries.
Writing as he did before the proliferation of monographic
literature on these topics, Morison's task was a difficult one. By
necessity, therefore, as well as by choice, he depended heavily on
such primary materials as customs-house papers, newspaper
marine lists, logbooks, and journals. With typical candor he explained the problem in his bibliographical essay. "No history of
Massachusetts pays the slightest attention to the maritime aspect
after the colonial period," he wrote. "[With few exceptions]
local histories of the maritime towns are usually inadequate or
misleading on all maritime activities save privateering." On
more specific topics he concluded that there was "no wholly
satisfactory account of the Massachusetts fisheries," that the
whaling industry was in "need of a comprehensive
history . . . paying due attention to the labor and business
aspects," and that Henry Hall's Report on the Shipbuilding Industry (Washington, 1884) "is a most unsatisfactory work."
Searching for documentary materials brought its own frustra-
tions: privately held manuscript collections were regularly
discarded as trash; customs-house records were destroyed by fire;
newspapers in the smaller ports offered disappointingly little*

maritime material. In the face of all these obstacles Morison had largely to make his own trail as a pioneer maritime historian.

In the second place Morison's work stands out because of its scope. The author well knew the extent to which maritime history involved political and social matters along with its more obvious economic implications. He touched upon many significant historical themes long before later scholars would examine them in more detail. In the first edition of The Maritime History of Massachusetts *one could have read of the politics of deference more than thirty years before the debate surrounding Robert E. Brown's* Middle-Class Democracy and the Revolution in Massachusetts, 1691-1780, *of ethnic heterogeneity a generation before Oscar Handlin's* Boston's Immigrants, *of the relationship between seaport and hinterland nearly twenty years before Robert G. Albion's* Rise of New York Port, 1815-1860.

The Maritime History of Massachusetts *has already taught several generations of students and other readers how pervasive the sea's influence is on American history. Without the growth of seaport and overseas markets the farmers of Massachusetts (and by implication other regions as well) could not have expanded production as they did and thereby enjoy a rising standard of living. Without the capital generated by seaborne commerce the development of manufacturing would have been delayed. Without the availability of low-cost shipping the flow of immigrants into America would have been seriously impeded. Morison is careful not to claim too much for his subject, however, and his view of maritime history is startlingly realistic. His privateers are not the financial bonanzas one reads about in lesser books. His whaleships stink and his fishermen sweat. And albeit a little reluctantly perhaps, he calls his clipperships "monuments carved in snow," which "disappeared with the sudden completeness of the wild pigeon."*

Yet another reason for the work's enduring value is that it is so well written. A look at but a few of his descriptions reveals his vivid imagination: Boston, sprawling in the lap of Massachusetts

Bay, "long since outgrown the small rocky peninsula of her birth, and ever in need of a new suit of clothes"; Robert Bennet Forbes, whose brief residence in France may have accounted for "his frank, impetuous nature, so foreign to his Scots blood and Yankee upbringing"; the clippership, of which "the Flying Cloud *was our* Rheims, *the* Sovereign of the Seas *our* Parthenon, *the* Lightning *our Amiens." I know that Morison's language is sometimes too flowery for many of today's students just as many of his references sail unappreciated over their heads, but almost all of his young readers are in the end delighted to discover that history can be a joy to read.*

On nearly every page Morison relates an anecdote that both illuminates the point he is making as well as enlivens the text. There is Captain Benjamin Crowninshield returning to Salem with high-value coffee against his orders to bring back pepper, whose price had fallen. Or the Brewster ship captain, Elijah Cobb, risking his life in the turmoil of revolutionary France to reap a profit on his cargo of provisions. Morison never forgot what Senator Beveridge told him when asked why his Life of John Marshall *was so popular. "The trouble with you professors," he explained, "is that you write for each other. I write for people almost completely ignorant of American history. . . ." So did Morison, and with far more success than any other American historian of this century.*

The Maritime History of Massachusetts *stands as a monument to a great American historian. Factually sound, bold in its interpretations, and written with clarity and vigor, the book is a model for all historians, whether they occupy arm-chair, desk-chair, or professorial chair.*

Benjamin Woods Labaree

Mystic Seaport, Connecticut
September 1979

Here is no catalogue of ships, reader, nor naval chronicle, but a story of maritime enterprise; of the shipping, sea-borne commerce, whaling, and fishing belonging to one American commonwealth. I have chosen to catch the story at half flood, when Massachusetts vessels first sought Far-Eastern waters, and to stay with it only so long as wind and sail would serve. For to one who has sailed a clipper ship, even in fancy, all later modes of ocean carriage must seem decadent.

Having written these pages for your enjoyment, I have not burdened them with citations; but, having discovered much sunken historical treasure, and taken of it but sparingly, I have added some sailing directions and soundings thereto in a bibliography. Therein also, that this preface may be short, I have thanked the many persons who have aided me in the search. But I cannot close without particular acknowledgment to Captain Arthur H. Clark, author of "The Clipper Ship Era," for bearing with my constant demands on his time, patience, and memory; and to Dr. Octavius T. Howe, who placed freely at my disposal the results of many years' research on the Argonauts of forty-nine.

S. E. MORISON

Harvard University, February 1921

Forty years have passed; and the "sea-captains young or old" with whom I sailed in other days, and who gave me a vast amount of sea lore, have departed on their final voyage. Many mistakes in the earlier editions have been rectified, and the data in recent books, especially Carl C. Cutler's "Five Hundred Sailing Records" (1952) and "Greyhounds of the Sea," have been incorporated.

Boston, March 17, 1961

Essex County includes Salem, Marblehead, Cape Ann, Newburyport, and all the seacoast north of Boston and its suburbs. Hingham and the South Shore (except Cohasset) are in Plymouth County, which also includes a few towns on Buzzard's Bay. Barnstable County is synonymous with Cape Cod. Bristol County includes New Bedford, Fairhaven, and the Taunton valley. Nantucket is a separate county, and Martha's Vineyard and the Elizabeth Islands constitute the "County of Dukes County." It will be understood that the term "town," in this book, has no urban connotation, being used in its New England sense of a territorial and political unit.

When three dimensions are given for a vessel, they are length on deck, greatest breadth of beam, and depth of hold.

CHAPTER I

COAST AND SEA

MASSACHUSETTS has a history of many moods, every one of which may be traced in the national character of America. By chance, rather than design, this short strip of uninviting coast-line became the seat of a great experiment in colonization, self-government, and religion. For a generation, Massachusetts shared with her elder sister, Virginia, leadership in the American Revolution. For another generation, with her offspring Connecticut, she opposed a static social system to the ferment of revolutionary France. With the world peace of 1815 she quickened into new life, harnessed her waterfalls to machine industry, bred statesmen, seers, and poets, generated radical and revolutionary thought. The Civil War rubbed smooth her rough corners, sapped her vitality to preserve the Union and build the Great West, and drew into the vacuum new faiths and peoples.

Through every phase and period, save the last, breathes a rugged faith and blows the east wind. For two hundred years the Bible was the spiritual, the sea the material sustenance of Massachusetts. The pulse of her life-story, like the surf on her coast-line, beat once with the nervous crash of storm-driven waves on

I

granite rock; but now with the soothing pour of ground-swell on golden sands. Now and again a greater wave rolls in with crested menace, but ends in harmless curl of foam on shelving beach.

Massachusetts proper (for I do not speak of her first-born, Maine, whose maritime history deserves a special volume) has a coast-line of some seven hundred and fifty miles, following the high-water mark. It begins "three English miles to the northward" of a "great river there commonly called Monomack river, alias Merrimack river," as King Charles I determined. The Merrimac now means whirring spindles, sordid tenements, and class struggles. But for two centuries and more its tidal waters, flowing between towns that bear the old-world names of Salisbury, Amesbury, Haverhill, and Newbury, midwifed hundreds of noble vessels; and Newburyport was the mart for a goodly portion of interior New England.

From the river mouth to Cape Ann, the long sandy finger of Plum Island protects a region sung by Whittier, where

Broad meadows reached out seaward, the tidal creeks between, And hills rolled wave-like inland, with oaks and walnuts green.

Here even the agriculture was maritime; not creaking wains, but broad-beamed "gundalows" collected the harvest of salt hay. Yet seagoing vessels could make their way up to Rowley and Essex, and the white spires of old Ipswich.

Once past the gleaming dunes of Castle Neck, and across Squam River (which may lead us, if we will, to Gloucester's back door), we are fairly on Cape Ann. This rocky fist of Massachusetts, like the slender, sandy arm of Cape Cod, has led whole generations of boys afishing. Hotels and villas and granite quarries now crowd its shores, once white with drying codfish, and more funnels than sails now break the horizon. But on its seaward thrust you may still find spots where, but for the wail of whistling buoy, and the twin light towers of Thatcher's, nothing has changed since the "spectral host, defying stroke of steel and aim of gun," assaulted the Cape Ann garrison.

Cape Cod and Cape Ann are the two horns of Massachusetts Bay; two giant limbs thrown seaward, like the wings of a fish-weir, to guide sea-borne commerce into Boston's fruitful embrace. But Cape Ann and its southern base (together called the North Shore of Massachusetts) contains certain pockets, Gloucester and Salem and Marblehead, which for two centuries managed to cull from the choicest of the catch. Neither imposing nor spectacular, this North Shore; yet the massed and multi-colored rocks, with bits of beach or shingle nestling between, have a subtle charm that every summer attracts thousands of city-dwellers from all parts of America. Factory cities and yachting centers have now replaced the fishing villages; Italian gardens and palaces blot out even the memory of the rugged seashore farms.

In the lap of Massachusetts Bay sprawls Boston; long since outgrown the small rocky peninsula of her birth, and ever in need of a new suit of clothes. Point Shirley at the north, Hull at the south, and the rocky barrier of the Brewsters, as tough as the Puritan elder whose name they bear, shield a gracious, island-dotted bay, and a deep, landlocked inner harbor. The Blue Hills of Milton, unchanged from the day they caught the first white man's searching gaze, make a serene background to the nervous, bustling activity of the modern seaport.

With Nantasket Beach begins the South Shore,

ending at Plymouth in the armpit of Cape Cod. In Cohasset the granite skeleton of Massachusetts protrudes for the last time, making a small fishing harbor behind a cluster of tide-swept rocks, from which Minot's Light, flashing one-four-three, warns shipping. Beyond we cross the southern boundary of the Massachusetts-Bay Colony, and enter the "Old Colony," as it is still called, of Plymouth Plantation. This South Shore is a complete contrast to the North, even in climate; a succession of barrier-beaches in flattish curves, backed by salt marshes and wooded country with gentle contours. There is another tiny harbor at Scituate, between which township and Marshfield the North River admits a thin stream of tidewater well inland. Then come Salt-House or Duxbury Beach and the Gurnet, Saquish and Long Beach, protecting Plymouth Bay from the Atlantic rollers. But Plymouth Bay, a series of tortuous channels between shoals and grassy flats, could not serve a great trading community. In compensation, Pilgrim grit and native white oak made of its shores and the North River banks, a great shipbuilding center.

Once past the wooded bluffs of Manomet, we are on the biceps of "th' Cape," Cape Cod. East twenty-five miles into the Atlantic, then north by west another score, pushes this frail spit of sand, ending in a skinny finger forever beckoning seaward the sons of Massachusetts. The Cape is unique, this side of Brittany. It has been the greatest nursery of seamen in North America, but its offspring have had to sail from other ports than their own. Save for the great haven within its finger-tip, the Cape has no harbor fit for larger than fishing vessels; and Provincetown, in its ocean-walled isolation, could never become a center of commerce.

The Bay side of Cape Cod is to-day the most un-

4

spoiled maritime section of the Massachusetts mainland. From the car-shops of Sagamore to the artist-
fishing colony at Provincetown, not one smoking factory chimney, and only a handful of summer palaces,
mar the simplicity of beach, dune, and marsh. Shin-
gle-sided cottages of the ancient style, shell-white
or weather-rusted, line the sandy roads; slim spires
spindling up from a mass of foliage betray a village;
low pine-clad hills break the sky-line. As we proceed
northward, the Cape grows wilder and bleaker, up
to the wind-swept highlands of Truro, the topgallant
forecastle of Massachusetts.

At Chatham, on the "back side" of the Cape, we
reach once more the summer estates' "No Trespass-
ing" signs, which hardly end before our circuit of the
Massachusetts coast is concluded at Westport. Narragansett Bay belongs to Rhode Island; but one of its
tidal tributaries, the Taunton River, has from time
immemorial sent shad and alewives up into the heart
of the Old Colony; and in times historic, floated down
ships.

Detached from the mainland, annexed to Massachusetts only in 1691, since held by the slenderest of
political ties, is a diadem of island jewels — the Elizabeth Islands and Martha's Vineyard; Chappaquiddick
and Muskeget, Tuckernuck and Nantucket. Hardly
a spot on the New England coast lacks passionate
devotees; but the worshipers of Nantucket form a cult
of positive fanatics. Anchored on the edge of the Gulf
Stream, this bit of terminal moraine has a unique
climate, flora, landscape, and population. On her
south shore endlessly breaking, the southwest swells
impart their surge to the long grasses of Nantucket's
flower-starred moors. Under their lee nestles the one
unspoiled seaport town of New England; a town in

5

which every house built before 1840 — and many later, were sired by the sea. For this island, peopled by Quaker exiles from Puritan persecution, created that deep-sea whaling, whose peculiar blend of enterprise, dare-deviltry, and ruthlessness forms one of the most precious memories of our maritime past. New Bedford, and the minor ports of Buzzard's Bay, were but mainland colonies of Nantucket; although in course of time, like the colonies of ancient Greece, they surpassed their mother state.

Yet for all this wealth of coast-line and abundance of good harbors, maritime Massachusetts enjoyed no natural advantage over other sections of the Atlantic coast. Cape Breton and Newfoundland are nearer the Grand Banks; hundred-harbored Maine offers better anchorage. Chesapeake Bay is more deeply indented, more richly supplied with agricultural wealth, more centrally placed, and seldom obstructed by snow or fog. No great river comparable to the St. Lawrence, the Hudson, or the Delaware, tapping the wealth of a mighty interior, makes a great trading city on the Massachusetts coast inevitable. Boston has always felt this handicap; her persistent place among the greater American cities, in spite of it, is a miracle of human enterprise. The back country, limited by a political frontier in the north and a mountain barrier in the Berkshires, produced no staple to compare with those of the middle and southern colonies. Boston is two hundred miles nearer northern Europe than New York: but Nova Scotia is nearer still. Boston Harbor freezes but once a generation: but Massachusetts Bay in sailing-ship days was dangerous water in dirty weather. Its irregular bottom gives the lead-line no clue. When a northeast snowstorm obscured Boston Light, a mistake of a quarter-point fetched up many a good ship on Cohasset rocks or the Graves. Before the days of cheap chronometers, when a slight mistake in longitude meant Nantucket South Shoals, vessels from the West Indies, South America, and the Orient dared approach Boston or Salem only by the long détour of Vineyard Sound, Nantucket Sound, and the back side of the Cape. Returning East-Indiamen were sometimes detained for weeks in Wood's Hole or Vineyard Haven, awaiting a chance to weather Monomoy and Pollock Rip, whilst fair wind and sheltered waters pled the advantages of New York. The Pilgrims began to agitate for a Cape Cod canal as soon as they discovered the head of Buzzard's Bay; but it was not until 1914 that the canal was built.

Nature seemed to doom Massachusetts to insignificance; to support perhaps a line of poor fishing stations and hardscrabble farms, half-starved between the two hungry mouths of Hudson and St. Lawrence. Man and a rugged faith have made her what she is. With but a tithe of the bounty that Nature grants more favored lands, the Puritan settlers made their land the most fruitful not only in things of the spirit, but in material wealth. Even Nature's apparent liabilities were turned into assets. The long-lying snow gave cheap transport inland, the river rapids turned grist and fulling mills, then textile factories; even granite and ice became currency in Southern and Oriental trade.

The ocean knows no favorites. Her bounty is reserved for those who have the wit to learn her secrets, the courage to bear her buffets, and the will to persist, through good fortune and ill, in her rugged service.

CHAPTER II

THE COLONIAL BACKGROUND

1602-1760

THE maritime history of Massachusetts, so far as white men are concerned, began when some Basque or Norman or "Portingale" unknown, blown off Grand Banks by an easterly gale, found shelter under the lee of Cape Cod or Cape Ann. Finding the Indians ready to truck, and the adjacent waters teeming with fish, he and his kind returned. By the time the *Mayflower* sailed, one could find men in any fishing port from Bristol to Bilbao who could tell the bearings of Cape Ann from Cape Cod, and compare the holding-ground in every harbor from Narragansett to Passamaquoddy. When the Pilgrims were casting about for a permanent settlement, the *Mayflower's* pilot recommended "a good harbor on the other headland of the bay, almost right over against Cape Cod . . . in which he had been once." They would have fared better had they taken this seaman's advice.

Bartholomew Gosnold visited Cape Cod and the Elizabeth Islands in 1602, and named them. De Champlain, two years later, made a good harbor chart of Gloucester ("le Beau Port"), fought with natives at Nauset ("Mallebarre"), and looked in at the site of Boston; but New France he preferred to build along the mighty outlet of the Great Lakes. The *Onrust* sailed around Cape Cod to Nahant, and returned to Manhattan.

Captain John Smith, in 1614, was the first English-man to examine the Massachusetts coast, and to give

8

it that name. Erecting his fish-flakes (wooden frames for drying fish) on the Island of Monhegan, he sent one shipload to England, and another to Spain, where it fetched five Spanish dollars the quintal. The six months' voyage cleared fifteen hundred pounds. In the meantime he explored the coast, and told the world about it in his "Description of New England," a sane, conservative exposition of the natural advantages of Massachusetts. For his pioneer work, sound advice, and hearty support of the Pilgrim colony, John Smith should rightly be regarded as the founder of maritime Massachusetts. Yet in all our glut of tercentenaries, this honest, valiant captain has been wellnigh forgotten in the region that he served so well.

Stirred by Captain Smith's writings, and still more by his success, English fishermen began to crowd their Celtic rivals from New England waters. Now, Smith himself had urged his countrymen to save time and "overhead" by basing the fisheries in New England, and combining them with fur-trading and shipbuilding; rather than sending out fresh crews and equipment every summer. In 1623 the "Dorchester Adventurers," a group of West-County capitalists, endeavored to put his suggestion into practice. A crew of men landed at the site of Stage Fort Park on Gloucester Harbor, built huts, flakes and a fishing stage, commenced tillage, and drew plans for a fishing-trading colony, with church, school, and shipyards. The immediate experiment failed (though not before a full fare had been sent to Spain); but the promoters were reorganized as the "Governor and Company of the Massachusetts-Bay," with a title to all land between the Merrimac and the Charles, from sea to sea.

In the meantime, the Plymouth Colony had arrived.

The Pilgrim fathers sailed with high hopes and a burning faith, but with few preparations and no clear idea of how to make a living on the Atlantic coast. Intending to "finde some place aboute Hudsons river for their habitation," the "deangerous shoulds and roring breakers" about Monomoy forced the *Mayflower* to "bear up againe for the Cape." Had the sands of Cape Cod afforded a sustenance, they might well have tarried at the site of Provincetown. But the cleared Indian cornfields across the bay, vacant through a providential pestilence, tempted them to the spot named Plymouth on Captain Smith's map.

Save for the overwhelming need of saving precious lives, this choice was unfortunate. Plymouth was deeply embayed, devoid of a dry landing place or anchorage for large vessels; and ill provided with back country. The Pilgrims learned the secrets of fur-trading and fishing only after costly failures. They were mercilessly exploited by English financiers. For two generations they owned no great shipping. Reënforced by the Puritan emigration of a later decade, they eventually spread out along Cape Cod, the South Shore, and Buzzard's Bay. Their faith and courage are beyond disparagement; but had Massachusetts been peopled alone by the Pilgrim seed, it would long have remained a mere slender line of cornfields, trucking posts, and fishing stations.

In 1630, ten years after its settlement, the Plymouth Colony contained but three hundred white people. At that time the Colony of Massachusetts-Bay, founded only at the end of 1628, had over two thousand inhabitants. Within thirteen years the numbers had reached sixteen thousand, more than the rest of the continental colonies combined; and the characteristic maritime activities of Massachusetts — fishing, shipping, and West India trading — were already well under way.

It was not the intention of the founders of Massachusetts-Bay to establish a predominantly maritime community. The first and foremost object of Winthrop and Dudley and Endecot and Saltonstall was to found a church and commonwealth in which Calvinist Puritans might live and worship according to the Word of God, as they conceived it. They aimed to found a New England, purged of Old England's corruptions, but preserving all her goodly heritage. They intended the economic foundation of New England, as of Old England and Virginia, to be large landed estates, tilled by tenants and hired labor.

In this they failed. The New England town, based on freehold and free labor, sprang up instead of the Old English manor. And for only a decade was agriculture the mainstay of Massachusetts. The constant inflow of immigrants, requiring food and bringing goods, enabled the first comers to profit by corn-growing and cattle-raising. This could not continue. "For the present, we make a shift to live," wrote a pessimistic pioneer in 1637; "but hereafter, when our numbers increase, and the fertility of the soil doth decrease, if God discover not means to enrich the land, what shall become of us I will not determine."

God performed no miracle on the New England soil. He gave the sea. Stark necessity made seamen of would-be planters. The crisis came in 1641, when civil war in England cut short the flow of immigrants. "All foreign commodities grew scarce," wrote Governor Winthrop, "and our own of no price. Corn would buy nothing; a cow which cost last year £20 might now be bought for 4 or £5 . . . These straits set our people

on work to provide fish, clapboards, plank, etc., . . .
and to look out to the West Indies for a trade . . ."

In these simple sentences, Winthrop explains how
maritime Massachusetts came to be. The gravelly,
boulder-strewn soil was back-breaking to clear, and
afforded small increase to unscientific farmers. No
staple of ready sale in England, like Virginia tobacco
or Canadian beaver, could be produced or easily obtained. Forest, farms, and sea yielded lumber, beef,
and fish. But England was supplied with these from
the Baltic, and by her own farmers and fishermen. Unless a new market be found for them, Massachusetts
must stew in her own juice. It was found in the West
Indies — tropical islands which applied slave labor to
exotic staples like sugar-cane, but imported every necessity of life. More and more they became dependent
on New England for lumber, provisions, and dried
fish. More and more the New England ships and merchants who brought these necessities, controlled the
distribution of West-India products.

Massachusetts went to sea, then, not of choice, but
of necessity. Yet the transition was easy and natural.
"Farm us!" laughed the waters of the Bay in May-
time, to a weary yeoman, victim of the 'mocking
spring's perpetual loss.' "Here thou may'st reap
without sowing — yet not without God's blessing;
't was the Apostles' calling." And with sharp scorn
spake the waters to an axeman, hewing a path from
river landing to new allotment: "Hither thy road!
And of the oak thou wastest, make means to ride it!
Southward, dull clod, and barter the logs thou would'st
spend to warm thy silly body, for chinking doubloons,
as golden as the sunlight that bathes the Spanish
main."

Materials and teachers for a maritime colony were

already at hand. The founders had been careful to secure artisans, and tools for all useful trades, that Massachusetts might not have the one-sided development of Virginia. Fishing had not ceased with the failure of the Gloucester experiment. Dorchester, the first community "that set upon the trade of fishing in the bay," was little more than a transference to New England soil of Dorset fishing interests. Scituate was settled by a similar company. The rocky peninsula of Marblehead, with its ample harbor, attracted fisherfolk from Cornwall and the Channel Islands, who cared neither for Lord Bishop nor Lord Brethren. Their descendants retained a distinct dialect, and a jealous exclusiveness for over two centuries. Marblehead obeyed or not the laws of the Great and General Court, as suited her good pleasure; but as long as she 'made fish,' the Puritan magistrates did not interfere. Literally true was the Marblehead fisherman's reproof to an exhorting preacher: "Our ancestors came not here for religion. Their main end was to catch fish!"

Equally true was Marblehead's protest against an export tax in 1669. "Fish is the only great stapple which the Country produceth for forraine parts and is so benefitiall for making returns for what wee need." The firm-fleshed codfish of northern waters is unsurpassed for salting and drying. Colonial Massachusetts packed three grades. Dun fish, the best, was 'made' by alternately burying and drying the larger-sized cod until it mellowed sufficiently for the taste of Catholic Europe. Portugal and Spain, where Captain John Smith sold his first fare, Southern France and the 'Western' and 'Wine' Islands, were the markets for dun fish; and for barrel- and pipe-staves as well. In exchange, Cadiz salt; Madeira and Canary wine; Bilbao iron and pieces of eight; Malaga grapes and

13

Valencia oranges were carried to English and colonial markets. When Charles II began tightening up colonial trade, Sir George Downing, of Harvard's first graduating class, saw to it that this Mediterranean traffic was allowed to continue. The middling grade of dried codfish, easy to transport, to keep, and to prepare, was a favorite winter food of colonial farmers. The lowest-grade dried fish, together with pickled mackerel, bass, and alewives, was the principal medium in West-India trade. As John Smith predicted, "Nothing is here to be had which fishing doth hinder, but further us to obtain." Puritan Massachusetts derived her ideals from a sacred book; her wealth and power from the sacred cod.

Shipping was the other key industry of the colony. Fishing would have brought little wealth, had Massachusetts depended on outside interests for vessels — as she must to-day for freight-cars. Distribution, not production, brought the big returns in 1620 as in 1920. Massachusetts shipbuilding began with the launching in 1631 of Governor Winthrop's *Blessing of the Bay*, on the same Mystic River that later gave birth to the beautiful Medford-built East-Indiamen. By 1660 shipbuilding had become a leading industry in Newbury, Ipswich, Gloucester, Salem, and Boston. The great Puritan emigration brought many shipwrights and master builders, such as William Stephen, who "prepared to go to Spayne, but was persuaded to New England." A four-hundred-ton ship *Seafort* [1] was built

[1] The method of computing tonnage in colonial times was the number of "tuns" (double hogsheads) of wine a ship could carry. From the Revolution to 1865, tonnage meant a vessel's capacity in tons of forty cubic feet each, estimated by the following formula (L = length on deck, B = greatest breadth, D = depth of hold):

$$\frac{(L - 3/5\ B)\ X\ B\ X\ D}{95}$$

at Boston in 1648, but wrecked on the Spanish coast, decoyed by false lights ashore.

Few Massachusetts-built vessels were so large as this; four hundred tons meant a great ship as late as 1815. The colonial fleet for the most part consisted of small single-decked sloops, the usual rig for coasters, and lateen-rigged ketches, the favorite rig for fishermen, of twenty to thirty tons burthen, and thirty-five to fifty feet long.[1] Good oak timber and pine spars were so plentiful that building large ships on order or speculation for the English market soon became a recognized industry. Rope-walks were established, hempen sail-cloth was made on hand looms, anchors and coarse iron-work were forged from bog ore, and wooden 'trunnels' (tree nails) were used for fastening planking to frame.

The English Navigation Act of 1651, restraining colonial commerce to English and colonial vessels, gave an increased impetus to New England ship-building; for the Dutch, with their base at New Amsterdam, had been serious competitors. In another generation, vessels built and owned in New England were doing the bulk of the carrying trade from Chesapeake Bay to England and southern Europe. "Many a fair ship had her framing and finishing here," wrote Edward Johnson about 1650, "besides lesser vessels, barques and ketches; many a Master, beside common Seamen, had their first learning in this Colony."

Half the breadth was generally used in lieu of depth after the War of 1812, and sometimes so used as early as 1789. William Stephen in 1661 contracted to build for Salem parties a two-decked ship, 91 × 23 × 9½ at £3.5 per ton. Her tonnage would be 190. The *Mayflower's* was 180 (according to Bradford), but she was probably somewhat shorter and deeper.

[1] See the model of the ketch *Sparrow-Hawk*, which brought forty passengers to Plymouth Colony in 1626, in the Peabody Museum, Salem; and her very ribs, preserved for two centuries in Cape Cod sand, now in the basement of Pilgrim Hall, Plymouth.

The shipmaster's calling has always been of high repute in Massachusetts. Only the clergy, the magistracy, and the shipowning merchants, most of whom were retired master mariners, enjoyed a higher social standing in colonial days. The ship *Trial* of two hundred tons, one of the first vessels built at Boston, was commanded by Mr. Thomas Coytmore, a gentleman of good estate, "a right godly man, and an expert seaman," says Governor Winthrop — who made his fourth matrimonial venture with Captain Coytmore's widow. The foremast hands were recruited in part from English seaports, but mostly from the adventure-loving youth of the colonies. When Captain John Turner came back from the West Indies in a fifteen-ton pinnace, with so many pieces of eight that the neighbors hissed "Piracy!"; when the *Trial* "by the help of a diving tub," recovered gold and silver from a sunken Spanish galleon; what ploughboy did not long for a sea-change from grubbing stumps and splitting staves? When gray November days succeeded the splendor of Indian summer, the clang of wild geese overhead summoned the spirit of youth to wealth and adventure

> "Là-bas, où les Antilles bleues
> Se pâment sous l'ardeur de l'astre occidental."

A sea voyage, moreover, was an easy escape from the strict conventions and prying busybodies of New England towns. Not even Cotton Mather could extend the long arm of Puritan elder into cabin and forecastle. "It is a matter of saddest complaint that there should be no more *Serious Piety* in the *Sea-faring Tribe*," states his "Sailours Companion and Counsellor." "Old *Ambrose* called the Sea, *The School of Vertue*. It afflicts all the vertuous here, that the *Mari-*

16

ners of our Dayes do no more to make it so." His subsequent enumeration of seamen's vices suggests that the clipper-ship crews could have taught little to these sons of pious Puritan households. "No Sundays off soundings" doubtless held good in the seventeenth century as in the nineteenth.

Edward Randolph, an unfriendly but accurate English observer, describes Massachusetts in 1676 as a thriving maritime colony. Thirty of her merchants have fortunes of ten to twenty thousand pounds. The colony feeds itself, and produces a surplus for export to Virginia and the West Indies, as well as "all things necessary for shipping and naval furniture." Four hundred and thirty vessels between thirty and two hundred and fifty tons burthen "are built in and belong to that jurisdiction." They traffic with the West Indies, and with most parts of Europe, carrying their own or other colonies' produce, distributing return ladings throughout continental colonies and West Indies, "so that there is little left for the merchants residing in England to import into any of the plantations." They pay no attention to the English laws regulating trade. They have even sent ships to 'Scanderoon' (Alexandretta); to Guinea, the slave mart; and to Madagascar, the pirate rendezvous. Randolph's conclusion is significant. "It is the great care of the merchants to keep their ships in constant employ, which makes them trye all ports to force a trade, whereby they abound with all sorts of commodities, and *Boston may be esteemed the mart town of the West Indies.*"

Colonial Massachusetts, then, was a chain of prosperous trading towns and fishing villages, separated from the wilderness by a belt of farming communities. The key industries were fishing and shipbuilding.

The secret of maritime success was that persistent enterprise which led her merchant-shipowners to "trye all ports" and to risk all freights.

Even farming Massachusetts clung to coast-line or Connecticut River, a feeder of the Sound ports. Worcester County was a wilderness until 1730. For over a century after the *Mayflower's* voyage, few Massachusetts farms were more than thirty miles distant from tidewater, and all felt the ebb and flow of sea-borne commerce. "If the merchant trade be not kept on foot, they fear greatly their corne and cattel will lye in their hands," writes Edward Johnson. A Yankee farmer prospered only through foreign markets for his industrial by-products, such as bar-reled beef and pork, hewn lumber and staves; bowls, buckets, brooms, ox-bows, axe-helves, and the like, whittled out by firelight in long winter evenings. The influence of West-India trade and the fisheries pene-trated the remotest frontier settlements of New England.

*

* *

The half-century of peace and virtual independence, which permitted this extraordinary development, was followed by forty years of war, Indian massacres, pestilence, witchcraft, and loss of liberty. In 1691 the Massachusetts-Bay Colony was combined with Plymouth, the islands of Martha's Vineyard and Nantucket, and the provinces of Maine and Sagadahoc, under a royal charter as the "Province of Massachusetts-Bay." Imperial control was tightened, but not enough to prevent another outburst of prosperity after the Peace of Utrecht in 1713.

That date begins a general broadening-out in all

lines of marine activity. In codfishing it marks an era, both by the launching of the first schooner at Gloucester, and the British acquisition of Newfoundland and Nova Scotia, with their convenient shores and teeming waters. Admission to the French West Indies in 1717 extended our fish market, and increased our importations of molasses, until sixty-three Massachusetts distilleries were running full time. New England rum replaced beer and cider as the favorite American beverage, and supplanted French brandy as medium in the 'Guinea trade.' Slaving — popular tradition and Faneuil[1] Hall to the contrary notwithstanding — never became a leading interest of Massachusetts; Boston and Salem as slaving ports were poor rivals to Newport. But most Boston merchants owned slaves as house servants, and bought and sold them with other merchandise.

Massachusetts also traded with the mainland of South America. At Surinam fish and lumber were exchanged for the products of the Dutch East Indies; at Honduras logwood and mahogany were cut for the London market. New England provisions even found their way into Brazil by way of Madeira.

Shipbuilding increased so rapidly that in 1724 several master builders of London petitioned the Lords of Trade "not to encourage ship building in New England because workmen are drawn thither." Duxbury shipbuilding began in 1719, when Thomas Prince built his first vessel of wild cherry wood; and the North River became a serious competitor to the Merrimac.

In 1713, the merchants of Boston proposed "the Erecting of a Light Hous and Lanthorn" at the

---

[1] Properly pronounced "Funnel," and so spelled on Peter's tombstone. But the last generation of schoolma'ms has taught us to call it "Fan-you-well."

harbor entrance; and three years later Boston Light, the first lighthouse in the new world, was completed. "A great Gun to answer Ships in a Fog" was shortly added to its equipment. Marine insurance began at Boston a few years later. Offshore whaling was perhaps the most important development of the half-century before the Revolution. Cape Cod taught Nantucket how to harpoon whales, but Nantucket went her teacher one better when in 1715 Christopher Hussey fitted out a vessel to pursue sperm whales, and tow them ashore. A few years later, by erecting brick try-works on shipboard, the Nantucket whalers were able to extend their cruising radius to the coast of Brazil and the Arctic Ocean.

Massachusetts enjoyed peace for three-quarters of the period from 1713 to the Revolution. In war-time her fishing fleet was dismantled, but the fishermen found exciting employment on armed merchantmen bearing letters of marque and reprisal. A typical Massachusetts-built vessel of the larger class, subject of our unique pre-Revolutionary ship portrait, was the *Bethel*, owned by the Quincy family.[1] Armed with fourteen guns and carrying thirty-eight men, she captured in 1748 by sheer Yankee bluff a Spanish treasure ship of twenty-four guns and one hundred and ten men, "worth the better part of an hundred thousand pounds sterling." So congenial, in fact, did our provincial seamen find privateering, that many could not bear to give it up when peace was concluded. In consequence, not a few were hanged in chains on Bird Island or Nix's Mate, whereby every passing seaman might gain a moral lesson.

Boston increased in population from about seven thousand in 1690 to about seventeen thousand in 1740.

[1] The *c* in this name is pronounced like *s*.

THE COLONIAL BACKGROUND

It was the largest town in the English colonies until
1755, when passed by Philadelphia, and "the principal
mart of trade in North America" for a much longer
period. "Boston Pier or the Long Wharf," built in
1710, extended King (now State) Street some two
thousand feet into deep water. Wealthy merchants
came from overseas to share the results of Puritan
thrift and energy. Thomas Amory, of London, after
visiting Lisbon, Amsterdam, Charleston, Philadelphia,
and New York, found Boston their superior in commercial activity, and settled there in 1720.

A fresh tide of immigration was beginning to flow
into Massachusetts Bay, and a good part of it was non-
English. The Yankee race, in fact, had never been all
English. Were I asked to mention two Massachusetts
families who generation after generation sent their
sons to sea, I should name the Devereux and the
Delano, both of French origin. In Mr. Whitmore's
blue-book of Boston provincial society, about one-
third of the families are of non-English origin; principally French and Scots, like the Faneuils and Bow-
doins, Shaws and Cunninghams, but including Germans like Caspar Crowninshield and Dutchmen like
John Wendell. Irishmen like Patrick Tracy, of Newburyport, and Captain James Magee, of Boston, rose
to eminence in maritime pursuits, and married into the
old Puritan families. Thomas Bardin, a Welshman,
founded the Hanover forge where North River vessels
obtained their anchors and ironwork. Another Welshman taught Lynn to specialize in women's shoes,
which before the Revolution became an important
medium in the coasting trade.

Equally false are two contrasting notions: — the
one that New England was of 'pure Anglo-Saxon
stock' at the Revolution; the other that the Revo-

21

lution was an Irish movement. These are the pet lapdogs of modern race snobbery. The seventeenth-century stock completely absorbed its eighteenth-century accretions, both English and non-English. To outsiders, as late as 1824, the population of seaboard Massachusetts seemed, and was, racially homogeneous as that of Brittany. But the race was not Anglo-Saxon, or Irish. It was Yankee, a new Nordic amalgam on an English Puritan base; already in 1750 as different in its character and its dialect from the English as the Australians are to-day. A tough but nervous, tenacious but restless race; materially ambitious, yet prone to introspection, and subject to waves of religious emotion. Conservative in its ideas of property and religion, yet (in the eighteenth century) radical in business and government. A people with few social graces, yet capable of deep friendships and abiding loyalties; law-abiding yet individualistic, and impatient of restraint by government or regulation in business; ever attempting to repress certain traits of human nature, but finding an outlet in broad, crude humor and deep-sea voyages. A race whose typical member is eternally torn between a passion for righteousness and a desire to get on in the world. Religion and climate, soil and sea, here brewed of mixed stock a new people.

From 1740 to the Revolution, Boston declined slightly in population — owing probably to frequent epidemics, high taxes, and high cost of fuel — but the smaller seaports came up. A glance at the Georgian mansions of Michael Dalton and Jonathan Jackson at Newburyport; of John Heard at Ipswich; of Winthrop Sargent at Gloucester; of George Cabot at Beverly; of Richard Derby and Nathaniel Ropes at Salem; of Jeremiah Lee and 'King' Hooper at Marblehead, and the latter's country seat in Danvers, will convince the most skeptical that wealth and good taste came out of the sea, into these little towns; mere villages they would be called to-day. Marblehead in 1744 had ninety vessels in active service, two hundred acres covered with fish-flakes, and an annual catch worth £34,000 sterling. In 1765, with just under five thousand inhabitants it was the sixth town in the thirteen colonies; behind Newport, but ahead of Salem, Baltimore, and Albany.

Why was maritime Massachusetts so prominent in the American Revolution? Because she was so democratic! answers the bright scholar. Here is another fallacy I would puncture in passing. American democracy was not born in the cabin of the *Mayflower* or in Boston town meeting, but on the farming, fighting frontier of all the colonies, New England included. Seaboard Massachusetts has never known such a thing as a social democracy; and in seaboard Massachusetts, as elsewhere, inequalities of wealth have made political democracy a sham. Few town meetings have been held near tidewater where the voice of shipowner, merchant, or master mariner did not carry more weight than that of fisherman, counting-room clerk, or common seaman. Society in seaboard New England was carefully stratified, and the Revolution brought little change save in personnel. The 'quality' dressed differently from the poor and middle classes, lived in finer houses, expected and received deference, and 'ran' their communities because they controlled the working capital of ships and goods. The only difference from old-world society lay in the facility in passing from one class to another.

Marblehead has always had a reputation for democracy, especially after the departure of 'King'

Hooper. But Bentley, apropos the death of Colonel Glover in 1805, remarked, "The leading men had power nowhere else known in N. England." Visiting Andover, the same keen observer noted the young people assembling to dance, "in classes according to their ages, not with any regard to their condition, as in the Seaport Towns." Manchester, a poor fishing village, voted as the Boston merchant who handled its catch dictated. Even in Cape Cod, there was a great gulf between squire and fisherman. "Was Cape Cod democratic?" I asked an aged gentleman from Barnstable, who had gone west before the Civil War. "Why, yes; it was n't like Boston — everybody *spoke* to everybody else." — "But was it democratic like Wisconsin?" — "No! by no means!"

The sea is no wet-nurse to democracy. Authority and privilege are her twin foster-children. Instant and unquestioning obedience to the master is the rule of the sea; and your typical sea-captain would make it the rule of the land if he could.

Since the merchants ruled society and politics in Massachusetts almost from the beginning to 1825, when they were forced to divide with the manufacturers, it were well to be sure we know what a merchant was. Down to the Civil War, the word was understood as Dr. Johnson defines it: "one who trafficks to remote countries." A merchant was no mere shopkeeper, or commission dealer. He bought and sold, at home and abroad, on his own account, and handled 'private adventures' on the side. He owned or chartered the vessels that carried his goods. Specialization came only within a generation of 1860. The provincial merchants owned not only merchant ships, but fishing craft, whalers and coasters, sent their vessels to the other continental colonies, England, the

Mediterranean, the West Indies, and the Spanish
main for all sorts of commodities; sold their return
ladings at wholesale, and at retail from their own
shops; speculated in wild lands, did a private banking
business, and underwrote insurance policies. Many of
them were wealthy, for the time. Thomas Boylston,
the richest man in Provincial Massachusetts, was supposed to be worth about $400,000 just before the
Revolution; and Colonel Elisha Doane, who maintained a country estate and a perpetually sandbound
coach at Wellfleet on the Cape, was a good second.

These colonial merchants lived well, with a spacious
brick mansion in Boston and a country seat at Milton
Hill, Cambridge, or as far afield as Harvard and Hop-
kinton, where great house parties were given. They
were fond of feasts and pageants, of driving out to
country inns for a dinner and dance, of trout-fishing,
and pleasure cruises to the Maine coast. They carried swords, and drew them if not granted proper deference by inferiors. Their wives and daughters wore the
latest London fashions, and were painted by Smibert,
Blackburn, and Copley. Their sons went to sea on a
parental ship, or, if they cared not for business, to
Harvard College. Nor was this 'codfish aristocracy'
ashamed of the source of all these blessings. The
proudest names in the province appear in "Boston
Gazette" or "Post-Boy" offering for sale everything
from fish-lines to broadcloth. The Honorable Benjamin Pickman placed a half-model of a codfish on every
front stair-end in his new Salem mansion.

The backbone of maritime Massachusetts, however,
was its middle class; the captains and mates of vessels,
the master builders and shipwrights, the ropemakers,
sailmakers, and skilled mechanics of many different
trades, without whom the merchants were nothing.

25

Benjamin Franklin was a typical product of this class, the son of an English-born tallow-chandler, and a Folger of Nantucket. As the broad humor of that island puts it, "Ben's keel was laid in Nantucket, but the old lady went to Boston to launch him." His first childish invention was a cob-wharf in the Boston millpond marsh, as a fishing station for minnows; his first imprints were broadside ballads on Blackbeard, and the shipwreck of Captain Worthilake, which he hawked about the crooked streets. In all his varied career the New England salt never worked out of Franklin's blood. One remembers the Gulf-Stream chart, which he persuaded a Nantucket cousin to sketch, in the vain hope of dissuading British shipmasters from bucking that ocean river. His "Maritime Suggestions" contain some practical hints that were later followed up by shipbuilders. It was this Yankee middle class of the water-front, keen, ambitious, inventive, courageous, that produced the great merchants and shipmasters of later generations; that gave maritime Massachusetts its characteristic flavor.

CHAPTER III

REVOLUTION AND RECONSTRUCTION

1760-1788

A DOGGEREL tory poet made no bad analysis of the
Patriot party in the northern colonies, as a coalition
of 'John Presbyter,' 'Will Democrack,' and 'Nathan
Smuggle':

> John answer'd, Thou art proud,
> Brittania, mad and rich,
> Will d——d her, with his Crowd,
> And call'd her, 'Tyrant ——.'
> While Nathan his Effusions bray'd
> And veaw'd She ruin'd all his Trade.

Boston became the headquarters of the American
Revolution largely because the policy of George III
threatened her maritime interests. "Massachusetts-
Bay is the most prejudicial plantation to this kingdom," wrote Sir Josiah Child. Instead of trading only
with the mother country, and producing some staple
which she could monopolize, Massachusetts would
spite the Acts of Trade and Navigation, would "trye
all ports," would trade with England's rivals, and
drive English ships from colonial commerce.

Of course she had to do all this in order to live and
prosper; and every penny won from free trade (as she
called it) or smuggling (as the English called it) was
spent in England. Until 1760, Englishmen saw the
point and let well enough alone; but the ministers of
George III believed it their duty to enforce the stat-
utes, and make Massachusetts a colony in fact as in
name. Not only their policy, but their method of exe-

cuting it was objectionable. Loyalty was chilled, and a fighting spirit aroused, by incidents such as this:

On Friday last a Coaster belonging to Scituate was passing one of the Ships of War in this harbour, when they dous'd their mainsail, but it not being quite to the satisfaction of the commanding officer of the Ship, they sent their boat on board and upon the Officer's stepping upon the Sloop's deck he immediately drew a cutlass with which he struck the master of the Coaster on the cheek, which cut a gash near three inches long, after which he damn'd him for not showing more respect to the King's Ship and then cut the halliards of the mainsail and let the sail run down upon deck.[1]

The American Revolution in eastern Massachusetts was financed and in part led by wealthy merchants like John Hancock, Josiah Quincy, James Bowdoin, Richard Derby, and Elbridge Gerry.[2] When the crisis came in 1775, a minority of the merchants, alarmed at mob violence, preferred law and order to liberty and property; but the majority risked the one to secure the other — and obtained both. They may, too, have been moved by the same high ideals which, spread broadcast by the voice and pen of Adams and Otis, Hawley and Warren, set interior Massachusetts ablaze. But their interests as well were at stake. If American trade were regulated by corrupt incompetents three thousand miles away, Massachusetts might as well retire from the sea.

In consequence, the Revolution in eastern Massachusetts, radical in appearance, was conservative in character. The war closed with little change in the social system of provincial days, although the change in personnel was great. Maritime interests were still supreme. The Constitution of 1780 was a lawyers' and merchants' constitution, directed toward some-

---

[1] *Boston Gazette and Country Journal*, Sept. 25, 1769.
[2] The *G* in this name is hard.

thing like quarterdeck efficiency in government, and the protection of property against democratic pirates.

The maritime history of Massachusetts during the War of Independence would make a book in itself; it has already lent color to many books. We must pass by the marine Lexington in Machias Bay, the state navy fitted out in 1775, the British attacks on Gloucester, Portland, and New Bedford. Just a word, however, on privateering. Her success in this legalized piracy was probably the greatest contribution of seaboard Massachusetts to the common cause. Six hundred and twenty-six letters of marque were issued to Massachusetts vessels by the Continental Congress, and some thousand more by the General Court. Privateers were of little use in naval operations, as the disastrous Penobscot expedition proved; but they were of very greatest service in preying on the enemy's commerce, intercepting his communications with America, carrying terror and destruction into the very chops of the Channel, and supplying the patriot army with munitions, stores and clothing at Johnny Bull's expense.

From an economic and social viewpoint, privateering employed the fishermen, and all those who depended on shipping; taught daring seamanship, and strengthened our maritime aptitude and tradition. Privateers required speed; and the Massachusetts builders, observing, it is said, the scientifically designed vessels of our French allies, did away with high quarterdecks, eased water-lines, and substituted a nearly U-shaped cross-section for the barrel-shaped bottom and unseemly tumble-home of the old-style ships. Commerce continued with the West Indies, France, and Spain in letter-of-marque ships, armed merchantmen with a license to take prizes on the side.

The letter-of-marque ship *General Pickering* of Salem, Captain Jonathan Haraden, fourteen guns and forty-five men, but heavily laden with sugar, beat the British privateer *Achilles* of three times her size and armament off Bilbao, in one of the most gallant sea-fights of the Revolution. On the back side of Cape Cod, whalemen with swivel-armed boats kept watch on Nantucket and Vineyard Sounds, the sea-lane to the British base in New York. With an impudent daring that astounded the enemy, they swooped down on his vessels when becalmed, or cut them out of Tarpaulin Cove and Holmes Hole at night-time. On Salem, in particular, the Revolution wrought an entire change in commercial spirit. Before the war Salem was mainly a fishing port. Privateering gave her seamen a broader horizon, and her merchants a splendid ambition.

In the earlier years of the war, large profits were made from privateering by every one connected with it. A favorite speculation for merchants was to buy, in advance of his cruise, half a privateersman's share of his forthcoming prizes. But in the last year or two of the war the British tightened their blockade, captured a large part of our fleet, and drove the rest into port. The insurance rate from Beverly to Hayti and back was forty per cent in 1780. The Derbys of Salem are said to have been the only privateering firm to retain a favorable balance, when peace was concluded.

But it was a great war while it lasted!

Then came the worst economic depression Massachusetts has ever known. The double readjustment from a war to a peace basis, and from a colonial to an independent basis, caused hardship throughout the colonies. It worked havoc with the delicate adjustment of fishing, seafaring, and shipbuilding by which Massachusetts was accustomed to gain her living. By

1786, the exports of Virginia had more than regained their pre-Revolutionary figures. At the same date the exports of Massachusetts were only one-fourth of what they had been twelve years earlier.

The fisheries had to be reconstructed from the beginning. Owing to the diplomacy of John Adams, Massachusetts codfishermen retained access to their old grounds; but they lacked vessels, gear, and capital. It is generally assumed that our fishing fleet had been transformed into privateers, and needed only reconversion to go out and catch cod. But the fishing schooner of that period was a slow, unwieldy craft, of little use in privateering. Such of them as had been converted, for the most part were captured; the rest, high and dry for seven years, needed expensive repairs. The whaling fleet of Nantucket and Dartmouth [1] had been wiped out. Only four or five remained out of two hundred sail; the rest had been lost, burned, or captured.

Independence deprived the Massachusetts cod-fisheries of their greatest market, the British West Indies; and the whale-fisheries of their only foreign market, England. Johnny Bull naturally slammed his colonial doors in Jonathan's face; would receive his ships on no terms, nor even his salt provisions and cod-fish in British vessels. He intended to build up his own fisheries and lumber trade. France and Spain excluded recent allies from their colonial preserves. The Dutch, Danish, and Swedish islands remained; not important markets, but good centers for smuggling. But until the new ropes were learned, the returns to New England fishermen were meager indeed. After four years of peace, about four-fifths of the Grand Banks fleet

[1] Dartmouth until 1787 included New Bedford, Fairhaven, and Westport.

31

was in commission; but the men were not earning enough to see their families through the winter. By 1789, only one-third of the whaling tonnage of 1773 had been restored.[1]

The coasting trade was under a similar handicap, for Massachusetts had been accustomed to pay for her imports of tobacco and Southern produce largely with West India goods. Almost the only thing that could be done was to send small sloops and fishing vessels to peddle out local produce along the shores of Chesapeake Bay, Albemarle Sound, Pamlico Sound, and Cape Fear River, for corn, tobacco, and naval stores. For example, three fishing schooners cleared from Beverly for Maryland and North Carolina during the first two weeks of December, 1787. The *Swallow*, forty-five tons, takes bricks, butter, fish, rum, potatoes, and "6 Tons of English Hay here produced." The *Woodbridge*, Seward Lee master, takes "5 hhd. salt, 12 q. dry fish, 5 hhd. molasses, 4 bbl. Mackerell, 6 doz. buckets, 9 Setts wooden measures, 3 half-pecks, 11 buckets with covers, 6 hhd. & 6 bbl. N.E. Rum, 8 boxes chocolate, 3 doz. common cheeses, 2 cases Earthen ware, 1 doz. axes, 36 bbl. potatoes, 1 doz. setts Sugar Boxes"; and "all the above are the Growth and Manufacture of this state." With such typical cargoes of "Yankee notions," pathetic in their homely variety, the smaller seaports of Massachusetts were wooing the prosperity which had already returned to the South.

And what of the slave trade? A dark subject, indeed; one which I have endeavored in vain to illuminate. The "Guinea trade" had never been an important line of commerce in Massachusetts. It was forbidden, under heavy penalties, by an act of the General Court

[1] See table in Appendix.

in 1788. Yet it did not entirely cease. Felt, in his "Annals of Salem," prints the instructions of an owner to a slaver which left that port in 1785. Dr. Bentley, who had a keen scent for this nefarious traffic, notes in his diary the names of at least eight Salem shipmasters who engaged in it, at one time or another, between 1788 and 1802. A mutiny in the middle passage disposed of one; another was killed by a negro in revenge; one, "of a most worthy family," died at Havana, another cut his own throat. Only one seems to have been arrested, and he was released for lack of evidence; although an extant log of one of his voyages, from Salem to the Guinea coast and the West Indies, bears witness to his guilt. Salem had a regular trade with the West African coast, rum and fish for gold dust, palm oil, and ivory; and it would be surprising if an occasional shipmaster did not yield to the temptation to load 'black ivory' as well.

The statistics of slave imports at Charleston, between 1804 and 1808, disclosed by Senator Smith, of South Carolina, in the latter year, state that seventy of the entering vessels belonged to Great Britain, sixty-one to Charleston itself, fifty-nine to Rhode Island, only one to Boston, and none to any other Massachusetts port. But this does not include the West-Indian slave trade; and an interesting insurance policy, dated June 13, 1803, suggests how it could be carried on without breaking either the laws of Massachusetts or of the United States. One of the most eminent and famous firms of China merchants, acting as agents for one Robert Cuming, of St. Croix (Danish West Indies), insures for $33,000 at ten per cent, his ship *Hope* and cargo from the coast of Africa to Havana, under Danish colors. "The assurers are liable for loss by insurrection, but not by natural mortality. Each slave is valued at

33

two hundred dollars." This policy is underwritten by seven of the most respectable Boston merchants, and negotiated by an eighth.

William Lloyd Garrison exposed a domestic slave-trader of Newburyport in 1829, one who took slaves as freight from Baltimore to New Orleans. Even later the New Bedford whaling masters occasionally engaged in the African trade. Only a thorough examination of our court records, and of the archives of such foreign seaports as Havana, would reveal a measure of the full truth. Yet I believe the statement warranted that the slave trade, as prosecuted from Massachusetts or by Massachusetts capital after the Revolution, was occasional and furtive, rather than a recognized underground traffic. Certainly it played no prominent part in the commercial prosperity of the community; and the assertion, often disproved but as often repeated, that Massachusetts was "the nursing mother of the horrors of the middle passage," is without any foundation in fact.

Shipbuilding came to a standstill shortly after the Revolution. With no British market for our bottoms, and British colonial ports closed to the American flag; with French, Austrians, Germans, Dutch, and Swedes competing for our carrying trade, and no government capable of granting protection; the shipping supremacy of Massachusetts seemed forever ended. According to an official report of the French consul at Boston, about one hundred and twenty-five vessels had been launched annually in Massachusetts before the war. In 1784, only forty-five vessels left the ways; and twelve of them, built for the French East-India service, were so poorly constructed that no more outside orders came. Between 1785 and 1787, only fifteen to twenty were built annually. A goodly fleet of merchantmen, and several new privateers like the *Astrea* and *Grand Turk*, constructed during the last year or two of the war, were on hand; but there was little employment for them. Instead of sending her fleet to all Europe, as optimists predicted, Massachusetts found her own harbors thronged with foreign flags, and her wharves heaped high with foreign goods.

Between May and December, 1783, twenty-eight French vessels, and almost the same number of English merchantmen, brought cargoes, worth almost half a million dollars, into Boston Harbor alone. Consisting largely of luxuries, they were nevertheless snapped up (on credit, of course) by the merchants of this war-stricken town of ten thousand inhabitants. Peace brought a riot of luxury such as Massachusetts never saw again until 1919. The war debt was enormous, the need of production imperative; but privateering, speculation, and the continental currency had so undermined Yankee thrift and energy that many persons thought the character of the race had completely changed. Travelers commented on the vulgar display of the profiteers, and the reckless spending of farmers and mechanics. We hear of artisans buying silk stockings, and 'jeunes paysannes' coming into Boston market, wearing 'chapeaux Montgolfiers.'

Worst of all, civil conflict was impending. For some years before the Revolution, central and western Massachusetts had been increasing rapidly in population, and acquiring class consciousness. The farmer no longer blessed the merchant, but cursed him as an exploiter. All classes and sections had allied to resist British imperialism; but the war brought about much friction. Mutual accusations of profiteering and slacking were frequent. Berkshire County refused obedience to the Boston government until 1780; and few

35

debts or taxes were paid in western Massachusetts for seven years.

By 1783 the farmers had acquired a higher standard of living, and a heavy burden of debts. European creditors began to press Boston merchants; who turned to their country storekeeper debtors, who began to distrain on the farmers, who then called upon government to establish a moratorium for debts, and to issue cheap money. But maritime Massachusetts controlled the government, by the simple device of apportioning the state senate according to taxable wealth. Every effort of the representatives to relieve the farmers died in the upper house.

The merchants even shifted the burden of taxation to those who could least bear it. Forty per cent of the state expenses were raised by poll-taxes, which fell equally on rich and poor, merchant prince and plough-boy. The customs duties were low, and largely evaded; Samuel Breck tells in his "Recollections" how the best people would smuggle in a good proportion of each cargo, as if the customs were still the King's.

Owing to the dislocation of the West-India trade and the departure of the French and British armies, there was no longer a market for the farming and domestic produce of central New England. Prices and common labor fell to almost nothing. At this crisis, the state government began to distrain on tax delinquents, and the merchants on their debtors. The courts became clogged with suits. Farms which had been in one family for generations, were sold under the hammer at a fraction of their real value, to pay debts contracted at inflated prices, or a few years' overdue taxes. The situation became intolerable to men who had fought for liberty.

In the summer of 1786 the storm broke. The up-country yeomanry, under the leadership of Revolutionary officers like Daniel Shays, began breaking up sessions of the courts, in the hope of a respite from confiscations until the next state election. Government ordered them to disperse, and preached "frugality, industry and self-denial." The yeomanry persisted, and the tide of lawlessness rolled nearer Boston. Governor Bowdoin proclaimed the rebel leaders outlaws. They then resolved to be outlaws indeed, and attacked the Springfield arsenal in search of better weapons than pitchforks and Queen's arms. One 'whiff of grapeshot' dispersed the ragged battalions to the bleak hills of western Massachusetts. Loyal militia and gentlemen volunteers from the seaboard, advancing through the deep snow of a hard winter, broke up the remaining bands, early in 1787. It was a victory of property over democracy; of maritime Massachusetts over farming Massachusetts.

Notwithstanding these civil disorders, some brave efforts were made both by the Commonwealth and by private individuals, in the years near 1786, to make the state more self-sufficient. The Massachusetts Bank, first in the state, was chartered in 1784. A small manufacturing boom set in about the same time. The "Boston Glass House" was established by a group of local capitalists in 1786, and received a state monopoly for manufacturing window-glass. The Cabot family established the Beverly Cotton Manufactory in 1787. Most of these experiments closed their doors in a few years' time. But the Charles River Bridge from Boston to Charlestown, opened on the eleventh anniversary of the battle of Bunker Hill, was a financial success, and encouraged the building of several other toll-bridges that greatly increased the facilities of the seaport towns.

In the meantime, commerce was slowly reviving. Yankee skippers [1] were learning to outwit both Barbary corsairs and West India regulations. Orders in Council changed neither the Jamaican appetite for dried codfish, nor the Yankee thirst for Jamaica rum. A Massachusetts vessel putting into a British port "in distress" was likely to obtain an official permit to land its cargo and relieve the "starving population." France, thanks to Jefferson's diplomacy, gradually reopened her insular possessions; and Spain permitted direct trade with Havana, Trinidad, and New Orleans. St. Eustatius, St. Bartholomew, and the Virgin Islands became *entrepôts* for illicit traffic. Much New England lumber and whale oil found its way to the West India and English markets by acquiring a "British" character in Nova Scotia. Despite the English disposition to "cramp us in the Cod-Fishery," as Stephen Higginson put it, and the bounties paid by France to her *pêcheurs d'Islande*, the West Indies took a greater proportion of our dried codfish in 1790 than in 1775. But the total exports were still far below those of the pre-Revolutionary era.

By 1787 the West-India trade was in a measure restored. Beverly, for instance, imported about 3100 gallons of foreign rum, 7000 gallons of "other foreign distilled spirits," 400 pounds of cocoa, 3500 pounds of sugar, and 50,000 pounds of leaf tobacco, between April 1 and July 1, 1787. The benefits of a reopened market for farm produce and wooden ware, percolating into the interior, did more to salve the wounds of Shays's Rebellion than all the measures passed by the Great and General Court.

---

[1] This term is correctly used only for the masters of fishing vessels, coasters, and small craft such as traded with the West Indies. A document of 1775 in the Beverly Historical Society speaks of "the chuner Mary thomas Rusel Skiper & oner."

But the general commercial situation in Massachusetts was still most unsatisfactory. Every state, under the Confederation, had its own customs duties and tonnage laws. When Massachusetts attempted to discriminate against British vessels, her neighbors received them with open arms; and British goods reached Boston from other ports by coasting sloops. Not even the coasting trade was confined to the American flag; and the port dues were constantly changed. More commercial treaties were needed with foreign powers. Federal bounties were needed to revive fishing. Shays's Rebellion, fortunately, sent such a thrill of horror through the states, that conservative forces drew together to create a more perfect union.

In the struggle of 1788 over the ratification of the Federal Constitution, Massachusetts was a pivotal state. The voters returned an anti-Federalist majority to her ratifying convention. By various methods, enough votes were changed to obtain ratification. A meeting of four hundred Boston mechanics (following, it is said, a promise by local merchants to order three new vessels upon ratification) drew up strong Federalist resolutions, which turned the wavering Samuel Adams. Governor Hancock was reached by methods less direct. Boston hospitality had its influence. "I most Tel you I was never Treated with So must politeness in my life as I was afterwards by the Treadesmen of Boston merchants & every other Gentlemen," wrote a backwoods member. Finally the Convention ratified, by a majority of 19 out of 355 votes. The sectional alignment was significant. The coast and island counties of Massachusetts proper cast 102 votes in favor, and only 19 against, ratification. The inland counties [1]

[1] Including Middlesex and Bristol, the bulk of whose population was agricultural at this period.

cast 60 in favor, 128 against. For the third time in ten years, maritime Massachusetts won over farming Massachusetts.

On her proper element, maritime Massachusetts was already winning a cleaner fight: — victory over lethargy and despair; victory over powers who would cramp her restless energy, doom her ships to decay, and her seamen to emigrate. Some subtle instinct, or maybe thwarted desire of Elizabethan ancestors who, seeking in vain the Northwest Passage, founded an empire on the barrier, was pulling the ships of Massachusetts east by west, into seas where no Yankee had ever ventured. Off the roaring breakers of Cape Horn, in the vast spaces of the Pacific, on savage coasts and islands, and in the teeming marts of the Far East, the intrepid shipmasters and adventurous youth of New England were reclaiming their salt sea heritage.

CHAPTER IV

PIONEERS OF THE PACIFIC

1784–1792

MARITIME commerce was the breath of life for Massachusetts. When commerce languished, the commonwealth fell sick. When commerce revived even a little, the hot passions of Shays's Rebellion cooled just enough to permit a ratification of the Federal Constitution. Prosperity, not only of the seaport towns, but of the agricultural interior, depended as of old upon the success of seafaring Massachusetts. Without prosperity, emigration would follow, and slow decay, and death. The codfishermen must exact tribute from the Banks; the whalers must pursue their 'gigantic game' around the Horn, the merchants and trading vessels must recover their grip on the home market and the handling of Southern exports; must find substitutes for the protected trade of colonial days; must elude the Spanish *guarda costas* along the circumference of South America; must compete with English, Scots, and Dutchmen in the Baltic and the Indies; and must seek out new, virgin markets and sources of supply in the Pacific. All this had to be done, that Massachusetts retain her position among the brighter stars of the American constellation. The doing of it determined her political orientation; transformed a revolutionary community, the most fecund source of political thought in the western world, into a conservative commonwealth, the spearhead of the aggressively reactionary Federalist party.

"From 1790 to 1820, there was not a book, a speech

41

a conversation, or a thought in the State," wrote Emerson. Speaking relatively and broadly, he was right. The Yankee mind, engrossed in the struggle for existence, neglected things spiritual and intellectual during this Federalist period of its history; and the French Revolution made thought suspicious to a commercial community. Yet thought there was, even though the Sage of Concord might not call it by that name; the thought that opens up new channels of trade, sets new enterprises on foot, and erects a political system to consolidate them. By such thought, no less than the other, the grist of history is ground.

Every seaport of Massachusetts proper from Newburyport to Edgartown was quickening into new activity in 1789; none more so than the capital. The Boston of massacre and tea-party, of Sam Adams and Jim Otis, of uproarious mobs and radical meetings, was in transition to that quiet, prosperous, orderly Federalist Boston, the Boston of East-India merchants and Federalist statesmen; of Thomas Handasyd Perkins, Charles Bulfinch, and Harrison Gray Otis.

In appearance, the Boston of 1790 was unchanged since 1750. Charles Bulfinch had returned from Europe, but his native town had barely taken up the slack of the turbulent era; some accumulation of wealth was needed to employ his architectural talents. The eighteen thousand inhabitants were not crowded on their peninsula of seven hundred and eighty acres — about nine-tenths the area of Central Park, New York. As one approached it by the Charles River Bridge in 1790, Boston seemed "almost to stand in the water, at least to be surrounded by it, and the shipping, with the houses, trees, and churches, have a charming effect." Beacon Hill, a three-peaked grassy slope, still innocent of the gilded dome, dominated the town. From its

42

base a maze of narrow streets paved with beach stones, wound their way seaward among ancient dwellings; dividing around Copp's and Fort Hills to meet again by the water's edge. One of them, to be sure, led to "landward to the west," but at spring tides even that, too, went "downward to the sea." Buildings crowded out to the very capsills of the wharves, which poked boldly into deep water. The uniform mass of slate and mossy shingle roofs, pointed, hipped, and gambreled, was broken by a few graceful church spires, serene elders of the masts that huddled about the wharves. As for the people, "Commerce occupies all their thought," writes Brissot de Warville in 1788, "turns all their heads, and absorbs all their speculations. Thus you find few estimable works, and few authors." But "let us not blame the Bostonians; they think of the useful before procuring themselves the agreeable. They have no brilliant monuments; but they have neat and commodious houses, superb bridges, and excellent ships." To Timothy Dwight, of New Haven, the Bostonians seemed "distinguished by a lively imagination. . . . Their enterprises are sudden, bold, and sometimes rash. A general spirit of adventure prevails here."

One bright summer afternoon in 1790 saw the close of a great adventure. On August 9, Boston town heard a salute of thirteen guns down-harbor. The ship *Columbia*, Captain Robert Gray, with the first American ensign to girdle the globe snapping at her peak, was greeting the Castle after an absence of three years. Coming to anchor in the inner harbor, she fired another federal salute of thirteen guns, which a "great concourse of citizens assembled on the various wharfs returned with three huzzas and a hearty welcome." A rumor ran through the narrow streets that a native of

"Owyhee" — a Sandwich-Islander — was on board; and before the day was out, curious Boston was gratified with a sight of him, marching after Captain Gray to call on Governor Hancock. Clad in a feather cloak of golden suns set in flaming scarlet, that came halfway down his brown legs; crested with a gorgeous feather helmet shaped like a Greek warrior's, this young Hawaiian moved up State Street like a living flame.

The *Columbia* had logged 41,899 miles since her departure from Boston on September 30, 1787. Her voyage was not remarkable as a feat of navigation; Magellan and Drake had done the trick centuries before, under far more hazardous conditions. It was the practical results that counted. The *Columbia's* first voyage began the Northwest fur trade, which enabled the merchant adventurers of Boston to tap the vast reservoir of wealth in China.

*

*   *

The history of this discovery goes back to the close of hostilities, and reveals a thread of optimism and energy running through years of depression. In December, 1783, the little fifty-five-ton sloop *Harriet*, of Hingham, Captain Hallet, sailed from Boston with a cargo of ginseng for China. Putting in at the Cape of Good Hope, she met with some British East-Indiamen who, alarmed at this portent of Yankee competition, bought her cargo for double its weight in Hyson tea. Captain Hallet made a good bargain, but lost the honor of hoisting the first American ensign in Canton, to a New York ship, the *Empress of China*.

Although the capital and the initiative were of New York, the direction of this voyage was entrusted

to the supercargo [1] of the *Empress*, Major Samuel
Shaw, of Boston, one of the few sons of New England
mercantile families who had served through the entire
war. The *Empress of China* arrived at Macao on
August 23, 1784, six months out from New York; and
despite Shaw's inexperience brought home a cargo that
proved America need pay no further tribute for teas
or silks to the Dutch or British. Major Shaw's report
to the government was published, stimulating others to
repeat the experiment; and he freely gave of his experience to all who asked. After receiving the purely
honorary title of American consul at Canton, he returned thither in 1786, on the ship *Hope* of New York,
James Magee master, to establish the first American
commercial house in China. He was also one of the
first in the East-India trade. A short residence in
Bombay so affected his liver, that he died on a homeward voyage in 1794, in his fortieth year. Of Samuel
Shaw it was said by that rugged shipmaster of Duxbury, Amasa Delano, that "he was a man of fine talents and considerable cultivation; he placed so high
a value upon sentiments of honor that some of his
friends thought it was carried to excess. He was candid, just and generous, faithful in his friendships, an
agreeable companion, and manly in all his intercourse."

Shortly after her arrival at Canton, the *Hope* was
joined by the *Grand Turk*, of Salem, Captain Ebenezer
West, the first Massachusetts vessel to visit the Far

---

[1] A supercargo was the representative on shipboard of owners and
consigners. He took no part in navigation, but handled the business side
of the voyage. A captain often acted as supercargo, especially when a
relative of the owners; in such cases he generally carried a clerk to keep
the books. Promotion of a supercargo to the command of a vessel was
called "coming in through the cabin window"; promotion of a foremast
hand, "coming in through the hawse-hole."

East. Her return to Salem on May 22, 1787, brought fabulous profits to her owner, whetted the appetite of every Massachusetts merchant, and (what was equally important) fixed his good wife's ambition on a chest of Hyson, a China silk gown, and a set of Canton china.

Although America was outstripping every other nation in China trade, save Britain, she could not long compete with Britain without a suitable medium. The Canton market accepted little but specie and eastern products. British merchants could import the spoil of India and the Moluccas — opium and mummie and sharks' fins and edible birds' nests. Yet Britain paid for the major part of her teas and silks in silver. Massachusetts, on the morrow of Shays's Rebellion, could not afford to do this. Ginseng could be procured and sold only in limited quantities. Unless some new product were found to tickle the palate or suit the fancy of the finicky mandarins, the *Grand Turk's* voyage were a flash in the pan. To find something salable in Canton, was the riddle of the China trade. Boston and Salem solved it.

The ship *Columbia* was fitted out by a group of Boston merchants who believed the solution of the problem lay in the furs of the Northwest Coast. Captain Cook's third voyage, the account of which was published in 1784, and John Ledyard's report of the Russian fur trade in Bering Sea, gave them the hint. Possibly they had also learned from Samuel Shaw that a few Anglo-Indian traders, whom Captain Gray later met on the Coast, had already sold Alaskan sea-otter at Canton.

Although privately financed, with fourteen shares of $3500 each,[1] the voyage was conceived in the public

[1] The shareholders were Joseph Barrell, Samuel Brown, and Captain Crowell Hatch, prominent Boston merchants; Charles Bulfinch the

spirit of the old merchant adventurers. A medal was struck to distribute among the natives. An expert furrier, a surgeon, and (luckily for us) an artist were taken. John Kendrick, of Wareham, commanded both the expedition, and the ship *Columbia*, eighty-three feet long, two hundred twelve tons burthen, built at Hobart's Landing on the North River, Scituate, in 1773. Robert Gray, born of Plymouth stock in Tiverton, Rhode Island, and a former officer in the Continental navy, was master of the ninety-ton sloop *Lady Washington*, which accompanied the *Columbia* as tender. Both vessels made an unusually long passage, and encountered heavy westerly gales off Cape Horn, which they were the first North American vessels to pass. On April 1, 1788, in latitude 57° 57' south, they parted company. Gray reached the coast of "New Albion" eleven months out of Boston, and was joined by the *Columbia* at Nootka Sound, the fur-trading center on Vancouver Island. It was too late to do any trading that season, so both vessels were anchored in a sheltered cove, while the crew lived ashore in log huts and built a small boat. In the summer of 1789, before a full cargo of skins had been obtained, provisions began to run low. Captain Kendrick therefore remained behind, but sent Gray in the *Columbia* to Canton, where he exchanged his cargo of peltry for tea, and returned to Boston around the world.

The *Columbia's* first voyage, like most pioneering enterprises, was not a financial success. Fourteen American vessels preceded her to Canton, and most of them reached home before her. Four of them, belonging to Elias Hasket Derby, of Salem, had approached the China market from a different angle and with

architect, John Derby, son of E. H. Derby, of Salem, and J. M. Pintard, a merchant of New York.

greater success. The ship *Astrea*, Captain James Magee,[1] carried a miscellaneous cargo, which had taken almost a year to assemble. The barques *Light Horse* and *Atlantic* exchanged provisions at Mauritius (Ile de France) for bills which at Bombay, Calcutta, and Surat bought a good assortment for Canton; the brig *Three Sisters*, Captain Benjamin Webb, disposed of a mixed cargo at Batavia, where she was chartered by a Dutch merchant to carry Java products to Canton. She and the *Atlantic* were there sold, and the entire proceeds invested in silks, chinaware, and three-quarters of a million pounds of tea, which were loaded on the two larger vessels.

Elias Hasket Derby, ignorant even of the arrival of his vessels at Canton, was beginning to feel a bit nervous toward the end of May, 1790, when a brig arrived with news of them. On June 1, the *Astrea* was sighted in Salem Bay. But Mr. Derby's troubles were not yet over. On June 15, the *Light Horse* appeared; but for lack of wind was forced to anchor off Marblehead. In the night an easterly gale sprang up. The vessel was too close inshore to make sail and claw off. Early in the morning her crew felt that sickening sensation of dragging anchors. Astern, nearer, nearer came the granite rocks of Marblehead, where the ragged population perched like buzzards, not displeased at the prospect of rich wreckage at Salem's expense. "King Darby" hurried over in his post-chaise to watch half his fortune inching toward disaster on his very doorstep. Finally, with but a few yards to spare between rudder and rocks, the anchors bit, and saved the *Light*

---

[1] Captain James Magee (1750–1801), described as "a convivial, noble-hearted Irishman," during the Revolution commanded the man-of-war brig *General Arnold*, which was wrecked in Plymouth Bay. He married Margaret Elliot, sister of Mrs. Thomas Handasyd Perkins, and lived in the old Governor Shirley mansion at Roxbury.

Horse until a shift of wind brought her to the haven where she would be.

Two months later, Captain Gray entered Boston with a damaged cargo to find Captain Magee advertising China goods in the Boston papers. But the *Columbia* had opened a channel to fortune that her rivals were quick to follow.

As supercargo of the *Astrea*, Mr. Derby had chosen Captain Magee's young brother-in-law, Thomas Handasyd Perkins. The Boston " Herald of Freedom " for January 6, 1789, announced that all persons "wishing to adventure" aboard the *Astrea* "may be assured of Mr. Perkins' assertions for their interest." Those who accepted were not disappointed; and the pedigrees of many Boston fortunes can be traced to that China voyage and its consequences. Young Perkins inherited an aptitude for the fur trade from his grandfather, Thomas Handasyd Peck, the leading fur exporter of the province; and he had learned the mercantile business at his mother's knee. The widow Perkins, one of those remarkable New England women of the Revolutionary period, carried on her husband's business with such success that letters used to be received from abroad addressed to "Elizabeth Perkins, Esq." No wonder that, with such forbears, Thomas Handasyd Perkins became the first of Boston merchants, both in fortune and in public spirit.

On returning to Boston in 1790, young Perkins bought the little seventy-ton brigantine *Hope*, and sent her under Captain Gray's former mate, Joseph Ingraham, to the Northwest Coast. In a single summer she collected fourteen hundred sea-otter skins. The *Columbia* started on her second voyage in September, 1790, and the brigantine *Hancock*, one hundred fifty-seven tons, Samuel Crowell master, two months later.

49

Lieutenant Thomas Lamb and his brother James, merchants, joined Captain Magee in building at Boston, the ship *Margaret*, one hundred fifty tons, which sailed under the latter's command on December 24, 1791, "bound on a voyage of observation and enterprise to the North-Western Coast of this Continent." Others quickly followed.

By 1792 the trade route Boston–Northwest Coast–Canton–Boston was fairly established. Not only the merchantmen of Massachusetts, but the whalers (of whom more anon), balked of their accustomed traffic by European exclusiveness, were swarming around the Horn in search of new markets and sources of supply. It was on May 12, 1792, that Captain Gray (according to the seventeen-year-old fifth mate of the *Columbia*, John Boit, Jr.) "saw an appearance of a spacious harbour abreast the Ship, haul'd our wind for it, observ'd two sand bars making off, with a passage between them to a fine river. Out pinnace and sent her in ahead and followed with the Ship under short sail, carried in from 1/2 three to 7 fm. and when over the bar had 10 fm. water, quite fresh. The River extended to the NE. as far as eye cou'd reach, and water fit to drink as far down as the *Bars*, at the entrance. We directed our course up this noble *River* in search of a Village. The beach was lin'd with Natives, who ran along shore following the Ship. Soon after, above 20 Canoes came off, and brought a good lot of Furs, and Salmon, which last they sold two for a board Nail. The furs we likewise bought cheap, for Copper and Cloth. They appear'd to view the Ship with the greatest astonishment and no doubt we was the first civilized people that they ever saw. At length we arriv'd opposite to a large village, situate on the North side of the River, about 5 leagues from the entrance. . . . Capt.

Gray named this river *Columbia's* and the North entrance Cape Hancock, and the South Point, *Adams*. This River in my opinion, wou'd be a fine place for to set up a *Factory*. . . . The river abounds with excellent *Salmon*."

On her first voyage, the *Columbia* had solved the riddle of the China trade. On her second, empire followed in the wake.

CHAPTER V

THE NORTHWEST FUR TRADE

1788–1812

BEFORE the *Columbia* returned again, another rash enterprise of Boston merchants, an attempt to enter the Canton market through imitation of the British East India Company, had failed. The ship *Massachusetts*, of almost eight hundred tons burthen, the largest vessel constructed to that date in an American shipyard, was built at Quincy in 1789 for Samuel Shaw and other Boston merchants. Her model and dimensions were taken from a British East-Indiaman, and her equipment and roster, with midshipmen and captain's servants, imitated the Honourable Company so far as Yankee economy permitted. Under the command of Captain Job Prince, the *Massachusetts* sailed from Boston on March 28, 1790. She carried a general cargo, which her owners expected to exchange at Batavia for goods suitable for Canton. But the Dutch authorities (as one might have foreseen) refused a permit. When the *Massachusetts* arrived at Canton with an unsalable cargo, after a long and tempestuous voyage, Samuel Shaw gladly seized an opportunity to sell her for $65,000 to the Danish East India Company. This experience prejudiced American shipowners against vessels larger than five hundred tons, and determined the merchants of Boston to concentrate on the Northwest fur trade.

"The habits and ordinary pursuits of the New Englanders qualified them in a peculiar manner for carrying on this trade," wrote one of them, "and the embarrassed state of Europe gave them . . . almost a monopoly of the most lucrative part of it." Salem merchants preferred the Cape of Good Hope route, over which they attained their first success; Englishmen, Philadelphians, and New Yorkers soon dropped out; and by 1801, out of sixteen ships on "The Coast" (as Boston called it this early) all but two were Bostonian. The masters and mates, and at first the crews, were for the most part Bostonian, and the vessels of Boston registry. So it is no wonder that the Chinook jargon, the pidgin English of the Coast, names United States citizens "Boston men" as distinguished from "Kintshautsh (King George) men."

The most successful vessels in the Northwest fur trade were small, well-built brigs and ships of one hundred to two hundred and fifty tons burthen (say sixty-five to ninety feet long), constructed in the shipyards from the Kennebec to Scituate. Larger vessels were too difficult to work through the intricacies of the Northwest Coast. They were heavily manned, in case of an Indian attack; and copper-bottomed by Paul Revere's newly invented process, to prevent accumulating barnacles and weeds in tropic waters. The Winships' *Albatross*, which neglected this precaution, took almost six months to round Cape Horn, and found her speed reduced to two knots an hour. Clearing from Boston in the autumn, in order to pass the high latitudes during the Antarctic summer, they generally arrived on the Coast by spring.

"The passage around Cape Horn from the Eastward I positively assert," wrote Captain Porter, of the frigate *Essex*, "is the most dangerous, most difficult, and attended with more hardships, than that of the same distance in any other part of the world." A passage in which many a great ship has met her death:

53

in which the head winds and enormous seas put small vessels at a great disadvantage. Yet, so far as I have learned, not one of these Boston Nor'westmen failed to round the Horn in safety.

To obtain fresh provisions and prevent scurvy, the Nor'west traders broke their voyage at least twice · at the Cape Verde Islands, the Falklands, sometimes Galapagos for a giant tortoise, and invariably Hawaii. For these were leisurely days in seafaring, when a homeward-bound vessel would stand by for hours while the crew of an outward-bounder wrote letters home. Captain Ingraham on his passage out in the *Hope*, in 1791, discovered and named the Washington group of the Marquesas Islands, whose women (so he informed the jealous officers of the *Columbia*) were "as much handsomer than the natives of the Sandwich Islands as the women of Boston are handsomer than a Guinea negro."

After the soft embrace of South Sea Islands, the savage grandeur of the Northwest Coast threw a chill on first-comers. Behind rocks and shingle beaches, on which the long Pacific rollers broke and roared incessantly, spruce and fir-clad mountains rose into the clouds, which distilled the sea-borne moisture in almost daily showers. The jagged and picturesque coast-line — a Maine on magnificent scale — offered countless harbors; but behind every beach on the outer margin was a mass of dank undergrowth, impenetrable even for the natives, whose dugout canoes served for hunting and fishing, transport and war.

On making his landfall, a Boston Nor'westman came to anchor off the nearest Indian village, bartered so long as he could do business, and then moved on to one after another of the myriad bays and coves until his hold was full of valuable furs. It was a difficult and hazardous trade, requiring expert discrimination in making up a cargo, the highest skill in navigation, and unceasing vigilance in all dealings with the Indians.

The Northwest Indians were dangerous customers. Captain Kendrick, on parting with Gray during their pioneer voyage, wrote him, "treet the Natives with Respect where Ever you go. Cultivate frindship with them as much as possibel and take Nothing from them But what you pay them for according to a fair agree‑ ment, and not suffer your peopel to affront them or treet them Ill." Gray obeyed, although he found the Indians already treacherous and aggressive; the result, he believed, of English outrages. The Boston men, both from interest and humanity, endeavored by just and tactful dealings to win the natives' confidence. But their work was hampered by irresponsible fly-by-nights who would pirate a cargo of skins, and never return.

In the early days, scarcely a voyage passed without a battle. Captain Kendrick lost a son, and was once driven from his own vessel by an Indian Amazon and her braves. The *Columbia* lost her second mate, and several members of her crew at "Murderers' Harbor." In 1803, the natives near Nootka Sound attacked the Amorys' ship *Boston*, Captain John Salter, and slaughtered all the ship's company but two; one of whom, John Jewitt, lived to write a narrative that thrilled generations of schoolboys. Given a firm master and stout crew, the Nor'west trading vessels could take care of themselves. Beside swivel-guns on the bulwarks, they were armed with six to twenty cannon, kept well shotted with grape, langrage or canister; and provided with boarding nettings, muskets, pistols, cutlasses and boarding pikes. The quarterdecks were

loopholed for musket fire, the hatches were veritable
'pill-boxes.' When a flotilla of dugouts surrounded
the vessel, only a few natives were permitted on board
at one time, and men armed with blunderbusses were
sent into the cross-trees, lest the waiting customers
lose patience.

Even peaceably inclined, the natives were hard to
please. "They do not seem to covet usefull things,"
writes Captain Gray's clerk, "but anything that looks
pleasing to the eye, or what they call riches." They
rated a fellow-Indian socially by his superfluous
blankets, by copper tea-kettles that were never used,
and by bunches of old keys worn like a necklace and
kept bright by constant rubbing. When rebuked by
Captain Sturgis for this wasteful display, an Indian
chief anticipated Veblen by adverting to the Boston
fashion of placing brass balls on iron fences, to tarnish
every night and be polished by the housemaid every
morning!

The Indians evidently had more discrimination than
generally acknowledged, for on her first voyage the
Columbia carried large numbers of snuff-bottles, rat-
traps, Jews'-harps, and pocket mirrors, which (except
for the last) were a dead loss. Her second cargo, in
1790, is typical of the Northwest fur trade as long as it
lasted. From Herman Brimmer were bought 143
sheets of copper, many pieces of blue, red, and green
'duffills' and scarlet coating. Solomon Cotton sold
the *Columbia's* owners 4261 quarter-pound 'chissells';
Asa Hammond, 150 pairs shoes at 75 cents; Benjamin
Greene, Jr., blue duffle trousers at 92 cents, pea
jackets, Flushing great coats, watch-coats and 'fear-
noughts';[1] Samuel Parkman, 6 gross 'gimblets,' and

---

[1] A stout woolen cloth, used for outside clothing at sea. The chisels
were merely short strips of iron. Duffles, also a coarse woolen, had been

12 gross buttons; Baker & Brewer, striped duffle blanketing; Samuel Fales, 14 M 20d. nails; and the United States government, 100 old muskets and blunderbusses.[1] Very few of these articles were manufactured in Massachusetts, and sometimes a Nor'westman would make up a cargo in England before starting for the Coast. New England rum, that ancient medium for savage barter, is curiously absent from the Northwest fur trade. Molasses and ship-biscuit were used instead of liquor to treat the natives.

The principal fur sought by Boston traders was that of the sea-otter, of which the mandarins had never been able to obtain enough from Russian hunters. Next to a beautiful woman and a lovely infant, said Captain Sturgis, a prime sea-otter skin two feet by five, with its short, glossy jet-black fur, was the finest natural object in the world. Its price varied considerably. Captain Gray's mate obtained two hundred skins at Queen Charlotte's Island for two hundred trade chisels (mere bits of strap iron); but at Nootka Sound the price was ten chisels apiece, or six inches square of sheet copper. Most vessels took a metal-

used by New Englanders in the beaver trade since the seventeenth century.

[1] Most Boston business firms who do not figure in the invoices are found among those supplying the outfit. John Derby, part owner, furnished 4 cannon and 8 swivels (probably from one of his father's former privateers), and Captain D. Hathorn (great-uncle of Nathaniel Hawthorne) freighted them from Salem. S. & S. Salisbury furnished twine and lead pencils; John Joy, one medicine chest; Thomas Amory Jr. & Co., 14 bbls. pitch and turpentine; J. & T. Lamb, 6 anchors; Josiah Bradlee, horn 'lantherns,' tin kettles and a coffee pot; Samuel Whitwell, a blacksmith's bellows; J. Lovering & Sons, 27 lb. tallow; Elisha Sigourney, 71 lb. grape shot; J. L. & B. Austin, cordage; Jonathan Winship, 135 bbls. beef; Mungo Mackay, 3 hds. N.E. rum; Lewis Hoyt, 2 hds. W.I. rum and 3 kegs essence of spruce; Wm. Boardman Jr., 3 ironbound casks; Robt. & Jos. Davis 20 bbls. cider, 6 of cranberries, 2 of barberries and 10 pigs. (*Columbia* MSS., 59.)

worker to make tools and weapons to order. Captain Ingraham's armorer made iron collars and bracelets, which became all the rage on the Coast and brought three otter skins each. Captain Sturgis, observing that the Indians used ermine pelts for currency, procured five thousand of them at the Leipzig fair for thirty cents apiece. On his next voyage he purchased one morning five hundred and sixty sea-otter skins, worth fifty dollars apiece in Canton, at the rate of five ermines, or a dollar and a half, each. But he so inflated the currency that it soon lost value! Later, noting that war-captives were a recognized form of wealth among the Indians, some Boston traders began buying them from tribes which were long on slaves, and selling them to tribes which were short. This form of speculation in foreign exchange was sternly reproved by George Lyman, and forbidden to his vessels and shipmasters.

The first white men to attempt a permanent establishment in the Oregon country were the Winship brothers of Brighton — Abiel, the Boston merchant, Captain Jonathan, Jr., and Captain Nathan, who commanded the family ship *Albatross*. On June 4, 1810, she sailed forty miles up the Columbia River and anchored off an oak grove, where her crew broke ground for a vegetable garden, and started work on a log house. But the Chinook Indians, the fur middlemen of Oregon, would brook no competition. Having no warships or marines to back them up, the Winships were forced to evacuate. It was a sad disappointment. Jonathan Winship, Jr., whose hobby was horticulture, "hoped to have planted a Garden of Eden on the shores of the Pacific, and made that wilderness to blossom like the rose." Others fulfilled his dream, bringing slips from the very rose-garden of Brighton where Captain Jonathan spent the long tranquil years of retirement he had earned so well.[1]

Unless exceedingly lucky, vessels remained eighteen months to two years on the Coast, before proceeding to Canton, and it was commonly three years before Long Wharf saw them again. Small brigs and sloops were sent out, or built on the Coast, to continue the collection of furs during the absence of the larger vessel.

The Sandwich Islands proved an ideal spot to refresh a scorbutic crew, and even to complete the cargo. Captain Kendrick (who plied between Canton and the Coast in the *Lady Washington* until his death in 1794) discovered sandalwood, an article much in demand at Canton, growing wild on the Island of Kauai. A vigorous trade with the native chiefs in this fragrant commodity was started by Boston fur-traders in "the Islands"; leading to more Hawaiian visits to New England, to the missionary effort of 1820, and eventually to annexation.

Another variation to the standard China voyage was contraband fur-trading along the coast of Spanish California. According to H. H. Bancroft, the first American vessel to anchor in California waters was the ship *Otter* of Boston, one hundred and sixty-eight tons, Ebenezer Dorr, Jr., master, which put in at Monterey for provisions in 1796. All trade and intercourse between Boston men and Californians was contraband; but both seized every opportunity to flout the Laws of the Indies.

---

[1] "Solid Men of Boston" (MS.), 70. Jonathan, Jr., founded the beef-slaughtering business at Brighton in 1775, and supplied the American army and French fleet during the Revolution. Charles Winship, another brother in this remarkable family, died at Valparaiso about 1800, when in command of the brigantine *Betsy*, bound for the Northwest Coast. A second Captain Charles Winship, son of a fifth brother, died at Valparaiso in 1819 or 1820 when in command of a sealing voyage.

Boston vessels generally carried a *Carta de Amistad* from "Don Juan Stoughton, Consul de S.M.C. para los Estados Unidos de New Hampshire, Massachusetts," etc. This was to be used if forced to put into one of His Catholic Majesty's ports "par mal Tiempo o otre acontecimiento imprevisto" — which exigency was pretty sure to occur when the land breeze smelt sea-otterish. Richard J. Cleveland, of Salem, owner and master of the brig *Lelia Byrd*, tried to make off with some pelts under the very nose of Commandant Don Manuel Rodriguez, who retaliated in the bloodless "Battle of San Diego" on March 21, 1803. But untoward incidents were rare. At his next port, San Quintin, the *Lelia Byrd's* people got on beautifully with a group of mission fathers who came down to trade and gossip. They spent two merry weeks together on this lonely shore, dining alternately in tent and cabin, inaugurating a half-century of close and friendly relations between Puritan and Padre on the California coast. Nothing like a common interest in smuggling to smooth religious differences!

Captain Joseph O'Cain, of Boston, in a ship of two hundred and eighty tons named after himself and built on North River for the Winships, inaugurated a new system of otter-hunting in 1804. Putting in at New Archangel (Sitka), he persuaded Baranov, the genial Russian factor, to lend him a hundred and fifty Aleut Indians, on shares. These expert otter-hunters, putting out from the ship in their skin canoes, like Gloucester fishermen in dories, obtained eleven hundred sea-otter pelts for Captain O'Cain in his first California cruise. Kills were made under the very walls of the San Francisco presidio. Three years later, O'Cain chartered his ship *Eclipse* of Boston to the Russian-American Company, traded their furs at

Canton, visited Nagasaki and Petropavlovsk, lost the
vessel on the Aleutian Islands, built another out of the
wreck, and returned to trade once more.[1] California
sea-otter and fur-seal hunting, combined with contraband mission trade, was pursued with much success
for about ten years, when the Russians declined
further aid to their competitors.

Another class of Pacific fur-traders were the "sealskinners." About 1783, the ship *States*, owned by a
Boston woman,[2] was fitted out for a voyage to the
Falklands in search of fur-seal and sea-elephant oil.
Some of the sealskins obtained were carried on a
venture to China, and the result encouraged others to
follow. Although sealskins brought but a dollar or two
at Canton, such quantities (even a hundred thousand on a single voyage) could be obtained merely by
landing on a beach and clubbing the helpless animals,
that vessels were especially fitted out to go in search
of them, and the smaller Nor'westmen occasionally
picked up a few thousand on their way to the Coast.
Connecticut was more conspicuous in this trade than
Massachusetts; but several vessels were commanded
by Nantucketers, and others were owned there and in
Boston or Salem. As in whaling, the men were generally shipped on shares, and often cheated out of
them. Masafuero, in the Juan Fernandez group, was
the center for seal-killing; but other islands off the
Chilian coast, St. Paul and Amsterdam Islands in the

[1] One would like to know more of this Captain O'Cain. He was an
Irishman whose parents lived in Boston, and first visited the Coast in
1795 on an English vessel, whose master, at his request, left him at
Santa Barbara. He managed to return to Boston in time to be married
there in 1799.

[2] 'Lady' or 'Madam' Haley, as she was called in Boston, was a sister
of the famous Jack Wilkes: for second husband, she married Patrick
Jeffery, a Boston merchant.

Indian Ocean, South Georgia, the Farralones and Santa Catalina off California, were visited before 1810. Gangs of sealers would be left on some lonely island in the South Pacific, while the vessel smuggled goods into Callao, Concepcion, Valparaiso, and smaller places like Coquimbo and Pisco. Amasa Delano, of Duxbury (private, U.S.A., at fourteen, privateersman at sixteen, master shipbuilder at twenty-one, second mate of the ship *Massachusetts*), with his brother built the sealers *Perseverance* and *Pilgrim*, and sailed as far as Tasmania, where they matched rascalities and exchanged brutalities with one of the British convict colonies. It was a Boston sealskinner, the Dorrs' *Otter*, which rescued from Botany Bay Thomas Muir, one of the victims of Pitt's Sedition Act. Eighty years later, New Bedford whalers were extending the same courtesy to exiled Fenians.

The first commercial relations between the United States and the west coast of South America, were established by sealers, Nor'westmen, and whalers putting in "under stress of weather" to obtain provisions, and indulge in the favorite Yankee pastime of swapping. To a certain extent they imported ideas; Richard J. Cleveland made a point of spreading republican propaganda at Valparaiso. The manner of their reception depended on the official mood. Bernard Magee in the ship *Jefferson* had only to present his ship's papers, signed by Washington, to receive the freedom of Valparaiso from Governor-General Don Ambrosio O'Higgins. Others were not so fortunate, and many a poor sailor, forced against his will into smuggling, spent in consequence a term of years in a South American calaboose.

Whaling was another industry of maritime Massachusetts that renewed its strength in the Pacific. But we must postpone our whaling voyage lest we lose sight of the Canton market, the golden lodestone for every otter-skin, sealskin, or sandalwood log collected on Northwest Coast, California. or Pacific Islands.

CHAPTER VI

THE CANTON MARKET

1784–1812

THE Northwest trade, the Hawaiian trade, and the fur-seal fisheries were only a means to an end: the procuring of Chinese teas and textiles, to sell again at home and abroad. China was the only market for sea-otter, and Canton the only Chinese port where foreigners were allowed to exchange it.

Major Shaw's description of the Canton trade in 1784 would fit any year to 1840. After a voyage of several weeks from Hawaii, a Yankee trader passed between Luzon and Formosa, made Lintin Island, ran a gantlet of piratical junks, paused at the old Portuguese factory of Macao, and sailed up-river past the Bogue forts to Whampoa, the anchorage for all foreign merchantmen. There the Hoppo came aboard to receive gifts for wife, mother, and self, and measure the ship for her 'cumshaw-duty.' Thence her cargo was lightered in chop-boats twelve miles upstream to Canton, landed at Jackass Point, and stored in a factory or hong hired from one of the twelve Chinese security merchants, who had a monopoly of foreign trade, and acted as commercial godfathers to the Fan-Kwae, or foreign devils.

To Yankee seamen, fresh from the savage wilderness of the Northwest, how marvelous, bewildering was old Canton! Against a background of terraced hongs with their great go-downs or warehouses, which screened the forbidden City of Rams from foreign devils' gaze, flowed the river, bearing a city of boats the like of which he had never dreamed. Moored to the shore were flower-boats, their upper works cunningly carved into the shape of flowers and birds, and strange sounds issuing from their painted windows. Mandarin boats decorated with gay silk pennants, and propelled by double banks of oars, moved up and down in stately cadence. Great tea-deckers, with brightly lacquered topsides and square sail of brown matting, brought the Souchong, Young Hyson, and Bohea from up-river. In and out darted thousands of little sampans, housing entire families who plied their humble trades afloat. Provision dealers cried their wares from boats heaped high with colorful and deadly produce. Barbers' skiffs announced their coming by the twanging of tweezers, emblem of their skippers' painful profession. Twilight brought the boat people to their moorings, a bamboo pole thrust in oozy bottom, and paper lanterns diffused a soft light over the river. For color and exotic flavor there was no trade like the old China trade, no port like Canton.

Boston traders, in contrast to the arrogant officials of Honourable John, were welcomed by the Chinese; and on their part acquired an esteem for the Chinese character that has endured to this day. Russell Sturgis, who traveled and resided in many lands, said that he never knew better gentlemen than the Hong merchants. Houqua's name was a household word in Boston merchants' families. They never tired of describing old Houqua tearing up the $72,000 promissory note of a homesick Bostonian, with the remark, "You and I olo flen; you belong honest man only no got chance. . . . Just now have setlee counter, alla finishee; you go, you please." But trade did not always go on in this princely manner. The Chinese were able to instruct even Bostonians in the pleasant art of smuggling. There was much clandestine trade in otter-skins from Yankee ships in Macao Roads, or the near-by Dirty Butter Bay; good training for opium-running at a later period.

The strange laws and customs of the Chinese led to the creation of Boston mercantile agencies at Canton in order to ease the way for American traders. Major Shaw established the first, Shaw & Randall, on his return to Canton as American consul in 1786. The *Columbia's* cargo was handled by him, and a commission of seven and one-half per cent charged on the return lading. Competition later reduced this to two and one-half per cent, of which one was returned to the supercargo. The most famous house of our period was Perkins & Co., a branch of J. & T. H. Perkins, of Boston. Established in 1803, the illness of the chief put this concern under the charge of his sixteen-year-old clerk, John Perkins Cushing. The young man's letters were so precocious that his uncles made him permanent head man, and took him into partnership. Except for two brief visits home, Cushing remained at Canton thirty years, and became the most wealthy and highly respected foreign merchant in China.

What with the commissions, duties, presents, and graft that must be yielded at every step to hoppo, comprador, or linguist, the cost of doing business at Canton was very heavy. The *Columbia's* first lading, of one thousand and fifty sea-otter skins, sold for $21,404.71; but after fees, expenses, and repairs were deducted, only $11,241.51 remained to invest in a homeward cargo. Even after the ropes were learned, it was a clever captain who expended less than six thousand dollars at Canton. Yet the American demand for tea, nankeens, crapes, and silks increased so fast, and Boston merchant-shipowners proved so efficient in the cheap handling and distribution of China goods to all parts of the world, that the trade grew by leaps and bounds. The value of imports at Canton on American vessels rose to over five million dollars in 1805–06; of this over one million was accounted for by 17,445 sea-otter, 140,297 seal, and 34,460 beaver-skins, and 1600 piculs of sandalwood. Most of the remainder was specie brought directly from Boston, New York, and Philadelphia. The same year American vessels exported almost ten million pounds of tea from Canton. It was a constant marvel to Europeans, who conducted the China trade in great ships owned by chartered monopolies, how the Americans managed to survive these heavy charges with their small, individually owned vessels. Yet the American, and particularly the Boston way of China trading was the more economical. Free competition, and elimination of pomp and circumstance, more than made up for the small craft's disadvantage in 'overhead.'

When the winter season brought favoring winds, the ships quickly completed their lading, obtained the Grand Chop that passed them down-river, and caught the northeast monsoon down the China Sea. Off the coast of Borneo began several hundred miles of dangerous waters: shoals, reefs, and fantastic islands, baffling winds and treacherous currents, among which one had the feeling that Conrad describes, of being constantly watched. Let a vessel but touch on submerged reef, and hundreds of Malay proas come swarming to take her life's blood. Through Gaspar Passage or Banka Straits the vessel reached a welcome stretch of open water, and before long the sight of Java Head. A stop for fresh provisions was made off the village of Anjer, where Java "rose from level groves of shore palms to lofty blue peaks terraced with rice and red-massed kina plantations, with shining streams and green kananga flowers and tamarinds, and the land breeze, fragrant with clove buds and cinnamon, came off to the ship like a vaporous dusk." [1] There, the ship was quickly surrounded by a swarm of canoes plied by naked Malays, and laden with cocoanuts, oranges, mangoes and mangosteen; with Java sparrows, parrots, monkeys, green turtles, and Malacca-joint canes.

From this enchanted spot the ship threaded the Sunda Straits, full of dangerous rocks that rose out of seventy-fathom depths, toward which the currents irresistibly drew becalmed vessels. "Thank God we are clear of Sunda Straits," confided a Boston shipmaster to his sea journal on November 19, 1801. "'T is surprising to see the joy depicted on every one's countenance at getting clear of these horrid straits. Many of the sailors who had never been off duty was now obliged to take to their beds. Many a time they had to support themselves on a Gun while doing their duty. Still they would not give out till we got clear. Such men as these deserve my best regards."

Once a vessel was clear of the straits, a quartering southeast wind stretched her across the Indian Ocean to Madagascar and the Cape of Good Hope. Simon's Town was frequently visited for a little smuggling. Then, after a last call at St. Helena, the China trader squared away for Cape Cod.

*
* *

"There are better ships nowadays, but no better seamen," wrote an aged Boston merchant in 1860; and his words still hold good. Of these gallant Nor'west-men, who thought no more of rounding the Horn than their descendants do of rounding Cape Cod, Captain

[1] Hergesheimer, *Java Head.*

THE CANTON MARKET

'Bill' Sturgis was one of the best. A tough, beetly-browed son of a Cape Cod shipmaster, he left Boston for the Coast in 1798 as sixteen-year-old foremast hand on the ship *Eliza*, belonging to T. H. Perkins, his young but wealthy relative. He returned to Boston five years later as master of the Lambs' ship *Caroline*, and of the fur trade. On his third voyage, in command of Theodore Lyman's new ship *Atahualpa* with $300,-000 in specie on board, he beat off an attack of sixteen pirate junks in Macao Roads. Returning, he formed with John Bryant, of Boston, the firm of Bryant & Sturgis, which after the War of 1812 revived the Northwest fur trade, and opened the hide traffic with California.

William Sturgis became one of the wealthiest merchants of Boston, and lived to hear the news of Gettysburg; but no one dared call him a merchant prince. Owing perhaps to the caricature of leisure-class display he had seen among the Northwest Indians, Captain Sturgis refused to surround himself with paintings, bric-à-brac, and useless furniture. Throughout the worst period of interior decoration, his simple mansion on Church Green remained as neat and bare as a ship's cabin. When he occupied a Boston seat in the Great and General Court, one of the professional orators of that body got off a long Greek quotation. Captain Bill replied in one of the Indian dialects of the Northwest Coast, which, he explained, was much more to the point, and probably as well understood by his colleagues, as that of the honorable and learned gentleman. Public-spirited without self-advertisement, writing and lecturing with salty emphasis on the Oregon country, an honored member of learned societies, yet proud that he came in through the hawse-hole; William Sturgis was the finest type of Boston merchant created by these far-flung adventures of Federalist days.

Another famous Nor'westman, who had neither the background nor the connections of William Sturgis, was Captain John Suter. Born of Scots parents near Norfolk, Virginia, in 1781, left a penniless orphan at the age of eight, he made his way to Boston on a schooner. The child was befriended by a Boston pilot, who taught him to hand, reef and steer, to read his Bible, and to live straight. At seventeen he began his deep-sea voyages. The next two years brought adventures enough to have dampened any one's ardor for seafaring; privateering against France, capture, and a Brest dungeon; a West-India voyage, impressment into a British frigate, an attack of smallpox, and one of 'yellow jack.' Yet no sooner was the boy back in Boston than he shipped as foremast hand on the ship *Alert* outward bound to the Northwest Coast and Canton.

Without education, family, or anything but his own merits to recommend him, John Suter did so well on his first Northwest voyage that on his second, in 1804, he sailed as mate and "assistant trader" on the ship *Pearl*. On her return, he was promoted to master and supercargo, and made a most successful voyage to the Coast and Canton. The value of ship, outfit, and cargo, judging from statistics of other voyages, could not have exceeded forty thousand dollars.[1] In spite of some unpleasantness with the Indians — who once had to be cleared from the *Pearl's* decks by cross-fire from the loopholes — Captain Suter collected enough furs

[1] The cargoes of twelve vessels which cleared from Boston for the Northwest Coast between 1797 and 1800 were invoiced between $7500 and $19,700. (*Solid Men of Boston*, 76.) The *Caroline* in 1803 asked only $14,000 and obtained but $13,000 insurance for ship, cargo, and outfit. The rate was seventeen per cent, covering risk "against the Natives and as well on shore as on board."

and sandalwood to pay all expenses at Canton, and lay out $156,743.21 in goods. His return cargo is so typical of that trade and period, that I give it in detail, from the Captain's own manuscript memoranda, with the prices realized at auction sale in Boston.

SALES OF SHIP PEARL'S CARGO AT BOSTON, 1810

50 blue and white dining sets, 172 pieces each....	$ 2 290.00
480 tea sets, 49 pieces each......................	2 704.80
30 boxes enameled cups and sauces, 50 dozen each	1 360.00
100 boxes Superior Souchong tea...	795.87
100 chests Souchong.............................	3 834.66
235 " Hyson.............................	13 290.65
160 " Hyson Skin..........................	5 577.40
400 " other teas..........................	13 668.48
200 chests Cassia of 2208 "matts" each..........	8 585.52
170 000 pieces 'Nankins'...........................	118 850.00
14 000 " (280 bales) blue do....................	24 195.00
5 000 " (50 ") yellow do.................	6 800.00
2 000 " (50 ") white do..................	2 580.00
24 bottles oil of Cassia.......................	466.65
92 cases silks (black 'sinchaws,' black 'sattins,' white and blue striped do. dark brown plains, bottle-green and black striped 'sattins for Gentlemens ware'........................	56 344.61
And sundries, bring the total to....................	261 343.18

Expenses of sale, including auctioneer's commission, wharfage, truckage, "advertising in *Centinel* and *Gazette*, 5.50," "advertising and crying of sales, 30.31," "liquors, 5.88".................................	2 129.06
Captain Suter's 'primage,' 5% on balance............	12 960.70
Balance to owners................................	246 253.42

On this were paid customs duties, within 12 months...	39 602.95
Net profit on voyage..............................	206 650.47

Having proved himself both a keen trader and an able master, Captain Suter was offered by George

Lyman a 'primage' of ten per cent, with the usual 'privilege' and salary, to succeed Captain Sturgis on the *Atahualpa*. He accepted, and took a sixteenth share in ship and cargo as well.

Owing to his ruthless repulse of a band of Indians who had boarded the *Pearl*, Captain Suter returned to the Coast a marked man. One day an Indian chief came on board, ostensibly to trade. Immediately a flotilla of dugouts, containing over two thousand warriors, issued from behind a wooded point and surrounded the *Atahualpa*. They found a worthy successor to Captain Sturgis on her quarterdeck. Suter took the chief by the throat, put a pistol to his head, and told him to order the canoes away or he would blow his brains out. The order was given. Deliberately weighing anchor, Captain Suter made sail, and when free of the canoes released his prisoner, who turned out to be the very Indian who had successfully attacked John Jacob Astor's *Tonquin*.

Owing to the War of 1812 and the presence of British cruisers in the Pacific, Captain Suter sold the *Atahualpa* at Hawaii at considerable sacrifice; but he got enough furs into Canton to send home, after peace was concluded, a cargo that netted the owners almost $120,000 on their original adventure of not over $40,000.

Would that we could reproduce the language, expressions, and motions of that extinct breed, the Nor'-westman of Boston! Of John Suter, little survives but bare facts, and one anecdote. He was more deeply religious than most New England-born sea-captains, and read the Bible aloud daily on shipboard. One young scamp of a supercargo amused himself by putting back the bookmark at the conclusion of every day's reading, until the Captain remarked mildly that he seemed to be having head winds through the Book of Daniel! After a sixth and a seventh voyage around the world, Captain Suter settled down in Boston to the tranquil joys of home and family, church and lodge, that he had fairly won from sea and savage barter.

"Sir, you'l please to let my mama know that I am well, Mr. Boit [the fifth mate, aged seventeen] also requests you'l let his parent know he is in health." This postscript to a letter of John Hoskins, clerk of the *Columbia*, to her principal owner, reminds us how young were the Yankee seamen of that period. It seems that the generation of Revolutionary privateersmen was so quickly absorbed in our expanding merchant marine as to call the youngest classes to the colors. A famous youngsters' voyage to Eastern waters, many times described, was that of the Derby ship *Benjamin*, of Salem, in 1792–94. Captain Nathaniel Silsbee, later United States Senator from Massachusetts, was but nineteen when he took command of this vessel; yet he had followed the sea for five years, served as Captain Magee's clerk on the *Astrea*, and commanded two voyages to the West Indies. His first mate, Charles Derby, was but one year older; his clerk, Richard J. Cleveland, but eighteen. The second mate, an old salt of twenty-four, proved insubordinate and was put ashore!

With a miscellaneous cargo, including hops, saddlery, window glass, mahogany boards, tobacco, and Madeira wine, these schoolboys made a most successful voyage to the Cape of Good Hope and Ile de France, using sound judgment as to ports, cargoes, and freight, amid embargoes and revolutions; slipping their cables at Capetown after dark in a gale of wind to escape a British frigate; drifting out of Bourbon with the ebb tide to elude a French brig-o'-war; spending a few days fishing, shooting wild goats, and catching turtles at Ascension; returning to Salem after nineteen months' absence, with a cargo which brought almost five hundred per cent profit to the owner, and enabled the young master to make a home for his mother and sisters.

Captain Silsbee was by no means the youngest shipmaster on record. James Howland, 2d, of New Bedford, was given a merchant ship by his father on his eighteenth birthday, and as her captain went on a honeymoon voyage to the Baltic with his still younger bride, before the year elapsed.

But the most remarkable youthful exploit in this bright dawn of Pacific adventure, that has come to my notice, is John Boit, Jr.'s voyage around the world, in the eighty-nine-ton sloop *Union*, of Boston.

At the age of nineteen, on August 1, 1794, he sailed from Newport as master of this sixty-foot craft and her crew of twenty-two, with ten carriage guns, eight swivels, and a full cargo and outfit for the Northwest Coast. The voyage south was pleasantly broken by catching green turtles and shooting albatross — one measuring sixteen feet tip to tip; by celebrating Christmas Day, and stopping at St. Iago and the Falklands, to save the crew from scurvy, and to hunt wild hogs. The *Union* rounded the Horn safely in thick, blowy weather, reaching 57° 42' south latitude on February 4, 1795. On May 16, two hundred and sixty days out, she sighted land, and the next day dropped anchor in "Columbia's cove, Bulfinch's Sound," on Vancouver Island. Here, young Boit tells us, he felt quite at home. The natives recognized him, and inquired after each and every member of the *Columbia's* crew. Furs were double the price of 1792, but trade was brisk, and the sloop went as far north as 54° 15' to complete her cargo.

THE CANTON MARKET

On June 20, when lying at anchor in Puget Sound, the *Union* was attacked by several hundred Indians under Chief Scootch-Eye. With husky savages swarming around the sloop and over his bulwarks, Captain Boit and his crew kept their nerve, and without a single casualty to themselves killed the chief and forty of his warriors. When they got under way, and stood in toward the nearest village, the Indians came out trembling, waving green boughs and offering otter-skins in propitiation.

After a fruitless attempt to cross the bar at the mouth of the Columbia River, the *Union* went north again to Queen Charlotte's Island, and left the Coast for Canton on September 12, 1795. One month later, Captain Boit sighted "Owhyhee," at a distance of thirty leagues. The next day, sailing alongshore, the sloop was visited by native canoes bringing hogs and pineapples, and "the females were quite *amorous*." On December 5, the sloop joined seven larger American vessels at Whampoa. After exchanging his sea-otter for silk and nankeens, and taking freight and passengers for the Ile de France, he got under way in company with the American fleet on January 12, 1796. It was a two months' sail through the China Sea, the Straits of Sunda, and the Indian Ocean to Mauritius. Completing his cargo there with coffee and pepper, Captain Boit began the last leg of his voyage at the end of March, 1796. After passing the Island of Madagascar, he found the sloop's mast sprung, and had to fish it and apply preventer backstays while under way. Then came a four days' westerly gale, which stove in part of the *Union's* bulwarks, and swept the hen-coops off her deck, as she lay to. Early in May she rounded the Cape of Good Hope, and caught the southeast trades. Off Georges Bank, she was brought to by the French sloop-of-war *Scipio*, but allowed to pass "with the utmost politeness." Near Boston Harbor the British frigate *Reason* fired a shot through the *Union's* staysail, and forced the young master to come aboard with his papers, but "finding they could not make a prize of the sloop, suffer'd me to pass, after treating me in a rough and *ungentlemanlike* manner." At last, on July 8, came the welcome gleam of Boston Light. Castle William, as seafaring men still called Fort Independence, saluted the returning sloop with fifteen guns, which she returned. Anchoring in the inner harbor, she saluted the town, and got "three huzzas of welcome" from the wharves. The *Union* made a "saving voyage," beat most of the fleet home, and was the first, possibly the only, sloop-rigged vessel ever to circumnavigate the globe.

In view of the newspaper publicity given nowadays to men of twice Boit's age and experience for crossing the Atlantic in vessels no smaller than the *Union* and far better equipped, it is refreshing to note the scant attention he got. "Sloop Union, Boit, Canton," in small type at the end of 'Arrivals' in the "Boston Centinel." That was all![1]

*

* *

Many a Boston family owes its rise to fame and fortune to the old Nor'west and China trade; and not a few of them were founded by masters who came in through the hawse-hole, like Sturgis and Suter. Emoluments were much higher than on any other trade route. Masters and mates received only twenty to twenty-five dollars monthly wages; but each officer

[1] Another Boston paper reports his experience with the men-of-war, but makes no comment on his voyages.

had the 'privilege' of one-half to five tons (twenty to two hundred cubic feet) cargo space on the homeward passage for his private adventures in China goods; beside 'primage,' a commission of from one to eight per cent [1] on the net proceeds of the voyage. It was only prudent for owners to be generous with their ships' officers, on a route where the opportunities for private trading and fixing accounts were so great. Even with half the luck of John Suter, a master could clear twenty-five hundred dollars a year, and pyramid his profits by taking a share in the next voyage he commanded.

These wages and allowances were sufficient to attract the best type of New Englander. Nor'westmen's officers were almost exclusively native-born or adopted Yankees, and the men recruited largely from Cape Cod, Boston, and 'down East.' But every forecastle contained a few foreigners. [2]

No Richard Dana has told the story of the Nor'-westmen from the foremast angle. Unless the records of our admiralty courts yield something, the common seaman's side is lost. Certain it is, that the Northwest fur trade, until it existed no more, enjoyed a greater prestige and popularity among New England seamen than any other route. [3] Mutinies occurred, but

[1] Suter's primage of ten per cent on the *Atahualpa* was exceptional. On his next voyage, in the *Mentor*, he received but seven and one-half. The *Mentor's* chief mate had twenty dollars wages, one per cent on net sales at Canton, and two and one-half tons 'privilege' home.

[2] See chapter VIII.

[3] Dana tells a good story illustrating this, in his *Two Years Before the Mast*. On her homeward voyage from the California coast, with a cargo of hides, the *Alert* spoke a Plymouth brig, and sent a boat aboard to procure fresh provisions. Her Yankee mate leaned over the rail, and asked where they were from. "From the Nor'west Coast!" said sailor Joe, wishing to gain glory in the eyes of this humble West-India trader. "What's your cargo?" came next. "Skins!" said Joe. "Here and there a *horn?*" said the mate dryly, and every one laughed.

mutinies prove little. One that Captain Suter suppressed in Honolulu Harbor, with his strong right arm and cutlass, was caused by gambling among the crew. Many deserted in the Sandwich Islands, but who would not? Rumors have come down of unscrupulous owners, who in order to save money abandoned men on the Northwest Coast and substituted Kanakas. Captain James Magee brought the first Chinaman to the United States, but he was a student, not a sailor. And few such made the voyage twice. As "China Jack" (the favorite Whampoa factotum for American vessels) remarked after essaying a round trip to Boston, "Too muchee strong gale, sea allsame high mast head — no can see sky!"

CHAPTER VII

THE SALEM EAST INDIES

1790–1812

THE most formidable rival to Boston in the contest for Oriental wealth lay but sixteen miles "to the east'd," as we say on the Massachusetts coast when we mean north. Salem, with a little under eight thousand inhabitants, was the sixth city in the United States in 1790.[1] Her appearance was more antique even than that of Boston, and her reek of the salt water, that almost surrounded her, yet more pronounced. For half a mile along the harbor front, subtended by the long finger of Derby Wharf, ran Derby Street, the residential and business center of the town. On one side were the houses of the gentry, Derbys and Princes and Crowninshields, goodly gambrel or hip-roofed brick and wooden mansions dating from the middle of the century, standing well back with tidy gardens in front. Opposite were the wharves, separated from the street by counting-rooms, warehouses, ship-chandlers' stores, pump-makers' shops, sailmakers' lofts; all against a background of spars, rigging, and furled or brailed-up sails. Crowded within three hundred yards of Derby Street, peeping between the merchants' mansions and over their garden walls like small boys behind a police cordon, were some eighteen or nineteen hundred wooden buildings, including dwellings of pre-witchcraft days, with overhanging upper stories, peaked gables, small-paned windows, and hand-rifted clapboards black with age.

[1] Not including Beverly, which with three thousand, three hundred inhabitants in 1790, was combined with Salem as a port of entry in 1789.

79

A few steps from the merchant's mansion lies his counting-room and wharf, where his favorite vessel is loading Russia duck, West-India sugar, New-England rum and French brandy for anywhere beyond the Cape of Good Hope; to return with goodness knows what produce of Asia, Africa, and the Malay Archipelago, which you may then purchase at wholesale or retail from the selfsame wharf. From his front chamber the merchant may watch the progress of his new vessel in the near-by shipyard; but unless he be a privileged character like 'King' Derby, with "an intuitive faculty in judging of models and proportions," he had best not interfere. Shipbuilding, an ancient industry in Salem, is now growing fast; the China voyages of the *Grand Turk* and *Astrea* produced such a demand for new tonnage that Enos Briggs, a master builder of Pembroke in the Old Colony, has come to Salem, and at the head of Derby Wharf is constructing a new *Grand Turk* of five hundred and sixty tons, for which the new duck manufactory is weaving sailcloth. Next year he shall astonish the natives by launching a vessel sideways from the wharf; all Salem, summoned by town crier, helping or cheering. Ebenezer Mann, another North-Riverite, has the barque *Good Intent* on the stocks for Simon Forrester; and a vessel is rising on every slip of the ancient yard where Retire Becket carries on the business of his ancestors.

A Salem boy in those days was born to the music of windlass chanty and caulker's maul; he drew in a taste for the sea with his mother's milk; wharves and shipyards were his playground; he shipped as boy on a coaster in his early teens, saw Demerara and St. Petersburg before he set foot in Boston, and if he had the right stuff in him, commanded an East-Indiaman before he was twenty-five.

THE SALEM EAST INDIES

Whenever a Salem lad could tear himself away from the wharves, he would go barefoot to Juniper Point or pull a skiff to Winter Island, and scan the bay for approaching sail. Marblehead was a better vantage-point; but it was a lion-hearted Salem boy indeed who dared venture within the territorial waters of Marble-head in those days! The appearance of a coaster or fisherman or West-India trader caused no special emotion; but if the stately form of an East-Indiaman came in view, then 't was race back to Derby Wharf, and earn a silver Spanish dollar for good news. The word speeds rapidly through the town, which begins to swarm like an ant-hill; counting-room clerks rush out to engage men for unloading, sailors' taverns and board-ing-houses prepare for a brisk run of trade, parrots scream and monkeys jabber, and every master of his own time makes for cap-sill, roof-tree, or other vantage-point.

Let us follow one of the privileged, an old-time provincial magnate now in the East-India trade, as with powdered wig, cocked hat, and scarlet cloak, attended by Pompey or Cuff with the precious tele-scope, he puffs up garret ladder to captain's walk. What a panorama! To the east stretches the noble North Shore, Cape Ann fading in the distance. No sail in that direction, save a fisherman beating inside Baker's. Across the harbor, obscuring the southerly channel, Marblehead presents her back side of rocky pasture to the world at large, and Salem in particular. Wind is due south, tide half flood and the afternoon waning, so if the master be a Salem boy he will bring his ship around Peach's Point, inside Kettle Bottom, Endeavors, Triangles, and the Aqua Vitæs. We adjust the glass to the outer point where she must first appear, and wait impatiently. A flash of white as the sun catches foretopgallant sails over Naugus Head; then the entire ship bursts into view, bowling along at a good eight knots. Her ensign's apeak, so all aboard are well. A puff of smoke bursts from her starboard bow, and then another, as the first crack of a federal salute strikes the ear. Fort William replies in kind, and all Salem with a roar of cheering. Every one recognizes the smart East-Indiaman that dropped down-harbor thirty months ago.

"Is the front chamber prepared for Captain Richard?" asks our elderly merchant, as he descends to greet his son — just in time, for the ship, hauling close to the wind, is making for Derby Wharf. Within ten minutes she has made a running moor, taken in her sails, and warped into the best berth. The crowd parts deferentially as master and supercargo stalk ashore, gapes at a turbaned Oriental who shipped as cabin boy, exchanges good-natured if somewhat Rabelaisian banter with officers and crew, and waits to see the mysterious matting-covered bales, shouldered out of the vessel's hold.

To conclude this picture of Salem at the dawn of her period of greatest prosperity, read this abstract of the entries and customs duties during a period of twenty days, from May 31 to June 18, 1790, as I found them in the old custom house on Derby Street; and remember that these are foreign entries only, not including the fishermen, and the coasters that distributed Salem's winnings to a hundred American ports.

May 31. Brig *William & Henry*, B. Hodges master, from Canton. Tea, coffee, silks, spices and nankeens for Gray & Orne, Benj. Hodges, George Dodge, Jno. Appleton, Samuel Hewes Jr., Simon Elliot, Robt. Wyer, Mark Haskoll $9,783.81

June 2. Schooner *Betsy*, William Wooldridge master,

from Cadiz. Lemons, feathers, raisins, oil and salt for
William Gray.................................... 114.30

June 3. Schooner *Active*, Seward Lee master, from
Lisbon. Wine, salt, lemons, and feathers for William Gray 171.47

June 5. Schooner *Lark*, Saml. Foster master, from
Cadiz. Salt, Lemons, figs, &c. for Brown & Thorndike.... 35.40

June 5. Schooner *Bee*, Hezekiah Wallace master, from
Lisbon. Wine, salt and feathers for William Gray...... 166.92

June 5. Ship *Astrea*, James Magee master, from Canton. Tea, silks, China ware, nankeens and other merchandise for O. Brewster, J. Powers, Wm. Cabot, Webb & Brown, E. Verry, A. Jacobs, David Barber, B. Pickman, J. McGregore, G. Dodge, E. H. Derby, S. Parkman, D. Sears, E. Johnson, N. West, J. Gardner Jr., T. H. Perkins, Jno. Derby Jr., Webb & Bray, Magee & Perkins, J. Magee, T. H. Perkins & Co., J. Magee & Co........ 27,109.18

June 11. Schooner *Experiment*, Joseph Teel master, from St. Eustatia. Sugar, rum, gin and salt for R. Beckett & J. Teel..................................... 123.64

June 11. Brig *Three Brothers*, John Collins master, from the West Indies. Sugar, rum, iron and salt for John Collins... 207.82

June 12. Schooner *Nancy*, Sam. McIntire master, from the Isle of May.[1] Salt for Samuel Page.......... 96.12

June 14. Schooner *Hanah*, Rich. Ober master, from Lisbon. Salt, wine, and lemons for Hill & Ober........ 55.23

June 15. Ship *Light Horse*, Ichabod Nichols master, from Canton. Tea, silks and China ware for E. H. Derby, Hy. Elkins, J. Crowninshield, I. Nichols, Jno. Derby Jr., E. Gibaut.. 16,312.98

June 17. Schooner *Dolphin*, Thos. Bowditch Jr. master, from Port au Prince. Salt, sugar, and coffee for Norris & Burchmore............................. 56.97

June 17. Schooner *Sally*, John Burchmore master, from Port au Prince. Sugar and molasses for Jno. Norris & Co. 323.93

June 18. Schooner *Lydia*, Gabriel Holman master, from Aux Cayes. Molasses for Sprague & Holman...... 70.43

June 18. Schooner *Sukey & Betsey*, Thos. Bowditch master, from Martinico. Molasses, raisins & limes, for Saml. Ingersoll.................................. 101.97

[1] Maia, in the Cape Verde Islands.

June 18. Schooner *John*, Nehemiah Andrews master, from St. Lucia. Sugar, coffee, cocoa and molasses for N. West... 297.42

June 18. Brig *Favorite*, William Bradshaw master, from Lisbon. Salt, wine, and lemons for Joshua Ward & Co.. 113.13

Boston was the Spain, Salem the Portugal, in the race for Oriental opulence. Boston followed Magellan and the *Columbia* westward, around the Horn; Salem sent her vessels eastward after the *Astrea*, around Africa, along the path blazed by Vasco da Gama. Trace a rough curve from the Chinese coast along 20° north latitude, pull it south before reaching Hawaii, to join 120° west longitude at the equator, and you have a rough line of demarcation between the two. Everything north and east was preëmpted by Boston. Salem never entered the Northwest fur trade, and her first circumnavigator was a humble sealskinner in 1802. But to the southward and westward of this line, in the Dutch East Indies, Manila, Mauritius, both coasts of Africa, and the smaller islands of the Pacific, *Salem* had the same connotation as *Boston* on the Northwest Coast; it stood for the whole United States. As late as 1833, Po Adam, the wealthiest merchant of Quallah Battoo, "believed Salem to be a country by itself, and one of the richest and most important sections of the globe." Boston vessels competed at Calcutta; Salem vessels sometimes attained Canton; the fleet met off Java Head and returned home together; but for the most part each respected the other's territory, and left little to divide between Providence, New York, Philadelphia, and Baltimore.

The usual Salem method of making a trading voyage was to start off with a mixed cargo, assembled from Southern ports, the Baltic, the West Indies, and New England; peddle it out at the Cape of Good Hope,

Mauritius, and various ports in the East Indies; picking up oddments here and there, taking freight when occasion offered, buying bills of exchange on London or Amsterdam, and like as not making three or four complete turnovers before returning home. A typical outward cargo was that of 'King' Derby's ship *Henry*, one hundred ninety tons, which cleared from Salem for the Ile de France (Mauritius) in 1791. Pottery and ale, iron and salt fish, soap and gin, hams and flints, whale oil and candles, saddles and bridles, lard and tobacco, chocolate and flour, tables and desks made up her manifest. Her twenty-one-year-old master, Jacob Crowninshield,[1] was one of four brothers, each of whom commanded a vessel at about the same age. Their father, George Crowninshield, had but recently retired from the sea at the age of fifty-five, and was soon to rival 'King' Derby as merchant-shipowner. Captain Jacob had a great career before him; crowned by an offer, thirteen years later, of the Navy Department by President Jefferson. Ill health from long voyages in tropical waters obliged him to decline; but the same high office was subsequently conferred on a younger brother by President Madison.

The *Henry* obtained most of her return lading at Mauritius. But British sea power gradually strangled this eastern emporium of France, and Salem vessels were obliged to go to the source of supplies. This led to Massachusetts men taking up their residence in the seaports of British India. Samuel Shaw found his friend Benjamin Joy already established at Calcutta, on his return from China; and Thomas Lechmere, of Salem, became an alderman of Bombay.

In this sort of commerce, a large discretion was left to shipmasters and supercargoes. A typical letter of

[1] Pronounced 'Grounsell' at that period, but now as it is spelled.

instruction is one of 1792 from William Gray, another Salem rival of the Derbys, to Captain William Ward, of the brig *Enterprise*, one hundred sixty-four tons. He will dispose of his Russia duck, 'coles' (from Liverpool), and anything that he may think proper, at the Cape of Good Hope. There he is to pick up wine, brandy, raisins, and almonds for the Ile de France, where the whole cargo ought to sell for one hundred per cent profit, provided the *Enterprise* arrives before a certain Boston vessel. Captain Ward is to purchase there anything that will pay cent per cent at Salem, according to a list of prices current furnished him. His next stop should be Calcutta to take on sugar, saltpeter, and "Bandanno silk Handkerchiefs" at the same rate. Otherwise he must try to get a 'cheep' cargo of teak to exchange at Canton for China goods. He may even sell the brig, if a good opportunity offers. As Captain Ward did not find prices low enough for his owner's modest expectations, he took freight from India to Ostend, and there filled his hold with European merchandise.

Until 1811, when British regulations (surprisingly liberal at first) forbade all but direct voyages between India and the United States, the East-India trade was susceptible of infinite variety. Benjamin Carpenter, the Salem master of the Boston ship *Hercules*, wrote in 1794 that profits might be pyramided indefinitely by freighting goods between Ceylon, Bombay, Calcutta, and Madras, and by judicious turnovers at Rangoon, Bengal, and Coromandel. That is, provided one tipped heavily, and behaved like a gentleman. "From the Governor to the meanest citizen, I have made it my study to please. Let a man's occupation be what it will, you may have occasion for his aid. I have known a present of 10 s. to be the means of saving £100. Good language will have the same effect, therefore exert

86

yourself as much as possible this way and set apart £20 for these purposes."

During the European war, Madeira acquired an important relation to the East-India trade. Salem and Boston merchants exchanged general cargoes there for Madeira wine, which found a ready sale in Calcutta. They also began the pleasant practice of laying in a few pipes [1] for home consumption, the long voyage in southern waters improving its flavor. A typical voyage was that of the Maine-built ship *Herald*, three hundred twenty-eight tons, commanded by Nathaniel Silsbee (formerly of the *Benjamin*), and owned by himself, Samuel Parkman, and Ebenezer Preble. She sailed from Boston in January, 1800, with a cargo consisting of butter, beef, tobacco, codfish, rum, nankeen from China, two hundred thirty-six pipes of French brandy that had run the British blockade, and a large quantity of silver dollars and bills of exchange. Most of the provisions, the nankeen and the liquor were exchanged at Madeira for two hundred sixty pipes of "India market" wine and a score of "choice old London particular" for Boston. This genial cargo was carried around the Cape of Good Hope to Madras, where the India market wine was sold, and pepper, blue cloth, 'camboys' and 'Pulicate' handkerchiefs taken aboard. At Bombay and Calcutta, the bills and specie purchased pepper, sugar, ginger, and a bewildering array of India cottons, for which the fashions of that day, and the absence of domestic competition, afforded an excellent market in the United States.[2] The *Herald's*

[1] A pipe was a double hogshead, containing 110 to 125 gallons.

[2] In the "Beverly Shipping Documents," I, at the Beverly Historical Society, is an important letter of 1796 from Benjamin Pickman, of Salem, to Israel Thorndike, of Beverly, advising him how best to lay out $20,000 at Calcutta, with samples of several different cottons attached. It appears from this that Beerboom Gurrahs, a stout white sheeting, cost

invoice shows 'Callipatti Baftas,' 'Beerboom Gurrahs,' 'Allabad Emerties,' and a score of different weaves. Madras chintzes and seersuckers are the only names recognizable to-day.

Calcutta, lying eighty miles up the Hoogly River, was a port most difficult of access before the days of tugboats. After passing the Sand Heads — a considerable feat of navigation in itself, at times — it often took weeks to beat up-river. The anchorage at Calcutta was dangerous on account of the tidal bores, which in certain seasons worked havoc with ground-tackle and shipping. In the southwest monsoon season of 1799, writes William Cleveland, of Salem, insurance from Calcutta to Hamburg was sixteen per cent; but premiums would be written for half that rate from the Sand Heads to Hamburg.

The *Herald* left the Hoogly in company with three vessels from Philadelphia and one from Baltimore. Outside competition was evidently becoming serious. It was the period of our naval hostilities with France. When the Americans fell in with a British East-Indiaman, under fire from a French privateer, they decided to bear a hand, and formed line-of-battle. The master of the vessel abreast the *Herald* expressed a keen desire to leave, his speed being sufficient to elude the privateer. Captain Silsbee roared through his speaking-trumpet, "If you do, I'll sink you!" To which his colleague replied, "Damn you, Silsbee, I know you would!"; and saw the action through to a successful finish.

Small "private adventures" for the officers' and

about twelve cents a yard, white print cloth seven to eleven cents, and "mock Pulicat Handkerchiefs," eighty-four to ninety-five cents for eight. William Tileston, of Boston, known as 'Count Indigo,' did an extensive business printing India bandannas at his dyehouse in the old feather store, Dock Square, and at Staten Island. The duty saved by importing plain goods made this profitable.

owners' friends, varying in amount from a box of codfish to several thousand dollars in specie, were carried
both by China and East-India traders. Captain Gibaut,
of Salem, in 1796, "had private orders to execute in his
ship at Canton amounting to $4000, for the little ele-
gancies of life . . . so rapid are our strides to wealth and
luxury," notes the Reverend William Bentley. On the
brig *Caravan*, of Salem (two hundred sixty-seven tons),
early in 1812, Captain Augustine Heard took two thousand silver dollars to invest for his father, the same for
each brother, and from twenty to one hundred dollars
for sundry maiden aunts and retired Ipswich sea-captains. Numerous friends requested him to purchase
for their wives red cornelian necklaces, camel's-hair
shawls, pieces of cobweb muslin or Mull Mull, straw
carpets, bed coverings, and pots of preserved ginger.
Henry Pickering wanted a Sanskrit bible, and three
children gave him a dollar each to invest in Calcutta.[1]
Besides there was a cargo valued at forty thousand
dollars, and the first consignment of missionaries, male
and female, sent by the Puritan Church of Massachusetts to "India's coral strand." But the Reverend and
Mrs. Adoniram Judson and Samuel Newell were not
wanted at Calcutta by the British authorities, and had
to be dropped at Mauritius.

Augustine Heard was a shipmaster whose cool daring
became legendary. Approaching the Sand Heads in an
onshore hurricane, having lost his best bower anchor,
and drawing a foot more water than there was on the
bar, Captain Heard shook a reef out of his topsails,
and laying the vessel on her beam ends, managed to

---

[1] One of the notes pasted in the *Caravan's* invoice book is: "Sir –
Please to purchase for Capt. John Barr — $200 — 2 Camels Hair Shawls
— White — 2 yards in Length & 1½ yards in width, with a Broad Palm
leaf Border mostly Green." A feminine hand has added, "narrow Border
round Edge avoid Red. If any Bal[ance] buy best Bandannas."

scrape across. Once, he is said to have run a pirate ship under in the China Sea. There are two versions of his return voyage in the *Caravan*, after the War of 1812 had commenced. According to one, he sold the *Caravan* and cargo to avoid capture in a South American port, and disguised as a shipwrecked mariner, with the specie proceeds in his sea-chest, took passage on a slaver to Rio de Janeiro, and thence to Boston. According to the other, the *Caravan* was captured off the coast of Madagascar by an English cruiser, which sent a lieutenant and prize crew aboard. All the Americans were placed in irons except the colored cook, and Captain Heard. Some days afterwards, a sudden and violent storm arose. While the English crew was aloft taking in sail, and the lieutenant busy giving orders, Heard went into the galley, got the cook, and with his aid knocked the irons off his own people. They then seized arms, rushed on deck, and as each English Jack descended the rigging, clapped him in irons and sent him below. Captain Heard then extended the courtesies of the cabin to the English officer, and brought him and his crew as prisoners into Salem Harbor.

On the Northwest coast of Sumatra, Salem found wealth and adventure such as Boston men obtained on the Northwest coast of America. Her merchant seamen, like the Portuguese before them, tracked Eastern spices to their source. It was at Benkulen, in 1793, that Captain Jonathan Carnes heard a rumor of wild pepper to the northwestward. Returning to Salem, he was given command of a fast schooner, and cleared for unknown destination. "Without chart or guide of any kind, he made his way amid numerous coral reefs, of which navigators have so much dread even at the present day, as far as the port of Analaboo."[1] His

[1] J. H. Reynolds, *Voyage of the U.S. Frigate Potomac* (1835), 201.

cargo, costing (with expenses) eighteen thousand dollars, sold for seven hundred per cent profit at Salem. The town went pepper mad. A dozen vessels cleared for Benkulen; but few of them got so much as a sneeze for their trouble. Gradually, however, the secret leaked out; and by 1800, years before there was a published chart of the Malay archipelago, the harbors of Analabu, Susu, Tally-Pow, Mingin, Labuan-Haji, and Muckie and all those treacherous waters now illuminated by the genius of Conrad, were as familiar to Salem shipmasters as Danvers River. Twenty-one American vessels, ten from Salem and eight from Boston, visited this coast between March 1 and May 14, 1803, bargaining with local datus for the wild pepper as the natives brought it in. Between the two northwest coasts there was little choice, in point of danger. Many a Salem man's bones lie in Sumatran waters, a Malay kreese between the ribs.

By way of reward, Salem became the American, and for a time the world emporium for pepper. In 1791, the United States exported 492 pounds of pepper; in 1805, it exported 7,559,244 pounds — over seven-eighths of the entire Northwest Sumatran crop; and a very large proportion of this was landed in Salem. Captain James Cook imported over one million pounds of pepper in one lading of his five-hundred-ton ship *Eliza*.

Some of the tinware that itinerant Yankees peddled throughout the Eastern States, was made from Banka tin, obtained by Salem traders from an island beside the Gaspar Straits. Batavia, the Tyre of Java, shortly

This is the usual version of the origin of the Northwest Sumatra trade. W. Vans, however, claims that he and Jonathan Freeman opened that trade in their brigantine *Cadet* in 1788. (*Life of William Vans* (1832), 4.) See forthcoming articles by Mr. George Putnam in Essex Historical Collections.

after the ship *Massachusetts* was refused entrance, opened her doors to American vessels, which brought home increasing amounts of sugar and coffee.

The famous *Astrea*, John Gibaut master, ventured into the harbor of Pegu, near Rangoon, in 1793, and was promptly commandeered by His Burmese Majesty. This enabled Captain Gibaut to travel up the Irawaddy River, collecting curiosities for the East-India Museum and for his Salem pastor, Dr. Bentley. He was undoubtedly the first American to take this classic road to Mandalay. No permanent trading connection, however, seems to have been established with Burma. A year later, one of the numerous Captain Hodges of Salem adventured a quantity of gum lacquer from Pegu, but was unable to dispose of it at any price.

"This day a letter from an Arabian Chief, Said Aimed," records Dr. Bentley on October 2, 1805, "by Mr. Bancroft, a Salem Factor in those seas. He mentioned the wish of a Jew to write to me in that country, from whom I may expect to hear by Capt. Elkins." That year Salem imported two million pounds of coffee from Arabia. So remote from the beaten track of vessels was Mocha, that the *Recovery*, of Salem, Captain Joseph Ropes, which opened the trade in 1798, was given a reception similar to that of Columbus in the new world. In 1806, the ship *Essex*, Captain Joseph Orne, with sixty thousand dollars in specie, adventured up the Red Sea to Hodeda. At Mocha he augmented his crew with some Arabs, who turned out to be 'inside men' of a notorious pirate. The *Essex* was captured, and her entire crew massacred. When the news reached the Salem owner, who was Captain Orne's uncle, he is said to have remarked, "Well, the ship is insured!"

A more cheerful story of the Mocha trade is the

maiden voyage of the well-armed ship *America*, owned
by George Crowninshield and his sons, and commanded by his nephew, Benjamin Crowninshield.
On July 2, 1804, she left Salem with very positive and
emphatic orders to proceed to Sumatra for pepper,
and nowhere else; for Captain Benjamin was too much
inclined to use his own judgment. "Obey orders if you
break owners," was a maxim of the old merchant marine. Yet this independent master received at Mauritius such favorable news of the coffee market that once
more he determined to disobey. On November 30, the
America passed "through the straits of Babelmandel,
and anchored off Mocha, the Grand Mosque bearing
E. by S." There, and at Aden and Macalla Roads she
took in coffee, gum arabic, hides, goatskins, and senna,
and cleared for Salem.

Now, by June, 1805, when the *America* was sighted
from Salem town, pepper had fallen and coffee risen
to such an extent that the owners were praying Captain
Ben had broken orders! Unable to restrain their im-
patience until she docked, the Crowninshield brothers
put off in a small boat. Approaching her to leeward,
they began sniffing the air. One was sure he smelled
the desired bean; but another suggested it might be
merely a pot of coffee on the galley stove. Finally, dis-
regarding all marine etiquette, Benjamin W. Crowninshield shouted, "What's your cargo?" — "Pe-pe-per!"
answered the Captain, who was enjoying the situation
hugely. "You lie! I smell coffee!" roared the future
Secretary of the Navy through his speaking-trumpet.

Once having found their way into the Pacific Ocean,
Salem shipmasters began to exploit its " Milky-ways
of coral isles, and low-lying, endless, unknown archi-
pelagoes and impenetrable Japans." The crews of Salem vessels, undismayed by the occasional killing and

eating of their comrades by Fiji cannibals, gathered edible birds' nests from surf-beaten rocks, employed native divers to fish tortoise-shell and mother-of-pearl; and gathered slimy sea-cucumbers ('beech de mer') from coral reefs, to make soup for the mandarins. Thus a new medium was obtained for purchasing China tea. One lonely group in the South Atlantic, Tristan de Cunha, was taken in formal possession by Jonathan Lambert, of Salem, remaining his private principality until his death in 1813.

A second ship *Astrea*, Henry Prince master, displayed her ensign in Manila Bay on October 3, 1796, and opened a trade in sugar, hemp, and indigo that continued as long as Salem men owned vessels. No Salem boy, in *seventeen* ninety-eight, thought the Philippines were canned goods! Most of our present insular possessions were visited by Boston or Salem ships before the nineteenth century — except Guam, which was saved for 1801. The barque *Lydia*, of Boston, Moses Barnard master, was chartered by the Spanish government to convey thither a new governor of the Marianas, with "Lady, three Children and two servant girls and 12 men servents, A Fryar & his servent, A Judge and two servents." The log of this voyage, by the *Lydia's* first mate, William Haswell, is among the most entertaining of the several hundred sea-journals preserved in Salem. The *Lydia* first put in at Zamboanga (Mindanao), a pleasant place which produced nothing but "Cocoa Nuts, water & Girls." Six of the latter were brought on board by the governor's sons, with "Music to Entertain us, but the Ship was so full of Lumber that they had no place to shew their Dancing in; how ever we made a shift to amuse ourselves till 3 in the Morning, the Currant then turning and a light breeze from the Northward springing up sent them all

94

on shore, they Singing and Playing their Music all the way." At Guam, officers and crew had royal entertainment. The governor and family wept copiously at their departure, and pressed livestock, fruit, and other gifts on the captain until they overflowed the deck, and had to be towed astern in the jolly-boat.

This commerce with the Far East, in pursuit of which early discoverers had scorned the barren coast of Massachusetts, was a primary factor in restoring the commonwealth to prosperity and power, in giving her maritime genius a new object and a new training, in maintaining a maritime supremacy that ended in a burst of glory with the clipper ship. By 1800, Massachusetts had proved the power of her merchants and seamen, when unrestrained by a colonial system; had given the lie to tory pessimists who predicted her speedy decay when detached from the British Empire. A tea party in Boston Harbor, at the expense of the British East India Company, brought on the American Revolution. Twenty years later, tea and spices earned through trafficking with savage tribes, carried in Massachusetts vessels and handled by her merchants, were underselling the imports of that mighty monopoly in the markets of Europe.

Note: Dr. Kenneth W. Porter, after research in the Heard Mss. and in contemporary newspapers, informs me that the stories about the *Caravan* related on p. 90, "cannot be true." I have retained them, however, as an example of romantic family tradition.

CHAPTER VIII

SHIPS AND SEAMEN

1790–1812

SHIPBUILDING, the ancient key industry of Massachusetts, expanded greatly during the Federalist period. Exactly how much, we have no means of knowing, for no record was kept of the many vessels built for other states and countries. But the total merchant and fishing fleet owned in Massachusetts (including Maine) almost doubled between 1794 and 1802,[1] and by 1810 increased another fifty per cent, attaining 500,000 tons, a figure not surpassed until after 1830.

The far-flung commerce of Salem and Boston was conducted in vessels that were small even by contemporary standards. 'King' Derby's entire fleet of six ships, one barque, four brigs, two ketches, and a schooner had a total tonnage of 2380, less than the clipper-ship *Sovereign of the Seas* a half-century later. William Gray owned 113 vessels first and last, before 1815; but only ten of them were over 300 tons burthen, and the largest was 425 tons. The average dimensions of six famous East-Indiamen of Salem, built between 1794 and 1805, are, length 99 feet, breadth 28 feet, burthen 336.[2] The second *Grand Turk* (124 feet long, 564 tons), Salem's "Great Ship," was sold to New York in 1795 for $32,000, as "much too large for our Port & the method of our Trade." Salem Harbor was so shallow that vessels drawing more than twelve feet

---

[1] Federal statistics before 1794 are inaccurate. See p. 166.

[2] The same length as, and a slightly greater breadth than the Boston mackerel schooner *Fannie Belle Atwood* in 1920.

96

had to unload by lighters; but in Boston, twelve feet could be carried up to Long Wharf at low tide. Yet Boston vessels seem to have been no larger than those of Salem, and the average Nor'westman was nearer two hundred than three hundred tons.

"A wise marchant neuer adventures all his goodes in one ship," wrote Sir Thomas More. Even those who could afford large ships preferred to distribute the tonnage among several small ones. For it is a great mistake to suppose that the danger of seafaring decreases as tonnage increases, beyond a certain point. Every square yard more sail area, in those days of single topsails, hemp rigging, and simple purchases, increased the difficulty of handling. Every foot more draft increased the danger of navigating uncharted seas and entering unbuoyed harbors. "Lost at sea with all hands," that frequent epitaph of the great clipper ships, was seldom if ever the fate of a Massachusetts vessel in the Federal period. The Crowninshields lost but four of their great fleet of East-Indiamen by 1806; two on Cape Cod, one on Egg Harbor bar, and one on the French coast. Massachusetts builders, moreover, had not yet acquired the technique to construct large vessels properly. Hence the superstition, current in New England seaports until 1830 or thereabouts, that five hundred tons was the limit of safety; that a larger vessel might break her back in a heavy sea. To round the Horn in a vessel under one hundred tons, as did several of the Boston Nor'westmen, was a remarkable feat of seamanship. But the boldest Yankee shipmaster of 1800, if given the choice, would rather have taken a Chebacco boat around Cape Stiff than a two-thousand-ton clipper ship.

Salem's fleet included vessels constructed on the North River, the Merrimac, or "Down East," but her merchants greatly preferred home-built ships, under their immediate supervision. A launching, "the noblest sight man can exhibit," thought Dr. Bentley, was a gala occasion. In his diary for October 31, 1807, he writes: "This day Mr. Brigs in South Fields launched a ship [the *Francis*] for Mr. Peabody, Merchant of this town of Salem, into South river. And about an hour afterwards Barker, Magoun & Co. launched at the entrance of the neck into the Lower harbour a Ship for Nathaniel Silsbee, Merchant of this Town. This last I saw. As the flats are level & the building ground low, the builders could not have the advantages of the two other yards which are steep banks of the rivers. But As soon as her stem block was taken away she began with a gradual increased motion to descend to the water, & without the least interruption or crack of anything near her, she rode upon the Ocean amidst the incessant shouts of the Spectators."

Most American seaports, including Boston, have shamefully neglected the splendid history of their maritime efforts. But Salem loved her ships, and cherished their memory. Hence she has taken first place by default, and her many writers have unconsciously given the modern public (as did their ances-tors the South-Sea islanders) the impression that Salem means America; that nowhere else in the world were built or owned such fast and wonderful vessels. The Peabody Museum ship portraits deepen this impression; for Salem employed the best artists of the day to depict her vessels — Antoine Roux, of Marseilles, *portraitiste de navires* unsurpassed for precision of detail and artistic effect; Michele Corné, whom the *Mount Vernon* brought from Naples in 1800, to pass the rest of his long life in New England seaports; and his pupil George Ropes. "In every house we see the ships of our harbor delineated for those who have navigated them," wrote Dr. Bentley in 1804; and the same holds true to-day. When Salem capital was transferred to cotton mills, her merchants, unlike those of Boston and New York, did not discard their ship pictures in favor of steel engravings after Sir Edwin Landseer, or dismal anonymous etchings of wintry trees.

Quaint and interesting the ships of the Federalist period certainly were, with their varied coloring (bright, lemon, or orange waist against black, blue, or dark green topsides, and a gay contrasting color for the inside of bulwarks); their carved 'gingerbread work' on stern, and 'quick-work' about the bows; their few large, well-proportioned sails (royals seldom, and skysails never being carried), and their occasionally graceful sheer. But strip off their ornaments, and you find, with few exceptions, a chunky, wall-sided model. The big ships of that day were built in Philadelphia and Europe; the small, fast clipper schooners and brigs, on Chesapeake Bay. New England builders obeyed the ancient tradition that "ships require a spreading body at the water's edge, both afore and abaft, to support them from being plung'd too deep into the sea." [1] The apparently sharp bow in some contemporary pictures is really nothing but deadwood, an ornamental cutwater preserving the tradition of a Roman galley's rostrum. The real bows were of the 'cod's head' type, bluff and full, buffeting a passage for the ship by sheer strength. And in no Massachusetts-built ship of this period whose dimensions are preserved, was the length as much as four times the beam.

[1] William Hutchinson, *Treatise on Practical Seamanship* (Liverpool, 1777), 12.

Several of these vessels made good, but not remarkable passages. The ship *Fame* (112 feet long, 263 tons), whose launching was a great event of 1802, once made Vineyard Haven in ninety-two days from Sumatra, completing the round voyage in seven months and seven days. But the full-bodied New York packet-ship *Natchez*, built in 1831, made her home port in sixty-seven days from Java Head, when driven by 'Bully' Waterman. The fastest Salem vessel of our period was the ship *America*, 114 feet long, 31 feet beam, and 473 tons burthen, built in 1809 by Retire Becket, with the aid of a local Scots draughtsman. Her beautiful portrait by Antoine Roux suggests easier lines than were then common. But her record day's run (over 240 miles) and bursts of speed (13 knots) were made as a privateer, with hull razeed to 331 tons, and a lofty rig that no mere merchantman could have carried. Another much-touted Salem-built vessel is the frigate *Essex;* but a careful reading of Captain David Porter's log of her Pacific cruise proves her to have been an uncommonly slow sailer for an American frigate. In the Peabody Museum, Salem, is an interesting half-model of the ketch *Eliza* (93 × 25 × 9 feet, 184 tons), built by Enos Briggs in 1794, and indicating a striving after speed. She has a curved stem, hollow water-lines, the stern of a modern navy cutter, and considerable deadrise; suggesting both a Baltimore clipper and the yacht *America*.[1] The *Eliza* once made a round voyage to India in nine months. She must have carried very little cargo compared with the usual chunky type, for which reason, possibly, the experiment led to nothing.

[1] Very likely her lines were copied from a Chesapeake Bay schooner. The "Fast-sailing Virginia built schooner Fox, 30 tons, 58 feet," is advertised for sale in the *Salem Gazette* of July 15, 1796.

SHIPS AND SEAMEN

It did not take much in those days to give a vessel a reputation for speed. In 1816, Augustine Heard, who had commanded Boston and Salem vessels for years, considered the brig *Hindu* fast, because on a voyage from Calcutta to Boston she sailed 7 to 7.5 knots an hour within six points of the wind, and 8.9 knots off the wind. Dr. Bentley notes that several Salem vessels, unable in their outward passage to breast the winds and currents off the coast of Brazil, were forced ignominiously to run home.

Until some competent naval architect makes a thorough study of American shipbuilding (and may the day come soon!) no one has a right to be dogmatic. But I venture the opinion that Salem-built vessels of the Federalist period were in no way superior to those constructed elsewhere in Massachusetts; that the builders of New York, the Delaware, and Long Island Sound were probably quite as competent as those of New England; and that the first real advance in the design of large American merchantmen, subsequent to the Revolution, came during or after the War of 1812.

The lower Merrimac from Haverhill to Newburyport was undoubtedly the greatest shipbuilding center of New England, at this period as in colonial days. Currier's rare monograph on Merrimac shipbuilding lists about 1115 vessels constructed and registered there between 1793 and 1815, inclusive; and a number constructed for outside parties are not to be found on his list. Twelve thousand tons of shipping were launched on the Merrimac in the banner year of 1810. As in other shipbuilding centers, all the cordage, sails, blocks, pumps, ironwork, anchors, and other fittings were made locally, employing hundreds of skilled mechanics. The jolly ropemakers of Salem used to outwit the Puritan taboo on a merry Christmas, by feasting St. Catherine of Alexandria, the patron saint of their profession, every December 25!

It was a Newburyport builder, Orlando B. Merrill, who in 1794 invented the lift or water-line model, probably the greatest invention in the technique of naval architecture between the days of Drake and the days of Ericsson. The lifts of the model, measured with a foot-rule, determined the dimensions of the vessel; and when she was completed, the model was neatly sawed amidships, one-half going to the owner, the other remaining in the builder's shop. Every builder was his own designer, as a matter of course. The technique was handed down from father to son; but there was such competition that no shipbuilder ever grew rich in the Federalist period.[1]

Medford, where the *Blessing of the Bay* was launched in 1631, became again a shipbuilding center in 1802. In that year Thatcher Magoun, of Pembroke, a pupil of his townsman Enos Briggs at Salem, examined the shores and bed of the Mystic River. Finding them free of obstruction, noting the noble oak groves in the neighborhood, and estimating that the Middlesex Canal, just completed, would enable him to tap the timber resources of the upper Merrimac, he decided to establish a shipyard at Medford. Calvin Turner, of Scituate, and another member of the house of Briggs, joined him in 1804. From the start, these Medford builders specialized in large ships and brigs — two hundred and fifty tons up — but until the War of 1812 they only built two or three apiece annually. After 1815, the vessels that he built for the China trade gave

[1] I have found little data on the cost of vessels at this period. The Merrimac-built brig *Enterprise*, 164 tons, cost $5000 to build in 1792, and the Maine-built ship *Wells*, 205 tons, sold when three years old for $7000 in 1804.

Thatcher Magoun a reputation second to none among American shipbuilders; and "Medford-built" came to mean the best.

Boston and Charlestown yards did little but naval construction and repairing during the Federalist period, although several fine ships were there built by Josiah Barker (of North River origin), and Edmund Hart, the master builders of the *Constitution*. The Boston fleet, three times as great as Salem's and second only to New York's, was largely procured from the Maine coast, the Merrimac, and the North River. That narrow tidal stream, dividing the towns of Marshfield and Pembroke from Scituate, Norwell, and Hanover, was like the Merrimac a cradle of New England shipbuilding.

The North River attained the height of its activity in Federalist days. Thirty vessels were completed here in 1801, and an average of twenty-three a year, 1799 to 1804. Looking downstream from the Hanover bridge, eleven shipyards were in view, filled with vessels in various stages of construction. Every morning at daybreak the shipwrights might be seen crossing the pastures or walking along the sedgy riverbank to their work, for a dollar a day from dawn to dark. When the sun rose above the Marshfield hills, like a great red ball through the river mist, there began the cheery clatter of wooden shipbuilding — clean, musical sounds of steel on wood, iron on anvil, creak of tackle and rattle of sheave; with much geeing and hawing as ox-teams brought in loads of fragrant oak, pine, and hackmatack, and a snatch of chanty as a large timber is hoisted into place. At eleven o'clock, and again at four came the foreman's welcome shout of "Grog O!" For it took rum to build ships in those days; a quart to a ton, by rough allowance; and more to launch her properly.

103

Standing on this same Hanover bridge to-day, it is hard to believe what the records show to be true, that within a few hundred yards, where there seems hardly water enough for a good-sized motor boat, were built for New York merchants in 1810–11 the ships *Mount Vernon* [1] and *Mohawk*, respectively 352 and 407 tons burthen. Farther down, near the *Columbia's* birthplace, even greater vessels were launched — poking their sterns into the opposite bank, and having to be dug out. Getting them down this narrow, tortuous river, full of rocks and shoals, was a ticklish business, entrusted to a special breed of North River pilots. Crews of men followed the vessel on both banks, with long ropes attached to each bow and quarter, hauling or checking as the pilot, enthroned between knightheads, commanded, "Haul her over to Ma'sh-field!" or, "Haul her over to Sit-u-wate!" Motive power was provided by kedging, heaving up to an anchor dropped ahead by the pilot's boat. Fourteen tides were sometimes required to get a vessel to sea, as the mocking river sauntered for miles behind the barrier beach, and dribbled out over a bar that taxed all Yankee ingenuity to surmount. When shipbuilding had ceased, a new outlet opened at the nearest point to the ocean.

The North River builders did much work for "foreign" (i.e., non-Massachusetts) order, and for the whalemen. Their vessels seem to have lacked even a local reputation for speed. Very few paintings of them have survived. One, of the ship *Minerva*, 223 tons, built by Joshua Magoun at Pembroke in 1808 for Ezra Weston and others of Duxbury, shows a vessel built in the best style of the day; gray-blue topsides

---

[1] Length 99 feet, 6 inches, breadth 28 feet, depth 14 feet, 3 inches. The largest vessel ever constructed on the North River was another ship *Mount Vernon*, 464 tons, built in 1815 for Philadelphia by Samuel Hartt.

and bulwarks, with bright waist, quarter-galleries, beautiful quick-work on the bows, and a finely proportioned sail plan.

Fishermen and other small vessels were constructed in Plymouth Bay at this period; and at Wareham and Mattapoisett on Buzzard's Bay were more children of North River, building three-hundred-ton whalers for Nantucket, and neutral traders for New Bedford. Fishing vessels were also built on Cape Cod, Cape Ann, and Essex, as well as in the larger centers. The presence in the Boston registry of the two-hundred-ton ship *Merry Quaker*, built at Dighton in 1795, proves that that center of religious dissent on the Taunton was up and doing. But having viewed the Merrimac, Salem, the Mystic and North Rivers, we have made the rounds of the greater shipyards in Massachusetts proper.

*

*　　*

And now for the sailors. A frequent occurrence in the New England of our period is illustrated by a pretty story of Cohasset. One spring evening young Southward Pratt, a farmer's barefoot boy, goes out as usual to drive the cattle home. But the cows are heard lowing at the pasture bars, long after their accustomed hour to be milked. There is no trace of the lad. Something called him from that rocky pasture; a sea-turn in the wind, perhaps; or a glimpse of Massachusetts Bay, deep blue and sail-studded, laughing in the May sunshine. True to his name, Southward obeyed the call.

Three years pass. The cows are now tended by young Mercy Gannett, who has come from Scituate to live with the Pratts as hired girl, in the friendly fashion of the day. One summer evening she comes running home from the pasture, frightened, breathless. A strange young man with bronzed face and lithe, free movements, had appeared at the pasture bars, and announced he would drive the cattle home that evening. Of course it was the prodigal son; and naturally he married Mercy, and lived happily ever after.

Southward's sudden departure, and his return, are both typical of the Massachusetts merchant marine. The Bay State, more seafaring in her taste (if one includes Maine) than any other American commonwealth, has never had a native deep-sea proletariat. Her fleet was manned by successive waves of adventure-seeking boys, and officered by such of them as determined to make the sea their calling. The European type of sailor, the "old salt" of English fiction, content to serve before the mast his entire lifetime, was almost unknown in New England. High wages and the ocean's lure pulled the Yankee boys to sea; but only promotion — or rum — could keep them there. If Southward or Hiram enjoyed his first voyage and made good, he was soon given an officer's berth, of which there were plenty vacant in a marine that increased from 98,000 to 435,700 tons (excluding fishermen [1]) between 1789 and 1810, which required one man at least to every fifteen tons, and in which the proportion of officers to seamen was not less than one to five. If quickly cured of his *wanderlust*, he went back to the farm, and was replaced by another boy. When the embargo tied up Salem shipping, the discharged crews returned to their villages — precisely as did the Russian workmen during the late Revolution. Speaking broadly, officers' berths in European ma-

[1] The figures for 1789 are an approximation. See p. 166. For the crews of fishermen see chapter x.

rines were class preserves, going by favor and influence to the sons of shipmasters, merchants, and their
dependents. Few European sailors had the education
to qualify themselves for command. But in the Massachusetts marine the great majority of masters came
in through the hawse-hole, and the vast majority of
seamen had sufficient command of the three R's to
post a log, draft a protest, draw up a manifest, and,
with a little instruction on shore or shipboard, find a
position at sea. Captain Zachary G. Lamson, of Beverly, tells of sailing as foremast hand on a Salem brigantine, every one of whose crew of thirteen rose to be
master of a vessel. With officers thoroughly trained in
the rudiments of their profession, and young, ambitious seamen culled from the most active element of a
pushing race, it is no wonder that the Massachusetts
marine achieved great things.

Never, save possibly at some colonial period, has
the Massachusetts marine been one hundred per cent
American. In Federalist days, it certainly contained an
appreciable minority of foreigners. How much, it is
impossible to say. Not until 1817 did federal law require two-thirds of a crew to be American. Even before 1793 we find a foreign minority in the crew lists
of some famous Pacific traders; [1] and after that date,

[1] On the ship *Massachusetts* in 1790, there were six petty officers from
Massachusetts, four from England, and one each from New Hampshire,
Ireland, Scotland, and Sweden. Before the mast were nineteen from
Massachusetts, seven from other New England states, ten from England,
six from Ireland, and one each from Scotland and Virginia (Delano, *Voyages*, 27). Eight nationalities were represented in the *Boston's* crew of
fifteen, in 1803 (Jewitt's *Narrative*); but this crew was enlisted in England. The New York brig *Betsey*, in the China trade, picked up her
crew at New Haven and Stonington (Edmund Fanning, *Voyages*, 1833
ed., 69). The *Margaret*, Captain James Magee, had two Swedes, one
Dutchman, and sixteen Americans before the mast. On the Boston
ship *Hercules*, in a voyage to Calcutta in 1792–94, all four officers, eight

when British subjects with forged naturalization papers, or birth certificates purchased from a discharged American, sought whatever protection the American flag afforded, these crew lists are open to suspicion. A Spanish boy named Benito, who joined the *Astrea* at Cadiz, shipped on his next voyage as Benjamin Eaton, of Salem. Captain Samuel Snow, of Cohasset, was really Salvador Sabate y Morell, brought from Spain many years before by Captain Ephraim Snow, of Truro. William Gray testified in 1813 that in his opinion one-fifth of the seamen in the American merchant marine were foreigners. Adam Seybert, the statistician, estimated one-sixth in 1807. Probably the proportion was less in New England, where the native supply was abundant. A British agent was told by Salem merchants in 1808 that they no longer employed British seamen, in order to avoid trouble from impressment. John Lowell asserts that only the vessels of the middle and southern states, where the native population had little maritime aptitude, employed foreigners to any extent. This statement must be taken with caution, as made for political effect; but the argument is reasonable. Only a careful examination and rigorous checking-up of the crew lists in our custom-house records can establish the truth.

Looking over these crew lists of registered vessels, one finds a small, constant minority of foreigners — not only Englishmen, but Germans, Scandinavians, and Latins — who acknowledge themselves such. But the great majority profess to be native-born Yankees, and probably were. Newburyport drew farmers'

out of nine petty officers, and fifteen out of twenty-five seamen were Massachusetts men. The other petty officer and one seaman were Irish, seven seamen were English, and two doubtful. (MS. Journals, Essex Institute.)

boys from the valley of the Merrimac and from all
southern New Hampshire. Marblehead's sailors were
mostly of the tough local breed. Salem drew upon her
own population, and all Essex County; her vessels also
include a large number of men from the Middle States
and Baltimore.[1] Boston's crew lists have been destroyed; but most Cape Cod boys seem to have gone
there for a start. The youthfulness of them is striking.
Most are in their teens and early twenties; seamen
over thirty are rare, and over forty almost unknown.
The few older men were probably victims of drink,
who squandered their wages at the end of each voyage,
in classic sailor fashion, and had no other recourse but
to reship.

Tradition, love of adventure, desire to see the world,
and the social prestige of the shipmaster's calling were
partly responsible for Yankee boys going to sea. Few
could grow up in a seaport town and resist the lure.
For boys in the inland towns, seafaring offered the
only alternative to clodhopping, the sole means of
foreign travel, and the best opportunity to gather
wealth. The West was not yet a word to fire the imagination. Hewing out a new farm in the Green Mountains or the Genesee Valley did not promise much
variety from home life. One could fight Indians on the
Northwest Coast — and play with the Kanaka girls
between fights. Ordinary life, to be sure, was not so
dismal in New England farming towns as the self-
styled experts in Puritanism would have us think.

[1] On the ship *Restitution* of Salem in 1804, out of nine seamen seven
give their residence as Baltimore, although two were born in Salem, two
in Germany, and one each in North Carolina, Rhode Island, and Philadelphia. On the ship *John* of Salem, 250 tons, in 1804 nine seamen give
their birthplace in Essex County, nine elsewhere in Massachusetts, three
elsewhere in New England, two in New Jersey, one each in Maryland,
"America," and Denmark.

There was a succession of husking-bees and barn-raisings and rustic dances and sleighing parties, well lubricated with rum. But imagine the effect of a young man returning with tales of pirates and sea-fights and South Sea Islands, with 'cumshaws' of tea and silk and Chinese carving for his mother and sweetheart, and a bag of silver dollars to boot.

For one of the chief attractions of seafaring was the high wages that were not only earned, but actually paid, in the Federalist period. The *Columbia*, on her first voyage, paid ordinary seamen but $5, and able seamen $7.50 per month; but she sailed in a period of unemployment. Wages quickly rose with commercial expansion. By 1799, J. & T. Lamb were paying boys $8 to $10, ordinary seamen $14 to $17, able seamen $18, and petty officers up to $24 per month, in the Northwest fur trade. The crew of their snow *Sea Otter* was paid off with $500 to $600 each, after deducting $100 to $150 for articles furnished from the slop chest, on which (if the Lambs followed the practice of Bryant & Sturgis) the men were charged at least one hundred per cent profit. In addition they could make a couple of hundred dollars on a judicious investment at Canton, stuffed into their sea-chests.

Data on wages in other trade routes are scarce, but what we have indicate a rise to a similar high level. Israel Thorndike, of Beverly, was paying ordinary seamen $4.50 and able seamen $7 per month in schooner voyages to the West Indies and Portugal in 1790. In 1794, the A.B.'s rate had risen to $10. On the U.S. frigate *Essex*, in 1799, boys and ordinary seamen got from $5 to $14, able seamen $17, besides prize money; at a time when an army private's pay was $3 per month. According to a French admiral in 1806, some seamen he impressed from an American brig were getting $17.

SHIPS AND SEAMEN

In the Russian trade in 1811, William Gray is paying his ordinary seamen $16 and his A.B.'s $20 and $21. Senator Lloyd, of Massachusetts, stated early in 1812 that the average pay of American seamen was $22.50 per month.

Shore wages, in comparison, were low. Common labor received but eighty cents to a dollar a day in New England between 1800 and 1810, and out of this had to feed and house itself. There were few opportunities for wage-earning, outside farm labor. Consequently many young men went to sea merely to lay by a little money to get married on, or buy a farm. But many of them never returned from their dangerous calling. Yellow Jack contracted in a West-India port disposed of many a stout ploughboy. We hear of schooners limping home from the Spanish Main, sailed only by one sickly man and a boy. Out of 634 members of the Essex Lodge of Free Masons in Salem, 293 were mariners and 246 master mariners; of these 50 were lost at sea and 42 died in foreign ports. "By the arrival of Capt. Phillips from Calcutta in the ship *Recovery*," writes Dr. Bentley, "we learn of the death of Winthrop Gray, the last of a company of jolly fellows at Salem. We hear of the death of several of our promising young seamen." Within a few yards of each other in the old graveyard at Kingston, overlooking Plymouth Bay, may still be seen the following memorial stones:

Erected in memory of Capt. Joshua Delano who died in Havanna April 2, 1800 aged 31 years.

Erected in memory of Capt. William Delano, who died on his passage home from Batavia Octr. 21, 1797, aged 27 years.

In memory of Peleg Wadsworth, who was drowned February 24th 1795 in Lat. 39 N. Long. 70 W. aged 21 years 6 months and 5 days.

MARITIME HISTORY OF MASSACHUSETTS

In memory of Amasa Holmes, who died in his passage from Cronstadt to Boston Jan'y 30, 1834, in the 24th year of his age.

In memory of Simeon Washburn who was drowned July 6, 1805, aged 24 years.

The only approach to a privileged class in the Massachusetts fleet was the supercargoes. This position — the business agent of the owners on shipboard — was often reserved for Harvard graduates, merchants' sons, and other young men of good family who had neither the taste nor the ruggedness for the rough-and-tumble of forecastle life. His position was no sinecure. The relationship with the master, between whose functions and the supercargo's there was no sharp line, required diplomatic qualities. Responsibility for selling and obtaining cargoes required self-reliance, and sound knowledge of world commerce and economics. John Bromfield, a supercargo with two generations of Boston merchants back of him, read Henry Colebrooke's "Husbandry and Commerce of Bengal," William Marsden's "History of Sumatra," Colonel Symes's "Embassy to Ava," Stavorinus's "Voyage à Batavia," and Wilcocke's "History of Buenos Ayres," to qualify himself for his business. As supercargo under Captain Bill Sturgis in the *Atahualpa*, he informed the master of the pirate junks' approach off Macao — his brother had been killed by Malay pirates a few years before — and fought like a lion during the action. Joseph W. Cogswell, one of that group of New England intellectuals who attended Göttingen, first changed his sky if not his mind as supercargo on William Gray's brig *Radius*, in the most difficult days of neutral trade. Patrick T. Jackson, pioneer cotton manufacturer and founder of the city of Lowell, learned his first lessons from the world as clerk to his brother Captain Henry

Jackson, on J. & T. H. Perkins's ship *Thomas Russell*, in the Mediterranean and East-India trade.

A supercargo was occasionally promoted to master mariner, as in the case of Dr. Bowditch; but there were few captains in the Massachusetts fleet who had not worked their way up from the forecastle. In spite of this democratic method of selection, New England shipmasters were distinguished for their gentlemanly qualities. The English merchant marine, in spite of privilege, was still officered by Captain Cuttles and Hatchways, of the type described by Smollett. If an English gentleman went to sea, he chose the navy. But in New England the social prestige of the merchant service remained as high as in colonial days. Gentlemen of family and education set the quarterdeck standards, to which homespun recruits conformed as best they could. Consequently we find American shipmasters received into the upper bourgeois society of the seaports where they traded; and not infrequently marrying Spanish or Italian girls of good family. Captain E. H. Derby, Jr., was entertained by Nelson aboard the *Victory*. The same wages and commissions were given generally as in the Canton trade,[1] although naturally the latter was the most lucrative, and obtained the best men. Thus the officers became partners in every voyage. Not infrequently a shipmaster retired at the age of thirty with sufficient capital to start a mercantile business of his own. The master mariners whose names are in the records of the Boston Marine Society before 1812, were the merchant-shipowners of the next generation.

Hitherto, Yankee shipmasters had never been conspicuous in navigation. In seamanship they were preëminent; in rigging, handling, and caring for their

[1] Chapter VI.

vessels — in getting the last ounce of speed and service out of them. Having no dockyards to depend on, they were used to turn engineer on occasion. Captain William Mugford received a gold medal from the American Philosophical Society, for the jury rudder he rigged on the ship *Ulysses*. They thought nothing of heaving down or careening a vessel on some lonely South-Sea beach, scrubbing her bottom, paying her seams, and making extensive repairs, while part of the crew stood guard against cannibals. When Captain Penn Townsend, by miscalculation, found his brig *Eunice* high and dry on St. Paul's Island (a favorite Salem resort in the Indian Ocean), his crew built a huge wooden cask around her hull, and rolled her off.

Dead reckoning, by compass, log, and dipsey lead, was the traditional New England method of finding one's position at sea.[1] That was all very well for Atlantic and West-India voyages, but not for circumnavigating the globe. The stately ship *Massachusetts*, in 1790, in all her padded equipment, had no chronometer, and no officer who could find longitude by any other method. Consequently she missed Java Head, and lost several weeks' time. But a Salem boy was already planning a remedy.

Nathaniel Bowditch[2] was born at Salem in 1773, the son of Habakkuk Bowditch, a shipmaster who had seen better days. His formal schooling was slight. The dawn of Salem's maritime expansion found him apprentice to a local ship-chandler. He fed a precocious passion for mathematics in the Philosophical Library,

---

[1] All the seaport towns had private schools of navigation in the seventeen-nineties. Even at as small a village as Wellfleet, "We have in the winter a number of private schools, by which means the greater part of the young men are taught the art of navigation," writes the Reverend Levi Whitman, of that place, in 1794.

[2] First syllable rhymes with 'how.'

the nucleus of which was an Irish scientist's collection
which a Beverly privateer had captured during the
Revolution. In 1796, he went to sea as captain's clerk
on the ship *Henry*, Salem to the Ile de France, and the
following year sailed as supercargo in the *Astrea*, to
Manila. On this voyage he not only spent every spare
moment in making observations, but taught twelve
members of the crew to take and work lunars, the only
method of getting longitude without a chronometer,
which no Salem vessel could afford. Working lunars
is a tricky business, for any error in the observation
brings a thirty-fold error in the result; and as young
Bowditch found no less than eight thousand errors in
the tables of the standard English book on navigation,
he decided to get one out of his own. Two more
voyages gave him the practice and the leisure for the
immense amount of detailed calculations; and in 1801
appeared the first edition of Bowditch's "Practical
Navigator," which has been translated into a dozen
languages, passed through countless editions, and still
remains the standard American treatise on navigation.

While the "Navigator" was making a market for
itself, its author went to sea, as master of the ship
Putnam, Beverly to the northwest coast of Sumatra.
At the close of this successful pepper voyage, he proved
his own theories by entering Salem Harbor on Christmas Eve, 1803, in a blinding northeast snowstorm,
without having picked up a single landmark. For
years to come, "I sailed with Captain Bowditch, Sir!"
was a Salem man's password to an officer's berth.

Notwithstanding the work of Bowditch, it took a
generation or more to wean most Massachusetts shipmasters from their dependence on dead reckoning, in
which primitive method they were adepts. An interesting incident of neutral trading illustrates this. In

1810, an American vessel was seized at Christiansand, and condemned by the admiralty courts of Denmark (then at war with England) on the ground that her lack of chart or sextant proved that her voyage commenced in the British Isles. The other American shipmasters in port then drew up a protest in which they assert, "we have frequently made voyages from America without the above articles, and we are fully persuaded that every seaman with common nautical knowledge can do the same."

Captain Jeremiah Mayo, of Brewster, about the year 1816, took the brig *Sally* of Boston, 264 tons, from Denmark through the English Channel to the Western Ocean in thick weather — without an observation or a sight of land. Bryant & Sturgis reprimand one of their East-India shipmasters, in 1823, for purchasing a chronometer for $250, and inform him he must pay for it himself. "Could we have anticipated that our injunctions respecting economy would have been so totally disregarded we would have sett fire to the Ship rather than have sent her to sea." Nathaniel Silsbee, in 1827, sailed to Rotterdam in a brig that had no chronometer, and whose officers knew nothing of lunar observations.

Still it was not Bowditch's fault if seamen did not use the means he offered; and an increasing proportion of them did. On his death, in 1838, the Boston Marine Society resolved, "As astronomer, a mathematician and navigator himself, a friend and benefactor has he been to the navigator and Seaman, and few can so justly appreciate the excellence and utility of his labours, as the members of this Society. . . . His intuitive mind sought and amassed knowledge, to impart it to the world in more easy forms."

Boston, Salem, and Newburyport all had their

marine societies, open to master mariners and sometimes shipowners as well, before the Revolution. But
at Salem in 1799 there was organized the East India
Marine Society, with membership restricted to Salem
shipmasters or supercargoes, "who shall have actually
navigated the Seas near the Cape of Good Hope or
Cape Horn." An exclusive club, perhaps; one whose
certificate of membership equaled a patent of nobility
in Essex County; but not a small or merely a social
club. Fifty-seven members were admitted during the
first two years. The Society furnished them with blank
duplicate sea-journals to be filled out and deposited
in the Marine Library at the close of each voyage.
Therein were faithfully noted all observations of latitude, with the position of ports, reefs, and headlands,
as "the means of procuring a valuable collection of
useful information." Blank pages were assigned for
"remarks on the commerce of the different places
touched at in the voyage with the imports, exports
and manner of transacting business." In this way the
community gathered strength from the achievements
of its members.

"Whatever is singular in the measures, customs,
dress, ornaments, &c. of any people, is deserving of
notice," continue the directions, which conclude with
an injunction to note down "any remarkable books in
use, among any of the eastern natives, with their subjects, dates and titles"; and to collect for the East
India Marine Museum, articles of dress and ornament,
idols and implements and all things vegetable, animal,
and mineral. At their annual meetings the members,
each bearing some Oriental trophy, passed in procession through the streets, preceded by a man "in Chinese habits and mask," and a palanquin borne by Salem negroes tricked out as natives of India, bearing a

proud Salem youngster in the habiliments of a native prince. To the public spirit of her shipmasters, Salem owes the nucleus of her famous Ethnological Museum, and records of her early commerce unsurpassed by any American seaport.

Note: Dr. Harold Bowditch, by studying the journals of Nathaniel Bowditch, and local meteorological data, has decided that the story of 1803 related on p. 115 is a myth.

CHAPTER IX

MERCHANTS AND MANSIONS

1782–1812

Divitis Indiæ usque ad ultimum sinum (of teeming Ind, to the uttermost gulf) was the appropriate motto on Salem's city seal. Wealth, her merchants certainly did acquire. Elias Hasket Derby, dying in 1799, bequeathed an estate of a million and a half dollars to his sons. Israel Thorndike, of Beverly, and Captain Simon Forrester, who came to Salem a poor Irish lad, each left about the same sum. 'Billy' Gray, when Jefferson's embargo caught him, was reputed to be worth three million dollars, and known to be the greatest individual shipowner in the United States. But more than this, the Salem merchants spent their money in a manner that enhanced the pleasant art of living, and permanently enriched the artistic content of America.

Puritanism, in its religious and social implications, stamped Federalist Salem. Puritanism is the reputed enemy of art and genial living. Yet the people of Massachusetts Bay, since their first struggle for existence on the fringe of the continent, had built a succession of goodly houses in oak and pine, and even brick, whose beauty improved as the sea yielded an increasing store. The spoil, accumulated through twenty years' voyaging to the uttermost limits of the Far East, produced at Salem the fairest flowers of American domestic architecture.

The presiding genius of this Federal architecture (as it should be called, rather than the loose and ill-fitting 'Colonial' or 'Georgian') was Samuel McIntire. Born at Salem in 1757, the son of a housewright, McIntire had as hard and meager a boyhood as Bowditch. Of his young manhood we know little. Probably he worked as a woodcarver, and exercised his talents not only on houses, but on the figureheads, cabin mouldings, and quick-work of vessels. Suddenly in 1782, the year of peace, he blossoms forth as the architect of the Peirce-Nichols house; with its out-buildings one of the finest architectural groups ever executed in wood in the United States.

This house was built for Jerathmeel Peirce, a merchant who saved enough out of the Revolution to prove an early success in the East-India trade. It marks a new type, the square, three-storied, hip-roofed, detached dwelling, which stamps the Federalist period in New England. Captain Peirce, after a frugal fashion of that day, had only half the interior completed at once. The rest was fortunately postponed until McIntire had acquired a new manner; the refined and delicate style of interior decoration introduced in London by the brothers Adam. The east parlor was completed in 1801, just in time for the marriage of Sally Peirce to Captain George Nichols.

This twenty-three-year-old shipmaster had followed the sea since the age of sixteen, and had many acquaintances at London, St. Petersburg, Calcutta, and Batavia. He brought his bride from Bombay, for her wedding dress, the most beautiful piece of striped muslin ever seen in Salem. After four weeks' honeymoon he was off again to Sumatra. At the age of twenty-nine he retired from the sea, and lived long enough in the beautiful house that his father-in-law built, to vote twice for Abraham Lincoln.

For twenty years after the building of the Peirce-

Nichols house, little notable construction was done in Salem. A few merchants, like E. H. Derby, employed the young architect to erect new and splendid dwellings, adorned by pilasters and surmounted by glazed cupolas whence approaching sail might be surveyed in comfort. But the greater number required a prudent accumulation, before deserting the ancestral gambrel. As they gathered wealth and the possibility of leisure, the mercantile families shrank from the raw east winds, and picturesque but embarrassing contacts of the waterfront. About 1801, they began to desert Derby Street and its tributaries for Essex Street, Washington Square, and above all, Chestnut Street.

On this broad, elm-shaded avenue — to-day the finest street, architecturally, in New England — McIntire and his nameless fellow-workers expended the endeavors of their fruitful years. The square, three-storied, hip-roofed house, constructed of warm red brick laid in flawless Flemish bond, prevailed. The front doors are framed in fanlight and sidelights, shaded by oblong or elliptical porches whose roofs are supported by attenuated columns, their capitals carved by the master himself. A Palladian window opens on a formal garden in the rear. The interiors are simply arranged, with four rooms to a floor, and decorated in a free and original adaptation of the Adam style. Stables, barns, and garden houses are designed with the same care as the mansion, that nothing might mar the general effect.

In his public buildings — the Court House, assembly halls, and South Meeting-House, McIntire was equally successful.

There was little in the architecture of these dwellings, save their uncompromisingly square mass, to suggest the character of their occupants. For very few of the shipmasters and merchants of Federalist Salem came of wealthy colonial families. They were a rugged race, with little of the polish that marked contemporary society in Boston or Philadelphia or Charleston. They were self-educated; for Salem then had miserable schools, and no boy destined for the sea went to Harvard. They were not ashamed to work with their own hands in garden or outlying farm; and in a run of ill-luck, their wives or sisters could without loss of caste open a little shop in a front room — as Hepzibah in "The House of the Seven Gables." Their ways were at best bluff and simple; at worst, harsh and blustering. Too many carried the manners of the quarterdeck into their Adam parlors. One wonders where they acquired the taste to erect such dwellings, or, if the taste was wholly their architects'[1] to enrich them with the beautiful furniture, porcelain, and glass that are still the pride of Salem. Everything made in 1810 was not good; Chestnut Street mansions might as well have been stuffed with vulgarized empire as with chaste Chippendale.

Salem society, like that of all our seaport towns, was stratified. Of the life of her middle and lower classes we know little save their occasional delinquencies. Salem is said to have had a greater per capita wealth than any American town; but hard winters always crowded the almshouse and demanded much charity of the well-to-do. All classes were bound together by a common interest in maritime prosperity. In 1790, the two hundred and twenty-eight heads of families (including widows) in Dr. Bentley's East Church, included thirty-five mariners, fifty-eight master mariners, nine

[1] For the sort of thing that the Salem architects avoided, see the engraving of "Mr. Dorsey's Gothic mansion" at Philadelphia, in Dennie's Portfolio, v, 124 (1811).

boat- or ship-builders, five rope- or sail-makers, and five fishermen. Even people whose principal occupation was independent of commerce, generally owned a share in a ship, or made private adventures. Nathaniel Richardson, who owned the largest tannery in Essex County, also owned four vessels; and his son Nathaniel, who "hurried into bold adventures," died in Malaga at the age of eighteen.

Unquestioned social preëminence was enjoyed by the merchant-shipowners, who with few exceptions had commanded vessels on East-India voyages. Their social life was simple rather than brilliant. Formal dinners were infrequent, balls given only by subscription, at stated intervals, in Hamilton Hall or Washington Hall, according as the company was Federalist or Republican. For the bitter politics of this period divided Salem society by a deep longitudinal chasm, across which the rival clans of Derby and Crowninshield glared defiance. Driving or sleigh-riding, with Nahant or some good tavern for objective, was a common diversion. But perhaps the favorite one for shipmasters' families was a fishing party in the bay, followed by landing on Baker's or Misery Island for a magnificent chowder, cooked, as a chowder should be, in iron pot over driftwood fire by a Salem African. Several families maintained small pleasure-boats. The finest of them, George Crowninshield, Jr.'s, thirty-six-foot *Jefferson*, rigged like a Chebacco boat, once took Dr. Bentley from Salem to Beverly harbor in fifteen minutes and back in thirty-four. Wealth cost that generation too much effort to be frittered in riotous living or wasteful display. Those Salem families who acquired a fortune in the days when every day brought a ship, have with few exceptions retained their position to this day.

Boston throughout the Federalist period was a commercial center of about three times the importance of Salem, whether one takes population, tonnage, or customs duties as the standard of comparison. The commercial activity of Boston Harbor was prodigious. "Upwards of seventy sail of vessels sailed from this port on Monday last, for various parts of the world," states the "Columbian Centinel" on Wednesday, October 26, 1791. In 1793 there entered and cleared eleven vessels from England, one hundred and nineteen from the West Indies, and one hundred and sixty-three from other foreign ports. "The harbour of Boston is at this date [November, 1794] crowded with vessels," wrote Thomas Pemberton. "Eighty-four sail have been counted lying at two of the wharves only. It is reckoned that not less than four hundred and fifty sail of ships, brigs, schooners, sloops and small craft are now in this port." The population increased from 18,320 in 1790 to 33,787 in 1810.

To take care of this expanding commerce and population, Boston began the process, which still continues, of making new land by filling in various coves that gave her so jagged a shore-line. A corporation began shoveling the crest of Beacon Hill into the Mill Pond, near the present North Station, about 1807; and another laid out Broad Street, somewhat straightening the harbor front. Other companies financed new wooden bridges to Charlestown, Cambridge, and South Boston, which opened up sections of the town never before utilized; and before the end of the War of 1812 work started on the Mill Dam, a continuation of Beacon Street across the Back Bay. Still, not very much was done before 1825 to take away the picturesque stabs that salt water made into old Boston. One tongue of the harbor came up to Liberty Square; and another to Dock Square, which was the market and retail center of the town. A few yards away was State Street, rapidly becoming lined with the new banks and insurance offices that commercial expansion required. Near by was completed, in 1808, the new Exchange Coffee-House, whose seven stories proclaimed Boston a town, merely because she was too proud to become a mere city! A Boston Loyalist who returned for a visit in 1808, wrote, "The great number of new and elegant buildings which have been erected in this Town, within the last ten years, strike the eye with astonishment, and prove the rapid manner in which the people have been acquiring wealth." Boston was practically re-built between 1790 and 1815, in a distinctive style of Federal architecture which the public persists in lumping with everything else built before 1840 as 'colonial.'

Like the merchants of Renaissance Italy, those of Federalist Boston wished to perpetuate their names and glorify their city by mansions, churches, and public buildings of a new style and magnificence. Luckily, among their number was a young man who had the training and the genius to guide this impulse into fruitful and worthy channels. Charles Bulfinch, in contrast to McIntire, had every advantage of birth, wealth, and education. The son and grandson of prominent physicians, he graduated at Harvard in 1781, and went to France and England to travel and to study architecture. On his return, in 1787, he found Boston more concerned in preserving its existing property from Dan Shays, than ambitious to build. With unerring instinct, he helped to launch the very voyage whose consequences made his career. The *Columbia's* great adventure was planned at his father's house, and Charles Bulfinch himself was one of her owners.

The merchants were soon ready for new houses, and the cramped condition of Boston compelled them to economize space. Only in "West Boston" (Cambridge Street) and Beacon Hill ("out of town") was it still possible to erect detached mansions. Hence the first important commission that came to young Bulfinch was to design the first solid block of residences in New England, the Tontine Crescent on Franklin Place.[1]

Crescents are common enough in English cities; but few had yet been built when Bulfinch sailed for Boston. He must have seen the Adelphi terrace of the Adam brothers, who taught him his sense of proportion, as they inspired McIntire's detail. Whatever the source, Bulfinch's handling of the problem was masterly. Sixteen three-story brick houses were built according to a plan that showed uniformity without tiresome repetition. The entrances were grouped by twos, the end groups advanced six feet beyond the others, and adorned by pilasters. Instead of breaking the crescent in its center, where another street entered Franklin Place, Bulfinch arched it over with a library, whose classic columns, Venetian window, and attic story pleasantly broke the uniform line of roofs. The middle of the oval in front was occupied by a grass plot and trees, with a classic urn in memory of Franklin; the opposite side was filled with another harmonious group of dwellings, and the approaches were given distinction by Boston's first theater, and first Catholic cathedral church, which the young master designed. The general effect of Franklin Place, as of all the Bulfinch school, suggests London of the Regency; but loyal Bostonians prefer to compare London to Boston — and the chronology bears them out!

Bulfinch also designed a new form of detached man-

[1] On the site of the curved portion of Franklin Street.

sion for the wide, elm-shaded spaces on Summer Street, and for Beacon Hill, where residences were springing up on the sunny slope of Copley's pasture. Bulfinch relieved the square mass of Georgian tradition by a bow in the center of side or rear, making place on the ground story for an elliptical dining-room. The best example, still extant, is the Governor Gore mansion at Waltham. His later city houses gained light and distinction by a double bow or swell front, accentuated by pilasters reaching to the cornice.

As architect of public buildings, from the capitol at Augusta to that of Washington, no American save Stanford White has ever surpassed Bulfinch. The Boston State House (1795), with its gilded dome, is his most famous early work; one should visit the old Representatives', and present Senate Chamber, to appreciate the full measure of his genius at the age of thirty-two. In his later work, like the New South Meeting-House (1814), and University Hall at Harvard (1815), he found in hammered granite a fit medium for his chaste lines, as a gray dress for a Puritan maiden. Most interesting of his public works, from our viewpoint, was the brick block of thirty-two stores, with counting-rooms or warehouses overhead, which he designed for the new India Wharf in 1805, giving the water-front an air of solidity and permanence more common to European than American ports.[1] It was the boldest bit of harbor development yet undertaken in the United States. Sixty years later, Atlantic Avenue ploughed its way through the middle of India Wharf, disrupting the graceful archway with attic story that broke the long slate roof. The remaining portion, its red brick mellowed by the east wind, still

[1] A part of India Wharf may be seen at the right of the photograph of shipping in chapter XXII.

maintains a frigate-like dignity amid motor trucks and excursion steamers.

In repairing and enlarging old buildings, like Christ Church and Faneuil Hall, Bulfinch showed a reverence for the old forms, of which his own work seemed a natural development. He and his school gave Boston architecture a stamp of distinction that even the imitators of Romanesque, Gothic, and French Renaissance have been unable wholly to efface. One is tempted to ascribe his pure taste and perfect proportion to an ocean origin; but, curiously enough, land architecture grew steadily worse in Massachusetts as naval architecture reached perfection in the clipper ships.

Boston society differed from that of Salem, as the graceful curves of Bulfinch's dining-rooms and spiral staircases differ from the straight lines of McIntire's interiors. Boston society was less simple, both in its manners and its composition; and quite as aristocratic as that of Philadelphia or London. "The *better* people are all aristocrats," wrote John Singleton Copley, Jr., from Boston in 1796. "My father is too rank a Jacobin to live among them." Well-to-do professional men like Harrison Gray Otis, Federalist politicians like Josiah Quincy, retired capitalists like Christopher Gore, and wealthy shopkeepers like Samuel Eliot and David Sears, formed as conspicuous a portion of the social upper crust as merchant-shipowners; and few names were included which had risen to prominence since the Revolution. Social life was formal and brilliant, with private balls and cotillion parties, and immense dinners. Several merchants maintained country seats in the neighborhood, like their colonial forbears; but most of them found Boston a good enough summer resort. Few traces of Puritanism were left among the gentry. It was a period of religious tolerance, before Protestant and Catholic had renewed, or Orthodox and Unitarian begun their quarrels. But political feeling was exceedingly bitter, and any deviation from Federalist orthodoxy was punished by social ostracism. East-India voyages seemed to mellow manners, and Madeira wine; but to sharpen political prejudices.

The merchants themselves did not form a social unit, as in smaller towns. Their portraits by Gilbert Stuart have a sort of family likeness, a complacent air and ruddy face suggesting a seafaring youth, with a plenty of "choice old London particular," that had passed the equator four times before its final ripening under the eaves. Those who inherited wealth, or had begun business before the Revolution, were more highly regarded than the self-made man who had traced new trade-routes; but certain families combined both distinctions. There was a distinct class of merchant princes, who lived in magnificent style, surrounded by suggestions of Oriental opulence. The Honorable Thomas Russell was a sort of marshal of this mercantile nobility, and passed on his baton to Thomas Handasyd Perkins. On a social pinnacle of their own making were the mercantile *émigrés* from Essex County — the Lowells, the Higginsons, and the Jacksons, who (according to Colonel Henry Lee) "came up from Newburyport to Boston, social and kindly people, inclined to make acquaintances and mingle with the world pleasantly. But they got some Cabot wives, who shut them up." Another distinct group was composed of plain, hard-working men, toilsomely accumulating a fortune and a name; men like Nathaniel Goddard, of a poor farmer's family of Brookline, who made his first capital by tending a lonely trading post on Passamaquoddy Bay; Josiah Marshall, a farmer's boy from Billerica, who attained Franklin

Place *via* Coast and Islands; Josiah Bradlee, the most extensive advertiser in the Federal press, spending in his entire lifetime, from 1778 to 1860, but one night outside Boston, and that at Nahant; a merchant of whom it was said that if he sent a shingle afloat on the ebb tide bearing a pebble, it would return on the flood, freighted with a silver dollar!

The merchant princes clung to the ways and fashions of colonial days, or of 1790 at the latest, unwilling to admit even by the cut of a waistcoat that Robespierre could change their world. At eight or eight-thirty the well-to-do Boston merchant appeared among his family in China silk dressing-gown and cap, as Copley had painted his father. Short family prayers, and a hearty breakfast by a blazing hickory fire. Then the mysteries of the toilet, performed by body servant or, preferably, by a neighborhood Figaro, a San Domingo refugee who discreetly gossips while he performs the rite of shaving. Hair is dressed, tied in a queue, and powdered; unless there is a white wig to be nicely adjusted. A fresh white cravat with long lapels, is folded and skillfully tied. Then for the nether limbs. Linen drawers are tied down, silk stockings pulled up smooth, and gartered against all chance of ungentlemanly wrinkling; buff nankeen breeches arranged neatly over them and silver buckle drawn tight. Low-hung waistcoat and broad-skirted coat of light-colored broadcloth come next. After a few parting suggestions to his lady, Master takes a stout gold-headed Malacca-joint cane, three-cornered hat, scarlet cloak if chilly, and sallies forth on foot, followed by Cicero, the colored butler, with huge market-basket. For it is the simple custom of the day, on one's way to business, to choose the materials for one's dinner, in the neighborhood of Faneuil Hall.

MERCHANTS AND MANSIONS

Suppose one of those sharp, bright winter days, following a fresh snowfall that has etched the outlines of new brick shops and black old gabled houses with high lights. Huge "pungs" (ox- or horse-drawn sledges), the connecting links between ocean commerce and New England farms, are drawn up in Dock Square three deep and piled high with butter, cheeses, fresh and salt meat, game, winter vegetables, wooden ware, and barrels of cider and perry, from some of which small boys are sucking through a straw until the owner shouts — "Hey, you've had your penny-worth!" Through this cheerful activity strolls our merchant, and having chosen his joint and poultry and game and fixings, sends his servant home, and continues to his counting-room on India Wharf, or near by.

If it is winter, there is not much to do; for the larger vessels are away; but there are always accounts to be made up, tea and silks to be withdrawn from bond, and plans for next season discussed with master builders. At eleven, Henry the chief clerk mixes a stiff jorum of Jamaica rum, to get himself and master through the morning. At half-after twelve or one, the business day ends, save for the genial institution of 'Change. This is a meeting of all the merchants, on the sidewalk of State Street if weather permits, otherwise in tavern or insurance office, to talk shop, ships, and politics for a half-hour or so.

By two o'clock the merchant is at home again, and at two-thirty comes dinner. Perhaps it is a formal feast, in the oval dining-room, with some fellow-merchants, a state senator or two, a judge, and their respective ladies; begun by a hot punch handed to the gentlemen in a China loving-cup; continued through several substantial courses, washed down with sherry, madeira, and (rarely) champagne; prolonged into can-

131

dlelight after the ladies retire and the cloth is removed, by port, brandy, political gossip, and damning the Jacobins. If an ordinary family dinner, it is followed by a sleigh-ride, or, in long summer days, a family drive in coach or high English phaëton, behind fat bays, to take tea and fruit at some country seat — with Harry Otis at Oakley, or Kitty Gore at Waltham, or John Lowell at Roxbury, or Ben Bussey at Jamaica Plain. A ball or evening supper party, perhaps; otherwise a cold supper and glass of madeira at home, 'and so to bed.'

Federalist Boston was full of small gentlemen's clubs, which met at each others' houses or at taverns, for evening talk and cheer. Several of them were fire societies, each member maintaining a pair of leathern buckets, a canvas bag for saving valuables, and a bed key; which articles had to be solemnly inspected every so often, as an excuse for a party. In addition, there were large public dinners, followed by formal toasts, accompanied by music, and (on the Fourth) discharges of artillery — such as the annual feast of shells on Forefathers' Day, the festivities of election week, and the annual dinner of the Boston Marine Society. The meetings of this society were common ground where all Bostonians interested in seaborne commerce met. The secretary describes it in 1811 as "composed of upwards of one hundred former shipmasters who have retired from sea with adequate fortunes, many of whom are largely interested in the insurance offices and as underwriters, and about fifty of the most respectable merchants and shipowners and gentlemen of the highest stations in the commonwealth. The rest of the Society is composed of the more active and younger mariners who still follow the seas as a professional business." These last were the men who made the name of Boston famous from Archangel to Smyrna, and east by west to the River Plate and Calcutta. Too busy, as yet, to care for social life or Bulfinch mansions, the next generation was their harvest season.

CHAPTER X

THE SACRED CODFISH

1784–1812

On March 17, 1784, Mr. John Rowe, of Boston, merchant, arose from his seat in the Representatives' Hall of the Old State House, and offered a motion, "That leave might be given to hang up the representation of a Codfish in the room where the House sit, as a memorial of the importance of the Cod-Fishery to the welfare of this Commonwealth, as had been usual formerly." Leave was accordingly granted; and the same wooden emblem presented by genial Johnny Rowe, having followed the Great and General Court to Beacon Hill, still faces the Speaker's desk.

Massachusetts still retains her supremacy in the American codfisheries; but in 1790 this industry was in the parlous state that the war had left it. Relief came quickly from the federal government. On July 4, 1789, Congress granted a bounty of five cents on every quintal of dried fish or barrel of pickled fish exported. Elbridge Gerry, of Marblehead, and Benjamin Goodhue, of Salem, had a good deal to do with obtaining this favor; but there was no opposition from other parts of the country. Charles Cotesworth Pinckney, of South Carolina, in the debates of the ratifying convention in his state, had generously urged the distress of the New England fisheries as a reason for closer union. In 1791, the General Court of Massachusetts begged additional protection. Thomas Jefferson, Secretary of State, issued a friendly but rather non-committal report; but Senator George Cabot, formerly the owner of Beverly fishermen, framed and put through the act of February 9, 1792, granting a bounty of one dollar to two dollars and a half per ton (depending on the size) to vessels engaged in the codfishery four months in the year; three-eighths of the bounty to go to the owner, the rest to be divided among the crew.

Under the influence of federal bounties, and the general expansion of commerce in the late eighteenth century, the Massachusetts codfishery began to look up again. The tonnage of her fishing fleet (including that of Maine) gradually increased from about 10,000 in 1790 to 62,000 in 1807, when Jefferson's embargo brought another check.

The Grand Banks of Newfoundland fisheries were renewed in what was left of the pre-Revolutionary fleet — old-fashioned barrel-bottomed schooners of not over seventy tons, called "heel-tappers" on account of their low waists and high quarterdecks.[1] Fishermen, the most conservative of seafarers, seem to have made no improvement in their models until after 1815. Methods were unchanged. Bankers made two or three fishing trips a year. The spring fare was either brought home in time for election day (the last Wednesday in May), or dried on "any of the unsettled bays, harbors and creeks of Nova Scotia, Magdalen Islands and Labrador," as Article III of the Treaty of Peace (thanks to John Adams) permitted, but most of the curing was done on the sands or ledges of the home port.

The only innovation of the Federalist period was a wider range. The "Bay" (of Chaleur) and Labrador shore fisheries, secured in the same treaty, were first

135

visited shortly after the war, and immediately became popular. Almost a thousand sail passed through the Strait of Canso in 1807, outward bound —

> Where Anticosti lies
> Like a fell spider in its web of fog, . . .
> And frost-rimmed bays and trading stations seem
> Familiar as Great Neck and Kettle Cove,
> Nubble and Boon, the common names of home.

On Sundays, the New England fishermen "swarmed like flies" on the shore of the Gulf of St. Lawrence, said a British observer, whose reports were largely responsible for his government's efforts to restrict these grounds in the negotiations at Ghent. By 1808, three-quarters of the dried fish exported from Massachusetts came from the Bay and Labrador coast; less than one-quarter from the Grand Banks, which required larger vessels and more expensive outfits. The Bank fishermen, however, were able to export their own fares, when cured, to France, Spain, Portugal, or the West Indies in the winter season.

Encouragement of the New England fisheries was often justified on the ground that they contributed both men and vessels to the navy and merchant marine. In time of war, when unarmed Bankers would fall certain prey to the enemy, their crews perforce enlisted in the navy or on a privateer. But on the merchant marine their influence was slight, except in so far as their produce furnished freight and a medium for trade. The more ambitious youths of fishing towns entered the merchant marine — Captain Cressy, for instance, of the *Flying Cloud* clipper, was a Marblehead boy. But notwithstanding popular belief and congressional oratory, ex-fishermen were seldom found among the crews of deep-sea merchantmen, at any period of our

136

history.[1] "They make troublesome merchantmen," writes Bentley of the Marblehead fishermen in 1816. "But no men are equal to them in the things they know how to do from habit."

Fishing was a specialized form of maritime enterprise. The small amount of capital required, the short voyages (enabling a man to live at home with his family at least half the year), and the share system of rewarding crews, appealed to a class of men who could not afford the expense of mercantile ventures, and would not submit to the wage system, the discipline, and the lengthy voyages of merchant vessels. The Yankee liked fishing 'on his own hook' — the phrase originated here, before the Revolution, to describe a system in which each member of the crew supplied his own gear, bedding, and food. Fishermen had their own customs and costumes,[2] types and traditions which were handed down from generation to generation.

A fisherman's son was predestined to the sea. As soon as he could walk, he swarmed over every Banker or Chebacco boat that came into port, began 'hand-lining' for cunners off wharves and ledges, and begging older boys to teach him to row. At six he was already some aid in curing the catch, and he helped his mother with the household work, in order to qualify as sea-cook. Boys of nine to twelve years did the cooking in Marblehead and Gloucester fishermen at this period,

[1] R. B. Forbes is most emphatic on this point. Captain Arthur H. Clark backs him up. The author of *The Mate and his Duties* (Liverpool, 1855), p. 24, states, "It is in general much easier to make a good sailor out of a landsman than a fisherman." Fishermen were not used to discipline or to quick movements, and were apt to shy at laying out on yardarms.

[2] The New England fisherman's costume, until about 1830, when oilskins were adopted, was a sheep- or goat-skin jacket, and 'barvel' (leather apron), baggy calfskin trousers, yellow cowhide "churn boots," and tarred canvas hat, shaped like the modern sou'wester.

137

and on Cape-Codders even later. After a voyage or two he handed over his cooking utensils — a single iron pot and long spoon — to a younger brother or cousin, became an apprentice, learned the secrets of luring codfish to hook, and the art of heading, splitting, and salting with quick precision. A strong boy of fifteen or sixteen might be as accomplished a fisherman as any; a 'high-liner' of the fleet. To save enough to acquire a fishing vessel, and live ashore on her earnings, was his highest ambition. Otherwise he grew gray in the service of the sea. When rheumatic arms could no longer haul on sheet or cable, and eyes grew dim from straining through night, fog, and easterlies, he retired from deep waters, and puttered about with lobstering, shore fishing, or clam-digging.

Marblehead, a scant three miles from Salem, was as different in its appearance, its commerce, and the character of its people, as if it lay overseas. Built on ground so hilly and boulder-strewn that there seemed hardly place for the weather-beaten houses; peopled by descendants of the peculiar old stock; the harbor open to northeast gales, which sent in great wicked rollers that tore up the stoutest ground tackle; Marblehead yet remained the premier fishing port of Massachusetts.

Few seaport towns in America had lost more by the Revolution. Before the war, Marblehead had rivaled Salem in population and foreign commerce. But 'King' Hooper and Benjamin Marston had become tories, and the elder Ornes, Lees, Pedricks, and Gerrys had died or removed to more prosperous centers. Their sons remained (for this being Marblehead the ordinary laws of emigration did not hold); but they had no capital to renew the foreign trade; and indeed it would have been useless to compete with Salem.

There was nothing left but the fisheries, and even they were at the lowest ebb. Average gross earnings per vessel had fallen from $483 in 1787 to $273 in 1789. There were 459 widows and 865 orphans, mostly dependent for support on the taxpayers, in this town of 5500 people. Houses and fish sheds were tumbling to pieces, and the sea threatened to make a clean breach through the Neck and ruin the harbor.

Marblehead stiffened her back, organized a lottery to relieve the poor, founded an academy in time to fit Joseph Story for college, acquired a bank and insurance company, and was rewarded with a partial return of prosperity. Her fishing schooners were the largest and best of the New England fleet. With the aid of small brigantines and topsail schooners like the *Raven*, their local catch was exported to France, Spain, and the West Indies, where high prices prevailed. "We got about one dollar for every fish we carried out" to Bilbao, one voyage, remembered an old fisherman.

When the Napoleonic wars raised freights to unheard-of figures, the Marblehead schooners and brigantines from seventy-five to one hundred and fifty tons burthen found it profitable to engage in the carrying trade. In 1792, Marblehead had only three entries from Europe; in 1805, the old impost book at the custom house records sixteen entries from Bilbao, one from Lisbon, four from Bordeaux, three from Nantes; one from La Rochelle, one from Alicante, two from Tönning (Holstein), one from St. Petersburg, and eight, with salt, from the Cape Verde Islands. In addition, there were the same year ten entries from Martinique, three from Havana, and one each from Guadeloupe and Dominica. In 1806, Marblehead had her first entry from the East Indies; the brigantine *Orient* (187 tons), Edmund Bray master, from Calcutta, with cottons, gunny bags, ginger, sugar, segars, bandannas, carpets, cords and blinds for Robert Hooper and several others. The customs duties annually collected at this little port rose from $22,300 in 1801 to $156,000 in 1807, when her fleet had a tonnage of 21,068; more than half that of Salem, but less than Newburyport or New Bedford.

Notwithstanding these impressive figures,[1] Marblehead never recovered her provincial affluence. Her newly won wealth went mostly to swell Salem and Boston fortunes. Her fishermen, less thrifty than the Puritan stock of Beverly and Cape Cod, frolicked away every winter the remembrance of their summer toils, and kept in debt to the vessel owners. Her population increased only by 239 souls from 1790 to 1810, which means, in view of the notoriously large families of Marblehead fishermen, that considerable emigration took place.

Jefferson's embargo achieved the ruin of Marblehead as the first fishing port of New England; and the War of 1812 found her much as the Revolution had left her, poor but proud, sullen but excitable. Happy the visiting 'furriner' from Salem, Lynn, or Boston, who escaped a 'squaeling' from her ragged urchins![2] In 1808 occurred the regrettable incident of Skipper Benjamin (not Floyd) Ireson, for his crew's cowardice and lying (not for his hard heart), tarred and feathered and carried in a dory (not cart) by the fishermen (not

---

[1] Due partly to Oriental imports in Boston vessels, consigned to Boston and other outside merchants. One such cargo, in the ship *Liverpool Packet*, W. T. Magee master, from Canton, consigned to George W. Lyman and James Morgan, paid over $72,500 duties in 1811.

[2] 'Squaeling,' in Marblehead dialect, meant hurling a stone, or other hard object. "I don't remember any one being squaeled," said an old lady of Marblehead to a friend of mine not many years ago — "unless 't were a Lynn man!" she added, thoughtfully.

the women) of Marblehead. Mr. Roads told the facts in his history, and Mr. Whittier acknowledged, "I have no doubt that thy version of Skipper Ireson's ride is the correct one."

T' other side Salem from Marblehead, not fifteen minutes' ride across Essex Bridge (completed in 1788 at the colossal cost of sixteen thousand dollars), was the ancient town of Beverly. Here were the stately homes of the Cabots, Lees, and Thorndikes, who, in combination with the clever lawyers of Newburyport, the orators of Boston, and the tea barons of Salem, controlled Massachusetts politics for the coming generation. History has not been kind to Beverly. After teaching Boston how to bake beans, the metropolis usurped the credit. After showing Salem how to fish and privateer, the larger port absorbed her neighbor in 1789 as a place of entry and registry. But the records of the state custom house, during the 'critical period,' throw light on her commercial economy. Apart from the operations of her distinguished triumvirate, Beverly was a fishing port, and the only fishing port which by 1790 had increased her catch and tonnage over pre-Revolutionary figures. In 1785, she was the proud possessor of thirty schooners and a sloop, from twenty to fifty tons burthen, including two *Pollys* two *Larks*, three *Betsys*, three *Swallows*, a *Two Friends*, a *Three Friends*, a *Three Brothers*, an *Industry*, a *Cicero*, and a *Hannah*. Every summer they made from two to four fares of fish, and every winter traded with the South and the West Indies, and the Cape Verde Islands. Within ten years Beverly's tonnage had doubled. Dr. Dwight, of Yale, judged her fishermen "distinguished for good order, industry, sober manners, and sound morals." The records of the Beverly Farms Social Library, organized in 1806, bear him out; for we find that Skipper Charles

Dodge took to sea with him Bishop Gardiner's 'Life,' Henry's 'Meditations,' and Baxter's 'Saints' Rest'; while Skipper Gamaliel Ober, for light summer reading on the Grand Banks, chose Jonathan Edwards on 'Religious Affections,' the third volume of Josephus, and Drelincourt on 'Death.'

Whilst Marblehead reverted from trading to fishing, and back again, Gloucester declined as a fishing port, but revived her foreign trade. In 1790, she already owned four ships, nine brigs, and twenty-three schooners, beside fishing vessels. Gloucester's specialty was a commerce in fish and molasses with Surinam. Why Gloucester should have gotten a grip on this trade, which was common to all the fishing ports in colonial days, is a mystery; but certain it is that until well on in the nineteenth century, Gloucester vessels were better known in Dutch Guiana than those of any other North American port. The wealthier merchant families of Gloucester Harbor — Sargents and Parsons and Pearces — aspired to higher things. They formed an association to carry on the East-India trade in the ship *Winthrop and Mary*, but the total loss of this vessel on her homeward passage from Sumatra in 1800 ended the experiment. Nevertheless, Gloucester was a thriving and prosperous town in the Federalist period, boasting a bank with a vault carved out of solid rock, a schoolhouse with cupola, and a two-story "artillery house" or armory, with four field pieces and a bell procured from Denmark. "They excell in their parties, their clubs, and also in their military parades," wrote Dr. Bentley, after being entertained by the Gloucester people in 1799.

Inability to man her Bankers, owing to the popularity of the Bay, Labrador, and offshore fisheries, was responsible for Gloucester's temporary decline as a fishing port. These minor fisheries were the specialty of Gallop's, Folly, Pigeon, Long, and Loblolly coves on Sandy Bay and the north side of Cape Ann.[1] They were prosecuted not in Bankers of a size requiring capitalist backing, but in smaller boats, which the fishermen themselves could build and own on shares. The typical Cape Ann fishing vessel of the Federalist period was a Chebacco boat (ancestor of the Down East 'pinkies' of to-day) — so called from the Chebacco Parish of Ipswich where the type was invented and built. Double-ended, 'pink' (sharp) sterned, rigged with two pole masts, stepped well forward so that no headsail was needed, and not over thirty feet long, the Chebacco boats were easy to handle and rode the waves like a duck. They were seaworthy enough for a Labrador voyage, but for the most part sought cod, haddock, or pollock on the banks and submerged ledges along the Maine coast, or within a hundred miles of Eastern Point — Old Man's Pasture, Matinicus Sou' Sou' West, Spot o' Rocks, Saturday Night Ledge, Kettle Bottom, Cashe's Ledge, and the Fippennies. In 1792, Cape Ann owned one hundred and thirty-three Chebacco boats of eleven tons burthen on an average; and by 1804 the number had increased to two hundred and the tonnage doubled.

Yet the Cape Ann fishermen were as a class miserably poor, and generally in debt to some storekeeper at Gloucester Harbor. The picturesque coves where their tiny cottages clustered, afforded poor anchorage and protection. At any sign of a northeast storm every Chebacco boat had to leave its tree-root moor-

---

[1] These villages were all in the township of Gloucester, until 1840, when some of them were set off as the town of Rockport. Gloucester village, now the city, was called "The Harbor," to distinguish it from other villages in the township.

143

ing, and slip around Cape Ann, to the protection of Gloucester Harbor.

Chebacco (incorporated the town of Essex in 1819) owned a fleet of about forty local boats. At Ipswich, up a narrow, winding river where nothing larger than a motor boat ventures nowadays, the Farleys, Tread- wells, Lakemans, and others owned a fleet of Bankers, Bay fishermen, and West-Indiamen. In ascending the river, they had to be warped around Nabby's Point by cables bent onto iron rings set in the rocks. Ipswich, in spite of her lace industry and fishing fleet, was somewhat of a decayed town during the Federalist period; an example of what Salem would have been without the East-India trade.

Reserving Newburyport for another chapter, let us coast by the fishing ports south of Boston. The South Shore was at a standstill during the Federalist period; but whatever life it had came from fishing. Cohasset with but 817 inhabitants in 1790, barely passed the thousand mark in 1820. Scituate increased by less than three hundred between 1776 and 1810. "The whole region," observed Dr. Dwight, "wears re- markably the appearance of stillness and retirement; and the inhabitants seem to be separated, in a great measure, from all active intercourse with their coun- try." But Dr. Dwight did not visit the active ship- yards on the upper North River. Plymouth Bay was slightly more progressive; but the combined popula- tion of Duxbury, Kingston, and Plymouth, including considerable farming country, hardly exceeded that of Marblehead or Gloucester in 1800, and "about half the inhabitants live by husbandry." Their fleet was almost annihilated by the Revolution. Before the war, these towns marketed their catch at the West Indies or through Boston, but about 1790 a Plymouth merchant opened an export trade to the Mediterranean. Plymouth Bày then built up a considerable fleet — sixty-two schooners of thirty-eight to one hundred and thirty-six tons burthen by 1807. Two of them belonged to Joshua Winsor, of Duxbury, whose house, warehouse, wharf, and other possessions are shown in the attached illustration, the work of some itinerant painter. Fish-flakes of the ancient pattern — woven platforms of alder branches, on posts about thirty inches above the ground — lined the shores for two miles either side of Plymouth Rock. And as a neutral trading port, Plymouth Bay was not far behind Marblehead.[1]

Cape Cod, which had never permitted the war to shake its thrift and frugality, recovered a modest prosperity through a combination of fishing and salt-making. This latter industry began at Dennis early in the Revolution, when the British fleet cut off our supply of salt — a necessity for curing fish, and preserving meat in pre-cold-storage days. After the war, it was necessary to cheapen the process in order to compete with imports. One Cape-Codder harnessed the wind, to save pumping; and another harnessed the sun, with an ingenious arrangement of wooden vats and sliding covers, to save fuel. By 1800 there were one hundred and thirty-six salt-works between Sandwich and Provincetown, yielding twenty-five to thirty-three per cent profit from their sales of marine and Glauber salts, despite the heavy imports from Maia, Lisbon, and Turks Island. Dr. Dwight in his travels was impressed by the "tidy, comfortable appearance" of the Cape Cod cottages, and with the surprisingly fruitful yield of Cape Cod agriculture. Barnstable, for instance, exported about fifteen thou-

[1] See below, chapter xii.

145

sand bushels of flax annually. "But husbandry is pursued with little spirit," wrote the minister of Chatham; "the people in general passing the flower of their lives at sea, which they do not quit till they are fifty years of age, leaving at home none but the old men and small boys to cultivate the ground." In Wood's Hole, Barnstable, and other harbors vessels were fitted for combination fishing and whaling voyages, sailing to the Gulf of St. Lawrence prepared to catch anything from a herring to a Greenland whale. The population of Cape Cod increased from seventeen thousand in 1790 to twenty-two thousand in 1810; and the fishing fleet in proportion. But Provincetown, in 1810, still had less than one thousand inhabitants; and Cape civilization did not reach full bloom for another generation.

Going fishing or to sea was looked forward to by every Cape Cod boy. Elijah Cobb, later an eminent Brewster shipmaster, embarked at Namskaket on the packet-schooner *Creture* in 1783, to seek his fortune at Boston, paying his passage with two bushels of home-grown corn. He felt lucky to be shipped as cook and cabin boy for Surinam, at $3.50 per month; and brought his mother twenty silver dollars, more than she had seen since the death of her husband at sea, years before. Osborne Howes, a prominent Boston merchant of Cape origin, describes the thrifty life in a North Dennis shipmaster's family, about 1812. Deborah, his mother, made all the clothing for herself and the five children. Cotton and wool were purchased in Boston, and made into yarn on the family spinning-wheel during the winter. When the days became longer, she and the older children spent an hour or more weaving every morning before feeding the stock or preparing breakfast; and in this way every child had a new woolen kersey suit, and two of striped or checked cotton cloth every year. Yet she was always bright and joyous, and received or gave visits three or four times a week. The Cape had to work hard for its daily bread, but what it got was good. The minister of Chatham gives us the typical menu of fishermen's families, toward the end of the eighteenth century. Breakfast: tea or coffee, brown bread (of home-grown 'rye and injun'), and salt or fresh fish. Dinner: one or more of the following dishes: roots and herbs, boiled salt meat, wild fowl in autumn, fresh fish, boiled or fried with pork, shellfish, boiled salt fish, indian pudding, pork and beans. Supper: the same as breakfast, plus cheese, cakes, gingerbread, and pie. "Some have pie for breakfast." Thank God for that!

"In the seaports of Massachusetts Bay, one-quarter of the people live on fresh fish," wrote Stephen Higginson in 1775. Every seaside village sheltered a number of boat fishermen, who supplied the population with fresh fish, especially in the winter season. Of this industry no statistics and few records have been preserved. Every locality had its favorite type of boat, the larger using the mainsail and foresail rig of the Chebacco boats (as shown in the picture of Mr. Joshua Winsor's house at Duxbury and the wood cut of Provincetown in 1839); the smaller hoisting a spritsail, as shown on the certificate of the Salem Marine Society. One also finds frequent mention of canoes.[1] These were neither dugouts nor birch-bark

[1] For instance, "Went adrift, a small canoe last week, supposed to have been taken up by some Vessel — a spritsail, driver and Gibb, two oars, &c on board." (Boston *Independent Chronicle*, July 2, 1798.) The birch-bark canoe was very little used in colonial Massachusetts, which lay south of the range of the canoe birch. The square-sterned skiffs carried at the taffrail on seagoing vessels, as shown in several of our illustrations, were called "Moses boats."

canoes, but a small one-man type of lapstreak rowboat, which was used for pilot boat or yacht tender down to about 1880. On Cape Ann, when winter kept the Chebacco boats at home, the Sandy Bay boys put out in small flat-bottomed wherries, ancestors of the modern dory, and sold their catch to local storekeepers. Swampscott, a snug little village on the bight between Marblehead and Nahant, used a similar model to supply the shoemakers of Lynn. Cape Cod and Buzzard's Bay used the lapstreak, round-bottomed whaleboat, and the Block Island or Vineyard sailboat, a fast, able flat-bottomed type with a Chebacco rig.

We must not forget the humble shellfish, whose praises were sung by William Wood in his "New England's Prospect":

> The luscious Lobster, with the Crabfish raw,
> The Brinish Oister, Muscle, Periwigge,
> And Tortoise sought for by the Indian Squaw,
> Which to the flats daunce many a winters Jigge,
> To dive for Cocles, and to digge for Clamms,
> Whereby her lazie husbands guts shee cramms.

Wellfleet, on Cape Cod, specialized in oysters. The enterprising people of this place, when some marine epidemic depleted their oyster-beds, procured fresh stock from Chesapeake Bay; and by 1800 some sixty thousand bivalves were annually transplanted in order to acquire the Wellfleet flavor. When properly fattened, they were transported by locally owned vessels to the markets of Boston, Salem, and Portland.

Swampscott claims the invention of the lobster trap in 1808, previous to which one could pick up enough lobsters at low tide to supply the Boston market. Orleans specialized in the humble industry of clamdigging, the product of which, shucked and salted and packed into barrels, provided bait for codfishing.

THE SACRED CODFISH

Another Cape industry which profited by the shipping expansion of Federalist days was "moon-cursing," or plundering wrecks. Gossipy Dr. Bentley, apropos the snowstorm of 1802 in which several of his parishioners were lost on Peaked Hill Bar, recalled the story of the Reverend Mr. Lewis of Wellfleet. During his sermon one Sabbath, this sporting parson saw through the window a vessel going ashore. He stopped his sermon, descended the pulpit stairs, and with a shout of "Start fair!" led his congregation pell-mell out of the meeting-house door. A few years later, Dr. Bentley had to acknowledge his Cape Ann neighbors no greater respecters of flotsam than the men of Cape Cod. A richly laden East-Indiaman, running ashore on Thatcher's, was quickly relieved of her cargo. But note the inexorable workings of divine justice. The local market became so glutted with India cottons that the wreckers' wives could sell no product of their looms for almost a year!

Dark traditions have come down of the inhabitants of Cuttyhunk and Tarpaulin Cove, decoying vessels ashore by false lights, and murdering the crew. But the people of Cape Cod and Cape Ann always treated shipwrecked mariners with the utmost humanity. Zachary G. Lamson, in his autobiography, describes running ashore on the back side of Cape Cod, on the last night of the year 1801. The schooner drove over the shoals onto the beach, so that the crew was able to walk ashore over the bowsprit; but after wandering about in the small hours of a frigid morning, in vain search for shelter, two fell exhausted on the beach. The others crawled over the schooner's gunwale as she lay stranded by the tide, and turned in, with clothes frozen stiff. That afternoon some men of Orleans and Chatham, who had seen the vessel from the hills, pulled them out of bed, and dug their shipmates out of the snow. A tough breed, these Beverly seamen. Peter Woodbury and John Low, after lying twelve hours in the snow without boots or mittens, plus a six-mile boat journey, encrusted with ice like a tongue in aspic, were restored by kind Chatham women applying hot blankets steadily for seven hours. A day or two later, they walked all the way home to Beverly; and Peter served as master's mate on the *Constitution* during the War of 1812.

Although the codfisheries no longer played a stellar rôle in the pageant of maritime Massachusetts, their lesser part was no less indispensable. Pacific and Baltic trade required other currency than fish; but much of that currency was obtained in the first instance from fish. The sacred cod still fed the West-India and Mediterranean trades. He and his humbler cousins provided the seaboard population with cheap food. Pursuit of him employed thousands of people who must otherwise have emigrated; restored prosperity to the minor seaports, and preserved their pristine vigor.

Note on the "moon-cussers" (p. 149): During the course of years I have heard identical stories — the wreck-happy parson and false lights attached to tethered goats — at St. George's, Bermuda, in Cornwall, and on Achill Island, Ireland; and a friend of mine reports a monument to the victims of shipwreck somewhere on the coast of Scotland, with the inscription "This Monument was Erected by the Humane and Generous People of this Parish with Part of the Money Taken from the Pockets of the Deceased."

CHAPTER XI

NEWBURYPORT AND NANTUCKET

1790–1812

NEWBURYPORT was unique among Massachusetts sea-ports of Federalist days, in that she acquired considerable wealth without aid of Oriental trading. This compact little town, covering one square mile at the mouth of the Merrimac, recovered prosperity through a thrifty combination of shipbuilding, fishing, West-India and European trading, distilling, domestic manufactures, and internal improvements. Her population doubled between 1776 and 1810, her fleet increased from 118 vessels of twelve thousand tons in 1790 to 176 vessels of thirty thousand tons in 1806. Duties collected on imports tripled in ten years.

Much human effort was required before Newbury-port could reap full advantage of her position at the mouth of the Merrimac. The entrance lay over a bar with only seven feet of water on it at low tide; a bar that broke in easterly gales. An intricate system of day and night signals, shown from the lighthouses on Plum Island, warned approaching sail when it was unsafe to enter. Newburyport opened inland communication with Hampton by a canal through the salt marshes. Her capitalists organized, in 1792, the "Proprietors of the Locks and Canals on Merrimack River," who in four years' time completed a canal around the Pawtucket Falls between Chelmsford and Dracut.[1]

---

[1] It was this corporation which, in the hands of Boston capitalists of Newburyport descent, became the corporate overlord of the manufacturing city of Lowell.

By this means, Newburyport became the emporium for lumber, firewood, and country produce of northeastern Massachusetts and southern New Hampshire. At the same time the Chain Bridge, built three miles above the town, induced seagoing vessels to end their voyages at Newburyport instead of ascending higher.

It was this canal, tapping new sources for oak and pine, plus inherited aptitude, which enabled the lower Merrimac to hold its own in shipbuilding. There were two shipyards at Haverhill in 1800, others at Amesbury, Salisbury, and Old Newbury, and at least six at Newburyport, owned by Jackmans, Curriers, and other ancestors of the clipper-ship builders. Twelve thousand tons of shipping were launched on the Merrimac in 1810, and practically all their cordage, sails, blocks, ironwork, and fittings were made locally.

Newburyport specialized in the Labrador and Bay fisheries, in which sixty vessels were engaged in 1806. Her other hundred and sixteen vessels were employed in coasting, West-Indian, and European trade — of which more anon. Newburyport was also noted for rum and whiskey distilleries, for Laird's ale and porter, and for goldsmiths; Jacob Perkins having discovered a cheap method of making gold-plated beads, which were then in fashion. Even after the war-time depression there were ten jewelers' and watchmakers' shops at Newburyport. Here were printed and published the numerous editions of Bowditch's "Navigator," and Captain Furlong's "American Coast Pilot."

Newburyport boasted a society inferior to that of no other town on the continent. Most of the leading families were but one generation removed from the plough or the forecastle; but they had acquired wealth before the Revolution, and conducted social matters with the grace and dignity of an old régime. When Governor Gore, in 1809, made a state visit to Newburyport, where he had once studied law, he came in coach and four with outriders, uniformed aides, and a cavalry escort; and when the town fathers informed his ancient benefactress, Madam Atkins, that His Excellency would honor her with a call, the spokesman delivered his message on his knees at the good lady's feet. We read of weekly balls and routs, of wedding coaches drawn by six white horses with liveried footmen, in this town of less than eight thousand inhabitants. When personal property was assessed, several Newburyport merchants reported from one thousand to twelve hundred gallons of wine in their cellars.

Federalist architecture has here left perhaps her finest permanent trace. High street, winding along a ridge commanding the Merrimac, rivals Chestnut Street of Salem, despite hideous interpolations of the late nineteenth century. The gambrel-roofed type lasted into the seventeen-nineties, when the Newburyport merchants began to build square, three-storied, hip-roofed houses of brick, surrounded with ample grounds, gardens, and 'housins.' The ship carpenters who (if tradition is correct) designed and built these houses, adopted neither the graceful porches nor the applied Adam detail of McIntire; but their tooled mouldings on panel, cornice, and chimneypiece have a graceful and original vigor. They also invented, or perhaps acquired from provincial Portsmouth, an ingenious form of stairway, branching, Y-shaped, to serve front and rear. Although inferior to Boston and Salem in public buildings, "the steeple of the First Church lately built" in Newburyport, asserts the critical and much-traveled Dr. Bentley, "rivals anything in New England." It certainly does, to-day.

Timothy Dwight, who visited Newburyport about 1800, wrote: "The houses, taken collectively, make a better appearance than those of any other town in New-England. Many of them are particularly handsome. Their appendages, also, are unusually neat. Indeed, an air of wealth, taste and elegance, is spread over this beautiful spot with the cheerfulness and brilliancy, to which I know no rival. . . . Upon the whole, few places, probably, in the world, furnish more means of a delightful residence than Newburyport."

*

*　　*

When 'Lord' Timothy Dexter, Newburyport's famous eccentric, sent his consignment of warming-pans and woolen mittens to the West Indies, he knew what he was about. The warming-pans, as every one knows, were sold for syrup ladles; and the mitts made a suitable speculation for some Massachusetts vessel that was leaving for Russia.

This Russian trade was an innovation of the Federalist period. Massachusetts began it, and until the Civil War retained over half of it, through her facilities for handling the West-India goods of which Russia stood in need. George Cabot of Beverly opened this commerce in May, 1784, by sending his ships *Bucanier* and *Commerce* to the Baltic and to St. Petersburg. In 1788 the *Astrea* was disposing of tea, Bourbon coffee, New England rum, Virginia flour and tobacco at Gothenburg. They brought back canvas, duck, hemp, Russian and Swedish iron, which, with household linen, were the staples of the Baltic trade for the next fifty years. These articles were used in the New England shipbuilding industry, and also entered largely into cargoes exported to the Far East. No inconsiderable part of the goods exchanged by St. Petersburg and Riga with India and China went in Massachusetts vessels, *via* Salem and Boston. And it will doubtless surprise many people to learn that Salem was importing candles and soap from Archangel in 1798.

Dipping casually into the old custom-house records of Newburyport, I find on top of a neat bundle of coastwise manifests for 1810, that the locally owned ship *Nancy*, Moses Brown master, paid $3279.25 in duties on eighty-eight boxes of sugar from Pernambuco. It was shipped to Boston in the sloop *Mary*, and exported thence to St. Petersburg in the brig *Industry*. The next document traces a parcel of Russia linen sheetings. Imported from Cronstadt into Newburyport by the ship *Merrimack*, William Bartlett master, it was shipped in the sloop *Blue Bird* [1] to Boston, and re-exported thence in the brig *Betsey* to Havana. There, it was doubtless exchanged for sugar, the most valuable medium for our Baltic trade. Not only did this triangular commerce give quick turnover and large profits; it supplied maritime New England with the iron, hemp, and linen duck, which, until replaced by the products of Pennsylvania, Manila, and Lowell, were indispensable to her shipbuilding, fisheries, and navigation. The vessels engaged in it were called "Russiamen."

* *

The first white settlers of Nantucket, in the seventeenth century, were Quakers and harborers of Quakers who fled from persecution at Old Newbury. With Whittier as pilot, let us follow Goodman Macy's little shallop across the harbor bar, by the golden sands of

---

[1] This small coasting packet, when wrecked in 1805, had a cargo aboard worth $90,000. She was refloated, but the cargo lost.

Plum Island, and watch the sun drop behind the rounded Ipswich hills. The garrison's watch-fire guides us around Cape Ann; keeping the North Star over our port quarter brings us to Cape Cod. After a pause in Provincetown Harbor for a good chance, an offshore breeze takes us around the Cape, through the dangerous shoals and rips which deflected the *Mayflower* from her course; and to Nantucket.

Before 1775, the descendants of the Macys and Coffins and Folgers and Husseys had spread the fame of this island by their boldness and enterprise as whalemen. Then came the war. Nantucket lost one hundred and fifty vessels by capture and shipwreck, leaving only two or three old hulks out of her entire fleet. The whaling village of Bedford, her young mainland rival, was equally depressed. The British had burned its warehouses and thirty-four sail in the harbor; and only two or three survived of its whaling fleet of forty or fifty.

The English government, hoping to force the Islanders to remove to Nova Scotia, placed a prohibitive duty on whale and sperm oil, cutting off their principal market; and in 1785 the French government invited them to settle at Dunkirk. Beggars were crying for bread in the streets of Nantucket; but only nine families accepted this invitation, and even less went to Dartmouth, Nova Scotia. But over two hundred of the men, either during or after the Revolution, were forced to accept commands of British or French whalers. Others turned to codfishing, founding picturesque but profitless settlements on the south shore of the island, at Siasconset, Sasacacha, and Weweeder. One group attempted an East-India voyage, with disastrous results. For the most part the people waited for better times, "taking in each others' washing" for a living, according to the classic jest — and it was something more than a jest in the Nantucket of 1790, with no less than one hundred and eighty-five widows unable to support themselves.

The commonwealth, out of its poverty, granted a bounty on whaling products; England gave up trying to sink Nantucket; and the old whaling masters began to fit out old vessels, and to have apple-bowed, square-sterned ships of two to three hundred tons burthen built for them on the North River.[1] By 1789, Nantucket had eighteen vessels engaged in the northern right-whale fishery, and an equal number pursuing the more valuable sperm whale off the coast of Brazil; Dartmouth (including New Bedford and Westport) and Cape Cod had fifty-seven small right-whalers of sixty tons, and nine sperm-whalers.

It was a British whaler manned by exiled Nantucketers that first pursued the sperm whale into the Pacific Ocean. Four years later, in 1791, six Nantucket whalers, and one from New Bedford, took the same course. They found good hunting along the Chilian coast, and returned in time to profit by a good market in France.

From that time on, smoky glare of whalers' try-works was never absent from the vast spaces of the Pacific. Before the end of the eighteenth century, the whalemen began that exploration of the South Sea which is still recorded by islands named for Starbucks, Coffins, Bakers, Folgers, Husseys, and Howlands of Nantucket and New Bedford.

[1] The *Maria*, 202 tons, built at Pembroke for William Rotch, in 1782, was still whaling in 1872. Oil acted on the timbers as a preservative. The ship *Rousseau* was in commission ninety-seven years, the barque *Triton*, seventy-nine; and in the summer of 1920 the barque *Charles W. Morgan*, built in 1841, was fitting out for another whaling voyage at Fairhaven.

On the Island of Santa Maria in the Galapagos group, was the 'whalers' post-office'; a box on a tree where letters and two-year-old newspapers were exchanged. Even Australasia lay within their scope. By 1804, our whalemen and sealskinners had made themselves so comfortable along the north coast of Tasmania that the governor of Australia issued a proclamation against their building vessels on his shores.

Whaling crews at this period were recruited entirely from Nantucket and the Old Colony. Gay Head Indians were preferred as harpooners, and many local negroes were shipped as green hands; but a whaling skipper generally knew the record if not the pedigree of every man who sailed under his command. Wages were not paid to whalemen. The old share or 'lay' system of the seventeenth century continued; and for the first time was recorded in written contracts. The workers' share was far more generous than in the so-called golden age of whaling, a generation later. The usual 'lay' for a three-boat ship of twenty-one men, about 1804, was three-fifths of the catch to the owners, one-eighteenth to the master, one-forty-eighth to the "ends men," one-seventy-fifth to each able seaman, one-eightieth or ninetieth to each negro hand, and a one-hundred-and-twentieth to the cabin boy.

Prices of whale products ruled fairly high during the Federalist period, and a good export trade was built up; England being our best customer for sperm oil, and France and Spain for whale oil. But the ground lost in the Revolutionary War was not entirely recovered.[1] Americans had become so used to tallow candles during the war, that they had to be educated to appreciate the excellent spermaceti article turned out by Nantucket. The European war, with its spoliations

[1] See table in Appendix.

and embargoes, greatly hampered whaling, while it gave inflated profits to the merchant marine. The harbor, with only seven and a half feet on the bar at low tide, was a serious handicap as the size of whalers increased, and eventually proved Nantucket's undoing.

Nantucket, however, by handling and marketing her own products, prevented 'off-islanders' from reaping the fruits of her industry. By 1810, when a Philadelphia traveler made the accompanying sketch, the town had every earmark of thrift and prosperity. It had doubled its pre-Revolutionary population, and acquired some fifteen thousand tons of shipping, most of which was absent on the Pacific Ocean when the sketch was made. Several sail of whalers, however, are lying at the wharves, and the Falmouth packet-sloop has just passed in between Brant Point Light and Coatue.

Even before the famous foundation of her distinguished exile, Admiral Sir Isaac Coffin, Nantucket had better schools than many mainland seaports. She had fifteen to twenty candle-works and refineries, ten rope-walks, a bank, a museum, an insurance office, and a Free Masons' hall "with Ionick pilasters in front." The Lisbon bell, whose sweet tones to-day greet off-island visitors, will soon be hung in the stumpy tower of the old North Church. Tidy clapboarded houses, painted white or green, with 'captains' walks' atop, were beginning to replace the shingled dwellings of colonial days. Almost the entire male population of Nantucket followed the sea; and the rest were dependent on it. Even the cows, apparently, came down to the harbor's edge to browse, and take in the scene of marine activity!

CHAPTER XII

FEDERALISM AND NEUTRAL TRADE

1789–1807

FEDERALISM has opposite connotations in Europe and America, and a very special meaning east of the Hudson. New England Federalism was at once a political system, and a point of view. Sired by Neptune out of Puritanism, the teacher of its youth was Edmund Burke. Washington, Hamilton, and Fisher Ames formed the trinity of its worship. Timothy Pickering was the kept politician of New England Federalism, Harrison Gray Otis its spellbinder, Boston its political and Hartford its intellectual capital, Harvard and Yale the seminaries of its priesthood. New England Federalism believed that the main object of government was to protect property, especially commercial and shipping property; and it supported nationalism or states' rights according as the federal government protected or neglected these interests of maritime New England. It aimed to create and maintain in power a governing class, of educated, well-to-do men. Regarding Jeffersonian democracy a mere misbegotten brat of the French Revolution, New England Federalism directed its main efforts toward choking the parent, hoping thereby either to starve the progeny, or to wean it from an evil heritage.

Federalism did not attain the rigidity of a system until the early nineteenth century; but the economic block that formed its basis was already formed in 1790. All the maritime interests of New England were in reality one interest, that must stand or fall together.

FEDERALISM AND NEUTRAL TRADE

No one of her sea-borne industries was self-sufficient, and many of the greater merchants were directly concerned in all of them. By 1790, Boston and Salem were no mere market towns for salt fish and country produce, but *entrepôts* of world commerce. The outward cargoes to the East Indies were first obtained through trading with the West Indies, the Mediterranean, and northern Europe; and the success of Yankee vessels in these markets depended as much on their skillful handling of Southern produce, as on the ancient Massachusetts staples of fish, lumber, whale-oil, and rum. Although the use of tea, coffee, spices, and imported sugar became general among all classes of the New England population at this period, the bulk of the Oriental cargoes brought into Salem and Boston was reëxported. No section of the edifice could be touched without disturbing the rest. Yet every block was composed of white oak, the raw material of New England shipping. In final analysis, the power of Massachusetts as a commercial state lay in her ships, and the men who built, owned, and sailed them.

*

* *

All matters of shipping and navigation fell within the scope of the federal government's protecting arm. Massachusetts promptly ceded her seven lighthouses[1] to the United States, which assumed the burden of maintaining them, and of building new ones. For these few, dim whale-oil lights did not satisfy com-

---

[1] Portland Head (Maine), Plum Island Lights near Newburyport, Cape Ann Lights on Thatcher's Island, Boston Light, Plymouth Lights on the Gurnet, Brant Point and Great Point Lights on Nantucket. There were only eight more in the whole United States.

mercial interests. Vessels from the South, the West Indies, and the Far East approached Massachusetts Bay by way of Vineyard Sound, Nantucket Sound, and the back side of the Cape. On a fair westerly day in the seventeen-nineties, fifty or sixty sail could be seen from any point on this great ocean fairway. But imagine sailing this course at night, as the most leisurely of merchantmen might wish to do if the wind were fair, rather than risk a week's stay at Holmes's Hole. Leaving Great Point astern, one entered a dark chasm into which Cape Cod stretched its tentacles of death.

Petitions from the Boston Marine Society and other influential bodies induced the Government in 1797 to erect on the Clay Pounds, Truro, the Highland or Cape Cod Light. His powerful glare, varied by a comforting wink every sixty seconds, took vessels in charge before Great Point dipped under the horizon, and saw them safely around the Cape to within the scope of Boston Light or Thatcher's. Within a few years Gay Head Light was established at the entrance to this highway, the twins of Chatham Bar gave the line to a safe shelter, and Boon and Seguin were set up to guard the coast of Maine.

The approach to Salem Harbor is particularly difficult in thick weather or at night, on account of the many islands and submerged rocks in the bay. After a fatal storm in January, 1796, the federal government established a safe guide to the best channel, the Baker's Island Lights:

> Two pale sisters, all alone
> On an island bleak and bare,
> Listening to the breakers moan,
> Shivering in the chilly air.

FEDERALISM AND NEUTRAL TRADE

Four buoys at the mouth of the Merrimac were apparently the only such aids to navigation in Massachusetts waters until 1797, when Congress appropriated sixteen hundred dollars for sixteen buoys, "to be placed in and near the harbor of Boston." They were made of five-foot wooden staves bound by iron hoops, in the form of a truncated cone, and moored by the smaller end. Nantucket Harbor, so difficult of access as to require twice the pilotage rates of Boston, was buoyed before 1809. But the present efficient marking of ledges and channels developed very slowly.[1] Not until 1843 did the federal government begin a systematic coast survey.

Private enterprise supplemented the Government's efforts. The Boston Marine Society passed critical judgment on published charts, and examined candidates for Boston pilots. Nathaniel Bowditch brought out an excellent chart and sailing directions to Salem bay, based on surveys and soundings made by Captain John Gibaut and his pastor, Dr. Bentley. Before 1800 there was established a 'Telegraphe' system, which, by semaphores at Edgartown, Wood's Hole, Sandwich, Plymouth, Marshfield, Scituate, and Hull, notified Boston and Salem shipmasters of the arrival of their vessels at Vineyard Haven. The Humane Society of the Commonwealth of Massachusetts and the Merrimack Humane Society erected huts of refuge on dangerous and deserted stretches of the coast; a

[1] The method of establishing new buoys is shown by the following letter from H. A. S. Dearborn, collector of the port of Boston, to the collector at Barnstable, May 22, 1813: "Sir, I am directed by the Secretary of the Treasury to have a Buoy placed at the entrance of Barnstable Harbour, provided the expense does not exceed one Hundred Dollars. You are hereby authorized to have a Buoy made, & placed where it is most wanted. . . . Mr. J. L. Green has recommended Captain Prince Howe as a suitable person to do the work."

boon to shipwrecked mariners who often passed safely through the breakers only to perish of exposure and hunger on the sandy wastes of Cape Cod or Plum Island.

Shipwrecks on the New England coast still remained the principal form of casualty in the Massachusetts merchant marine. Peaked Hill Bar on Cape Cod took a heavy toll, even after Highland Light was established; for no light could penetrate the fog, rain, and snowstorms that inflict our coast. Four vessels were lost within sight of Salem, in a southeast rainstorm of February, 1807. The reefs off Cohasset were "annually the scene of the most heart-rending disasters," forty vessels being wrecked in one space of nine years, until the present lighthouse on Minot's Ledge, a site more difficult even than the famous Eddystone, was completed in 1860.[1] Nantucket Shoals lightship was not established until 1854. But the lighthouses erected and maintained by the United States, under the watchful care of Hamilton, saved many valuable lives and ships, and created a new bond of obligation between maritime Massachusetts and the administration.

Maritime Massachusetts expected something more from the federal government than 'lights, buoys and daymarks,' and she sent the right men to the capital to get it. Her senior senatorship was first conferred upon Caleb Strong, of Northampton, to conciliate the western counties. But when it came to choosing the junior senator, "the merchants made the Constitution," said James Sullivan, "and they should name the candidate." Tristram Dalton was accordingly chosen, and proceeded to New York in Newburyport style, in

[1] The first Minot's Ledge Lighthouse, completed in 1850, was demolished by a gale the following year.

his own four-horse coach, emblazoned with the Dalton arms, and attended by servants in the Dalton livery. "Everything that can affect shipbuilding I shall watch with a jealous eye," he wrote a constituent, when the first tariff debate began. Other jealous eyes were on the rum industry, and Vice-President Adams's casting vote once broke a Senate deadlock in favor of a low duty on molasses. Dalton was succeeded in the Senate by George Cabot, who had left Harvard before the Revolution to go to sea, and conducted a mercantile business at Beverly and Boston, beside taking an active part in the state government. Until 1816 the United States Senate contained a merchant of Boston or of Essex County, except for a period of five years, when Timothy Pickering upheld the same interest.

The merchants had worked for a more perfect union to obtain protection; nor were they disappointed. No section or interest in the United States was so favored by Washington's and Adams's administrations, as maritime Massachusetts. The fishing bounties, we have already mentioned. The first tariff acts (1789 and 1790) caused much grumbling, because of duties on iron, hemp, and molasses ($2\frac{1}{2}$ cents a gallon!); but no subsequent tariff proved of such benefit to Massachusetts shipping and commerce. The drawback system (refunding of tariff duties) was adopted for goods reëxported within a year; and Massachusetts became the greatest state for this branch of commerce. Foreign vessels had to pay ten per cent additional duty on ordinary goods, and about fifty per cent on teas.[1]

[1] Bohea tea, the cheapest grade, paid 10 cents a pound duty if imported in an American vessel from beyond the Cape of Good Hope; 12 cents if imported in an American vessel from Europe; 15 cents if otherwise imported. For Hyson tea the figures were 32, 40, and 50 cents. American registry at this period was confined to vessels owned wholly by American citizens and built in the United States.

Elias Hasket Derby petitioned, and Hamilton recommended a bonded warehouse system, which was adopted for teas in 1791. Customs duties could be paid as the teas were sold, at any time within two years of their importation. A similar privilege for shorter periods was extended in 1795 to importers of West-India and European goods.

Most important in their consequences were the tonnage duties, which were levied on vessels entering from foreign ports. American vessels paid six cents per ton burthen under the act of 1790; foreign vessels, fifty cents per ton. In the coasting trade an American vessel need pay this fee but once a year, but a foreign vessel had to pay it at every port.

The direct result of these discriminating duties was to drive English and other foreign vessels from American ports, in favor of those built and owned in the United States. Massachusetts shipbuilding was quick to benefit from the change. Her tonnage in 1792 was double[1] that of 1789, and amounted to a little over one-third the total American fleet. This extraordinary increase came before the Anglo-French war gave additional stimulus.

Most of these protective measures had been pushed through by Alexander Hamilton. His conscious policy was to favor the merchant-shipowner class, both to gain their powerful influence for strong government, and for the impost and tonnage duties, which accounted for ninety-two per cent of the revenues of the United States in 1791. His funding of the domestic debt, and assumption of the state debts, put money in the pockets of the merchants, who held large quantities

[1] An approximation. Professor Van Metre has pointed out that the Federal statistics of shipping from 1789 to 1793 are merely statements of shipping entering and leaving American ports, and that those for 1789 are low because the Federal collectors did not begin their work before midsummer.

of depreciated government securities. Consequently Hamilton's financial policy, which from the latitude of Charlottesville, Virginia, appeared unwarranted, unconstitutional, and anti-republican, seemed natural, necessary, and statesmanlike in Essex County, Massachusetts. It was just what maritime Massachusetts had ratified the Constitution to obtain! To the leaders of Bay State Federalism, Thomas Jefferson seemed a mutinous officer on the ship of state, and his democratic, strict-construction principles, the Jolly Roger of a piratical craft.

From 1789 to 1799 Hamilton dictated the financial and the foreign policies of the Washington and Adams administrations; and his privy council was the Essex Junto. This remarkable group of men, which guided the destinies of New England Federalism from its birth to its dissolution, was composed of practical and highly intelligent merchants and lawyers of Essex origin, who had migrated to Boston in search of greater opportunities. George Cabot and Fisher Ames were the Junto oracles, Stephen Higginson the practical merchant, Jonathan Jackson and John Lowell, Jr., of Newburyport, the elder statesman and pamphleteer, and Chief Justice Parsons the fount of legal learning. Timothy Pickering was the Junto mouthpiece in the United States Senate. Christopher Gore and James Lloyd hovered on the outskirts. Most of their families were intermarried, and their opinions, or rather prejudices, were the standard of 'right thinking' in eastern Massachusetts. Life and politics they regarded as from the quarterdeck of an East-Indiaman. Harrison Gray Otis and Josiah Quincy were little more than their political chanteymen, and all Massachusetts scurried to furl topsails when the Essex Junto roared the command.

The affiliations of maritime Massachusetts with British capital were equally significant. In 1783 the merchants renewed their ties with London merchant-bankers, like the firm of Lane, Son & Fraser, with whom they had traded before the war. With other firms, like the Baring Brothers (both of whom married daughters of a wealthy Philadelphia merchant), their relations became very close. Hamilton's United States Bank, and the several state banks organized at this period, by no means sufficed to float commercial operations.[1] It was from merchant-bankers of London

[1] The insurance of the Massachusetts merchant marine at this period was underwritten locally, however. Between 1799 and 1805 there were incorporated at least three marine insurance companies in Boston (in addition to seven private insurance offices), three each in Salem and Newburyport, two in Nantucket, and one each in Beverly, Marblehead, Gloucester, and New Bedford. Peter C. Brooks, one of the wealthiest of Boston merchants, made most of his fortune in marine insurance. I add some of the rates occasionally quoted in the Boston *Price-Current and Marine Intelligencer* showing the difference made by the French spoliations.

From Boston to	Sept.–Dec. 1796	Feb. 6, 1797
Any European port, except the following.....	2¼ @ 3	6 @ 7
Baltic and Mediterranean ports, warranted free from seizure.............................	3 @ 3½	5
Cape of Good Hope, Ile de France, &c.	5 @ 6	9 @ 10
Madeira, Canaries, C. Verde Is., &c.	2½ @ 3	5
Persia, India, with liberty to trade at any ports or places..................................	5 @ 6	10
China out and home........................	10 @ 12	20
Jamaica.....................................	2½ @ 3	17½
Other West-India Islands....................	2½ @ 3	9 @ 10
Nova Scotia and Newfoundland..............	2 @ 2½	5 @ 6
Quebec......................................	3½ @ 4	
New Orleans.................................	..3½ @ 4	10
St. Augustine and Bahamas.................	2	6
United States ports.........................	1½ @ 2	2½ @ 3

that the Boston shipowners obtained, on credit, their outward cargoes to the Northwest Coast. London, moreover, was the world's money-market. Exchange on Boston or New York was valueless outside the United States; but exchange on London was as good as gold throughout the western world. With proper banking connections in London, a Massachusetts shipmaster could buy bills with his cargo in a foreign port where no profitable return lading was available, and remit to his London banker; or instead of having to sell his outward cargo before reloading, he could leave it with a commission merchant, obtain a new venture by drawing against his London account, and be off without loss of time. Such relations were particularly useful when unexpected repairs or losses had to be met. They were equivalent to a Brown-Shipley or Baring Brothers letter of credit to-day, or to a checking account in making local purchases. Consequently her English connections were vital to maritime Massachusetts, and peace with Britain seemed worth almost any price.

Had Europe remained tranquil, had the Dutch Republic endured, and had French energy been guided into finance and industry, it is possible that Amsterdam or Paris would have replaced London as the financial center for American commerce. Many Massachusetts merchants deplored their too close dependence on English credit. The French Revolution served to draw the two countries together in trade as well as in thought, until its cataclysmic period began in 1792. From that time on the American trade with France and the French colonies became a colossal speculation, which appealed to the younger and more adventurous merchants, but appalled those who already had sound British connections. France, hemmed in by British

169

sea-power, threw open her colonial trade to neutrals. Famine, disorganization, and blockade raised the price of American provisions to unheard-of figures. Fortunes could be made in Paris by speculating in exchange, buying confiscated church or *émigré* estates, taking a share in French privateers, or bidding in their prizes. Such members of the younger generation as desired more refined adventure than the Northwest Coast afforded, hastened to France. The blithe spirit of these youngsters is well illustrated by a letter of twenty-one-year-old Ralph Bennet Forbes, who founded a great mercantile family of Boston:

Boston 1 *Nov.* 1794.

... I was hurried away in June ten days after my arrival in France (almost malgré moi) in order to close in the West Indies to the satisfaction of the two respectable houses who were concerned (James & Thomas H. Perkins & Stephen Higginson, Esq.) of these people I enjoy the confidence and I believe the esteem, this I hope is not lessened by having made a *great* voyage — this by the way — le temps passe, il faut tenir parole.

I have now in contemplation a voyage to France ... my plan is rather speculative and I may extend my personal excursion as far as l'Isle de France, this will depend on l'état actuel de la guerre, which I think will soon be finished. C'est le moment, mon cher, pour les jeunes gens de mon caractère de faire des mouvements rapides, de ramener quelques capitaux pour leur établissement après la paix. C'est alors qu'il faut des *Bases bien solides* pour être respecté dans le Commerce. . . . I find myself the loser by the Hispaniola Revolution of two hundred Joes (1600 Dollars); this affects me in beginning.

I must speak seriously of my intentions; after this voyage — it must be entirely between ourselves — I must be fixed in Boston for these reasons; my mother's property will constitute part of my capital, she will give it to me on no other terms. I have here a great many rich friends who though they might not launch out, would readily put their *marks* on the back of a note for an occasion, this is a good introduction to the Bank, of course, a key to the *False Capital* mode of Operation. I am determined to have a Southern Connection, on account of French business; they are not fond of cold

170

fingers. I am resolved never to connect myself, but with men stamped from infancy with Industry and determined like myself to devote every instant of time to business. My connections in Jamaica are *King's Contractors* — they will commission whomever established at the southward, with the purchase of flour and biscuit for that Island; this is an object I am determined never to see the West Indies again.

Many were the gay adventures enjoyed by young shipmasters like John Bailey of Marblehead, whose fresh, confident features are preserved for us in miniatures and portraits by French artists. One form of speculation was to purchase French prizes in American ports, and take them to Mauritius for sale. Such a one the captured English snow *George*, with a cargo of provisions invoiced at $25,000, was bid in at Boston in 1796 for $8000 by Crowell Hatch, one of the *Columbia's* owners, and placed under the command of his young kinsman John Boit, Jr., who had just returned from his remarkable voyage around the world. The *George* was foul, slow, and leaky. Near the Cape of Good Hope, Captain Boit got a spare topsail under her bows, which decreased the leak from 1500 to 400 strokes per hour; but as he neared Port Louis, Mauritius, the snow sailed more and more slowly, the leak gained, and the crew became weak from pumping. A signal of distress — the ensign in a wiff — brought out a naval detail from the French authorities, to relieve the men at the pumps, and saved her from foundering within sight of land. Captain Boit sold his cargo to the Government at a "ruinous advance," hove down his vessel, found the bottom worm-eaten and almost destitute of oakum, but cheerfully "painted the old Snow up as fine as a fiddle, & on the 20th of May del'd her up to Monsieur Hicks — a hard bargain on his side, I must confess! . . . God send I may

171

never sail in the like of her again!" He then laid out the proceeds in coffee and East-India goods, which he carried to Charleston, South Carolina, for another turnover, in a chartered ship.

It was easy enough to sell provisions in France at profiteer rates, but quite a different affair to collect payment. The adventures of Captain Elijah Cobb, of Brewster, illustrate the distinction. His brig *Jane* of Boston, on her way to Cadiz, was captured by a French frigate and sent into Brest, early in 1794. The prize court released her, and Cobb made a contract to sell his cargo of rice and flour for two hundred per cent profit, in bills of exchange on Hamburg. After waiting a month for the bills in vain, he sent the *Jane* home under the mate, and procuring a passport from Jean-bon St. André, went to Paris with an armed national courier, traveling day and night to escape brigands. At Paris the Terror was at its height. The authorities pretended never to have received the brig's papers, and deliberately mislaid the certified copies which the prudent master brought with him. There was nothing left but to interview Robespierre, who called him a *sacré coquin*, but gave the word that produced his papers and bills. Cobb left the capital just after the 9th Thermidor; but Joseph Russell, John Higginson, and Thomas H. Perkins, of Boston, witnessed the guillotining of Robespierre in the Place de la Concorde.

The death of his benefactor so reduced the market value of Captain Cobb's bills, that he went himself to Hamburg to collect. The French agent there had begun to protest payment, but by a good bluff Cobb had his accepted, and remitted the funds to T. Dickerson & Sons, London. On his next voyage to Havre, with flour, the same performance had to be repeated. Two visits to Paris, and five months' dancing attendance at the ministry of finance, were required to obtain full payment. Captain Cobb exchanged the silver ingots with which his debt was discharged, for three thousand Spanish doubloons, which he managed to smuggle out of France on his person despite the *chouans*, and a strict search at the frontier.

*
* *

American diplomatic history, in the period 1793–1815, is closely interlocked with that of commerce and of all maritime pursuits. Broadly speaking, one may say that in 1793 maritime Massachusetts was making up her mind on the American policy toward the European war. By 1795 she found her opinion to be flatly pro-British; in 1796 she imposed it on the rest of the state, and in 1797 on the rest of the nation.

British depredations on American commerce, in 1793–94, were irritating and costly. Other things being equal, maritime Massachusetts, a lusty young rival to the mistress of the seas, would have helped revolutionary France break British sea-power. But other things were not equal. American democracy, that nine-lived feline which the merchants had petted in 1775 — and repeatedly drowned since — now returned with a new lover, the battle-scarred French tomcat Jacobinism; and their amorous yowlings made sleep impossible for decent merchants in Franklin Place. They were disgusted and alarmed by Genet's impudence, and his American partisans' lawlessness. The successive upheavals in France showed that no substitute could there be found for the London money market; and in 1795 France engulfed Holland. Finally, the Reign of Terror and the *politique de l'an III* seemed to confirm Burke's warning, that the French Revolution was an international menace. Embattled France became an object of horror and loathing, as now Soviet Russia. To seat Jacobinism on Neptune's throne, because of British enmity to American shipping, would merely destroy all property. "Civilization" was the issue.

So reasoned New England Federalism; an alliance of merchant-shipowner, country squire and Congregational clergy, that carried everything before it in Massachusetts. The first test came with Jay's treaty. This pact of November, 1794, averted a war with England, and secured compensation for the British spoliations; but renounced neutral rights and commercial equality, in terms so humiliating "that some of our respectable men have . . . joined the Jacobins," wrote Cabot. Anti-British feeling flared to its highest point since the war. At a word from the French consul, a Boston mob sacked and burned to the water's edge a Bermudian privateer in the harbor. But the merchants soon saw the deeper issue of England, law, and order against France, Jacobinism, and terror. The eloquence of Harrison Gray Otis wooed the Boston democracy into agreement. Thereafter, Boston regularly delivered a Federalist majority in state and national elections. The clergy cowed their country congregations with tales of French atheism and atrocity. The treaty was ratified and carried into effect.[1] John Adams was

---

[1] "In consequence of the disposition shown in the House of Representatives of the Union not to grant the supplies for carrying the British treaty into effect, business has been very slack for these two weeks. All new appropriations are entirely suspended. The alarm is very general lest the dearest interests of our country — *peace and national honor* — should be sacrificed to party-spirit and Antifederalism." (J. & T. H. Perkins to one of their correspondents, April 30, 1796.) Although Jay's treaty, as ratified, did not permit American ves-

elected President, and Timothy Pickering, of Salem, became Secretary of State.

French spoliations in 1797 and Talleyrand's treatment of the American mission discredited Jefferson, made the Federalists dangerously popular, and enabled them in the name of patriotism to enforce conformity by sedition trials, social pressure, and other means now sadly familiar. There would, in fact, have been a war with France in 1799, had not President Adams defied Hamilton and the Essex Junto by suddenly adopting a pacific policy. Thereby began the feud between the Adams family and State Street.

Although war was not declared against France, a state of war existed on the sea, and was very popular in the Massachusetts seaports. By local initiative the sloop-of-war *Merrimack* and the frigate *Essex* were built at Newburyport and Salem. The frigate *Constitution* (Boston-built, but Philadelphia-designed) had been launched in view of an immense, enthusiastic crowd the previous year. A subscription loan of $136,-500 from the Boston merchants floated the frigate *Boston* in 1799. Acts of Congress, now completely under the control of Hamilton and the Essex Junto, permitted American merchantmen to strike back at their French tormentors, and to make prize of any French armed vessel.

A typical cruise for a half-fighter, half-trader, was that of the letter-of-marque ship *Mount Vernon* of Salem, 355 tons, 20 guns and 50 men. She belonged to 'King' Derby, and was commanded by his son, E. H. Derby, Jr. Leaving Salem on July 14, 1799,

sels to trade with British colonies, the regular quotations of insurance rates to Jamaica, Bahamas, Quebec, Nova Scotia, and Newfoundland, in Boston papers of 1796–97, proves that the trade was going on nevertheless.

with a complete outfit of light sails, including fore- and main-topgallant studdingsails, square spritsail on the jibboom, ringtail and steering-sail rigged below the spanker, she made Corvo in the remarkably short time of eight days, seven hours. After a running fight with a French frigate, a brush with a heavily armed lateener, and a regular battle with another off Algeciras, she made Gibraltar in seventeen days, twelve hours, from Salem. Her last assailant struck ensign and pennant. Captain Derby did not stop to take him, but put into Gibraltar with the satisfaction of having "flogged the vessel in full view of the English fleet."

At Gibraltar colonial produce such as sugar, with which the *Mount Vernon* was laden, was a drug in the market. Captain Derby therefore joined John Williams, of Baltimore,[1] in chartering and loading a brig; and on August 10 the two vessels left for the Levant. Touching at Palermo, but finding the market poor, they continued to Naples, where Captain Derby sold the *Mount Vernon's* cargo, valued at $43,275, for $120,000. "My sales have been handsome, though not so great as I could have wished," he wrote his father.

Exchange on London being disadvantageous, Captain Derby made an investment of his gains, typical of this troubled period. Fifty thousand dollars were laid aside for wines and silks; but it was some time before they could be delivered. Yet even the hospitality of Nelson, and the smiles of Lady Hamilton, could not tempt Captain Derby to tarry in Naples. He purchased two new polacca-rigged ships for sixteen thou-

[1] Probably of the Roxbury Williamses, who settled in Baltimore at this period. Amos Williams, of Baltimore, was part owner with the Peabodys of the schooner *Equality* of Salem.

sand dollars, and convoyed them in the *Mount Vernon* up the Adriatic (beating off two Turkish pirates *en route*), to Manfredonia. There he loaded wheat, which was carried around Italy and sold at Leghorn. The profits on this venture paid for the two polaccas with thirty thousand dollars to boot, only two and a half months after their purchase. In less than eleven months' time Captain Derby had made a net profit of over a hundred thousand dollars on an investment of forty-three thousand.

The European war did not create, it merely expanded, this Massachusetts-Mediterranean traffic, which dates back to Captain John Smith. The reëxport thither of Oriental goods began about 1790, when the glut of tea at Salem and Boston forced their merchants to seek new outlets. But this coasting trade of the *Mount Vernon* was new, and typical of war conditions. Schooners of seventy tons or under — like the *Raven* of Marblehead and the *Lidia* of Newburyport — crossed the Atlantic with a cargo of salt fish, sugar, and rum, bought goods cheap in one European port, sold them dear in another, and if they were so lucky as to avoid capture, cleared several times their cost in one voyage. Frequently they were sold abroad to avoid capture, and sometimes their officers and men stayed with them. The brig *Salem* of Boston, for instance, after a voyage to Amsterdam, Cadiz, and San Sebastian, was sold to French parties at Bordeaux. Captain Jeremiah Mayo, using her American papers, then took a cargo of claret to Morlaix, where it brought three or four times its cost in the Gironde.

Wheresoever in Europe a Massachusetts vessel was disposed of, it was easy for the officers and crew to pick up a passage home, as the following letter of a Beverly shipmaster relates:

177

Li[s]bon. May ye 18, 1793

Kind & Loving Wife

I now take this operty. to inform you of my well fair & good state
of health. Blessed be God for the same; hoping this will find you
& fammele in as good health as it Leaves me at preasent; after I sold
the schooner hope at Bilboa I wated for to get a passage to America but cold not get a passage in a vessel that was coming Directly
hoom; therefore I took passag with Capt. Joshua Orne to Lisbone
and from thence I expected to go with him to Marblehead; but finding a snow near bound for Boston which wanted a mate and so I
shipped with her, and shall sale tomorrow if nothing disapoints us,
I have sent you By Cap. Joshua Orne: 7 dozn & 10 silk handchafs 2
Long Looking glasses a dozn of knives & forks one half of which is for
your brother Beckford and a Little Gun and I Expect to send sum
other things which I shall put on bord this Night and you Go for
them or send sum boddey with an order. you may expect me in a few
days after you receive this if nothing happens to us . . .

from your ever loving husband till Death

JONATHAN BASEY

During the first half of the Revolutionary-Na-
poleonic wars, and until 1806, the yoke of Britain's
sea-power was an easy one. No interference was
made with broken voyages or with neutrals trading
between the Baltic, the Hanse towns, and France.
"I find several vessels have been advantageously employed in plying between Hamburg, Rotterdam, and
France, and that neutral vessels have been permitted
a free trade even from England," writes James Perkins to his brother at Bordeaux, in February, 1795.
He is sending out the ship *Betsy*, with a cargo of rice,
which is to serve as capital for continuing the carrying
trade between northern and French ports. American
entries at Hamburg increased from 35 in 1791 to 192
in 1799; and after Hamburg was closed to American
shipping in 1804, vessels entered at Tönning in Schles-
wig-Holstein, or at Lübeck. At Amsterdam there were
160 American entries in 1801.

This North-European trade was not without its cultural contacts. "This day my box from Hamburg arrived with the proceeds of my Coffee," writes Dr. Bentley in his Salem diary for 1806. "The good Professor has furnished me with great economy with some of the best Books which his country has yielded." Thus German erudition entered New England. Dr. Bentley was one of the American correspondents of Professor Ebeling, of Hamburg, buying for his learned friend numerous imprints of the smaller New England presses, which have disappeared in the country of their production. The books and coffee which the good Doctor cast upon the waters were indeed found after many days, and by his alma mater; for Professor Ebeling's incomparable collection of Americana was purchased by Israel Thorndike, merchant of Beverly, and presented to the Harvard College Library.

If Massachusetts had the same share of the Hamburg trade as of Baltic commerce, more than half the American entries were owned in her ports. For in 1802, out of eighty-one vessels that passed Elsinore during the open season, twenty-one belonged to Salem, fourteen to Boston, eight to Newburyport, eight to New York, seven to Providence, five to Marblehead, four to Gloucester, two to Charleston, and one each to Philadelphia, Norfolk, New Bedford, and Salisbury.[1] Many arrived not from their home port, but from Lisbon, Cadiz, the Western Islands, the West Indies, Amsterdam, and Bremen; bringing nankeens, pepper, sugar, fruit, coffee, tea, rum, wine, cotton, indigo, tobacco, and mahogany to Copenhagen and St. Petersburg. They cleared, laden with iron, hemp, flax, cordage and sailcloth, for all parts of the world. Several were schooners and brigantines under eighty tons

[1] From a "Sound list" brought home by one of the shipmasters.

burthen. This type of commerce is generally called the neutral carrying trade; but it was more than a carrying trade as the term is now understood, for the vessels did not merely take freight at inflated figures; they bought and sold goods on their owners' account, and made immense sums, which no statistics record, by the repeated turnovers.

The European trade was also vitally interlocked with the East-India and China trade, that was so rapidly expanding in the closing years of the eighteenth century. Unless an East-Indiaman made Madeira her first port of call, she generally acquired specie in Europe, or a cargo suitable for Bengal, by selling the proceeds of a former voyage, together with West-India goods, salt provisions, fish, and Southern staples, at any northern or Mediterranean port. "The speedy conversion of your present lading into dollars must be a governing object in your operation," state the instructions of J. & T. H. Perkins to one of their supercargoes, outward-bound with East- and West-India goods to the Mediterranean and Calcutta.

Hardly a port of Europe there was, from Archangel to Trieste where the Yankee trader was not as familiar as the seasons; hardly an occasion where he was not present, with something to swap. As Nelson's fleet lay licking its wounds after Trafalgar, who should heave in sight but the ship *Ann Alexander* of New Bedford, Captain Loum Snow, with a cargo of lumber, flour, and apples — just what the fleet needed! Supercargoes founded mercantile houses in foreign ports. Thomas Hickling, of Boston, settled in the Azores shortly after 1780. Preble & Co. (Ebenezer and Henry, brothers of the Commodore) were soliciting consignments at Dieppe, in 1804. George Loring, of Hingham, married a beautiful Spanish girl in the seventeen-nineties; his sons formed the firm of Loring Brothers of Malaga, which fifty years later was operating Massachusetts-built clipper ships under the Spanish flag.

*

* *

The seamen of colonial and post-Revolutionary Massachusetts thought they knew the ropes of European trade, but the war led their sons to new ports. Smyrna, the mart of Asia Minor, became the final residence of a loyalist member of the Perkins family, with whom J. & T. H. Perkins opened profitable relations before the end of the eighteenth century, obtaining Turkish opium for Canton. A convincing contrast of Yankee enterprise with Eastern lethargy, is the trade followed by Ebenezer Parsons for several years; loading coffee at Mocha in the Red Sea, and circumnavigating Africa to sell it at Smyrna, for three and four hundred per cent profit.

The west coast of South America had already made the acquaintance of Yankee whalers and fur-traders, when the Napoleonic wars opened the east coast as well to Massachusetts vessels. The first North American merchantman to enter the River Plate appears to have been the brig *Alert* of Salem, owned by Dudley L. Pickman and others, and commanded by Captain Robert Gray, of *Columbia* fame. She was captured by a French privateer and carried into Montevideo late in 1798. The Spanish officials fitted her out as a privateer under their own colors, but Captain Gray was released, and returned voluntarily in 1801 in command of the schooner *James*, after touching at Rio de Janeiro. Between February and July, 1802, eighteen Massachusetts vessels, and twenty-six from other North

American ports, brought mixed cargoes to the River Plate, and took away hides and specie; portending the great hides and lumber traffic of later years between New England, Argentina, and Uruguay. In 1810, William Gray was reëxporting "Buenos Ayres Hydes" and Peruvian bark from Boston to Tunis.

Several Massachusetts men entered the service of the new republics. Dr. Franklin Rawson, of Essex County, founded a distinguished Argentinian family. The name of Benjamin Franklin Seaver, of Boston, killed in battle while second in command of the Argentine fleet, is commemorated in a street of Buenos Aires; and William P. White, of Pittsfield, who established a mercantile agency there as early as 1804, gave such effective aid to the cause as to be called the "father of the Argentine Navy." A little later, Paul Delano, one of the twenty-one children of Nathan Delano, of Fairhaven, commanded the Chilean frigate *Independencia*, and applied his Yankee ingenuity to the construction of port works in open roadsteads. William Delano, of the same maritime family, served on the staff of General San Martin. Both remained in Chile, where their descendants are prominent citizens to-day.

Japan first saw the American flag in 1791, when the famous Boston sloop *Lady Washington*, Captain Kendrick, accompanied by the *Grace* of New York, Captain Douglas, entered a southern Japanese harbor in the hope of selling sea-otter. But the natives knew not the use of fur, and no business was done. It was the foreign policy of the French Committee of Public Safety that gained American commerce its first exchange with the forbidden kingdom. For almost two centuries the Dutch East India Company had enjoyed the exclusive right of sending one ship a year from Batavia to trade at Nagasaki, when, in 1795, French arms and propaganda transformed the Netherlands into the Batavian Republic, an ally and vassal to France. Fearing capture of its vessels by British warships, the Dutch East India Company for four successive years chartered American vessels for the annual cruise. The first, apparently, to have this honor was the ship *Eliza* of New York, of which there is a contemporary Japanese painting, showing her being lightered off a rock in Nagasaki Harbor, in 1798, by several dozen small boats. In 1799 the Perkins's ship *Franklin* of Boston, James Devereux master, was the lucky vessel; and of her voyage from Batavia to Japan and back we have a full account, from Captain Devereux's clerk, George Cleveland. On entering Japanese waters she hoisted the Dutch ensign, fired prescribed salutes of seven to thirteen guns each on passing seven different points, and another on anchoring in Nagasaki Harbor. The Yankee officers had to bend almost double when Japanese officials came on board, and to comply with minute and rigorous harbor regulations during their four months' stay. But they were allowed, carefully guarded, to visit the town, and to bring back private adventures of cabinets, tea-trays, and carved screens which are still treasured in Salem homes. In 1800 the ship *Massachusetts* of Boston received the annual charter for the colossal sum of $100,000, it was rumored; and in 1801 the ship *Margaret* of Salem pulled off the prize. She was apparently the last American vessel to be received in a Japanese harbor until Commodore Perry broke the isolation of Nippon.

*

*　　*

In 1801, with the election of Jefferson to the presidency, the national government fell into the hands of a combination partial to France, and professedly unfriendly to maritime commerce. But Jefferson's moderation agreeably disappointed maritime Massachusetts. The Hamiltonian system of fishing bounties, drawbacks, discriminating tonnage duties, and friendship with England continued unimpaired. Barbary corsairs were forced to respect the American flag. Jefferson chose his Attorney-General and his Secretary of War in Massachusetts, and but for the illness of Jacob Crowninshield, whose family had been consistently Republican, he would have had a Secretary of the Navy from the same state.

Early in 1802 Napoleon made peace with England, and the European trade slackened somewhat; but, of course, Massachusetts could not blame this on Jefferson. And in 1804, despite the raving of Federalist politicians, the commonwealth cast its electoral vote for the great Virginian. No doubt the maritime interests would have become reconciled to his administration had not a renewal of the war revived the passions and the difficulties of the previous decade.

England and Napoleon, by a series of Orders in Council and Imperial Decrees, began attempting to drive neutral shipping from each other's ports. As British sea-power tightened, and Napoleon extended his control over continental Europe, it became no longer easy for American shipping to play both sides. Hitherto, the British prohibition of neutral trading between her enemies and their colonies had been evaded by the "broken voyage" — bringing French colonial produce to Boston or Salem, paying duty, reloading it even on the same vessel, receiving the drawback, and proceeding to France. But in 1805 Sir William Scott made an example of the ship *Essex* of Salem,[1]

[1] The same vessel which met a tragic fate in the Red Sea, in 1806.

in a decision which remains a landmark in international law, so-called. Her voyage from Barcelona to Havana *via* Derby Wharf was declared one continuous voyage, and the cargo confiscated.

The merchants of Boston and Salem loudly protested. But before long they discovered that the bark of the *Essex* decision was worse than its bite. An old drawback book in the Plymouth custom-house records shows what indirect trade was going on in 1806 and 1807. The brig *Eliza Hardy* of Plymouth enters her home port from Bordeaux, on May 20, 1806, with a cargo of claret wine. Part of it is immediately reëxported to Martinique in the schooner *Pilgrim*, which also carries a consignment of brandy that came from Alicante in the brig *Commerce*, and another of gin that came from Rotterdam in the barque *Hannah* of Plymouth. The rest of the *Eliza Hardy's* claret is taken to Philadelphia by coasters, and thence reëxported in seven different vessels to Havana, Santiago de Cuba, St. Thomas, and Batavia. The brig *Rufus King*, about the same time, brought into Plymouth a cargo of coffee from St. Thomas. It is transferred to Boston, and thence reëxported to Rotterdam and Amsterdam in four different vessels. The barque *Hannah* also brought wine and brandy from Tarragona, which is reëxported from Boston to Havana and Madeira. The schooner *Honest Tom* left Plymouth for Bordeaux on December 21, 1806, with sugar and coffee that another vessel had brought from the West Indies. She returned to Plymouth on May 18, 1807, with wine and brandy which flowed from Boston to Demerara in the ship *Jason*, to the East Indies in the ship *Jenny*, and to San Domingo in the brig *Eunice*. Thus interposing a coastal voyage between the two ends of an essentially unneutral traffic evidently confused or satisfied the British admiralty.

President Jefferson stood up for neutral rights, and his representatives at London did their best to have the *Essex* decision rescinded. But before anything could be done, new and more stringent orders and decrees were issued by England and Napoleon; and in 1807 the country was stirred by an impressment outrage on the U.S.S. *Chesapeake.* Had Jefferson then called for a declaration of war, Massachusetts would have accepted war with good grace. Instead, he chose a policy which, without coercing the belligerent nations, sacrificed the commercial profits of Massachusetts and her political good-will. December 22, 1807, the date that Jefferson's embargo went into effect, begins a new period in American maritime history.

CHAPTER XIII

EMBARGO AND WAR

1807–1815

Our ships all in motion once whitened the ocean,
They sailed and returned with a cargo;
Now doomed to decay, they have fallen a prey
To Jefferson — worms — and embargo.

THUS jingled a newspaper poet at Newburyport in 1808. It was bad enough trying to feel out a channel between orders in council and imperial decrees: but to have one's fleet scuttled by act of Congress, on the pretense of protecting it, seemed outrageous and hypocritical.

The Embargo Act, which remained in force from December 22, 1807, to March 15, 1809, forbade any American vessel to clear from an American harbor for a foreign port, and placed coasting and fishing vessels under heavy bonds not to land their cargoes outside the United States. Another act, which went into effect at the same time, forbade the importation of many British goods. Nothing prevented American vessels then abroad from entering a home port, but once there, they could not legally depart for a foreign voyage.

There were many leaks in the embargo. For a time, by special dispensation of the President, merchants were allowed to send abroad for property they had already purchased. An immense smuggling trade went on over the Canadian and Florida borders. Vessels already abroad did not return until the embargo was repealed, if they could help it. The coast was more heavily guarded by federal officials and soldiers than

187

during the War of 1812, but nevertheless a number of vessels managed to slip out. Captain Charles C. Doten, of Plymouth, performed two notable feats of this sort. One dark night, in a southeast rainstorm that drove the water-front guards to cover, he re-rigged the schooner *Hannah*, which had been 'stripped to a girtline' by the collector of the port, with the sails and rigging of another vessel, and piloted her safely out of Plymouth Bay. Later he took the brig *Hope* out of Provincetown in a northeast gale, hotly pursued and fired upon by the revenue cutter; sold vessel and cargo of fish at St. Lucia for twenty-five thousand dollars, and brought it home in the form of Spanish doubloons, sewed into his clothing. The embargo did not kill Massachusetts commerce, then; but suspended at least half of it, and rendered the rest more furtive, difficult, and hazardous than it ever would have been under mere orders in council and imperial decrees.

At the time the embargo was laid, Massachusetts[1] was the principal shipowning commonwealth in America. Her total tonnage per capita was more than twice that of any other state. Her registered tonnage in foreign trade in 1807, 310,310 tons, was thirty-seven per cent of the total for the United States, and more than twice that of her nearest competitor, New York. In coasting trade she was also first, although her proportion was slightly less. Her fishing fleet, 62,214 tons, was eighty-eight per cent of the total; and although there was nothing in the embargo acts to prevent fishing, loss of the foreign market put the

[1] See statistics in Appendix. The figures here quoted for the state include Maine; those quoted for ports include minor ports in the custom district of that name. Whaling vessels are apparently included in the foreign tonnage.

greater part of the fleet out of commission. The same applied to the whaling. In all these branches of shipping the gains during the profitable years of neutral trade had been tremendous. Boston had passed Philadelphia, and become second only to New York for amount of tonnage owned. Following Baltimore and Charleston; Portland, Salem, and Newburyport were respectively the sixth, seventh, and ninth shipowning communities in the United States. The minor ports of Massachusetts, tempted by the rich freights and turnovers of neutral commerce, had increased their fleet considerably in the last few years.[1] Adopting Adam Seybert's estimate, that the American merchant marine in 1801 was earning at least fifty dollars per ton annually, the Massachusetts fleet of 1807 was bringing home about fifteen and a half million dollars a year in freight money alone, an amount far greater than the capital value of the fleet that earned it. Congress ordered the shipowners to forego this colossal income — equal to the entire federal revenue in 1806 — as well as the greater gains made by buying cheap and selling dear, in order to save their vessels from capture. Could the gain balance the loss?

This was a burning question in 1808, and continues to divide historians to this day. There were many in Massachusetts who agreed with Jefferson, but more who did not. John Bromfield, supercargo by profession and a Federalist in politics, wrote from London in

[1] Plymouth tonnage, for instance, had just doubled since 1800. In 1804 Plymouth had eleven entries from Portugal, one from Spain, one from Cape Verde Islands, two from Russia, ten from Martinique, and ten from smaller West Indian Islands — all schooners. In 1805 she exported almost half a million pounds of sugar to Holland. New Bedford had increased fifty per cent, to over 25,000 tons. Of her ninety to one hundred square-rigged vessels, only twelve were whalers. See chapters x and xi for the neutral trade of Marblehead and Newburyport.

189

1808, "It was certainly a very well-timed restriction upon our commerce, and has undoubtedly saved his political opponents from the loss of property to an immense amount." The Republican Crowninshields defended the embargo, and William Gray, a Federalist, and the largest individual shipowner in the United States, rallied to it as a necessary measure of self-protection. His Federalist neighbors retorted by accusing him of profiteering from his stock on hand. This charge he denied: and any statement from a man with the simple honesty and independence of William Gray carries weight. He sacrificed personal comfort and social position by his stand. Yet even Mr. Gray did not see fit to order home one of his vessels, the ship *Wells*, which left Salem eighteen days before the embargo was laid, and remained abroad making money for her owner while it endured. Marblehead remained faithful to embargo and Republicanism, despite her growing commerce. As Salem was Federalist, Marblehead was naturally the contrary;[1] but it seems that Marblehead was somewhat favored during the embargo. The local collector continued to issue San Domingo bonds, an indication that he was allowing vessels to clear for the West Indies.[2]

In general, the verdict of maritime Massachusetts was thumbs down on Jefferson and his "terrapin"

[1] Frequently, throughout the Federalist period, small seaports that were rivals to a near-by prosperous and Federalist center of commerce, voted Republican; Dorchester, Weymouth, Fairhaven, and Dighton, for example.

[2] Custom-house records, searched for me by Miss E. R. Trefry. The act of Feb. 28, 1806, required vessels clearing for certain parts of the West Indies to be bonded against trading with the Haytian rebels against Napoleon. But Marblehead had only twelve foreign entries during the embargo period, paying $35,000 duties, as compared with seventy for the year 1807, paying $156,000. The figures given in Dwight's *Travels in New England* are incorrect.

policy. The new British orders required some adjustment of trade routes, but as George Cabot said, profits were such that if only one out of three vessels escaped capture, her owner could make a handsome profit on the lot. It was still possible to ply neutral trade under British convoy, inspection, and license; a system degrading perhaps to national honor, but very similar to that which all neutrals, including the United States, permitted during the World War. Insurance rates were not prohibitive; and after the removal of the embargo Massachusetts shipping arose to a new high level despite the orders in council. As a pure business proposition, then, Jefferson's plea of protection made little appeal.

The embargo caused greatest hardship in the smaller ports, and among small shipowners and working people dependent on shipping. Newburyport, Salem, and Plymouth never recovered their former prosperity. Jefferson hastened the inevitable absorption of their commerce by Boston. Shipbuilding, with all its subsidiary industries, ceased altogether. Mechanics and master mariners had to resort to the soup kitchens established in the seaport towns, or exhaust their savings, or emigrate to Canada in search of work. The only consolation that Dr. Bentley, the stanch Republican pastor of Salem, could find in the embargo, was the stimulus it gave to pleasure-boating in Salem Bay! But few were so fortunately circumstanced as to seek solace from business depression in yachting life.

In 1807, the Federalist Party was *in extremis*. It had lost even the state government of Massachusetts. The embargo rescued it from the shadow of death, thrust into its palsied hands the banner of state rights, and sent it forth to rally the seafaring tribe. Politicians like Timothy Pickering hoped the embargo would re-

main in force until the "people recovered their true
sight" — and President Jefferson proved most accom-
modating. It was not difficult to persuade people of
the hypocrisy of his plea of protection, and to prove
that his real wish was to coerce England. With such an
object the Federalists had no sympathy. Their con-
viction that France was the center of disturbance and
unrest had deepened, although Napoleon did his best
to prove the contrary. Yet the Federalists were right
in believing that the restoration of peace and the hope
of liberty in Europe depended on the overthrow of
Napoleon; that any attempt to clip the British Sam-
son's hair was at that time internationally immoral,
and without sharp scissors, imprudent.

Not content with these arguments, the Federalists
asserted, with some plausibility, that Jefferson's ultimate object was to destroy New England's wealth and
power. How else could one explain, for instance, his
ban on East-India and China commerce? The orders
in council permitted our Oriental trade; Napoleonic
decrees were powerless in far eastern waters. Keeping
Salem's East-Indiamen in port merely helped English
shipowners. So abject a failure was the embargo as a
measure of coercion that Jefferson's persistent faith
in it could be explained only by enmity to American
shipping, or by pathological causes.

Fourteen months of embargo enabled the merchants
to recover their political supremacy, and to organize
a campaign of town-meeting resolutions that had the
ring of 1776. Deserted by his northern partisans in
Congress, Jefferson finally consented to sign the repeal
of the embargo on his last day in office — March 3,
1809. Prosperity promptly returned. But the embargo did a moral damage that determined New England's alignment in the coming war. It enabled the

EMBARGO AND WAR

Essex Junto, the most bigoted group of Federalist politicians, to endoctrine maritime New England with a blind hatred for the Republican Party; to regard the administration as a greater enemy than any foreign country. It bred a spirit of narrow self-complacency, a belief in the superior virtue, enterprise, and worth of Yankees as against New Yorkers, Pennsylvanians, and Southerners, that all but flared up into secession before the cause was removed.

After the embargo was lifted, a non-intercourse act with Great Britain remained in force three months; but this did not prevent the prompt reopening of Oriental, West-Indian, Baltic, South American, and Mediterranean commerce. Fortunes were made by supplying the British army in the Peninsular War. Shipyards awoke. Fayal in the Azores, where John B. Dabney, of Boston, was American consul and leading merchant, became a new St. Eustatius, a go-between for nations forbidden to trade with one another. Russia became almost our best customer, as Napoleon closed the ports of western Europe to our vessels. Almost two hundred United States vessels were now trading with Russia, over half of them, probably, belonging in Massachusetts.[1] Yankee shipmasters quickly adapted themselves to the new conditions. Wintering at Riga in 1810–11, they took part in the open-handed social life of the Balt nobility; skating carnivals, sleigh rides at breakneck speed over the flat country, *montagnes russes*, brilliant balls and Gargantuan dinners. To avoid the Danish privateers which were preying on American vessels, many made the long voyage around Norway to Archangel, whence their imports went a thousand miles overland to Moscow. But the ship-

[1] In 1803, fifty-four out of the ninety American arrivals in St. Petersburg belonged in Massachusetts. See also chapters XI and XII.

193

masters found Archangel rather exhausting, as the Russian merchants, after hibernating, expected their American customers to stay up and drink with them through the bright summer nights. The Boston ship *Calumet* penetrated the Black Sea to Odessa in 1810; shortly followed by the ship *America* of Salem, commanded by Captain Ropes. Profits in this Russian trade were immense. The ship *Catherine* of Boston, 281 tons, worth possibly $7000, cleared $115,000 net in one voyage of 1809.

President Madison's policy, at first favorable to commerce, won away from the Federalists a part of their previous gains. In 1810 William Gray was elected lieutenant-governor of Massachusetts. His friend John Quincy Adams, who likewise had been expelled from the Federal Party for supporting the embargo, was appointed minister to Russia, went out in one of the Gray ships, and proved a useful friend at court. William Gray was the principal Russian trader in the United States. He distributed Russian duck, sheetings, cordage, and iron (which sold for $115 a ton in Boston), to Philadelphia, Charleston, and New Orleans, there loading tobacco, sugar, and "cotton wool" for the Baltic market. Other vessels of his fleet took lumber and coffee to Algiers, and proceeded to Gallipolis to load olive oil for Russia. In addition, he was conducting a Mediterranean-Calcutta trade.

Napoleon considered the American Baltic fleet essentially British; and according to the British doctrine of neutral rights he was not far wrong. Certain vessels did a ferrying trade between Copenhagen and London; and all had to conform to British regulations, and accept naval convoy through the Belts. Even William Gray, who was continually protesting his innocence of British connections, used London bankers almost exclusively, and on one occasion chartered a British vessel. Napoleon, to complete his continental blockade, required the occlusion of neutral shipping from Russia, whose emperor was his nominal ally; and from Sweden, whose ruler was his former marshal. In the summer of 1810 he made the demand. Alexander and Bernadotte equivocated, and then refused. They had no intention of shutting off their subjects' supplies of West- and East-India goods. Then began Napoleon's preparations to invade Russia. Thus the Baltic trade of Massachusetts played an important if unconscious part in the chain of events that led Napoleon to Moscow and to St. Helena.

*

*   *

Within a week of the Grand Army's entrance into Russia, the United States declared war on Great Britain. To this War of 1812 maritime Massachusetts was flatly opposed. Her pocket and her heart were equally affected. She deemed the war immoral, because waged against the "world's last hope"; unjust, because Napoleon had done her commerce greater injury than had England; and hypocritical, because declared in the name of "free trade and sailors' rights" by a sectional combination that had neither commerce nor shipping. In Congress, a majority of the representatives from New England voted against the declaration of war, which was carried by a new group of representatives from the South and West, who were burning for a fight and anxious to conquer Canada.

Reviewing the diplomatic ineptitude of Madison's administration, the opposition of Massachusetts is not surprising. Napoleon's pretended revocation of his decrees had been exposed by Adams at St. Petersburg

195

as "a trap to catch us into a war with England." Every shipmaster knew that the French confiscations and sequestrations had continued. Secretary Monroe admitted as much in 1812, after war had been declared. By his own figures, the Napoleonic system had done more damage to American commerce than had British navalism. Yet the administration, on the ground that the "national faith was pledged to France," [1] adopted successively non-intercourse, embargo, and war against Great Britain. When the administration heard that England had repealed her orders in council, two days after our declaration of war, it decided to continue the war on the ground of impressment alone.

It was difficult to discover the true extent of impressment in 1812, and impossible now. Certain it is, however, that those seaboard communities of New England, which furnished the bulk of her merchant seamen, showed repeatedly by vote and deed their opposition to a war waged ostensibly in their behalf. Monroe's report of 1812, giving over six thousand cases of American seamen impressed into the English navy, was shot full of holes by a committee of the General Court of Massachusetts. Fifty-one of the leading shipowners of Massachusetts, who had employed annually over fifteen hundred seamen for the last twelve years, could remember but twelve cases of Americans being impressed from their vessels. Nor were all these witnesses Federalists. William Gray gave witness against his party, when he was able to recall but two cases of impressment from his great fleet of the last decade.

The truth probably lies somewhere between these

---

[1] By the Macon Act of 1810, which proposed that whenever either England or France should repeal their objectionable measures against the United States, non-intercourse should be adopted against the other.

extremes. A large number of impressed Massachusetts seamen spent the period of hostilities in Dartmoor Prison, rather than fight against their country. Contemporary newspapers, sailors' narratives and depositions, contain numerous and outrageous cases; none worse, however, than an instance of which Adams informed the Secretary of State, when twenty-two American seamen were seized by Napoleon's agents at Danzig, marched to Antwerp, and impressed into the French navy. Impressment gave sufficient cause for war, by modern standards. But war was no remedy, as the Peace of Ghent proved. A powerful navy was the only language England understood.

"Sir, if we are going to war with Great Britain," said Senator Lloyd, of Massachusetts, "let it be a real, effectual, vigorous war. Give us a naval force ... give us thirty swift-sailing, well appointed frigates ... and in a few weeks, perhaps days, I would engage completely to officer your whole fleet from New England alone." Yet the war congress adjourned without providing any increase of the weakened navy; without even proper appropriation for the vessels in commission. The navy department could not even afford to send the frigate *Constitution* to sea, after her escape from the British fleet; and had not William Gray dug into his own pocket for her supplies, she would not have met and defeated the *Guerrière*. Yet on the eve of war, Madison and Monroe squandered fifty thousand dollars of the nation's money on a worthless Irish adventurer, in the hope he would furnish proof of New England Federalist disloyalty. Is it surprising that the Federalist leaders cried out at this war for "free trade and sailors' rights," declared by "men who rarely ever saw a ship or sailor"; and that maritime Massachusetts followed Chief Justice Marshall rather than President Madison?

"The declaration of war has appeared to me," wrote John Marshall, "to be one of those portentous acts which ought to concentrate on itself the efforts of all those who can take an active part in rescuing their country from the ruin it threatens." Massachusetts agreed. "Organize a *peace party* throughout your Country," resolved her House of Representatives, *after* the declaration; and " let the sound of your disapprobation of this war be loud and deep, . . . let there be no volunteers except for defensive war." The Barnstable County peace convention, uniting many shipmasters sent by Cape Cod town meetings, declared the war to have "originated in hatred to *New England* and to commerce; in subservience to the mandate of the Tyrant of *France*." To sabotage the war, in the interest of an early peace, became the declared policy of maritime Massachusetts.

The community could not wholly refrain from enthusiasm at naval victories, especially when Boston's favorite frigate, the *Constitution*, was the victor. Hull and Bainbridge were banqueted by Boston merchants, and Perry presented with a service of plate. The Federalists even attempted to capitalize naval success, as the appended Boston ballot for the spring election of 1814 indicates.[1] But the State Senate, on motion of Josiah Quincy, refused a vote of thanks to Captain Lawrence for his capture of the *Peacock*, on the ground that "in a war like the present" it was "not becoming a moral and religious people to express any approbation of military and naval exploits." When Lawrence's body, after his glorious death aboard the *Chesapeake*, was brought back to Salem for burial, the North

---

[1] Ballots in these days were prepared by each party, and distributed at the polls. By law, they had to be written, not printed. A 'shaving-mill' meant a Jeffersonian gunboat.

Meeting-House was refused for the funeral ceremony, and its bell hung silent when the procession passed. The East-India Marine Society only by a vote of 32 to 19 decided to attend. A local militia company refused to do escort duty, and not a single representative of the state government attended in his official capacity.

Political sentiment being such, it is not surprising that Massachusetts did not show her former preëminence in privateering. As against fifty-eight privateers from Baltimore and fifty-five from New York, Boston only fitted out thirty-one, Salem forty-one,[1] and the smaller ports, probably not more than fifteen altogether. "Federalist ideas were so prominent" in Newburyport "that the fitting of privateers was opposed strongly," stated a contemporary. New Bedford, not only Federalist but Quaker, declared in town meeting on July 21, 1814, "we have scrupulously abstained from all interest and concern in sending out private armed vessels"; and resolved to quarantine for forty days any American privateer that polluted her harbor. The efforts of Salem's Republican minority, despite Federalists like Captain Ichabod Nichols, who read Marshall's "Life of Washington" through annually, explain her activity. Privateering was much the most popular form of service in maritime Massachusetts; it paid better wages, was safer, and more fun than the army or navy. Marblehead, which supported the war, provided 726 privateersmen, 120 naval seamen, and only 57 soldiers, not including the local militia.

[1] Rear-Admiral Emmons in 1853 estimated that 526 privateers were fitted out from the United States during the war; but this doubtless includes letter-of-marque vessels which were primarily traders, not commerce destroyers. Five of Salem's privateers were small open boats armed only with muskets, and only twelve were over one hundred tons burthen.

The first privateer to fit out from Salem was the new Gloucester-built Chebacco boat *Fame*, thirty tons, owned jointly by her master William Webb, and crew of twenty-four ex-shipmasters.[1] She put to sea on July 1, 1812, and returned eight days later with two prizes, a three-hundred-ton ship and a two-hundred-ton brig, taken off Grand Manan without firing a shot. George Crowninshield, Jr., decked over his thirty-six-foot yacht *Jefferson*, armed her with a gun or two, and sent her out with thirty men. "When I saw you landing, I could think of nothing else than so many goslins in a bread tray," said a Maine woman to the *Jefferson's* crew; but they sent in the second lot of prizes to Salem. There were rich pickings to be had on the Western Ocean that summer, before John Bull was fairly aroused. By the end of the year eighteen Salem privateers had captured eighty-seven prizes, of which fifty-eight, worth with their cargoes half a million dollars, were safely sent in. The local Federalist paper remarked that Salem property to the value of nine hundred thousand dollars had in the meantime been taken by the enemy. Perhaps the name of a new Salem privateer, the *Grumbler and Growler*, was a compliment to this unpatriotic sheet!

Most Salem privateering was done near the American coasts. But French ports offered a convenient base and refuge, as in the Revolution; especially in the latter year of the war, when the United States was blockaded. The schooner *Brutus* slipped out of Salem early in November. 1814. According to the log kept by her Nantucket sailing-master, Henry Ingraham Defrees, she took six prizes in six weeks' time; and near the coast of France, after a long stern chase, came up

---

[1] Maclay (*American Privateers*, 239) is in error in identifying this vessel with a Revolutionary privateer of the same name.

with the armed British ship *Albion*. At 3 P.M. "Bore down on the enemys Larboard quarter within pistol shot & gave him 2 broadsides, wore across his sterne & from thence under his Starboard quarter, gave her several broadsides, & musketry. At 3:30 she struck." Three days later, the captor put in at Quimper, Britanny, where one of her crew "was put in Irons for strikeing the 1st Seargent of Marines, he then insulted all the officers & to Prevent further insolence he was gagged for two hours with a pump bolt."

The most artistic ship picture in the Peabody Museum is Antoine Roux's portrait of the privateer brig *Grand Turk* [1] saluting Marseilles on her last cruise of the war. Her records give all the business details of commerce-destroying. The owners pay all expenses, and receive half the net proceeds of prizes. The remainder is divided into about one hundred and fifty shares, of which Captain Nathan Green gets ten, the first lieutenant, seven and a half; second lieutenant, sailing master, and surgeon, each six; secretary, paymaster, and pilot, each three; gunners and petty officers, each two or two and a half; and ninety-five seamen, each one. In addition, there is twenty dollars for whoever first sights a prize, and half a share extra for the first to board one. No seaman may sell more than half his share in advance.

Chesapeake-built clipper schooners, with their sharp ends, shoal draft, and cloud of canvas, were the most popular privateers in the War of 1812. Salem owned several of them; but a greater proportion were captured than of the home-built sort. During the war,

---

[1] Built at Wiscasset, Maine, 18 guns, 309 tons burthen. Maclay is again in error in identifying this vessel with the *Grand Turk* which made an early voyage to Canton. She was owned in Boston; but manned largely by Salem men.

Massachusetts builders probably began that process of drawing out the length of vessels and sweetening their lines, which in another fifteen years' time produced a much faster and handier type of merchantman than the Federalist period ever knew.[1]

Although the brig *Grand Turk*, according to Dr. Bentley, was considered the best sailer out of Salem, the Crowninshields' ship *America* was the most successful, as indeed she had been as a merchantman. Her new rig was enormous in comparison with her hull. Her main truck was 136 feet from the deck; her bowsprit, lengthened by jibboom and flying jibboom, 107 feet long; she had a 67-foot mainyard, and the total spread of her sail, from studdingsail boom-end to boom-end, was 104 feet.[2] Yet her length was only 108 feet, 7 inches, and breadth 30 feet, 8 inches. With her twenty-four guns and one hundred and fifty men she netted twenty-six prizes, which sold for over a million dollars. One of them was a Liverpool ship, by which the Irving family of New York was trying to smuggle English goods after hostilities had commenced. This explains why Tom Walker, in Washington Irving's story, on observing the name of Crowninshield, "recollected a mighty rich man of that name, who made a vulgar display of wealth, which it was whispered he had acquired by buccaneering."

[1] J. & T. H. Perkins to Perkins & Co., Canton, November 17, 1814, about their ship *Jacob Jones*, "Some insurance has been done on her, owing to her being a war built vessel, and having the reputation of a *swift sailor*, at fifty per cent ... Vessels built before the war cannot be insured at seventy-five per cent."

[2] The picture of her in chapter 8 shows her merchantman rig. There is a full-rigged model of her as a privateer in the Peabody Museum, and a reconstructed sail-plan in the Essex Historical Collections, xxxvii, 7. During her three last cruises she was commanded by James Chever, Jr., of Salem, who had started as her cabin boy in 1804, and had had a brother impressed into the British navy.

EMBARGO AND WAR

"Mr. Madison's war" interrupted the Pacific commerce of Massachusetts, to the profit of Great Britain. English letter-of-marque whalers, some manned by renegade Nantucketers, played havoc with our Pacific whaling fleet until Captain David Porter turned the tables with the frigate *Essex*. The salty narrative of her cruise, by this young Boston commander, is the best bit of sea literature of the period. Captain Porter gave his scorbutic seamen six months of heaven in Nukahiva Island, of which he formally took possession in the name of the United States, and rechristened the principal harbor Massachusetts Bay. Although Captain Ingraham of the *Hope* had discovered the island, the United States did not see fit to confirm Captain Porter's occupation; and the Marquesas fell to France.

The *Essex* never cruised far enough to protect our China and East-India traders. A number of them reached home safely during the first year of the war, giving small harbors their first and last contact with the Far East. Late in 1812 the ship *American Hero* from India put in at Barnstable. Early in April, 1813, the ship *Sally* from Canton learned from a fishing boat off Cape Cod that war had been declared the previous June. She also learned that two British frigates were waiting for her outside Boston Light. A favorable slant enabled her to slip into Plymouth Bay, and to give the Pilgrim capital its greatest sensation since the *Mayflower* landed. For not only did the *Sally's* rich cargo pay $133,731.47 in duties — more than that customs district had taken in since Jefferson's embargo — but she landed a Chinese passenger, who in full mandarin costume attended 'meeting' the following Sabbath. The collector of the port of Boston did his best to deprive Plymouth of the duties; but possession proved nine points of the law, and the *Sally's*

Canton goods were forwarded to her Boston owners in a fleet of wagons.

At Honolulu, early in 1812, the Winships of Boston had obtained a sandalwood monopoly from King Kamehameha I, in return for a percentage of the profits. Arrival of the first fragrant cargo at Canton was closely followed by news of the war, so that the Winships' agents, for fear of capture by English cruisers, had to ship the king's share of silk and specie in a slow Portuguese vessel. By the time she arrived at Honolulu, some British residents had so prejudiced Hawaiian royalty against Americans that the king showed signs of breaking the contract. To prevent this, Jonathan Winship, Jr. instructed the Portuguese captain to hold the specie until a new lot of sandalwood forthcame; unless indeed a British cruiser approached. In that event, the silver should be landed on the royal wharf, to avoid the possibility of seizure. A Hawaiian princess, overhearing the conversation, played a neat Yankee trick on the Yankee traders. At the lookout on Diamond Head, where the government maintained a signal station, her royal highness corrupted the human semaphore, who signaled to the inner harbor, "Big British warship coming!" The Portuguese captain hurriedly landed his cargo; and before the shipping intelligence proved false, Kamehameha had the specie, and snapped his fat fingers at Messrs. Winship, Winship & Davis. Not until another reign did Americans recover their influence at the Islands.

In order to send instructions to their blockaded vessels at Whampoa, the Boston China merchants dispatched three letters-of-marque, the brig *Rambler*, sixteen guns and fifty men, ship *Jacob Jones*, and schooner *Tamaamaah*.[1] All three reached Canton

[1] The common spelling at that time of Kamehameha.

safely, and took a few prizes off Lintin. Ordering the merchant vessels to remain until peace was announced, the three letters-of-marque, loaded deep with China goods, dropped down-river from Whampoa on the night of January 18, 1815, passing in the darkness two British men-of-war, and about twenty armed East-Indiamen, which fired guns and burned blue lights to no purpose. Keeping company through the homeward passage, they arrived at Boston on May 3 and 4, 1815, 108 and 109 days out from Whampoa, in time to get the high prices that prevailed just after the war.

During the first six months of the war, every Atlantic port of the United States traded with England, under license from the British blockading squadron. The ship *Ariadne* of Boston, owned by Amorys, Perkinses, Parsons, and Nathaniel Goddard, was a case in point. Obtaining informal permission from the Attorney-General and the Secretary of the Treasury, she took a cargo of provisions to Cadiz, under British license. It was currently believed in Massachusetts that tobacco from President Madison's own plantation went to England by this system, which Congress made no effort to restrain until the crops of 1812 had found profitable market. Much contraband trade went on over the New Brunswick and Florida frontiers, and part of the Massachusetts fleet took out Portuguese papers. Boston merchants made large profits from the enhanced price of foreign goods. John McLane cleared $100,000 by a corner in molasses soon after the declaration of war. Later, he established the McLane professorship of modern history at Harvard.

By 1813 conditions had changed. Only five American and thirty-nine neutral vessels cleared that year from Boston for foreign ports. On September 8 there lay idle in Boston Harbor, with topmasts housed and mastheads covered by inverted tar-barrels or canvas bags ("Madison's night-caps") to prevent rotting; ninety-one ships, one hundred and eleven barques and brigs, and forty-five schooners. And in December, 1813, Congress passed a new embargo act, which forbade all coastwise as well as foreign traffic, and was rigorously enforced. It is said that a man from the Elizabeth Islands, who brought corn to the New Bedford grist-mill, was refused clearance home for his bag of meal. Such a clamor arose against "Madison's embargo" that Congress repealed it in the spring of 1814; but no sooner was this done than the British blockade was extended from Long Island Sound to the Penobscot.

So completely did embargo and blockade stop coasting that a wagon traffic began between maritime Massachusetts and the South. Federalist wits expended their energy on this new form of commerce. Pungs and wagons were christened the *Jefferson's Pride* of Salem, and *Mud-clipper* of Boston. Newspapers reported, under "Horse-marine Intelligence," the entrance of fast-sailing wagons from New York and Albany, with news of vessels spoken *en route*, together with sundry searchings by customs officials and boardings by tithing-men, who vainly invoked blue laws against the deep-sea slogan of "No Sundays off soundings." Chanties were composed for the land navy:

> Ye waggoners of Freedom,
>   Whose chargers chew the cud;
> Whose wheels have braved a dozen years
>   The gravel and the mud.

Much commerce was also done in whaleboats which sneaked along the South Shore to Sandwich, and were then transferred overland with their cargoes to Buz-

zard's Bay, along the present route of the Cape Cod
Canal. An adept at this trade was Captain John Collins, of Truro, who later became a famous packet-ship
commander, and an organizer of the Collins line of
ocean steamers.

The British fleet made life very stimulating along
the Massachusetts coast, during the summer and autumn of 1814. Two frigates made their headquarters
at Provincetown, which the government had neglected
to fortify, and cruised constantly between Cape Cod
and Cape Ann. In August another British base was
established at Castine on the Penobscot. South of the
Cape, H.M.S. *Nimrod* ruled the waters of Nantucket
and Vineyard Sounds, and Buzzard's Bay. These
vessels captured, and often ransomed, such coasting
and fishing vessels as ventured out; their armed barges
made frequent forays and landings on the coast, to
destroy shipping and obtain fresh provisions. For defense, the Navy Department provided four Jeffersonian
gunboats, two at Newburyport and two at New Bedford, which were perfectly useless. The southern pair
spent most of its time safely hidden in the Acushnet
River, and even dared not attack the *Nimrod* when she
stranded on Great Ledge near New Bedford. When
the frigates raided Wareham, destroying buildings and
shipping to the value of many thousand dollars, the
gunboats bravely issued forth when it was all over —
and Wareham stopped counting her losses to laugh.
Otherwise, Massachusetts depended for defense on her
regular militia, stationed in small forts at most of the
larger seaports; and on volunteer companies of 'seafencibles.'

No part of the long coastline was unvisited by the
British frigates or barges. They landed a crew at
Thatcher's Island off Cape Ann, and dug potatoes; cut

fishing boats out of Kettle Cove; drove a schooner ashore on Mingo Beach, Beverly; took vessels from under the guns of Fort Sewall, Marblehead, and captured six coasters close by the Neck. In general, British landing parties had their will of Federalist towns, and were driven off by Democratic towns. "Provincetown received no small benefit from the English vessels, and some of the fortunes since acquired, had their beginning from this source," says the historian of Truro. Duxbury and Plymouth informed the commander of H.M.S. *Leander* that they considered the war none of their business; the Old Colony had not been consulted. But for the Gurnet garrison's perverse belligerency, Pilgrim neutrality might have been respected. Nantucket declared her neutrality in August, in order to procure food through the blockade. So near starving was the island, that a local wag asked his rich neighbor for a hammer to knock his teeth out — "he had no need of them, because he could n't get anything to eat!"

Captain Mathew H. Mayo, of Eastham, impressed as pilot on board a captured pinkie, managed by a series of clever stratagems to run her ashore within a mile of his own house. For this exploit the town of Eastham paid twelve hundred dollars to the British authorities, under threat of bombardment. Brewster was an easier mark. In September, 1814, Commodore Ragget, of H.M.S. *Spencer*, demanded four thousand dollars, to spare the village and the salt-works. Brewster had a company of artillery, with two field pieces; but the town meeting (whose moderator was Captain Elijah Cobb, that young shipmaster who had bearded Robespierre) calmly paid the money. Such non-resistance was quite unnecessary, for the British warships could not get within range of the bay-side Cape

cottages, and a good demonstration of militia usually
frightened away landing parties. Democratic Orleans
"promptly and indignantly rejected" a demand for
ransom, and was not molested. Two girls, left in
charge of the Scituate Lighthouse, frightened off a
British barge by retiring behind a hillock and playing
furiously on fife and drum.

Falmouth [1] best upheld the honor of the Cape. In
January, 1814, the commander of H.M.S. *Nimrod*
demanded that Falmouth surrender the Nantucket
packet-sloop, and several pieces of artillery which had
been used to good effect. Weston Jenkins, shipmaster
and militia captain, replied, "Come on and get them!"
The *Nimrod* then stood close in shore, and after granting two hours' truce to remove non-combatants, bom-
barded the houses from noon to nightfall. Eight cannon balls were lodged in one cottage alone; but beyond
smashing furniture and breaking salt-vats, little damage was done, and no lives lost. The entrenched militia prevented a landing. Later in the year Captain Jenkins, with a crew of neighbors in a small sloop, cut the
British privateer *Retaliation* out of Tarpaulin Cove.

Disaffection reached a dangerous point in all southern New England during the summer and autumn of
1814. In addition to its original grievance against the
war, maritime Massachusetts felt abandoned by the
federal government. Her volunteers were marched off
to the Canadian frontier, and her coast left defenseless;
while war taxes increased, and the administration
showed no sign of yielding its high pretensions, which
postponed the conclusion of peace. Interior Massachusetts was in general of like mind; and Connecticut
and Rhode Island as well. Secession from the Union
was openly propagated by the Federalist press; and

[1] The village now known as Wood's Hole.

there are various indications that secession sentiment had gone far among the people. According to the records of the Beverly artillery company, it "exercised the Gun as usual and fired a Royal Salute of 5 guns," on July 4, 1814. The Newburyport Sea Fencibles, composed principally of shipmasters and builders, flung a five-starred, five-striped flag to the breeze from Plum Island fort.

At the darkest hour of the war, when one British army was massed on the Lake Champlain front, another on its way to New Orleans, and the government of the United States a refugee from the destroyed capital, the General Court of Massachusetts summoned a New England convention at Hartford, to confer not only upon military defense against the enemy, but on political defense against the administration. Although the moderate Federalists conceived the Hartford Convention largely as a safety-valve to the passions they had helped arouse, the Essex Junto had other plans. Timothy Pickering, just reëlected to Congress by an all but unanimous vote, wished the Convention to draft a new constitution, and present it as a loaded pistol at the original thirteen states, with the alternative of an independent New England Confederacy. John Lowell paved the way, with articles and pamphlets defending the right of secession.

The unpatriotism of this programme needs no comment. However justified the Federalist opposition to the war in 1812, the war in 1814 had become a defensive struggle against the massed resources of the British Empire. Napoleon had been disposed of. The unwisdom of secession, for communities that depended for their very life on free intercourse with the other United States, is equally obvious. Politicians were perhaps more directly responsible for it than shipmasters; but the maritime interests of Massachusetts supported the politicians. And among the members of the General Court who voted for a convention at Hartford were merchants like T. H. Perkins, Israel Thorndike, Daniel Sargent, and Captain William Sturgis.

It seems strange that a people whose sails whitened every sea; whose two commercial cities, in many and remote parts of the world, stood for the United States; who talked familiarly of the Far West and Hawaii as The Coast and The Islands; should be so narrow and inflexible in their politics. Yet this attitude was natural and inevitable. *Cælum non animum mutant qui trans mare currunt.* They that do business in great waters have little in common with their land-plodding countrymen. Their native land is but a resting place between voyages; a wharf and shipyard and cottage by the sea. New England was but a broader Nantucket, where aged shipmasters could be found who knew half the coral reefs of the South Sea, but had never set foot in the United States. A sailor's daughter worked the creed of maritime Massachusetts into her sampler:

> Amy Kittredge is my name
> Salem is my dwelling place
> New England is my nashun
> And Christ is my Salvation.

The Union ceased to be valuable when fresh-water politicians took bread from the mouths of honest seamen. Better go it alone, a North American Denmark, than stifle under the rule of scatter-brained demagogues.

New England held her breath while the Hartford Convention secretly deliberated. Its report, appearing on January 6, 1815, showed that common sense and moderation had gained control. The administration was severely scolded, and nullification threatened if conscription were applied. But secession was calmly considered, and ruled out of practical politics.

Five weeks later, in the midst of a cold February that sealed the war-bound shipping in the idle ports, arrived the news of peace. From Newburyport to Provincetown sped the good news; shouted along the roads by stage-drivers through clouds of frozen breath, blared out by rusty fishhorns, and joyously tolled by meeting-house bells whose sullen silence no battle had broken. For maritime Massachusetts, peace meant the unlocking of prison doors; a return to the wide arms of her ocean mother.

CHAPTER XIV

THE PASSING OF SALEM

1815–1845

THE first few years of world peace were the severest test that maritime Massachusetts had ever met. New conditions, foreign and domestic, required a readjustment of her economic system. Europe at peace was recovering her own carrying trade. Only gradually did England open her colonial ports to Yankee ships, and a generation elapsed before new markets were found in California, Australia, and South Africa. At the same time the westward movement in the United States left Massachusetts more remote from the center of population; and it was difficult to find artificial means to surmount the Berkshire barrier. As places of exchange between the West and Europe, ports like New Orleans, Baltimore, and New York with the Erie Canal, had such obvious advantages over Boston and Salem that it was difficult to see how Massachusetts could survive as a commercial community. The futile, unpatriotic policy of New England Federalism made Massachusetts the butt and scorn of her sister states, and lost her, for the time being, all influence at Washington. A sullen pessimism was the prevailing attitude on State Street. The decline of Boston to a fourth-rate seaport, and the total extinction of Salem, were confidently predicted.

The younger and more far-sighted men put their money and brains into making Massachusetts a manufacturing state. Embargo and war had acted as a prohibitive tariff on English manufactures; and just be-

213

fore the war ended two scions of shipping families, Francis C. Lowell and Patrick T. Jackson, prepared against peace by setting up power looms at Waltham, in the first complete American cotton factory. Against the will of the shipping community, they obtained a protective tariff in 1816; and within a generation the manufacturing cities of Lowell, Lawrence, Chicopee, and Manchester, had been established by capital accumulated through neutral trading. Every country town with a good-sized brook or river set up a textile or paper mill or iron foundry; and a similar expansion in shoemaking altered the economy of fishing villages. The center of interest in Massachusetts shifts from wharf to waterfall; by 1840 she had become predominantly a manufacturing state.

Yet the same grit and enterprise that made this corner of the United States into a great workshop, managed to retain, and even to increase, its maritime activity. The merchants could no longer obtain special favors for their class. They were unable to maintain a distinct political party. Federalism, after a placid and powerless Indian summer, melted into dominant Republicanism by 1825. Daniel Webster, the child whom it had raised, seceded to high protection in 1828, and Boston ratified his change by electing Nathan Appleton to Congress against Henry Lee, a leading East-India merchant and brilliant writer on free trade. The mercantile and shipping community then made the best terms it could with the Whig Party. At the price of prohibitive duties on India cottons and cheap English woolens, and a heavy tariff on wool, hemp, and iron, it obtained low schedules for other Oriental goods, fruit and wines, and exotic products that did not compete with "infant industries." Manufacturing stimulated the import of wool

from Smyrna and South America, of coal from Philadelphia, and cotton from the Gulf ports and Charleston; it provided a new export medium, domestic cottons, which Yankee vessels introduced into the world's
markets; and it greatly increased the buying power of
New England. Many of the old mercantile families,
who became pioneer manufacturers, still remained
shipowners, reluctant to lose all touch with the element
that raised them from obscurity; and merchant-shipowners invested their surplus in manufacturing stock.
Ships lay idle when looms were still, and the ebb and
flow of commercial prosperity passed inland with the
east wind.

A surprisingly large tonnage managed to follow with
profit the old routes established in Federalist days;
proving that superior skill, not merely war conditions,
was at the bottom of the earlier prosperity. Boston
remained the principal North American emporium for
East-Indian, Baltic, and Mediterranean products until
the Civil War. And Massachusetts, though mutilated
by the separation of Maine in 1820, remained the leading shipowning state until 1843, when passed by New
York. Maritime history is punctuated by depressions,
when money was "tighter than the skin on a cat's
back," by periods of inflation, and by the panics of
1819, 1837, and 1857. But on the whole there was
progress, both in technique and in earnings. The usual
post-bellum inflation was liquidated in 1819. A toil-
some advance in the eighteen-twenties was followed by
perceptible speeding-up in the thirties, full-tide prosperity in the forties, and a glorious culmination in the
fifties, with the clipper ship.

Concentration was the order of the day. In her
struggle to keep pace with New York, Boston absorbed the foreign commerce and shipping of every

other Massachusetts seaport. The capital in twenty years' time recovered the losses from a decade of restrictions and war. Newburyport, Beverly, Salem, Marblehead, and Plymouth, after a brave effort to pick up, turned to manufacturing. New Bedford and Gloucester, Wellfleet and Provincetown, survived through specialization in whale, mackerel, and cod-fisheries.

"Newburyport has withered under the influence of Boston," wrote Caleb Cushing in 1825. Her population declined from 7634 in 1810 to 6375 in 1830. The Middlesex Canal, by tapping the Merrimac River at Chelmsford, diverted from Newburyport the lumber and produce of southern New Hampshire. Portland, Boothbay, and Bangor, in the thriving state of Maine, were exporting their lumber and fish direct, undermining her West-India trade. Gloucester absorbed a large part of her fisheries, and those of Ipswich as well. Deep slumber rested upon Newburyport. William Lloyd Garrison, the inspired printer's devil, tried to arouse her with a new journal, the "Free Press." High Street rubbed its eyes and rolled over, mumbling "Jacobin!" Then Garrison followed the white sails to Boston.

Marblehead made a brave, and partially successful, effort to revive her Baltic, South American, and West-Indian trade after the war. In August and September, 1821, she had three entries from St. Petersburg, two from Brazil, and two from Martinique; all of them schooners and brigantines from seventy-five to one hundred tons burthen.[1] But by 1840 her most success-

---

[1] One of them, the schooner *Sarah*, seventy-four tons, was the last command of John Roads Russell, who as a private in Colonel Glover's regiment had rowed the boat that ferried Washington across the Delaware.

ful merchants, such as Robert Chamblett Hooper, had moved to Boston; and the rest put their money into fishing schooners and shoe shops. Lucy Larcom has excited our pity for Hannah at a Window Binding Shoes in Marblehead, awaiting the return of fisherman Ben. Cold statistics, however, place Hannah among eleven hundred Marbleheaders producing annually over a million pairs of shoes, worth twice the average catch of the fishing fleet. Clearly, there were no economic grounds for Hannah's loneliness!

Salem as a seaport died hard. The merchant-shipping firm of Silsbee, Stone & Pickman, formed in the eighteenth century, lasted until 1893, when their (and Salem's) last square-rigger, the *Mindoro*, left Derby Wharf to become a coal barge. Yet Salem was prostrated by the war. Her overseas trading fleet declined from 182 sail in 1807 to 57 in 1815, and never again did she attain the tonnage or the entries of pre-embargo days. William Gray's departure to Boston in 1808 began a process that did not stop. The removal of another leading family of merchants and shipmasters —

> Old Low, old Low's son,
> Never saw so many Lows since the world begun —

to Brooklyn about 1825, where they established the merchant-shipping firm of A. A. Low & Brother, was a typical event of the period following 1815. "Nearly half our commerce and capital are employed in other ports," stated a Salem newspaper in 1833.

It became the practice for a Salem East-Indiaman to make two or three round voyages before returning to the home port, in the meantime piling up a balance for the owner at the London banking house of George Peabody. This famous son of Essex County was born of poor parents in 1795, in the part of Danvers afterwards given his name. His first fortune was made in a mercantile business at Baltimore, between 1815 and 1837, when he established himself in London as a competitor to Baring Brothers. Being a bachelor, George Peabody gave or bequeathed the bulk of his fortune, eight and a half million dollars, to the various funds, libraries, institutes, and museums that now bear his name. His partner and successor, Junius Spencer Morgan, left a son.

Joseph Peabody, a cousin of George, was the wealthiest merchant-shipowner of Salem between the embargo and 1845. He emphatically did not belong to the class described by Hawthorne, whose "ventures go to swell, needlessly and imperceptibly, the mighty flood of commerce at New York and Boston." His brig *Leander*, 223 tons, built at Salem in 1821, made twenty-six voyages to Europe, Asia Minor, Africa, and the Far East in the twenty-three years of her life. His ship *George* made twenty-one round voyages from Salem to Calcutta between 1815 and 1837, with such regularity that she was called the "Salem Frigate." [1] Salem vessels were always manned in part by local boys, but the *George* was a veritable training ship. No less than twenty-six mates and forty-five captains graduated from the forecastle of this floating bit of Essex County.

"Capt. West is respected & loved by every man on board," writes John Lovett, her Beverly supercargo, from Leghorn in 1818. "And I must say I think there is but few better men in Beverly, than Mr. Endicott [the first officer] is. We have an excellent crew — they are all young & very smart, & noisy enough. It is always 'drive on boys!' Whether to work, or to play, in the heat or cold, wet or dry. On the

---

[1] The ship *George* was 110 feet, 10 inches by 27 feet by 13 feet, 6 inches, 328 tons, and somewhat of a Baltimore clipper model. Built at Salem for a privateer in 1814, she was purchased by Mr. Peabody for $5250. It is said that she made Salem in forty-one days from the Cape of Good Hope in 1831.

passage the Capt. wished us to take care of ourselves, when the weather was bad the Ship was all under water and then he would call every man from the deck & forecastle to sleep in the cabin and then he was obliged to lay with us himself to keep peace that the Super-cargo & mates might sleep. We have discharged the principal part of our Cargo, and taken in some goods for Calcutta."

On arrival there, he writes, "There are now four ships in this port belonging to Mr. Peabody. . . . There are a great many Beverly men of my acquaintance in this place."

For several years Joseph Peabody competed in the China trade, and continued the famous pepper trade between Salem and Sumatra. It was in 1830 that his ship *Friendship* was attacked and captured by natives, off the village of Quallah-Battoo.

Salem had not yet spent her maritime energy. The palm-tree, Parsee, and ship on her new city seal repre-sented something more than a tradition. Salem men and Salem vessels were still seeking the spoil of Ind, *usque ad ultimum sinum.* They clung to their Oriental specialties, like the Northwest Sumatra pepper trade, as barnacles to a ship's bottom; and taught new black and brown peoples that Salem meant America. One of our most interesting books of American voyages, "The History of a Voyage to the China Sea," by Lieutenant John White, U.S.N., records a Salem adventure in the brig *Franklin*, which sailed up-river to Saigon in 1819, and opened Cochin-China to American commerce. The Fiji Islands were repeatedly visited, in spite of their danger. Nathaniel L. Rogers's brig *Charles Dog-gett*, William Driver master, lost five of her crew at Fiji in 1833. In the very same month that Mr. Knight, of Salem, chief mate of the *Friendship*, was done in by Malays at Quallah-Battoo, his brother Enoch was killed by Penrhyn Island savages on board Joseph

Peabody's ship *Glide*. In the interesting sailor's narrative of that disaster we find the best description of the Fiji trepang or beech-de-mer trade, which was monopolized by about six Salem vessels until the Civil War. Cannibal chiefs, warriors, women and children, tempted by trinkets and Yankee notions, came from a radius of a hundred miles to gather the delectable sea-cucumber, which the Salem men boiled in 'pot-houses' and cured in 'batter-houses' erected on shore. The resultant trepang, to the annual value of thirty thousand dollars, was carried to Manila or Canton, whence it found its way into soup at mandarin banquets. Occasionally the proletariat of Fiji would unite, and make Salem stew in the 'pot-houses,' but the survivors returned, and brought their wives.

Several of these brave ladies of the sea, to our ultimate profit, were bitten by the literary microbe so common in New England of their day. Mrs. Captain Wallis, of the barque *Zotoff*, published an interesting "Life in the Feejees." Miss Lowe, in a delightfully girlish journal, has described life in the foreign settlement at Macao; and her friend Mrs. William Cleveland made colored sketches of Macao types and incidents. A brief manuscript journal of her voyage to Timor, Macao, and Rio Janeiro also survives. Sailing from Salem in the ship *Zephyr* commanded by her husband, on October 29, 1828, they made Timor in the excellent time of eighty-nine days, and touched at various small islands and harbors to obtain sandalwood. At Dilli she sketched the process; the Portuguese governor, clad in a scarlet silk shirt and white nankeen pantaloons, is reclining in a hammock slung between two palm-trees, watching his subjects loading sandalwood logs on the *Zephyr's* tender.

"If the natives on the West Coast of Africa have

been temperate," remarks a historian of Salem, "they have been so in spite of the efforts of the Salem merchants to supply them with the materials for intemperance. . . . Salem has contributed largely to spread a knowledge of the virtue and good qualities of New England rum, of the astounding effects of gunpowder, and of the consoling influences of Virginia tobacco, among the savage tribes of the West Coast."[1] There were 558 arrivals at Salem from that part of the world between 1832 and 1864. It was an alongshore bartering business, to obtain ivory, gold dust, palm-oil, peanuts, and camwood. Small brigs and schooners, often commanded by their owners, made Africa somewhere about Sierra Leone, traded along the Guinea, Liberian, Ivory and Gold Coasts, and as far east as Akessa. At the larger places business was transacted through local merchants; but at the smaller trading stations the appearance of a Salem brig was a signal for the Kroomen to launch their long trading canoes through the surf. A sable potentate, dressed perhaps in a cast-off naval jacket, a hussar's helmet, and a loin-cloth, would be received on board and suitably 'dashed' (West Coast for tipped), to obtain his gracious permission for shipboard dicker, while the vessel lay at anchor or hove to. At Grand Bassam "we got a little ivory and camphor wood and a plenty of noise and begging," writes the mate of the African trading brig *Neptune* of Salem. "They always bring empty jugs with them if nothing else and plague a man's soul to death with entreaties to fill them with rum and gin and give them a little tobacco. A person may judge of the

---

[1] To which list they might have added cottons, wooden clocks, brass pans and other 'dicker' for the natives; and furniture, shoes, and provisions for the European residents. I have found no instance of Salem vessels engaging in the slave-trade at this period.

pleasure and satisfaction we have in trading with them by supposing himself on board a vessel and from one to three hundred naked niggers on deck and every one of them howling with the full strength of their lungs to make themselves heard."

This fever-infested coast was dangerous alike for seamen and for vessels. Harbors there were none, and the Salem brigs often needed their best seamanship to claw out of an anchorage that became a lee shore in a sudden change of wind, great rollers booming in at short notice, and breaking in forty feet of water. Yet the West Africa trade afforded a good living to many swapping Yankees, who had insufficient capital for the grand routes of commerce.

It was in the early thirties that the smaller Salem shipowners began trading with Madagascar, and with the neighboring island of Zanzibar. There they acquired the friendship of the Sultan, Seyyid Said, and monopolized the export of copal, a basic gum for varnish. An important local industry grew out of this trade. Jonathan Whipple discovered a new and cheap method of cleaning copal, about 1835, and about a million and a half pounds of the gum passed annually through his shop on the Salem water-front between 1845 and 1861.

Salem's vicinity to the Danvers tanpits and the cobblers' shops of Essex County, enabled her to hold a place in the South American hide trade, which led to the creation of a new American industry. According to local tradition it was Captain Benjamin Upton who brought from Para, Brazil, in 1824, the first consignment of pure gum 'rubbers.' Although heavy and clumsy, stiff as iron in cold, and liable to melt in warm weather, these overshoes proved just the thing for navigating the slushy streets of Salem in winter. The local merchants, sensing a new trade, sent Lynn lasts to Para, and thereby procured a better fit of rubber overshoes than the original native product. The Para customs records show that between 1836 and 1842, that port sent three quarters of a million pairs of pure gum overshoes to Salem, almost as much as to all other places combined. Thus began a new branch of the New England shoe industry, and the first step towards Charles Goodyear's momentous discovery, in 1839, of the vulcanization of rubber.

About 1845 the control of the Para rubber trade passed to New York, which gradually absorbed most of Salem's South American commerce, except a part of the hides needed for local consumption. Direct voyages from Salem to Manila continued until 1858; the ship *St. Paul*, owned by Stephen C. Phillips, making twelve round voyages in thirteen years. Salem clung desperately to her minor specialties, such as the trade with Fiji, Zanzibar, and the West Coast of Africa. But these were poor substitutes for the Calcutta, the China, and the Sumatra voyages, which ended with the death of Joseph Peabody in 1844. Although for fifty years thereafter a dwindling number of Salem firms traded with the Far East, Salem ceased to be an important seaport in 1845.

That was the very year when President Polk appointed Nathaniel Hawthorne surveyor of the port of Salem; in 1849 President Taylor removed him. In "The Scarlet Letter," which Hawthorne then wrote to replace official emoluments, he draws a true and enduring picture of Salem's gentle decay. The last entries from a dozen ports of world commerce had lately been recorded in the custom house, where Hawthorne dreamed away the idle days between the arrival of occasional hide ships, West Coast brigs, and Nova

Scotia wood schooners. In 1848, with the establishment of the Naumkeag Steam Cotton Mills, Salem entered the factory era; and a fluttering drone of spindles began to dominate the empty harbor and idle wharves.

CHAPTER XV

THE HUB OF THE UNIVERSE

1830–1845

BOSTON STATE-HOUSE is the hub of the solar system. You could n't pry that out of a Boston man if you had the tire of all creation straightened out for a crowbar. (*The Autocrat of the Breakfast Table.*)

WHILE foreign trade slipped away from the smaller seaports of Massachusetts, and riverside villages became manufacturing cities, Boston commerce increased to an extent undreamed of in Federalist days. Without annexing territory, Boston grew from forty-three thousand to sixty-one thousand souls between 1820 and 1830, passed the hundred-thousand mark about 1842, and increased over sixty per cent in the fifteen prosperous years that followed. In shipping and foreign commerce she managed to remain a good second to New York, despite the geographical advantages of Philadelphia, Baltimore, and New Orleans. Never before or since had Boston Harbor been so crowded, or the waterfront so congested with sailing vessels.[1] In 1806, the banner year of neutral trade, one thousand and eighty-three sail entered Boston from foreign ports. In the eighteen-thirties the yearly aver-

---

[1] Average annual arrivals from foreign ports at Boston, by decades:

1790–1800	1800–10	1810–20	1820–30	1830–35	1835–41
569	789	610	787	1199	1473

Annual arrivals of coasting vessels at Boston:

1830	1840	1844	1849	1851
2938	4406	5312	6199	6334

From Hazard's *U.S. Register*, VI, 32, and *Boston Shipping List and Price Current*, January 3, 1852.

225

age almost attained fifteen hundred, and the average size of vessels was growing as well. Coastwise arrivals increased in the same proportion; and by 1844, when a new and even greater era began, fifteen vessels entered and left the harbor for every day in the year.

At the same time Boston had become the financial center for New England manufacturing, with a banking system that withstood the panic of 1837; and itself a manufacturing city for Yankee notions, in both senses of the word. Next door to the Boston merchants lived the Boston reformers and poets. Not that they were any more welcome than before 1815; but somehow they appeared; and not infrequently in the midst of a shocked shipping family.

Old Boston was very young in 1840. "Here was the moving principle itself," wrote Emerson, "a living mind agitating the mass and always afflicting the conservative class with some odious novelty or other." Here, in 1832, young Emerson himself challenged the past by resigning the pastorate of the Second Church. Within a quarter-mile of State Street was the obscure hole where 'the freedom of a race began,' when in 1831 young Garrison composed, set up, and printed the first number of "The Liberator." Wendell Phillips, offspring of all that was worthy and respectable on Beacon Hill, became Garrison's convert after seeing him mobbed by counting-room clerks. Under the very hub itself began a new chapter in education, when Horace Mann, in 1837, became chairman of a new state board. The education of the blind had already begun through the concentrated brains, money, and benevolence of Samuel Gridley Howe and Thomas Handasyd Perkins. Longfellow, son of a member of the Hartford Convention, was domiciled under the Cambridge elms in 1836; and Prescott, whose father belonged to the same council of elders, produced his "Ferdinand and Isabella" the following year. In Faneuil Hall, in 1845, Charles Sumner flung down his challenge to militarism, which James Russell Lowell mercilessly satirized in the "Biglow Papers." Henry Thoreau, in the meantime, had found a new way of life at Concord, and Brook Farm had flourished and collapsed.

There is little connection, to be sure, between the maritime history of Massachusetts and these high lights of reform, revolt, and letters. Commercial Boston published their books, and financed such of their efforts as came under patchwork philanthropy; but for the most part ridiculed, condemned, or ignored. In all New England letters there is no genuine sea poetry; [1] nothing to equal the rollicking chanties that the common seamen improvised. Yet maritime Massachusetts became articulate in Dana's "Two Years Before the Mast" and Melville's "Moby Dick." What seafaring people, in the nineteenth century, has left prose monuments to compare with these? Dana, too, must be counted among the New England reformers. Many well-meaning people endeavored to save Jack's soul, philanthropists provided him with a snug harbor for his old age; Dana endeavored to obtain him justice.

New York was the only successful rival to Boston among North American ports, if one takes shipping as well as commerce into consideration. Her exports steadily advanced, while those of Boston remained stationary; for Boston, as usual, lacked a good export medium. [2] The imports of Boston increased, but New

[1] Longfellow's "Building of the Ship" and Whittier's "Legends of New England" perhaps might be stretched into this class, and Holmes's prose passage on "Sea and Mountains" in *The Autocrat*, paper XI. In general, however, the New England poets' attitude toward the sea is that of a summer boarder who is afraid to get his feet wet.

[2] New England manufactures were absorbed largely by the domestic

York's increased still more, and by 1845 the Empire State had a greater fleet than that of Massachusetts. To the extraordinary commercial growth of New York, the Bay State was a leading contributor. Many of the famous New York shipbuilders and merchants were Massachusetts men. "What aided in making great merchants in this city thirty years ago," wrote the author of "Old Merchants of New York City" in 1863, "was their having foreign or New England connections. Most of the shipping was owned in these eastern places, and consequently the merchant in New York who had the most extensive eastern connections did the largest business." "It is well known," writes another Manhattan expert in 1844, "that one-third of the commerce of New York, from 1839 to 1842, was carried either upon Massachusetts' account, or in Massachusetts vessels." Eighty-three per cent of Boston's imports were on local account; i.e., purchased abroad by Boston firms. But only twenty-three per cent of New York's imports were owned by New-Yorkers. Manhattan's geographical position was such that all the world poured gold into her lap. Boston's growth resulted entirely from local enterprise.

Shipping is the main explanation of Boston's successful rivalry with her other American competitors. A large proportion of the American merchant marine was still owned by Boston merchants, who preferred to handle the cargoes themselves rather than give Philadelphia or Baltimore the profits of distribution. The ability of her merchant-shipowners to earn freights, to

market. The average yearly export of domestic cottons from Boston was only about $2,250,000 between 1848 and 1856, although Massachusetts and New Hampshire together produced cotton goods to the value of $28,500,000 in 1850.

gather in cargoes from all parts of the world, and to find the right market, lay at the very root of Boston's success.

The old commercial spirit kept Boston abreast of modern improvements, provided harbor and railroad facilities, built larger and faster vessels, and established packet-lines. Boston's "principal advantage for the security of vessels," wrote a New-Yorker in 1844,[1] "and it is one that distinguishes this port from other principal ports of our country," is her "numerous docks, which are constructed with solid strength, and run far up into the city. These are bordered by continuous blocks of warehouses, either of brick or Quincy granite, which have an appearance of remarkable uniformity, solidity, and permanence. By the arrangement of these docks the numerous vessels, whose tracery of spars and cordage line them on either side, may unship their cargoes at the very doors of the bordering warehouses, and receive in return their supplies for foreign ports with the utmost security and dispatch."

Central Wharf, built in 1819, with fifty-four brick stores running down its center for a quarter of a mile, was a fitting companion to India Wharf. In its upper stories were three great halls for auction sales, and in its octagonal cupola the headquarters of the "Semaphore Telegraph Company," to which the approach of vessels was signaled from Telegraph Hill in Hull.[2] Below, as on India Wharf, were warehouses, wholesale stores, and counting-rooms of leading mercantile firms. Here cargoes from all parts of the world were bought and sold and accounted for, without the aid of steam heat, clacking typewriter, and office system. An

---

[1] James H. Lanman, in Hunt's *Merchants' Magazine*, x (1844).
[2] Central Wharf is shown on the left of Salmon's painting of the Wharves of Boston.

odor of tar and hemp, mingled with spicy suggestions from the merchandise stored above, pervaded everything. Respectable men clerks (*female* clerks, sir?— would you have female sailors?) on high stools were constantly writing in the calf-bound letter-books, ledgers, and waste-books, or delving in the neat wooden chests that enclosed the records of each particular vessel. Owners, some crabbed and crusty, others with the manners of a merchant prince, received you before blazing open fires of hickory or cannel coal, in rooms adorned with portraits and half-models of vessels. Through the small-paned windows one could see the firm's new ship being rigged under the owner's eye.

The invention and quick application of steam railroads was a great aid to the commerce of Boston. After playing with the idea of a Boston and Albany canal, Massachusetts wisely accepted the veto of her topography. In 1825 the Quincy Granite Railway, a short gravity tramway connecting granite quarries with tidewater, was financed by Thomas Handasyd Perkins. Further progress was delayed for several years, but by 1841 railroads spread fanwise from Boston to Salem and Portsmouth, New Hampshire, to Lowell and other manufacturing centers, to Providence and to Albany. Other local lines, like the Old Colony to Plymouth, soon followed. The Western Railroad, Boston's single connection with the West, was badly managed, and sent very little through freight to her wharves until after the Civil War, when the first grain elevator was erected on the harbor front. But the others, with water-front termini at Boston, and (in 1850) a belt-line connecting all with each other and the wharves, distributed incoming cargoes to inland points, and brought miscellaneous products of farm and forest, home workshop and factory, to Boston warehouses.

THE HUB OF THE UNIVERSE

More important than the railroads as distributing
agencies were the sailing packets. Every tidewater
village between Eastport and Provincetown, and many
beyond, had a packet-sloop plying to Boston. Even
nearby Hanover found it cheaper to send packet-sloops
down the tortuous course of the North River and
around the Cohasset reefs to Boston, than to use the
road. At Plymouth, in 1830 (a population of less than
five thousand), six sloops of sixty tons each were employed as Boston packets, exchanging local products
for raw materials used in the textile, iron, and cordage
factories; two schooners of ninety tons plied around
the Cape to Nantucket, New Bedford, and New York;
and three other vessels brought lumber from Maine.
A study of our coasting trade would reveal many
quaint characters, and curious trade routes. Skipper
Brightman, of Westport, for instance, collected fresh
eggs from the surrounding country, and took them to
Providence market in his sloop; he calculated that by
1840 he had transported at least three million and a
half eggs. Hingham maintained rival Republican and
Federalist lines of Boston packets; and so high ran
political feeling that if a Federalist missed his boat he
would spend the night on Long Wharf rather than
take the Jacobin sloop. The Federalist *Rapid*, built in
1811, long outlasted her party, continuing in service
until the Civil War.

Short local lines like these had existed since colonial
days, and in the Federalist era there had been "constant traders," as they were advertised, which took
freight to New York, Albany, Philadelphia, Alexandria, and Baltimore. Innovations of the era of peace
were regular packet-lines [1] to Southern ports and to

[1] A packet-line, as the term was understood before the Civil War,
meant two or more vessels whose owners advertised sailings to desig-

Liverpool. By 1844 we find advertised in the Boston papers the " Regular " line, with four vessels running to Havana, and others to Alexandria and Washington, to Savannah, and every ten days to New Orleans ("The ship has fine 'tween decks for dry goods, shoes, &c."). Allen & Weltch are running packets to Norfolk, Mobile, and to New Orleans ("elegant and extensive accomodation, no ice or lime taken"). Nathaniel Winsor competes for the New Orleans, the Savannah, and the Mobile traffic; Λ. C. Lombard's line runs to Charleston, Benjamin Bruce's to Mobile, W. B. Kendall's to Savannah, and Reed's to Norfolk, City Point, and Richmond; Baltimore is served by the Manufacturers', the Union, and the Despatch lines; four different lines run to Philadelphia, and at least five to New York.

Since colonial days there had been constant traders between Boston and Liverpool and London; but the famous Black Ball Line of New York, established in 1816, was the pioneer transatlantic packet-line under the American flag. The Boston & Liverpool Packet Company was founded in 1822, with four new ships named after jewels, one of which, the Boston-built *Emerald* [1] made an extraordinary passage from Liverpool to Boston under Captain Philip Fox, of Cohasset. Leaving Liverpool on February 20, 1824, at 3 P.M., she stayed with an easterly gale all the way, and carried sail enough to keep her lee rail buried until 3 P.M. March 8, when she hove to for a pilot off Boston Light, just seventeen days out. Three hours later she anchored below Fort Independence. The owners

nated ports, on schedules as regular as wind and weather permitted; and which depended for their profit on freight and passengers furnished by the public, rather than goods shipped on their owners' account.
[1] Length 110 feet, breadth 27 feet, tonnage 359.

thought she had returned from some mishap on her outward passage, and would hardly believe Captain Fox until he handed them some Liverpool papers of the day he sailed.

Captain Fox was an early example of that breed of sea-captains called 'drivers,' for in 1819 he had made a similar passage only a few hours longer, in the Merrimac-built ship *Herald*, 302 tons. Neither vessel ever showed much speed under other masters. To appreciate his achievement we must remember that the *Emerald's* record for a westward transatlantic passage was seldom, perhaps only once, surpassed by a sailing vessel, and then by a clipper ship five times her size.[1]

The Boston & Liverpool Packet Company failed very shortly, and was succeeded by a new line in 1827, for which several packet-ships of about 425 tons each were built to order at Medford and Boston. The accommodation plans of one of these, the *Dover* (121 feet long, built at Charlestown by John M. Robertson in 1828), show a forty-five foot main cabin with eleven staterooms about six feet square; a library, wine and spirit room, covered deck abaft the mainmast, for passengers' use and a "bathing room" (by the bucket method probably) on the port quarter. The charge for cabin passage was $140, including "mattresses, bedding, wines, and all other stores."

---

[1] Captain Clark (*Clipper Ship Era*, 247) states that the record is fifteen days Rock Light to Sandy Hook, made by the *Andrew Jackson* (1676 tons) in 1860. The famous *Dreadnought's* fastest westward passage was nineteen days. For a good example of the untrustworthiness of second-hand and subsequent statements of sailing ships' records, compare the yarns about the *Emerald's* passage in R. W. Emerson's *Journals*, III, 204 (told him in 1833 on shipboard); Nathaniel Spooner, *Gleanings from the Records of the Boston Marine Society* (1879), 98; H. A. Hill, *Trade and Commerce of Boston* (1894), 121, with Edmund P. Collier (who took the pains to examine contemporary and reliable sources), *Cohasset's Deep-Sea Captains*, 13.

Both packet-lines succumbed for the same cause: Boston's inability to furnish return cargoes. England, unlike the Baltic and Mediterranean, imported her East- and West-Indian goods in her own bottoms. No money could be made in the miscellaneous notions — sassafras, corn husks, cow horns, and rubber shoes — that Boston was shipping to Liverpool at this period. The packets were forced to Southern ports for an outward cargo of cotton; and this detour lost them their passenger business. Not until 1844, when the Train Line was founded, did Boston get a Liverpool sailing packet service of any vitality.

As early as 1825 the Boston merchants began to talk of a transatlantic steamship line. The matter had to wait until Samuel Cunard founded his North American Royal Mail Steam Packet Company, in 1839. Greatly to the delight of Bostonians, Mr. Cunard chose their city as his United States terminus. A wharf and docks at East Boston were leased to him rent free; and on June 2, 1840, the pioneer Cunarder *Unicorn*, 700 tons, entered the harbor. Boston had hardly recovered from the banquets given in her honor when the *Britannia* steamed in, bearing Mr. Cunard himself; and a new set of festivities commenced. A fortnightly schedule of side-wheelers was soon established, greatly to the disgust of New York, which had only one transatlantic steam packet to Boston's four. In January, 1844, when Boston Harbor froze out to Fort Independence — an event that comes hardly once a generation — the local merchants, to escape the jeers of New York, had a channel cut for the *Britannia* to get to sea.

The average length of the first thirty passages of Cunard liners to Boston, including the stop at Halifax, was one hour less than fifteen days. Within a decade, the time had been reduced by thirty hours. Rarely a sailing packet would make better time than this on an eastward passage; but for westward passages the *Emerald's* record was never surpassed by a packet-ship, and seldom approached. The average was nearer forty days. A great Train packet-ship in the fifties once took fifty-six days to make Boston against westerly gales, and a New York liner once required sixteen weeks. The sufferings of the Irish immigrants, who came to Boston in these and even less speedy and commodious sailing vessels, were hardly inferior to those of the seventeenth-century Puritans who founded our first settlements.

The maritime enterprise of Massachusetts seemed to crumple up before the problem of steam navigation. On western waters the steamboat became an established institution before the Peace of Ghent; but Yankees, for a generation after, regarded a steamer trip as a reckless form of sport. They felt much safer under sail. The shipwrecks on a lee shore, broachings-to and "all hands lost," of which the interior read with horror, seemed light risks in comparison with bursting boilers, scalding steam, and "burning to the water's edge." Even within my recollection, old ladies would ask for a stateroom on the Bangor boat "as far as possible from the boiler."

Coastwise steam packet-lines were established very slowly. In 1817 a group of Salem men built in Philadelphia the steamboat *Massachusetts*, and attempted to establish a route between Salem and Boston. Although they advertised liberally in the newspapers, offering the public a trip around the bay at a dollar a head, no 'write-up' appeared, or passengers either. The Salem "Gazette" even described a "melancholy occurrence" on the Potomac, a steamboat accident with details "too shocking to relate," at a time when the *Massachusetts* was trying to drum up trade. She was sold to the southward, and wrecked. A New Bedford–Nantucket service was attempted the next year in the *Eagle*, but withdrawn for want of patronage. A tiny steam tug, the *Merrimack*, was placed on the Middlesex Canal in 1818, and several times attained Concord, New Hampshire; but proved a financial failure.

Beyond a daily summer service to Nahant, which began in 1818, Boston had no steamboat facilities until 1824, when a Maine corporation established a line from Boston 'down East.' The New-York-built steamboat *Patent* left Boston every Tuesday for Portland and Bath. There one could transfer to the steamboat *Maine* (a local product of two schooners' hulls, fastened catamaran fashion), for Boothbay, Owl's Head, Camden, Belfast, Sedgwick, Cranberry Isles, Lubec, *and* Eastport. The entire journey consumed five days, spending the nights in harbors along the coast. A direct line to the Penobscot was established in 1833, with the steamboat *Bangor*. Replaced by a larger boat in 1842, and sold to the Turkish government, this 160-foot sidewheeler cheerfully proceeded to Constantinople under her own steam, calling for coal at Nova Scotia, Fayal, Gibraltar, and Malta.

The remaining story of Massachusetts steam navigation before 1860 is one of costly failures in transatlantic enterprises, ambitious projects that came to nothing, and a slow improvement in the down East, Nantucket and Long Island Sound service. Down to the Civil War steam played a very small part in the commerce of Massachusetts.

*
*   *

THE HUB OF THE UNIVERSE

Boston of 1830, already outgrown her original peninsula, was unable to make land fast enough to prevent both commerce and population spilling over into near-by islands and necks. Charlestown was more populous in 1860 than the whole of Boston in 1800; and East Boston, which as Noddle's Island had just twenty-four inhabitants in 1825, passed the fifteen thousand mark within thirty years. East Boston owed its sudden rise to a shipbuilding industry, which in twenty years' time produced the finest sailing ships that the world had ever seen. Owing to lack of timber, which all New England shipyards had drawn from their immediate neighborhood and back-country, Boston had declined as a shipbuilding center. In 1834 the pioneers of East Boston purchased land and erected a sawmill on Grand Island in Niagara River, transporting the timber to Boston by Erie Canal and Albany sailing packet. When Samuel Hall, of the old North River breed of master builders, established a yard at East Boston in 1837, the future of that place was assured.

No sooner had Boston acquired a municipal government than it resumed the process of pulling itself a few yards nearer the sea, by filling in the old Town Cove, whose creeks and docks ran up into the heart of the city. Josiah Quincy, the second mayor, turned out to be as far-sighted and enterprising in municipal affairs as he had been narrow-minded and reactionary in the affairs of the nation. His monument is Quincy Market and the surroundings; completed in 1827 at a cost of over a million dollars. Unlike modern municipal improvements, Quincy Market not only paid for itself, but has returned a handsome income to the city. A stone's throw from the market was a new town wharf, where market boats could land their provisions. Commercial Street was laid out to the northward along the heads of the wharves, filling up many a noisome dock on its way. To the southward, India and Broad Streets made the water-front until Atlantic Avenue cut off another bight of harbor in 1868.

Charles Bulfinch was employed in Washington from 1817 to 1830, and made few designs after his return. The mode of his successors in the public architecture of Boston, Isaiah Rogers, Ammi B. Young, and Alexander Parris, was the neo-classic, with heavy Doric pillars and pediment; their material, smooth Quincy granite, a stone without the mineral constituents to acquire an agreeable patina, but which takes on a certain dingy impressiveness with age. Their masterpiece was the "new Custom House" constructed between 1837 and 1848 at the head of the tongue of water between Central and Long Wharfs. Its classic pediment and monolithic granite pillars — each brought from Quincy by thirty-two yoke of oxen — now mask the foundations of the twentieth-century Custom House Tower.

The center of mercantile and municipal Boston in 1840 was the Old State House, at the head of State Street. Built in 1748 to house the Province government, its walls had once resounded with the eloquence of Otis and the Adamses. After the state government had moved to its Bulfinch front on Beacon Hill, the Old State House became the town, and subsequently the city hall. But there was plenty of room to spare. The small size, and still more the modest government of the Boston of 1840, is brought home to us when we find that this three-story brick building, 110 by 38 feet, housed not only the municipal government, but the post-office and a merchants' club. In the ground-floor room at the Washington Street end, Nathaniel

Greene, with fifteen other deserving Democrats, a messenger and a porter, handled Boston's mail. Overhead was the hall of the Common Council. Opposite, in the old Council Chamber, "the chief magistrate of the city, together with the City Clerk, remain through the day in the discharge of their ordinary duties," and the Board of Aldermen meet on Monday evenings. In the attic, and around the central stairs, were the offices of all other city officials. Under the aldermen's chamber, looking down State Street, was Topliff's News Room, a subscription club and reading-room for Boston merchants Newspapers and periodicals from all parts of the world, a complete register of entrances and clearances in American and foreign ports, and bulletins from foreign correspondents, were kept on file. Samuel Topliff had a system of signals from Long Island in the harbor to his house on Fort Hill, to inform him of arriving vessels, when a swift rowboat that he maintained would put out to obtain the latest foreign news. The Boston newspapers of 1840, lacking an Associated Press to give them such foreign news as seemed wise for the people to know, used Mr. Topliff as a news bureau.

The Boston merchants still continued their eighteenth-century custom of meeting on 'change, at one o'clock every week day, to discuss business and politics before going home to their two or three o'clock dinner. That formidable rite over, they 'took the air' in chaise or sleigh on the Mill Dam, or otherwise amused themselves while clerks carried on business in the counting-rooms. 'Change had been somewhat broken up into cliques by the practice of dispersing to adjoining insurance offices in wet or cold weather. In order to restore a community spirit, a new Merchants' Exchange building was erected on State Street in 1842.

Thither removed the Topliff News Room, and the previous year the municipal government had moved to the Court-House that Bulfinch built in 1810 on the site of the present City Hall. The Old State House was then given over to shops and offices.

During the generation following the war, fashionable Boston covered the open pastures and spacious gardens of Beacon Hill, with blocks of houses in smooth-faced red brick. Their architecture retained enough impress of Bulfinch to be vastly superior to anything that followed, but sacrificed his sense of proportion to a fashion for long, high-studded rooms, and ignored the fine detail that gave half its charm to Federal architecture. Louisburg Square, and the North side of Mount Vernon Street, are the best surviving examples of this style of the early thirties. In the flush days of the early fifties the newly rich turned toward the newer South End, where they surrounded graceful squares and lined broad avenues with brown-stone fronts and high stoops, which they speedily abandoned when the Back Bay was filled in. Western Avenue or the Mill Dam (now Beacon Street) was completed in 1821 across the Back Bay, which sheet of water, after a further cutting up by railroad embankments, became a veritable open cesspool. After prolonged litigation the filling in of the Back Bay ("with tomato cans and hoop skirts," as the ancient jest records) began in 1858.

Many of the leading merchants had remained faithful to the older South End, to be near their counting-rooms and the harbor. Summer Street, with provincial and Federal mansions surrounded by gardens and shaded by great elms, was the favorite residence of retired shipowners. A wall of Chinese porcelain screened the house of John P. Cushing from vulgar gaze; the door, opened by Chinese servants, disclosed a veritable museum of Eastern art. The first shop invaded Summer Street in 1847; Bulfinch's incomparable crescent on Franklin Place was replaced by granite business blocks between 1857 and 1859; and by the Civil War this section was almost wholly given over to business.

Despite the rise of manufacturing, merchants continued to dominate the social life of Boston. In the old directories one finds under the heading of "Merchants, principally ship owners and importers of cargoes of Russia, South America, Calcutta, Canton, European and West India Goods, etc.," most of the leading business men in Boston. Many left fortunes that are still intact; a few left some trace in local history.

Robert Bennet Forbes had the most original brain, and the most attractive personality of any Boston merchant of his generation. His first sea-voyage was made in 1811 as a six-year-old passenger with his mother in the fish-laden topsail schooner *Midas*, to join his father Ralph B. Forbes in France. The whole family, including the baby, John Murray Forbes, afterwards a famous railroad builder, returned in an armed Baltimore clipper in 1813, escaping the British blockading squadron by a running fight. Perhaps it was his short French residence that gave Bennet his frank, impetuous nature, so foreign to his Scots blood and Yankee upbringing.

Although a nephew of the great T. H. Perkins, young Bennet found no short cut to fortune. Shipping before the mast in the *Canton Packet* at the age of thirteen, "with a capital consisting of a Testament, a Bowditch, a quadrant, a chest of sea clothes, and a mother's blessing," he rose to be master at twenty, passed but six months ashore in ten years of China trading, and commanded his own ship at twenty-six.

At twenty-eight he entered the firm of Russell & Co., Canton, and rose to its head in eight years more. In 1840 he became merchant-shipowner in Boston; and engaged in various picturesque and benevolent side activities. An early convert to the screw-propeller and the iron steamer, he would have had Massachusetts lead in steam as in sail; he did introduce auxiliary steamers to the waters of China, and built the first ocean-going twin-screw iron tugboat, which was appropriately named *R. B. Forbes.*

The merchants of Boston were quick to respond whenever disaster came to the toilers of the sea. About 1840 a group of Boston gentlemen sent a cargo of provisions to famine-stricken Madeira, the product of whose vineyards had brought cheer to themselves and gout to their grandfathers. The grateful people returned the relief ship *Nautilus* laden with their choicest wine; and I have happily ascertained that the "Nautilus Madeira" is not yet entirely consumed. In 1841 a disastrous storm at Cape Ann brought charity nearer home. But the Irish famine of 1846–47 brought the greatest charitable 'drive' of this period. Early in 1847 a New England Relief Committee for the Famine in Ireland and Scotland was organized at Boston, with Mayor Quincy as chairman. Through free advertising and local committees, cash and provisions to the value of over $150,000 (of which $115,500 from Massachusetts) were quickly collected in New England, and a few hundred dollars additional came in from Yankees in the West, all forwarded to the wharves free of transportation charges. Congress, at the request of Robert C. Winthrop, lent the sloops-of-war *Jamestown* and *Macedonian.* The former began to load at Boston on St. Patrick's Day. Local Irishmen completed the work in record time, and on March 28 the vessel, laden to the danger point and officered by civilian volunteers under R. B. Forbes, caught a fresh northwest breeze from her wharf. Through northeast gales and with roaring westerlies in that boisterous season on the Western Ocean, Captain Forbes drove the *Jamestown* without mercy, mindful of the starving children of Erin. Fifteen days and three hours out from Boston, he let go both anchors in Cork Harbor. Few sailing packets at any season have made a faster passage. But she had only transported one quarter of New England's contributions. Captain Forbes, refusing flattering invitations to Dublin Castle and London, drove her back to Boston, and hastened to New York to load the *Macedonian*, which the New York relief committee had been unable to fill. Four merchant ships and two steamers were required to take the balance. Had Old England shown the same prompt generosity as New England, there need have been no famine in Ireland.

Once more, Boston's bread cast upon the waters returned after many days; in the stomachs of brawny Irishmen who came to build her railroads, tend her looms, and control her politics. Furthermore, the *Jamestown's* voyage began a regular grain trade between Boston and Great Britain.

Two years after this errand of mercy, Captain Forbes, now aged forty-five, was the hero of a collision at sea between the Cunard side-wheeler *Europa* and the barque *Charles Bartlett* of Plymouth, laden with emigrants. Leaping overboard, he passed the end of a rope around a fat German, and clung to him while both were alternately jerked out of water and plunged under it by the rolling of the ship to which the rope was fast. Then taking bow oar in a lifeboat, he helped pull more people out of water. This was only one of a series of adventures that make his "Personal Reminiscences" one of the best books of its kind.

Captain Forbes was also one of the pioneer yachts-men of New England. Yachting in Massachusetts re-sulted from a new custom of the merchants, a summer residence by the sea. In Colonial and Federalist days, Boston and Salem were so salty themselves that the few who felt the need of a "change of air" took it in-land, at a country seat. Horticulture was the gentle-manly hobby for a shipowner. But as Massachusetts turned inland for profit, she returned seaward for pleas-ure. Thomas Handasyd Perkins set a new fashion when, in 1817, he built a stone cottage just above the Spouting Horn at Nahant.

This rugged peninsula at the north margin of Boston Bay, a miniature, even rockier Marblehead, had re-mained a mere sheep-pasture for lack of a proper har-bor. After the war several Boston families began boarding in the few native houses, and in 1818 crowds of excursionists came by the steamboat *Eagle* to view Swallow Cave, Pulpit Rock, Natural Bridge, and other features that appealed to a romantic age in literature. Samuel A. Eliot erected a worthy example of the Greek revival in 1821; Frederic Tudor, the ice king, built a tasteful stone cottage in 1825, established a remark-able garden, and set out elm-trees.[1] The first Nahant Hotel, also of stone, was built on East Point in 1820, on the site of Senator Lodge's present voting residence; and quickly became the center of fashionable summer life on the New England coast. Other mercantile fam-ilies followed the dean of their order; and by 1860 Nahant exhibited every known atrocity in cottage

[1] Like almost everything else Mr. Tudor did, the setting out of elms was scoffed at — "no tree would grow on Nahant." The Tudor elms now make one of the most handsome avenues of trees in New England.

architecture, and had fairly earned its jocose subtitle of "Cold Roast Boston."

This peaceful capture of Nahant by the merchant princes began a process that has utterly transformed the New England sea-front. Swampscott, for example, was a poor fishing village until 1815, and mainly that for another forty years. 'Farmer' Phillips began taking a few summer boarders the year of peace. In twenty years this business had so expanded [1] that one of our earliest barrack-like summer hotels was erected, on the site of the present Ocean House. In 1842 a merchant of Boston offered four hundred dollars an acre for a farm next the hotel, and the astonished native threw down his rake and ran for a lawyer to get the deed signed before the Bostonian came to his senses! 'Cottages' began to spring up along the picturesque bluffs and beaches; and to-day Swampscott is part summer resort, part bourgeois suburb of Lynn and Boston.

The nucleus of the present Gold Coast from Beverly Cove to Eastern Point began between 1844 and 1846, when four Bostonians of mercantile stock, and a retired Salem shipmaster, purchased the better part of the shore-front of Beverly Farms; and Richard Henry Dana established the first summer estate in Manchester. The native who sold his hundred-acre seashore farm to Charles C. Paine for six thousand dollars (possibly a hundredth part of its value to-day), felt rather badly about the price. "These city men don't know nothing about farming land," he said, and threw in a yoke of white oxen to square the bargain with his conscience! It was not the fault of these newcomers that the North

---

[1] 'Aunt Betsey' Blaney, for room and board in 1830 charged three dollars a week, "which was considered high, as the boarders often waited upon themselves."

Shore eventually became a millionaires' club. They only asked to be let alone in their simple pleasures of boating and fishing, and driving along the twisty lanes of Essex County — weather-rusted houses of the seventeenth century with tiny detached shoe shops, elbowed apple-trees dropping their fruit over stone walls, dark pine woods where witches used to lurk, glimpses of sea and islands and white sails from close-nibbled sheep-commons.

About the same time the picturesque shore-line and excellent shooting at Cohasset attracted thither a few Boston families; and Daniel Webster maintained his magnificent physique by fishing and farming on his Marshfield estate. John M. Forbes acquired a ·foothold at Naushon in 1843, and the whole island fifteen years later.

"What can be more magnificent," wrote this same Forbes at sea in 1830, "than a strong gale (right astern, mind) of a clear winter's day — the ship springing forward under reefed topsails, and nothing to be seen but the white foamy tops of the waves. There is nothing that elevates the spirits so much as this, it is like riding a fiery horse,he goes at his own speed, but he carries you where you guide." Memories of these halcyon days led the Boston merchants to yachting, after their retirement from the sea. Others, like Captain Charles Blake, of the barque *Griffin*, returned to the ocean after acquiring from her bounty the privilege of leisure; trading about the Mediterranean and South Sea for the mere joy of it. Yachting, at best, is a poor imitation; yet even a sail in sheltered waters, if the breeze be brisk, gives something of that mental uplift of which Forbes speaks, and the skipper of the smallest sailboat that boasts a crew is kin to the proudest clipper ship commander.

THE HUB OF THE UNIVERSE

Apart from the two famous yachts owned by George Crowninshield, Jr., and small undecked pleasure boats, Massachusetts yachting begins in 1832 when Benjamin C. Clark, a Boston Mediterranean merchant who passed his summers at Nahant, purchased the pilot schooner *Mermaid*. John P. Cushing, just returned from China, then had built for him the sixty-foot pilot schooner *Sylph* and made his young kinsman Robert Bennet Forbes her sailing master. Her first cruise, with Captains 'Bill' Sturgis and Daniel C. Bacon as guests, was a night run from Boston around the Cape to Wood's Hole, which she made in fourteen hours. Before returning, the *Sylph* won the first recorded American yacht race, from Vineyard Haven to Tarpaulin Cove, against the schooner yacht *Wave*, owned by Commodore John C. Stevens, of Hoboken.

In 1835 R. B. Forbes was elected commodore of the Boat Club, an association of young merchant-shipowners and gentlemen of leisure, which owned a thirty-ton schooner yacht, the *Dream*. Three years later, with Daniel C. Bacon and William H. Bordman, Forbes built another schooner, the *Breeze*, which started her career by racing the *Dream* from Boston to Marblehead for lunch, and then home; the *Breeze* flying an empty champagne bottle in lieu of ensign. The following year came a famous ocean race, from Long Island to Halfway Rock off Marblehead and back, between the New York sloop *Osceola* and Mr. Clark's new thirty-six-foot schooner *Raven*, which won.

Off Nahant, on July 19, 1845, was held the first open yacht race in Massachusetts. A contemporary painting, here reproduced, gives a scene at this pioneer regatta. From left to right the contestants are the

247

Stars and Stripes, a Swampscott fisherman; the sloop *Evergreen*, owned by an aboriginal Johnson of Nahant; Mr. Clark's *Raven*, the schooner *Avon* (on the port tack), owned by Edward Phillips; the *Northern Light;* [1] and the schooner *Quarantine*, owned by the City of Boston. Of these only the *Avon* and *Raven* started in the race, but there were nine other contestants not shown in this picture. Wind was steady, from the S.S.E., the hotel was full of guests, the rocks covered with spectators, and a fisherman's dory race (shown in the foreground) furnished additional sport. The course was triangular, around a stake-boat off the Graves, around Egg Rock, and thence to the starting-line off Nahant. The schooner *Cygnet*, owned by John E. Thayer, a Long Wharf boatman, finished first, but the little *Raven* came in only four minutes later, and won on a time-allowance.

The fame of this regatta, the boats owned by her summer residents, and a huge new hotel, made Nahant the yachting center of Massachusetts Bay until the Civil War; although some very fast yachts, including the *Cygnet*, were kept for hire by the Long Wharf boatmen, who took many a party of jolly fellows for a Sunday cruise down harbor and bay. For many years almost all the yachts were of schooner rig, and differed not from the prevailing type of pilot-boat and clipper fishing schooner; indeed, a pilot-boat was often pur-

---

[1] This schooner yacht (62 feet, 8 inches, by 17 feet by 7 feet, 3 inches, 70 tons), designed by Lewis Winde, a Danish naval architect, settled in Boston, who made a specialty of pilot boats, was built at Boston in 1839 at a cost of $7000, and owned by William P. Winchester, a beef-packer. She was the largest and smartest yacht in Massachusetts waters for many years. Her bends were scraped bright and varnished, she had black topsides with a crimson stripe, and her crew wore red shirts and white trousers. She was lost in the Straits of Magellan in 1850, when on her way to San Francisco.

chased for a yacht, or *vice versa;* and several yachts were sent to Pacific waters to be used as pilot-boats or opium clippers.[1] Light sails and outside ballast were unknown. But in 1854 the centerboard sloop *James Ingersoll Day*, built at Stonington, Connecticut, came around the Cape, beat everything in Massachusetts Bay, and forced the local designers to create a yachting type. Although George Steers, of New York, with his *America* had the start of them, the Boston yacht designers pulled ahead after the Civil War. Corinthian yachting is the only maritime activity, save fishing, in which Massachusetts still retains her preeminence.

Summer vacations and summer yachting were the privilege of a very few, until after 1870. Almost every Boston boy learned to swim, to pull an oar, and to sail a small spritsail-rigged boat. His education was not complete until he had gotten lost in the fog, and spent the night on an island in Boston harbor. But another half-century passed before the income or the taste of bourgeois and mechanic allowed acquisition of summer camp and catboat.

Bourgeois Boston inhabited the West End, the filled-in Mill Pond land and South Cove, and overflowed to South and East Boston. The proletarian quarters were the Broad Street–Fort Hill section, and the North End, east of Hanover Street. Here were the sailors' boarding-houses and dance-halls, and here lived the longshoremen, truckmen, and Irish laborers. Over half were foreign-born; congestion and the infantile

---

[1] The pilot schooner *Fanny* (71 feet by 18 feet, 11 inches, by 7 feet, 2½ inches, 82 tons), designed by William Kelly and built by his brother Daniel at East Boston in 1850, made San Francisco *via* the Straits of Magellan in 108 days from Boston, and served as pilot-boat to the Golden Gate for twenty-six years.

death-rate were becoming a public scandal. For Boston had no city water supply until 1848,[1] nor until then one scrap of plumbing.

In North Square, the heart of the workers' district, Father Taylor set his net for sinners. This remarkable man was born in Virginia in 1793, went to sea at seven, and sailed the globe for ten years. In 1810, still a foremast hand, a vessel brought him into Boston. Strolling along Tremont Street, he heard the bell tolling in the new steeple of Park Street Church, where, to use his own words, he "put in, doffed hat and pennant, scud under bare poles to the corner pew, hove to, and came to anchor." A Methodist preacher completed his conversion. War followed, and Edward T. Taylor experienced privateering and Dartmoor. Returning to Boston, he peddled tinware about the country-side, exhorted sinners in the Old Rock school-house at Saugus, rode the Methodist circuit of eastern Massachusetts, and was called by the Boston Port Society to its seamen's chapel. A new Sailors' Bethel was erected for him on North Square in 1833, and for the next thirty-eight years he walked its pulpit like a quarterdeck.

"I have never heard but one essentially perfect orator," wrote Walt Whitman in his "November Boughs." "During my visits to 'the Hub,' in 1859 and '60 I several times saw and heard Father Taylor. In the spring or autumn, quiet Sunday forenoons, I liked to go down early to the quaint ship-cabin-looking church where the old man minister'd — to enter and leisurely scan the building, the low ceiling, everything strongly timber'd (polish'd and rubb'd apparently), the dark rich colors, the gallery, all in half-light — and smell the aroma of old wood — to watch the auditors, sailors, mates, 'matlows,' officers, singly or in groups, as they came in — their physiognomies, forms, dress, gait, as they walk'd along the aisles —

---

[1] Save a supply piped in hollow pine logs from Jamaica Pond, which reached comparatively few homes.

their postures, seating themselves in the rude, roomy, undoor'd, uncushioned pews and the evident effect upon them of the place, occasion, and atmosphere. . . .

"Father Taylor was a moderate-sized man, indeed almost small (reminded me of old Booth, the great actor, and my favorite of those and preceding days), well advanced in years, but alert, with mild blue or gray eyes, and good presence and voice. Soon as he open'd his mouth I ceased to pay any attention to church or audience or pictures or lights and shades; a far more potent charm entirely sway'd me. In the course of the sermon, (there was no sign of any MS., or reading from notes), some of the parts would be in the highest degree majestic and picturesque. Colloquial in a severe sense, it often lean'd to Biblical and Oriental forms. Especially were all allusions to ships and the ocean and sailors' lives, of unrivall'd power and life-likeness. Sometimes there were passages of fine language and composition, even from the purist's point of view. A few arguments, and of the best, but always brief and simple. . . . In the main, I should say, of any of these discourses, that the old Demosthenean rule and requirement of 'action, action, action,' first in its inward and then (very moderate and restrain'd) its outward sense, was the quality that had leading fulfilment.

"I remember I felt the deepest impression from the old man's prayers, which invariably affected me to tears. Never, on any similar or other occasions, have I heard such impassion'd pleading — such human-harassing reproach (like Hamlet to his mother, in the closet) — such probing to the very depths of that latent conscience and remorse which probably lie somewhere in the background of every life, every soul. For when Father Taylor preach'd or pray'd, the rhetoric and art, the mere words, (which usually play such a big part), seem'd altogether to disappear, and the *live feeling* advanced upon you and seiz'd you with a power before unknown. Everybody felt this marvellous and awful influence. One young sailor, a Rhode Islander (who came every Sunday, and I got acquainted with, and talked to once or twice as we went away), told me, 'that must be the Holy Ghost we read of in The Testament.' . . .

"I repeat, and would dwell upon it (more as suggestion than mere fact) — among all the brilliant lights of bar or stage I have heard in my time . . . I never had anything in the way of vocal utterance to shake me through and through, and become fix'd, with its accompaniments, in my memory, like those prayers and sermons — like Father Taylor's personal electricity and the whole scene there — the prone ship in the gale, and dashing wave and foam for back-

251

ground — in the little old sea-church in Boston, those summer Sundays just before the secession war broke out."

The fame of Father Taylor was more widespread than that of any Massachusetts author or statesman, for it penetrated every part of the world visited by ships and sailors. When he died in 1871, "just as the tide turned, going out with the ebb as an old salt should," Father Taylor was mourned by thousands of humble folk who had never so much as heard of Emerson and Webster.

*

* *

The coming of the Cunarders increased the morale of commercial Boston several hundred per cent. A New York paper admitted that Boston's trade with New Orleans and the Mississippi Valley equaled Manhattan's. Boston is "gaining rapidly on her great rival, New York," crows Hayward's Gazeteer in 1846. "In arrivals from foreign ports, New York exceeded Boston in 1839, 606 vessels . . . in 1844, only 34 vessels." So many of Boston's foreign entries were Nova Scotia schooners that the tonnage figures tell a different story; but her waterfront activity in the harbor, with close to three thousand foreign and six thousand coastwise entries a year, was prodigious. If Boston really expected to catch up with New York commerce, she was destined to disappointment; not even Yankee ingenuity could overcome the Hudson and the Erie. But in 1845 the most prosperous decade in the maritime history of Massachusetts was just beginning.

CHAPTER XVI

SHIPS AND SEAMEN IN SOUTHERN SEAS

1820–1848

LITTLE change can be observed in the routes or the methods of Massachusetts commerce between 1815 and 1850. Maritime commerce is still a tale of the West Indies and South America, of Mediterranean and Baltic, of East Indies and China and South Seas, and of small coasters that assembled and distributed cargoes. Certain routes, like the New Orleans and the South American, rise greatly in importance; others, like the Northwest fur trade, decline; but no new ones were established, for the excellent reason that our pioneer shipmasters of the seventeen-nineties had traced every ocean-way that could be pursued with profit, until new folk-migrations made new markets in California, Australia, and South Africa.

In 1815 the old crew merely picked up the lines which war had loosed, and continued hauling to the old chanties. The bulk of our overseas trading was done by merchant-shipowners as before, men who owned fleets of vessels both large and small, traded with many countries on their own account, chartered their vessels or took freight for others when opportunity offered, distributed their cargoes by auction sales on the wharf or through their own wholesale stores in Boston. Commerce was still dominated by the men who had learned its secrets as captains and super-cargoes before the war.[1]

[1] Of the twelve officers of the new Boston Chamber of Commerce founded in 1836, I recognize the names of all but three as prominent merchants and shipowners of the Federalist period.

253

Besides the establishment of packet-lines, which we have already noted, one noteworthy change took place in maritime technique between 1815 and 1850 — an improvement in the design, rig, and handling of vessels. A shipmaster, retired since 1819, who took passage fifteen years later on a recent Boston-built ship, was astonished at her ability to carry sail, to beat to windward, and to "tack in a pint o' water." The Medford builders, in particular, had quietly evolved a new type of about 450 tons burthen which, handled by eighteen officers and men, would carry half as much freight as a British East-Indiaman of 1500 tons with a crew of 125, and sail half again as fast. Such a ship cost, in 1829, seventy dollars a ton to build or thirty dollars to charter for a China voyage; she could earn forty dollars a ton freight out and home and the insurance rate was four per cent for the round passage, one per cent less than was charged Englishmen. More carrying capacity, and greater speed than older vessels of the same burthen, were obtained by greater length and depth in proportion to breadth, and a cleaner run. The bows are still bluff, but have sweeter water-lines than the older vessels. Longfellow has described the type in his "Building of the Ship":

> Broad in the beam, but sloping aft
> With graceful curve and slow degrees,
> That she might be docile to the helm,
> And that the currents of parted seas,
> Closing behind, with mighty force,
> Might aid and not impede her course.

Iron was superseding rope for permanent lashings such as trusses, parrels, and the gammoning of bowsprits. Sails were now made of Lowell cotton duck, instead of Russia linen or baggy, porous hemp; and there were many more of them. Vessels of this period, in fact, carried a loftier rig in proportion to their length than the clipper ships. Skysails appear for the first time in our merchant fleet, and royal studdingsails — so small that the seamen called them the 'tub o' dusters.' Russell Sturgis describes sailing from Manila to Gaspar Passage in 1844, with eleven sails set on the mainmast alone. Quarter-galleries, quick-work and gingerbread-work alike disappeared; leaving nothing of traditional adornment but a figure-head or billet-head, and a small scroll or shield on the transom. The clean, stripped, youthful-looking hulls, in marked contrast to the painted ladies of Federalist days, were clothed in dead black, relieved only by a bright waist, or white strip checquered by black ports.

In the shipbuilding boom that began about 1831, Maine overtook her parent Massachusetts. The great shipyards of the Sewalls and others on the Kennebec, St. George, and Penobscot rivers became serious competitors of the Mystic and Merrimac; and small coasting vessels were constructed all along the spruce-rimmed shore. Skeleton schooners and brigs crowded the shingle beaches at the head of rocky coves; then noisy with the cheerful clatter of shipbuilding, now silent from one year's end to another, save for scream of tern, and *quork* of blue heron.

Very different types of vessels were needed for different routes. For the cotton-carrying trade the old-fashioned converging topsides were preferred, to increase stability with so light a cargo. But most ship-owners wanted vessels-of-all-work, as it were, which could be sent to any part of the world where chances were good and freights high. The finest type of the period was the Medford- or Merrimac-built East-Indiaman; seldom over five hundred tons burthen, and usually smaller; for the size of vessels was just begin-

255

ning to increase. The *Alert*, which seemed so enormous to Dana after his California voyage in the brig *Pilgrim*, was but 113 feet long and 398 tons burthen. The *Rajah*, built by J. Stetson at Medford in 1836, 530 tons, 140 feet long, and 30 feet beam, is cited as "a fair specimen of our best freighting vessels." [1] They were not sharp ships, or clipper ships, or one-quarter the size of the most famous clippers; but they were the fastest and most economical ocean carriers of their generation. With their burly bows, lofty rig, flush decks, and bright waist or painted ports, these old Boston East-Indiamen have a certain charm that the clippers lack. Happy they, born in time to have seen such a ship rolling down from St. Helena, lee and weather studdingsails set alow and aloft, tanned and bearded sailors on her decks and Anjer monkeys chattering in her rigging, wafting an aroma of the Far East into the chilly waters of Massachusetts Bay.

From 1815 to 1840 Yankee seamen still existed. A strong minority, in some cases a majority, of foreigners, especially Johnny Bulls and Scandinavians, could be found in the forecastle of almost every Massachusetts vessel. But the greater part of most crews were native Yankee. 'Crimping' had not yet become the usual method of shipping a crew. Wages were lower

---

[1] In the Newburyport yards, the *Volant* of 457 tons, launched in 1810, held the record for size until 1836, when John Currier, Jr., built the *Columbus*, 594 tons, for the Black Ball Line. The next record-breakers in size were the *Flavio*, 698 (1839), *St. George*, 845 (1843), and *Castillian*, 1000 (1850). In the Medford yards, no vessel over 435 tons was built between 1810 and 1832. The first over 500 tons came in 1834, over 600 in 1837, over 800 in 1839, and the thousand-ton mark was touched in 1849. The yards of Bath, Maine, first passed the 500-ton mark in 1836. In 1841 the Sewalls built the *Rappahannock*, 1133 tons, for the cotton trade. She was too large to be profitable, and it is said that freight dropped a quarter of a cent a pound whenever she appeared at New Orleans. Not until 1852 did the Bath yards build another vessel above 1000 tons.

than in Federalist days — eight dollars a month for boys, ten for ordinary and twelve for able seamen on long voyages — but good men were still attracted by the chance to rise, for vessels were small, and the proportion of officers to men about one to four or five. It was not uncommon for youngsters of the best families to ship before the mast, although these ship's cousins, as the regular seamen called them, generally bunked in steerage or 'tween-decks, and played the gentleman ashore. "Sailors are the best dressed of mankind," wrote Emerson in 37° 4′ North, 36° 11′ West. They still wore a distinctive costume; shiny black tarpaulin hat, red-checked shirt, blue bell-mouthed dungaree trousers, navy-blue pea-jacket or watch-coat off the Horn; and for shore leave, a fathom of black ribbon for the hat, black silk kerchief in a neat sailor's knot around the neck, white ducks and black pumps.

The standard of seamanship was never higher. No man could be rated an able seaman until he became an expert in the beautiful splicing, seizing, parceling, graffing, pointing, worming, and serving which was included in the old-time art of rigging. Even an ordinary seaman was expected, "to hand, reef and steer, . . . to be able to reeve all the studdingsail gear, and set a topgallant or royal studdingsail out of the top; to loose and furl a royal, and a small topgallant-sail or flying jib; and perhaps, also to send down or cross a royal yard." Constant, hard work was the rule. No 'sogering' was allowed on Yankee vessels, and the treatment of the men was sometimes unnecessarily harsh, as Dana relates. Medicine chests were carried, and many a stern master nursed a sick seaman back to health in the cabin. But how these deep-sea sailormen must have laughed at the unconscious humor of Dr. Lowe's "Sailor's Guide to Health" which accom-

257

panied the medicine chests! Among the rules in this omniscient manual were, "Use tobacco sparingly if at all"; "Eat freely of vegetables, especially on long voyages"; "Observe regular hours for sleep"; and "Select an anchorage to the windward of the land."

It was no laughing matter, however, for a sick seaman who fell under the care of a captain's wife, so conscientious as Mrs. William Cleveland, of the Salem ship *Zephyr*. This good lady relates in her journal for 1829, how, "intending to be on the safe and cautious side," while in the fever-infested waters of Timor, she gave a chilly sailor "a powerful dose of Calomel and Jalap which was afterward followed by a dose of castor oil and numerous injections, blisters upon the calf of both legs after soaking them well in hot water, a blister on the breast, throat rubbed with Cinnamon, &c. He complained of no pain excepting the headache . . . soon after, delirium came on, which continued but a short time when he appeared to fall into a gentle quiet sleep . . ." — and passed away.

This voyage of the *Zephyr* is the earliest instance that has come to my notice of a Massachusetts shipmaster taking his wife to sea. The practice never became general until after the Civil War, but on short voyages was not uncommon in the forties. Captain Caleb Sprague, of Barnstable, master of the ship *North Bend*, writes from Bordeaux in 1844, "There is 9 American Vessels here and 5 of the Capts. have their Wifes. . . . we have had more invitations to dine than we have wish'd as the dinners in this Country are very Lengthy say from 3 to 4 houres before you rise from the Table and than not dry for Wine etc." No wonder Mrs. Sprague acquired a nautical turn of speech, remarking that an ill-fitting suit of clothes on her small boy "set like a shirt on a marlin-spike."

As for eating and drinking, the age of rum was passing, and the age of canned goods not arrived. Water, hard-tack, molasses, and 'salt horse' were the standbys. Colored sea-cooks compounded these maritime staples into the questionable amalgams which Rufus Choate described in one of his glowing periods as the "nutritious hash, succulent lob-scouse, and palatable dandy-funk." At Anjer, where hogs, chickens, and fresh vegetables were incredibly cheap, shipmasters laid in a store of them; but before long sarcastic grunts and crows informed the quarterdeck that Jack wanted his salt junk again. As one old shell-back asserted: "Yer may talk of yer flummadiddlers and fiddlepaddles, but when it comes down to gen-u-ine grub, there ain't nothing like good old salt hoss that yer kin eat afore yer turns in and feel it all night a-laying in yer stummick and a-nourishin' of yer."

Seafaring, at best, was a rough, dangerous calling, sometimes rendered unbearable by the brutality of master or mate. The humanitarian movement of the eighteen-thirties made a few feeble attempts to protect Jack from injustice and extortion. A federal statute of 1835 prescribed severe punishment for an officer who "from malice, hatred or revenge" shall "beat, wound or imprison" a member of his crew, or inflict "any cruel or unusual punishment." An act of 1840 gave a United States consul the power to discharge, with three months' advance pay, a seaman of whose cruel treatment he was convinced. It would seem, however, that those laws remained a dead letter, and that the shipmaster's despotism, benevolent or otherwise, remained unimpaired. Unscrupulous lawyers, inducing disgruntled seamen to bring action on flimsy grounds, so discredited the value of Jack's testimony that juries would seldom convict on it. And as

United States consuls in those days received no salary, but depended for their livelihood on commission business, they seldom had the courage to affront owners or officers.

Nevertheless, a foremast hand on a Yankee East-Indiaman was the best paid, best fed, and most competent sailor in the world, regarded by coasters, fishermen, whalers, and man-o'-war's-men, as the top-dog of his profession. And the officers must no more be judged by the brutality of Captain Thompson than other professions by their black sheep. A Yankee ship-master, in 1840, was the world's standard in ability and in conduct. The Massachusetts merchant marine was commanded for the most part by men of high character and education; navigators who could work lunars as well as Bowditch himself, and who inherited all the practical seamanship of the old school; "merchant-captains" who owned part of their vessel, and had full responsibility in trading. Most of the famous clipper-ship commanders had their training during the thirties and forties, which we may fairly call the golden age of the American merchant marine.

*

* *

The old Northwest fur trade was resumed in 1815 by several Boston firms which had long been engaged in it. Captain 'Bill' Sturgis, now head of Bryant & Sturgis, and Josiah Marshall, a countryman from Billerica who had built up an importing business at Boston during the Federalist period, were now the most active Nor'westmen. The letters of these firms show little change in method, but a decline in profits. Competitors were many; the Hudson's Bay Company, the Northwest Fur Company, American fur-traders who operated from St. Louis, and the Russians, who threatened to monopolize all. In consequence, the sea-otter became too scarce and high to continue an important medium for China. Between 1821 and 1830 the vessels annually engaged in the Northwest fur trade declined from about thirteen to two. For some years longer William H. Bordman, Jr., and Perkins & Co. found it profitable to carry supplies to Sitka and the Hudson Bay posts. But by 1837 the old Northwest fur trade, Boston's high-school of commerce for forty years, was a thing of the past.[1]

When the fur-traders departed, the settlers began to arrive. Hall J. Kelley, an energetic and erratic Boston schoolmaster, founded in 1829 an Oregon Colonization Society, which was supported by Edward Everett and other prominent men. His plans for peopling the banks of the Columbia with picked New Englanders came to naught, but his activities turned the minds of restless Yankees to that region. One of his associates, a Cambridge ice-man named Nathaniel J. Wyeth, led overland in 1834 the first group of permanent settlers to the Oregon country.

In the meantime another outpost of Massachusetts had been founded, at Honolulu. In 1819 a band of Congregational missionaries and three native Hawaiians, "formed into a Church of Christ" at Park Street, Boston, took passage around the Horn on the brig *Thaddeus*, to convert the heathen. On April 4, 1820, one hundred and sixty-three days out of Boston, this Hawaiian *Mayflower* anchored abreast the village of Kailua, where the king and queen, with hundreds

[1] In 1831 Captain Dominis, of Josiah Marshall's brig *Owhyhee*, tried the experiment of bringing pickled Columbia River salmon to Boston. It sold for fourteen dollars a barrel, but the Treasury Department made Marshall pay duty on it, as if purchased outside the United States, and the venture was not repeated.

of their subjects, were playing in the surf. Later in the day the royal family was entertained at dinner on the brig's quarterdeck. King Liholiho, dressed in a feather wreath, a string of beads, and a loincloth, was introduced to the missionaries' wives, while George Tamoree, a graceless native member of the party, furnished music for the meal on an orthodox bass viol.

The Boston missionaries arrived in the nick of time, partially to offset the demoralization introduced by Boston traders and Nantucket whalers. The latter were just beginning to use the Islands as a base; the traders, as we have seen, had been coming for a generation past. It so happened that the panic of 1819, making it difficult to procure specie for China, coincided with a new reign in the Sandwich Islands, which took the lid off the sandalwood traffic. Kamehameha I had conserved this important natural resource, so much in demand at Canton. But Liholiho, a weak-minded and dissolute prince, cheerfully stripped his royal domain in order to gratify tastes which the Boston traders stimulated. They sold him on credit rum and brandy, gin and champagne, carriages and harnesses, clothes and furniture, boats and vessels; until he had tonnage and liquor enough for an old-time yacht club cruise.

In 1820 Josiah Marshall sent out from Boston two small brigs, which were exchanged for sandalwood at Honolulu. Bryant & Sturgis dispatched under the command of Captain John Suter, the veteran Nor'-westman, a veritable fleet consisting of the ships *Tartar* and *Mentor*, brigs *Lascar*, *Becket*, and *Cleopatra's Barge*. The latter was a famous vessel. Built at Salem in 1816 for George Crowninshield, Jr., a young gentleman of leisure, she had taken him on a transatlantic yachting cruise. Sold for a song after his death, she made a trading voyage to Brazil, and was then purchased by Bryant & Sturgis. The Hawaiian monarch gave in exchange for her an amount of sandalwood worth fifty to ninety thousand dollars, and made her his royal yacht.[1] Her outward cargo, typical of the trade, is listed on the annexed bill of health. Possibly its rhythmic phrasing is accidental. But General Henry A. S. Dearborn, who as collector of the port of Boston signed this document, was something of a *littérateur*. Did the romantic name and history of the *Cleopatra's Barge* inspire him to premature effort in free verse?

The *Barge* was as long as the ship *Columbia*, but some of the schooners and brigs that our Pacific traders sent around the Horn to Hawaii were even smaller than Captain Ingraham's brig *Hope* or John Boit's sloop *Union*. James Hunnewell, of Charlestown, who established a famous mercantile firm at Honolulu, brought out in 1826 a crank, leaky little schooner called the *Missionary Packet*, only fifty-four feet long, thirteen feet beam, six feet depth, and thirty-nine tons burthen. His passage of the Horn almost ended his career, and the single voyage took nine months. While resting at Honolulu after his hard experience, Hunnewell was pulled out of bed by a party of rollicking whalemen, and induced to treat the crowd from his cargo of rum. Disliking the quality of the liquor, they forced the owner to sample it himself before letting him go!

This genial traffic continued about ten years, when sandalwood became a drug in the Canton market, and all but extinct on the Islands. In the meantime New

[1] A sketch made by Charles S. Stewart, one of the missionaries, in 1823, shows the *Cleopatra's Barge* under Hawaiian colors at Lahaina anchorage, island of Maui. Originally rigged as a brigantine or hermaphrodite brig, she was altered to a brig when she became a merchant vessel.

Bedford and Nantucket whalers were flocking to Hawaii, to 'recruit,' as they called it, with fresh provisions and Kanakas. As many as sixty put in at Honolulu in 1822, and in 1844 the total arrivals of whaling craft surpassed four hundred. Their presence greatly increased the difficulties of the missionaries, but proved a godsend to the merchantmen whose holds they lined with oil and whalebone, obtained in Arctic and Japanese whaling grounds. At the same time the native demand for American manufactures was increasing. Hawaii by 1830 had become the commercial Gibraltar of the Pacific; the basis of a trade, by Massachusetts merchants there established, with California, Canton, Kamchatka, and the smaller South Sea islands. Honolulu, with whalemen and merchant sailors rolling through its streets, shops filled with Lowell shirtings, New England rum and Yankee notions, orthodox missionaries living in frame houses brought around the Horn, and a neo-classic meeting-house built out of coral blocks, was becoming as Yankee as New Bedford. "Could I have forgotten the circumstances of my visit," wrote a visiting mariner in 1833, "I should have fancied myself in New England." [1] Even the first constitution of the Kingdom of Hawaii, issued by Kamehameha III under missionary influence, had a flavor of the old Massachusetts theocracy: "No law shall be enacted which is at variance with the word of the Lord Jehovah."

The Boston firms interested in Hawaii extended their operations to other South Pacific islands, violating the old demarcation line at the expense of Salem.

[1] Francis Warriner, *Cruise of the U.S. Frigate Potomac* (1835), 224. Daniel Webster about 1840 tried a case at Barnstable, Cape Cod, that involved the nature of the entrance to the "harbor of Owhyhee." It was unnecessary to call in experts, as seven members of the jury were intimately acquainted with said harbor.

Josiah Marshall's brig *Inore*, Eliah Grimes master,
even went to the Marquesas in search of edible birds'
nests, but without success. A typical South Sea voyage
was that of James Hunnewell's ship *Tsar*, Sam Kennedy master, a new vessel built for the Russian trade,
and purchased from J. William Ropes for $28,000.
Although of 470 tons burthen, the *Tsar* required no
more men to handle her than a Nor'westman of one-
quarter her size in the eighteenth century; for the
South Sea was becoming safer than the Caribbean.
Clearing from Boston in the spring of 1848, the *Tsar*
stopped four days at Rio Janeiro, rounded the Horn,
and let the trade-winds bring her to the enchanting
island of Tahiti. For six weeks she rode at anchor
in the landlocked harbor of Papeete (white crescent
beach, border of palms, orange and banana trees, half
concealing white cottages and thatched huts; back-
drop of verdure-clad mountains, and slumbrous pour
of surf on barrier reefs). Goods were sold to the
amount of $23,712.20, including codfish, lumber, rice,
Lowell and Amoskeag cottons, German glass, iron
safes, needles and thread, drugs and gravestones.
Some of the knobs dropped off the safes when swung
out of the hold; one of the packages marked "Tartar
Emetic" contained calomel; and one of the gravestones, intended apparently for the Salem market, was
already inscribed, "Sacred to the Memory of Maria
Peabody." Otherwise everything was in good order.

After selling all the market would take, Captain
Kennedy unloaded a large separate consignment, with
which Edward L. Gray, Jr., who sailed on the *Tsar*
with his wife and sister, opened an agency at Papeete.
Thence the ship proceeded to Honolulu, and discharged
the rest of her cargo, including Merrimack Prints,
Hamilton Ticking, Denims, fancy plaid linings, blan-

kets, salt provisions, groceries and umbrellas, shoes and saddlery, and — *palm-leaf hats.* Yankee merchants would carry coals to Newcastle, if Newcastle wanted them! Captain Kennedy had the owners' permission to proceed from the Islands on "any lawful trade to any part of the world at peace with our nation," according to his judgment; or even to sell the ship. But the whalemen at Honolulu offered him a return cargo of oil and bone, which with Hawaiian goat-skins and bullock hides, and some of the first gold-dust extracted from the California washings, gave him a valuable return freight.

When the Northwest fur trade died out, its place was taken by the hide traffic with California. The Coast from Cape Mendocino to Cape San Lucas had long been familiar to contraband fur-traders from Massachusetts, when, in 1822, California's adhesion to the Mexican Empire threw open her ports to legitimate commerce. Before the year elapsed, William Alden Gale, of Boston (*Cuatro Ojos* the Californians called him by reason of his spectacles), induced Bryant & Sturgis to send their *Sachem* to the Coast with a cargo of notions to exchange for hides. From that time to the Mexican War the Californians obtained most of their merchandise from Boston 'hide-droghers,' as these Pacific Coast traders were called; for their return cargoes took the bulk of California's hides into New England shoe shops. In addition to this direct trade from Boston the sea-otter business continued into the thirties; New Bedford whalers visited the Coast for fresh beef, doing a little smuggling on the side; Boston firms at Honolulu smuggled in merchandise by swift brigs, using Santa Catalina Island as a base; and the China merchants sent over Canton goods direct. R. B. Forbes, when visiting the Mission Dolores at

266

San Francisco in 1870, recognized among its 'old masters' some products of Hog Lane, Canton, which he had sold the padres thirty-five years before.

Secularization of the missions was regretted by the Yankee traders, from its unsettling effect on business. Protestants were not permitted to remain in Mexican California, but many Yankees of Puritan stock "left their consciences at Cape Horn," joined Mother Church, spoke Spanish with a down-east twang, married Californian heiresses, and absorbed the trade of the country. Dana found Massachusetts men established all along the Coast, from a one-eyed Fall River whaleman tending bar in a San Diego *pulperia*, to Thomas O. Larkin, the merchant prince of Monterey.

In the two years (1834–36) that Dana spent before the mast in Bryant & Sturgis's vessels, the California trade was at its height. All cargoes had to be entered at the Monterey custom house, Mexican duties were from eighty to one hundred per cent, and the regulations many. But the Mexican officials, knowing California's dependence on the Boston traders, let them off with a reasonable lump sum per cargo. The ships brought "everything that can be imagined, from Chinese fireworks to English cart-wheels," including even lumber (which the Californians were too lazy to cut for themselves), and shoes made at Lynn out of California hides. Part of the cargo was disposed of on shipboard, the cabin being fitted up as a variety store, to which dark-eyed señoras were conveyed in ship's boats. What they did not buy was placed in charge of a resident agent, who peddled it out at enormous profits (twenty dollars for a three-dollar piece of Lowell print-cloth) to the rancheros, against future deliveries of tallow at six cents a pound, and hides ('California bank-notes') at one to two dollars apiece, worth more than double in Boston. No contract was signed, for a Californian's word was his bond; but the agents employed *cuerreros*, or hide-brokers, to attend the *matanzas* (slaughters), receive the hides, and convey them in bullock-carts to an *embarcadero* on the coast. The Boston hide-droghers collected and carried them to San Diego. There each firm maintained salt-vats, where seamen and Kanakas cured the hides, and stored them until a shipload was accumulated. "Since the time when Queen Dido came the hide game over the natives at Carthage," wrote an irreverent grandson of Paul Revere, "it is probable that there has been no parallel to the hide-and-go-seek game between Boston and California."

Clean, slender ships anchored with slip-cable three miles offshore, gently swaying in the long Pacific swell, sails stopped with rope-yarns to break out and put to sea in a southeaster. No sound to break the eternal roar and roll of surf on endless beach, save tinny bells jangling out vespers from a white mission tower. Sailors waist-high in boiling foam, 'droghing' hides on aching head from beach to longboat, or hurling them down cliff at San Juan Capistrano. Sleepy Santa Barbara coming to life at the wedding of Doña Anita de la Guerra de Noriego y Corillo to plain Alfred Robinson, Bryant & Sturgis's agent. "Splendid, idle forties" for the Californians; not so idle for the Yankee seamen whose labor made cent per cent for owners, and fat primage for officers. Few survived to get into Bancroft's register of California pioneers. Dana's book is their only monument — who would wish a better?

*
* *

It was the very low price of California hides that made it worth while to send vessels for two years' voyages around the Horn in search of them. South America was the great source of supply for Massachusetts tanpits and shoe shops. In 1843, out of a total of 311,000 hides imported at Boston alone (and Salem took many thousand in addition), over 100,000 came from Buenos Aires and Montevideo, over 46,000 from Chile, 48,000 from New Orleans, and only 33,000 from California.

Many years before 1815, during the first struggles of the South American patriots, Yankee vessels flocked to their ports; and Massachusetts commission houses preceded American consuls in several South American cities.[1] Let historians seeking economic origins of the Monroe Doctrine look to the Northwest fur trade and to this early intercourse with South America!

The Lowell power looms at Waltham were making sheetings for the South America trade before 1824, and by 1850 that continent was taking over three-quarters of the total export of 'domestics' from Boston. The lumber trade to the River Plate increased, and old vessels on the point of falling to pieces were filled with Maine pine boards and sent to Buenos Aires to be sold for firewood. There was a sale for almost anything in South America, provided it could compete with British goods. In return, there was an excellent market in Boston, and all North American cities, for River Plate wool, hair, hides, sheepskins, and tallow, until the protective tariff system was applied to favor cattle ranches in the United States. The principal im-

[1] One of them, Richard Alsop, of the firm of Alsop, Wetmore & Cryder, at Valparaiso, with a branch at Lima, was making $100,000 a year by 1827. Others were Samuel Pomeroy at Arica, William Wheelwright at Guayaquil and other ports, the Thayers of Lancaster in Chile, Joseph W. Clapp at Montevideo, and Loring Brothers at Valparaiso.

porting and exporting firm at Buenos Aires was Samuel B. Hale & Co., whose founder, of a Boston mercantile family, first visited the River Plate in 1830 as super-cargo on a Boston ship. The firm at one time owned forty-six sailing vessels, and in addition Mr. Hale became a director of the first railway in the Argentine Republic.

Along the Central American coast small brigs and schooners peddled notions, bringing home cochineal, goatskins, and tropical woods. Pirates were a menace in the Caribbean as late as 1840. The brig *Mexican* of Salem was plundered of her specie in 1832, and only an opportune gale prevented the pirate crew from executing their captain's order — "Dead cats don't mew." Five of them were hanged in Boston two years later.

Rio de Janeiro was a favorite port of call for Yankee traders. "I shall never forget," wrote Osborne Howes, "the beautiful afternoon that we sailed into that magnificent harbor." It was November 25, 1833, and he was master of the little barque *Flora* of Boston, with flour and lumber to exchange for sugar.

We passed the fort shortly before sunset, were hailed and directed to proceed to the anchoring grounds some two miles distant, and were there boarded by the health officer. When the business with him was finished I went on deck. The land breeze had set in, bringing with it the fragrance of the orange-trees. The beautiful little islands rose abruptly from the water, on the tops of many of them were churches, the bells of which were ringing. West of us was a deep bay, some fifteen or twenty miles in extent, at the head of which were the Organ Mountains, with their peaks from five thousand to six thousand feet in height. Near us rose the Sugar Loaf, one thousand feet or more above the sea, and not far distant, the beautiful Corcovado Mountain. Small boats were passing across the bay, urged by sail or oar, and the negroes, as they pulled at the latter, were singing gayly. The lights of the city, some two miles distant, gleamed over the water, and these, brought out by the high moun-

tainous lands a little behind them, rendered the outlook most enchanting. The moon was shining brightly, and I remained on the
deck till midnight, enjoying the beauty of the scene.

A considerable coffee trade was built up with Brazil;
in 1843 Boston imported thence over four million
pounds, one-quarter of her total imports of the fragrant bean; and a million and a quarter more from
Puerto Cabello. A million more came from Cuba, and
eight and one half millions from Hayti. In this, as
in most branches of South American trade, Boston
was surpassed by other Atlantic ports of the United
States. but at Valparaiso the enterprise of Augustus
Hemenway gave Boston the bulk of North American commerce. This self-made merchant approached
South America by way of the Maine coast and the
West Indies. He owned a township in Washington
County, Maine, where pine was cut on his own land,
sawed into lumber at his own sawmill in Machias,
and carried to Cuba (where he owned a sugar plantation) or Valparaiso on his own ships, which returned
from the west coast laden with copper and nitrate of
soda.

Massachusetts merchants found South America a
good market for India shawls and China silk, which
suggested a direct trade from Canton in Boston vessels. R. B. Forbes, at twenty-one given command of
his uncle Perkins's brig *Nile*, disposed of a Canton
cargo at various ports from Bodega Bay to Buenos
Aires, where John M. Forbes, another uncle, was
chargé d'affaires.

As a feeder to New England's leading industry, as
an outlet for her products, and as a carrying trade,
this intercourse with South America became one of the
most important branches of Massachusetts commerce;
and it is one of the few branches that still continues

in sailing vessels. It was very similar to, and largely replaced the West-India trade of colonial days; with the important difference that it fed looms and shoe factories instead of slave coffles and distilleries.

CHAPTER XVII

CHINA AND THE EAST INDIES

1820–1850

RETURNING around the Horn, we find that the China trade until 1840 was carried on by the same unique methods and the same shrewd traders as before the war. Ships of all nations still anchored at Whampoa, and lightered their cargoes up-river to Jackass Point. Boston merchants of the old Nor'wester families maintained luxurious bachelor quarters in the Canton factories, and a summer residence at Macao. The only new element was the missionaries, among whom the Reverend Peter Parker, M.D., of Framingham, Massachusetts, deserves a passing mention for his pioneer work in founding native hospitals at Canton and Macao. There was little variation from decade to decade in the total volume of the American China trade, but a great change took place, even before 1840, in its character, and its relative importance for Massachusetts commerce.

Among the "flowery-flag devils," as the Chinese called our compatriots, the Perkins–Sturgis–Forbes connection remained all-powerful; for China trading required great experience in details, and sound financial backing. 'Ku-shing' (John P. Cushing), their Canton agent, with only two clerks to his establishment, did a business of millions a year, and returned a wealthy man in 1830 to his Summer Street mansion and his Belmont estate, attended by a retinue of Chinese servants. Perkins & Co., James P. Sturgis & Co., Russell, Sturgis & Co., and Russell & Sturgis of

273

Manila were finally consolidated into the firm of Russell & Co. of Canton, which had been founded by Samuel Russell, of Middletown, Connecticut, about 1818. Joseph Peabody, of Salem, as we have seen, maintained a foothold at Canton until 1840. Augustine Heard, at one time a partner of Russell & Co., established a separate house which remained in the hands of his nephews until well after the Civil War. Small firms were founded from time to time; but these "needy adventurers" and "desperadoes," as Captain Bill Sturgis called them, did not last long.

Russell & Co. did more business at Canton than any other American house. No small measure of this success was due to the friendship of Houqua, the Chinese hong merchant; a legacy of John P. Cushing. Houqua, as generous as he was wealthy, extended unlimited credit facilities to his Boston friends during the worst financial panics. He shipped his own teas to Europe and America on the Russell ships, and on one occasion sent John M. Forbes half a million dollars to invest in New England factory stock. In England the relations of the Boston China merchants with Baring Brothers, who had financed their early ventures to the Northwest Coast, became so intimate that Joshua Bates (who married a Sturgis) and Russell Sturgis (a great-nephew of T. H. Perkins) were successively admitted partners in that great merchant-banking house.

After 1815 the character of American imports from China gradually changed. Canton willow-ware, after a brief recovery, was crowded out of the Boston market by Staffordshire, Royal Worcester, and French porcelain. European imitations killed the nankeens. Crapes and silks declined with changes in fashion, and by 1840 teas made up over eighty per cent of American imports from China.

The greater part of this, even when shipped by Boston firms in Boston vessels, was sent into New York. Out of ninety-one vessels entering New York from Canton and Manila between 1839 and 1842, thirty-nine belonged in Massachusetts; and the entries from China at Boston and Salem averaged but five or six annually.

A one per cent state tax on auction sales, the customary method for disposing of China products, has been blamed for this exodus to Manhattan. This tax resulted from a temporary alliance in 1824 between retail grocers and the farmer vote. The former, for some obscure reason, wished to kill the auction system. The latter were looking for a new source of revenue rather than raise the state property tax from $75,000 to $100,000.

It was unwise to remove Boston's advantage (for New York already had an auction tax) at a period when the Erie Canal was pulling trade to Manhattan. But it is doubtful whether the tax drove any one from Boston. Some of her tea ships were already being sent to New York in 1824, and most of them continued thither when the tax was reduced one-quarter in 1849, and abolished in 1852. East-Indian, Russian, and Mediterranean imports continued to be sold principally in Boston, although disposed of by auction, and subject to the same duty. Both Boston and Salem maintained their early lead in the Manila trade, which was closely connected with the China trade, and carried on by the same firms. Four and a quarter million pounds of Philippine Islands sugar, and great quantities of Manila hemp and indigo, were landed at Boston in 1843. Similar commodities were imported from Batavia, where a Bostonian was the principal American merchant in 1850, and near which Boston interests acquired a large sugar plantation. Massachusetts also retained a considerable though irregular share of the Java coffee trade. For obvious geographical reasons New York, after the opening of the Erie Canal, was a better market for teas than Boston, so that when one China merchant began sending his ships there, the rest followed in self-defense. The same movement took place, twenty years later, in the wholesale cottons trade. Other shipping merchants and wholesalers who did not enjoy the social preëminence of the China merchants might have followed their example; after the Civil War most of them did. Until then they remained loyal to Boston. The fate of Salem warned Bostonians to retain control of distribution, as the condition of a healthy commercial life.

On the whole the China trade grew less important for Massachusetts year by year. It enriched but two or three family connections, and between 1820 and 1845 was not very lucrative even for them. Yet it produced a new type of vessel, the Medford-built East-Indiaman,[1] and provided an important outlet for New England manufactures. Our teas were no longer purchased with otter-skins and sandalwood. About 1817, the Boston merchants began to ship English goods to Canton, in competition with the British East India Company. Their success greatly irritated British merchants, excluded by the Honorable John's monopoly, and provided an additional incentive for Parliament throwing open the trade to all British subjects, in 1834. Already the Bostonians had begun to substitute Lowell cottons for the Lancashire; and ten years later the prosaic fruit of New England looms, to the annual value of a million and a half dollars, had replaced the lustrous and fragrant products of Coast and Islands.

[1] See previous chapter.

CHINA AND THE EAST INDIES

In spite of these new exports to China there still remained a heavy annual balance against Boston. The growing Chinese consumption of Indian opium created a demand at Canton for bills on London, which our China merchants began to supply, in place of Spanish dollars, about 1827. To a certain extent they supplied the forbidden drug itself, and made no secret of it. Since the opening years of the century, Perkins & Co. had made a specialty of carrying Smyrna opium to Canton; so did Joseph Peabody and every Boston or Salem merchant who could get it. But the total import of this inferior variety was inconsiderable, in comparison with the immense consignments of opium from British India — five hundred and seventy-eight thousand dollars' worth in the season of 1833–34, as compared with fourteen million dollars' worth of seductive Malwa and fragrant Patna, smuggled in by British ships.[1]

A small part, also, of the imports under the British flag were on the account of Russell & Co. and Augustine Heard. Within a few years' time, a fleet of Boston clipper schooners and brigs (like the 92-ton *Ariel*, which almost drowned R. B. Forbes on her trial trip, the 100-ton *Zephyr* and the 370-ton *Antelope*, built by Samuel Hall) was distributing opium along the China coast from Lintin Island, where the American firms maintained receiving ships. One small house at Canton was founded by a Salem mate and ship's carpenter who, taking advantage of Chinese respect for the dead, landed a large consignment of the forbidden drug in coffins supposed to contain departed shipmates! Olyphant & Co. of New York (derisively called 'Zion's

[1] The American ships at Canton this season numbered 70, as against 24 British East-Indianmen, 77 Country ships (vessels owned in British India), 37 Spaniards, and 45 of all other nations.

277

Corner' by their rivals) was the only Canton house that refused to participate in the opium trade; and their motive was not so much moral as practical. They feared that a traffic forbidden by the Chinese government, however countenanced by its officials, would breed trouble. They were right.

Having stated these facts, I must, in justice to the candid old China merchants and their descendants who made them public, warn the reader against exaggerating this opium traffic. For English firms, it was vital. For Boston firms, it was incidental, even in the China trade;[1] which trade was but a small and declining item in the commerce of Boston and Salem after 1815. Few, at the time, appreciated the moral and physical injury to the Chinese people they were committing through this traffic. Even Christian missionaries countenanced it, by taking passage on the opium clippers to ports they could not otherwise reach, and by accepting money from firms and individuals who dealt in the drug. It was commonly asserted that opium had no more effect on the Chinese than rum on Yankees. At the risk of appearing to black the kettle, I further submit that there is a difference between smuggling opium under the official wink and driving in opium with cannon and bayonet when officials are making a sincere if tardy effort at moral reform.

In England's opium war of 1840, Americans had no share; and few justified it save John Quincy Adams.[2]

---

[1] Opium made up over half of the British imports into China in 1831–32. Only one-fifteenth to one-twenty-fifth of the American imports at the same period were in Smyrna opium, and the amount of Indian opium imported in American vessels before 1850 must have been very small, so few were engaged in it. British opium imports exceeded greatly the total American trade.

[2] In a public lecture at Boston, that aroused a storm of protest; printed in *Chinese Repository*, XI, 274.

Many profited by it, nevertheless; both by absorbing the British trade during its course and sharing the fruits of its success. After England had extorted the Treaty of Nanking, which ended forever the old Canton methods and opened four new ports to European commerce, the United States government sent out Caleb Cushing, of Newburyport, as envoy extraordinary. In the treaty which he concluded on July 3, 1844, the United States disavowed all protection of opium smugglers.

The principal profits thereafter made by Boston capital in China were in tea, in steam freighting along the Yangtze River, and in clipper-ship freighting from the Treaty Ports to New York and London. A certain amount of opium smuggling continued. As late as 1872 fast steamers, some of Boston registry, were running it into Formosa, a thousand chests a trip; carrier pigeons conveying prices-current to interior correspondents. Russell & Co. removed to Shanghai, and finally went bankrupt in the nineties, by which time the Germans had crowded out the smaller Boston firms.

To-day no trace remains in Boston of the old China trade, the foundation of her commercial renaissance, save a taste for li-chi nuts, Malacca joints, and smoky Souchong.

*
* *

Do you remember, in the "Second Jungle Book," the adjutant bird's description of his frigid and wounded feelings, after swallowing a "piece of white stuff," which a man threw him from a great boat in the Ganges? And Mr. Kipling's explanation that the Adjutant had swallowed "a seven-pound lump of

Wenham Lake ice, off an American ice-ship"? Now, it cost one visionary Yankee some twenty-eight years' struggle to deliver that frozen sample of Wenham Lake, Massachusetts, to the Adjutant's crop.

When twenty-two-year-old Frederic Tudor proposed to ship ice to the West Indies from his father's pond in Saugus, Boston thought him mad; and seafaring men, fearing such a cargo would melt and swamp a vessel, with some difficulty were persuaded to handle his brig. His first venture was one hundred and thirty tons of ice to Martinique in 1805. On receiving news of its complete failure, he wrote in his journal, "He who gives back at the first repulse and without striking the second blow despairs of success, has never been, is not and never will be a hero in love, war, or business." By 1812 he had built up a small trade with the West Indies. The war wiped him out. After the Peace of Ghent he obtained government permission to build ice-houses at Kingston and Havana, with a monopoly of the traffic. It began to pay, and between 1817 and 1820 he extended the business to Charleston, Savannah, and New Orleans.

Frederic Tudor's letter-books (preserved in an old Boston office, under ship pictures and photographs of Tudor ice-houses in the Far East) reveal something of the pains, ingenuity, and persistence required to build up the ice-exporting business. Vessels had to be double-sheathed, to protect the ice from melting, and the captains had to be cautioned, with wearisome repetition, never to let the hatches be removed. Tudor experimented with all sorts of filling; with rice and wheat chaff, hay, tan-bark, and even coal-dust, before he settled upon pine sawdust as the best insulator. Instead of filling a long-felt want, he had to create a market at every new port; and to make the market pay, he had to educate not only the well-to-do, but the working people. He instructed Osgood Carney, supercargo of the barque *Madagascar* which took his first shipment to Rio de Janeiro, "If you can make a commencement for introducing the habit of cold drinks *at the same price* as warm at the *ordinary* drinking places . . . even if you *give* the ice . . . you will do well. . . . The shop frequented by the lowest people is the one to be chosen for this purpose." In addition, Mr. Carney must promote an ice-cream establishment, instruct people in the art of preserving ice at their homes, construct a temporary ice-house on shore, introduce it into the hospitals, and persuade the Brazilian government, on the ground of public health, to remit export duties on all products taken away by the Tudor vessels.

Nor did his pioneer work end with creating a market. No one in Southern ports knew how to store ice during hot weather. Mr. Tudor had to provide the materials for ice-houses, employees to construct them, and agents to take charge of distribution. Their carelessness and dishonesty was a constant trial. He became an expert in what nowadays is called the science of salesmanship. Playing on local excitement and curiosity, a high price was charged on first shipments. Gradually the price was lowered; and in order to stimulate steady sales, tickets were sold at a reduced rate, entitling the bearer to so many pounds on presentation at the ice-house.[1]

[1] At Charleston, South Carolina, in 1834, Tudor sold ice for 1¼ cents per pound, but ice tickets were sold at the rate of 1½ cents. Previously he had cut the rate to three-fourths of a cent in order literally to freeze out the Thayers of Boston, who endeavored to compete with him. At New Orleans, to which he paid from $435 to $600 for freight per small brig-load of ice, he was selling it for 2 cents; at Havana for 3 cents. The first price at Rio de Janeiro in 1833 was 12 pounds for a Spanish dollar.

In May, 1833, Tudor made his first venture to Calcutta; one hundred and eighty tons of ice in the ship *Tuscany*. "As soon as you have arrived in latitude 12° north," he instructed Captain Littlefield, "you will have carried ice as far south as it has ever been carried before, and your Ship becomes a discovery ship and as such I feel confident you will do everything for the eventual success of the undertaking; as being in charge of the first ship that has ever carried ice to the East Indies."

After sailing twice through the torrid zone, the *Tuscany* landed almost two-thirds of her chilly cargo in good order at Calcutta. Many are the yarns told of its reception. A Parsee asked the Captain, "How this ice make grow in your country? Him grow on tree? Him grow on shrub?" Indignant natives demanded their money back, after leaving a purchase in the sun. The poverty of the people made it difficult to establish a wide market; but the Anglo-Indian community quickly took to iced drinks, and paid large sums for the Baldwin apples, which were buried in the chilly cargoes. The trade was as genial for shipmasters as it was profitable for Mr. Tudor. While supercargoes dickered for return freight with the Babu Rajkissen Mitter, or Jamsetjee Jeejeebhoy & Co., the Boston captains moored their vessels to the banks of the Hoogly, and played host with drinks mixed Yankee-fashion, to all ships' officers in the port of Calcutta.

Mr. Tudor and his ice came just in time to preserve Boston's East-India commerce from ruin. Our carrying trade between Calcutta and Europe had declined almost to extinction. A precarious foothold in Bengal was retained by Boston and Salem houses only by importing specie, eked out with 'notions' such as spiced

Penobscot salmon, cods' tongues and sounds, coarse glassware, sperm candles and Cape Cod Glauber salts.[1] Our importing business from Calcutta had been "cut up by the roots" by the tariff of 1816, as Daniel Webster said; and within a few years the Massachusetts mills were making cotton cloth in sufficient variety to kill all demand for Allabad Emerties, Beerboom Gurrahs, and the like, so extensively imported in Federalist days. But the ice business increased to such an extent that by 1841, although pushed by fifteen competitors, and forced to lower the retail price to one cent a pound, Frederic Tudor was able to pay off a debt of a quarter-million contracted by his early experiments.

Between 1836 and 1850 the Boston ice trade was extended to every large port in South America and the Far East. When, at the Court of St. James, Edward Everett met the Persian ambassador, his first words were an appreciation of the benefits of American ice in Persia. For a generation after the Civil War, until cheap artificial ice was invented, this export trade increased and prospered. Not Boston alone, but every New England village with a pond near tidewater, was able to turn this Yankee liability into an asset, through the genius of Frederic Tudor.

The center of the business was Gray's (later Tudor's) Wharf, Charlestown. There the ice was brought by pung or train, as it was needed, from the ice-houses at Fresh Pond and other lakes in the neighborhood. In the winter of 1846 "a hundred Irishmen, with Yankee overseers, came from Cambridge every day to get out the ice" from Walden, where Thoreau was dividing his time between the study of nature and the Indian philosophers.

---

[1] The cargo of the *Emerald*, Captain Augustine Heard, in 1826. See also that of William H. Bordman's *Arbella*, next chapter.

"Thus it appears," he writes,[1] "that the sweltering inhabitants of Charleston and New Orleans, of Madras and Bombay and Calcutta, drink at my well. In the morning I bathe my intellect in the stupendous and cosmogonal philosophy of the Bhagvat-Geeta ... I lay down the book and go to my well for water, and lo! there I meet the servant of the Brahmin, priest of Brahma and Vishnu and Indra, who still sits in his temple on the Ganges reading the Vedas, or dwells at the root of a tree with his crust and water jug. I meet his servant come to draw water for his master, and our buckets as it were grate together in the same well. The pure Walden water is mingled with the sacred water of the Ganges. With the favoring winds it is wafted past the site of the fabulous islands of Atlantis and the Hesperides, makes the periplus of Hanno, and floating by Ternate and Tidore and the mouth of the Persian Gulf, melts in the tropic gales of the Indian seas, and is landed in ports of which Alexander only heard the names."

As might be expected, the Boston merchants found new East-India products with which to replace cottons, and turn over the profits they made on outward cargoes. "East-India goods," between 1830 and the Civil War, meant buffalo hides and jute; indigo and other dyestuffs; linseed and shellac; saltpeter; gunny-bags which Boston supplied to the corn-growers of the West, and gunny-cloth which was sent South for baling cotton. Colonel Francis Peabody, son of Joseph, established a linseed oil and jute factory near Salem about 1841, and began exporting its by-product of oil-cake to England. Adjoining Tudor's Wharf at Charlestown was his linseed oil and cake manufactory, and a shop where rice and gunny-cloth were prepared for the American market. In 1857 ninety-six out of the hundred and twelve vessels that loaded in Calcutta for the United States, landed their cargoes at Boston, earning an average freight of twenty thousand dollars.

The homeward voyage from Calcutta was not so pleasant as the cool outward passage. Various forms

[1] *Walden*, end of chapter XVI.

of insect life came aboard with the jute and gunnies, and propagated with surprising rapidity. Whoever left his boots outside his bunk (it is said) found nothing in the morning but the nails and the eyelets. An arrival from Calcutta in Boston (I have been told) was sometimes announced by a pack of terrified dogs running up State Street pursued by an army of Calcutta cockroaches!

In spite of these unpleasant if true incidents, the East-India trade (including, in the popular meaning of the word, the China, Manila, and Java trades as well as that of British India) enjoyed a greater prestige than any branch of Boston commerce since the Northwest fur trade died. An "East-India merchant," in ante-bellum Boston, possessed social *kudos* to which no cotton millionaire could pretend, unless previously initiated through Federalist commerce. To have an office on India Wharf, Boston, or to live in the India Row that comprised the fine old square-built houses of many a seaport town, conferred distinction. Among sailors, the man who had made an East-India voyage took no back-wind from any one; and on Cape Cod it used to be said of a pretty, well-bred girl, "She 's good enough to marry an East-India Cap'n!"

CHAPTER XVIII

MEDITERRANEAN AND BALTIC

1820–1850

WHILE Frederic Tudor was building a bridge of ice between Concord anarchy and Indian philosophy, the Mediterranean trade of Boston ferried Ralph Waldo Emerson to Malta, on his way to Florence and Ferney, Savage Landor and Carlyle. Let Emerson's own journal begin the story:

At Sea, January 2, 1833.

Sailed from Boston for Malta, December 25, 1832, in Brig Jasper, Captain Ellis, 236 tons, laden with logwood, mahogany, tobacco, sugar, coffee, beeswax, cheese, etc. A long storm from the second morn of our departure consigned all the five passengers to the irremedial chagrins of the stateroom, to wit, nausea, darkness, unrest, uncleanness, harpy appetite and harpy feeding, the ugly "sound of water in mine ears," anticipations of going to the bottom, and the treasures of the memory. I remembered up nearly the whole of Lycidas, clause by clause, here a verse and there a word, as Isis in the fable the broken body of Osiris.

Out occasionally crawled we from our several holes, but hope and fair weather would not; so there was nothing for it but to wriggle again into the crooks of the transom. Then it seemed strange that the first man who came to sea did not turn round and go straight back again. Strange that because one of my neighbours had some trumpery logs and notions which would sell for a few cents more here than there, he should thrust forth this company of his poor countrymen to the tender mercies of the northwest wind. . . .

The Captain believes in the superiority of the American to every other countryman. "You will see," he says, "when you get out here how they manage in Europe; they do everything by main strength and ignorance. Four truckmen and four stevedores at Long Wharf will load my brig quicker than a hundred men at any port in the Mediterranean." It seems the Sicilians have tried once or twice to bring their fruit to America in their own bottoms, and made the passage, he says, in one hundred and twenty days.

286

MEDITERRANEAN AND BALTIC

One hopes that the last item is nearer the truth than the wild yarns of the *Emerald's* record passage with which his homecoming captain stuffed Emerson. At Malta he left the brig *Jasper*, and she disappears into the fleet of undistinguished brigs and topsail schooners that traded from Boston to that part of the world.

Add lumber, 'domestics,' and East-India goods to the *Jasper's* cargo, and you have a typical outward lading from Boston to the Mediterranean for the period 1820–1850. The South European and Levantine peoples had by this time lost their taste for New England salt fish, but in compensation they had learned the good wearing qualities of Lowell cottons, and acquired a profitable thirst for New England rum. One Mediterranean firm ran a distillery in its Central Wharf store, importing the molasses and exporting the rum in its own vessels. But most outward cargoes had to be completed outside Massachusetts — in Maine and Chesapeake Bay, in the West Indies, South America, and the East Indies. Honduras logwood was in demand, to give that warm, rich color to Mediterranean wines. The ports of destination included Gibraltar, Malaga, Marseilles, Genoa, Leghorn, Sardinia, Gallipolis, Messina, Marsala, Palermo, Trieste, Zante, Volo, and Salonica. Return cargoes comprised oranges and lemons, wine and currants, nuts and raisins, corkwood, wool, olive oil, and a score of minor products. "I find that a large proportion of our trade with Genoa," wrote the American consul there in 1843, "has been carried on by Boston and Salem merchants. Some years, more than half the vessels entering this port have been owned by Robert Gould Shaw of Boston."

The letter-book of William H. Bordman, Jr., a young Boston merchant who had been to sea, shows

287

in some detail the indirect methods by which the Mediterranean trade was generally carried on, the way it fitted into other trade routes, and the unspecialized methods by which shipowners won wealth.

In 1824 Bordman ships domestic brown shirtings, Canton goods, soap, ham, and pickled Penobscot salmon, to the value of $1684, in one of his own vessels to South America. The supercargo is instructed to use his own judgment as to the port of sale, but is warned that Montevideo is overstocked with shirtings, and that the ship *Romeo* has just cleared for Buenos Aires with a similar cargo. The salmon will keep only twelve months, and must be sold before it spoils. Returns are left to the supercargo's judgment; but horsehair is suggested, and something must be shipped home "in time for me to take up my notes for the shirtings." The same year Bordman consigns codfish, cheese, and lard to Havana, in exchange for cigars of the "Dos Amygos or Cabañas brands, preferably of a light yellow color." Pipe, hogshead and barrel staves are then obtained at Norfolk, Virginia, where the cooperage inspection is more strict than in New England, for sale at Gibraltar and Cadiz. On vessels other than his own, he adventures 429 pairs of shoes, invoiced at $347.05, to New Orleans, where they sell for $850, less freight and expenses; and to Liverpool a consignment of sassafras — Gosnold's export from Cuttyhunk in 1602.

In 1826 Bordman sends his ship *Arbella* to Calcutta, laden with cigars and paint, currant jelly and shaving soap, cider, oakum and ham, Dutch, pineapple, and native cheese — the latter at three and a half cents a pound. The same year, when spices were scarce, one of his father's vessels enters from Sumatra with a cargo of pepper and Bourbon cloves, giving the Bordman family a corner. Part was shipped to Messrs. Perkins & Saltonstall at Baltimore, and the proceeds invested in "superfine Howard St. flour" at $4.12½. Part of this, together with more pepper and cloves, is sent to Hayti and Havana, and the proceeds invested in sugar. Three years later Bordman's vessels are taking sugar from Havana to Gothenburg for Swedish iron; and in 1830 he is sending pepper to the Mediterranean. His supercargo will decide the destination, when advised at Gibraltar on the state of the pepper market at Antwerp, Leghorn, Genoa, and Trieste; and may invest in a return cargo, or remit balance to London.

By 1830 Bordman has added a new arrow to his quiver — the Northwest Coast and Canton trade. The supercargo of his brig *Smyrna* is ordered to sell Northwest sea-otter at Canton, but to bring his acquisitions of beaver to Boston, where it is selling for eight dollars a pelt. Luckily the letter is not received, for by the time the *Smyrna* returns, enterprising Yankee hatters have popularized the silk hat, and beaver has fallen to four dollars. In search of the illicit medium for China trading, Bordman in 1832 sends a cargo of sugar from Havana to Smyrna for opium. "If on arrival the sugars will pay a profit, dispose of them at once, as I make it a rule never to speculate on certain gain." At this point the letter-book ends. From the manuscripts of Captain John Suter, who took a share in Bordman's vessels and ventures, we find that he was one of the last to enter and the last to leave the old Northwest fur trade. In 1833 he sent the ship *Rasselas* to Valparaiso and the Sandwich Islands, and the same year the brig *Smyrna* to Sumatra for pepper. Cost of vessel, cargo, and outfit was $28,218.09. Expenses of the fourteen months' voyage were $5050.82, including $854 wages to the Captain, and $1404.76 to the crew. Net sales amounted to almost one hundred per cent on the investment.

Massachusetts commerce, lacking a local export medium, was largely triangular, if not four- and five-cornered. For this reason, perhaps, we find that even those merchants who attempted to specialize in a single line participated in many others as well in order to assemble their outward cargoes and dispose of their acquisitions. On these secondary routes they sometimes employed their own vessels, but perhaps more often retained a share in a large number of vessels, in order to have some control over their movements and their cargo space. Specialization shows a marked increase about 1830, and by 1850 there was hardly a Boston merchant who did not confine his activities to one or two regions that fitted well together, such as China and East Indies, the Mediterranean and Smyrna, the South Sea Islands and South America, the Baltic and West Indies, or New Orleans, Havre, and Liverpool.

As yet there was no tendency to separate the ship-owning, purchasing, and distributing functions; and there were merchants who had even more irons in the fire than William Bordman. Ezra Weston built vessels in his own yard, opposite his paternal mansion on Powder Point, Duxbury, out of timber brought from Maine and the Merrimac in his schooners, or from Bridgewater and Middleborough on his own ox-teams. He rigged them with the products of his own ropewalk, sparyard, blacksmith shop, and sail loft at Duxbury; loaded them opposite his counting-room on Commercial Wharf, Boston; and sent them under his house flag to the Mediterranean, and all parts of the world.

MEDITERRANEAN AND BALTIC

As a distributing point for Mediterranean fruit and wine, Boston maintained its lead over New York until about 1850. As emporium for the varied products of the Near East, which found vent through Smyrna, it never had a serious rival. The same strange yearning for the Orient which pulled Boston ships around the Horn to Canton, drew her Mediterranean traders to this ancient mart of Lydia, since the dawn of history an outport of the hither East. Rounding the Peloponnesus, passing the white columns of Poseidon on Cape Sunium, and crossing the Ægean to Chios, the little brigs and barques of Boston or Plymouth, keeping a sharp lookout for Levantine pirates, entered a gulf that narrowed to a point where sits white Smyrna. Here, in an amphitheater of snow-crowned mountains, whose lower slopes were bright with orange and almond blossoms amid silver-gray olives, verdant fig orchards and somber cypress groves, they found a city in whose narrow streets Kurd and Anatolian rubbed shoulder with Armenian, Frank, and Greek; where Turkish rule rested lightly on survivors of ancient sea-powers — Tyrian and Hellenic, Frankish and Maltese, Genoese and Venetian. Easy it was at the bazaars to swap clocks and cottons, candles and rum, for the products brought in by camel-train, pack-mule, and felucca; easier still to sell them for vague promises of the same. In Smyrna, as in every Eastern port, business ceased to be robbery only when conducted by men who knew the local ways and customs.

It was a loyalist merchant of Boston, after long wanderings settling at Smyrna, who established the permanent connection in Federalist days. Two other Bostonians were resident there by 1816. Through them and their successors almost all the Mediterranean merchants of Central Wharf did a certain amount of business; but the bulk of the traffic was absorbed by two adopted citizens of Massachusetts. The Marquis Nicholas Reggio, of a Genoese family resident at Smyrna for centuries, and Joseph Iasigi, a Smyrniote Armenian, established themselves in Boston as merchant-shipowners about the year 1830. They imparted color to Boston society, and erected the statues of Columbus and Aristides in Louisburg Square. Their local, almost tribal connections, and instinctive knowledge of the devious, immutable methods of Smyrna, nailed Boston's supremacy in the Eastern Mediterranean for the rest of the sailing-ship era.

In a valley back of Smyrna are produced the best figs in the world, which, sun-dried and packed in drums, were shipped to Boston in sufficient quantities to supply all North America. Feluccas and camel-trains brought in coarse wool for the New England mills; gum-arabic and tragacanth, essentials for cotton printing; sponges and Turkey carpets, and drugs such as myrrh and scammony, which ante-bellum physicians loved to administer in generous doses. Smyrna opium we have already mentioned. The Mediterranean merchants imported it for the domestic drug trade, and the China merchants took it East by West; almost half the entire crop, about 1820, being handled by one Boston firm at Canton.

Naval architecture also profited by our Mediterranean trade. Baltimore clipper brigs and schooners were first used by Mediterranean merchants, to get their fruit to market in good season. By 1830 Massachusetts builders had created a type of deep, sharp brig with a rakish rig, which produced as much speed as the Chesapeake type and carried more cargo. Among the famous 'fruiters' were the brigs *Water Witch*,[1]

---

[1] Brig *Water Witch*, 86' 6" × 21' 3" × 10' 4", 168 tons; built by Joseph Clapp on the North River, Scituate, in 1831.

News Boy,[1] *Sea Mew,* and *Red Rover.* After bringing home grapes and oranges for the Thanksgiving and Christmas season, they would often make a winter voyage to Rio de Janeiro or to the West Indies. Captain Paxton, of the *Water Witch,* would return thence with bunches of bananas hanging from his main boom, for distribution among the friends of her owner, Benjamin C. Clark. Rivalry for each new crop of figs between the houses of Reggio and Iasigi led to a competitive building of swift barques. Iasigi & Goddard's *Osmanli,*[2] painted in the port of Smyrna by a local artist, is here shown; in the clipper ship era the Reggios' *Smyrniote* was only surpassed by Iasigi's *Race Horse,*[3] which also distinguished herself in the San Francisco trade.

*

* *

Fayal in the Azores, where in any year (save three) between 1807 and 1892 one would discover the principal merchant to be a Dabney of Boston, was an outpost of the Mediterranean trade. The outward-bound whalers stopped there to pick up cheap labor, and to unload their early acquisitions of oil, which the Dabneys then shipped to Boston in their own vessels, bringing back foodstuffs and notions for the Western Islanders. Oranges and Pico wine were local products that found their way to the Boston market. When his Dabney brother-in-law served him "Pico Madeira,"

[1] Brig *News Boy,* 111' × 26' 2" × 11' 5", 299 tons, designed by D. J. Lawler and built at Thomaston, Maine, for Frederic Cunningham in 1854.

[2] Barque *Osmanli,* 106' 2" × 24' 5" × 15', 287 tons; built by Waterman & Ewell at Medford in 1844.

[3] Barque *Race Horse,* 125' × 30' 3" × 16', 514 tons; designed by Samuel H. Pook, and built by Samuel Hall at East Boston in 1850.

Lewis Cunningham exclaimed, "Charles, I am very fond of you, but d——n your wines!" Like other Bostonians, he preferred the genuine article from Funchal, ripened in the hold of an East-Indiaman. Happily for our Fayal trade, only connoisseurs could tell the difference. Many a pipe of honest Pico was reshipped from Boston as "Choice old London particular."

Baltic-bound vessels would often stop at Fayal to top off their cargoes with oranges, whale-oil, and wine. For Massachusetts approached Russia, as in Federalist days, by a long détour in Southern waters, and her merchants managed to maintain their early supremacy in the Baltic until the Civil War.[1]

Sugar, shipbuilding, and cotton were the three keys to this triangular trade. Boston vessels took mixed cargoes to Havana, and there loaded sugar for the Baltic. By this means they paid for the Russia hemp and Baltic iron, which until the Civil War were essential raw materials for American shipbuilding. Manila was used on our merchantmen for sheets and halyards, lifts and braces; but the stout, inelastic Russia hemp was required for bolt-rope and standing rigging. Russia hemp upheld the lofty spars of our clipper ships, and indeed of all our vessels, until wire rigging was introduced in the sixties. Russian iron was preferred by the harpoon-makers of New Bedford; Swedish iron was used for the metal-work of wooden

[1] In 1820 seventy-seven American vessels passed the Sound on homeward passage. Of these twenty-nine were destined for Boston, eight for Salem, two for Newburyport, one for Marblehead, Gloucester, Plymouth, Beverly, and New Bedford. In 1840, out of sixty-four American vessels entering St. Petersburg, forty-nine belonged in Massachusetts; and out of sixty-five vessels entering the United States from St. Petersburg and Riga, thirty-two came to Boston and twelve (five of which belonged in Massachusetts) to New York. See also statistics in Appendix.

ships, and in the ironworks of Plymouth County, which had fairly exhausted the native ore. From Russia, too, came a superior grade of iron boiler-plate, the secret of whose composition eluded the Pennsylvania ironmasters for fifty years; also bristles for the brush factories, rags for the paper-mills, crash and linen for the housewives of New England, and expensive furs sewed up in leather trunks.

Boston remained the American emporium for Baltic products partly because it was the natural distributing point for shipbuilding materials, but mostly from the enterprise of her merchants. We have already seen, in William Bordman's letter-book, how a Baltic voyage fitted into the activities of a typical shipping merchant. Brigs and small ships were especially built for the trade. The itinerary of one such, the brig *Cronstadt* (100 feet long, 273 tons), built on the North River in 1829 for Thomas B. Wales and others of Boston,[1] shows that even vessels as small as the usual Mediterranean fruiter could be profitably employed. Baltic-bound cargoes were commonly owned in thirds by the shipowner, the Cuban sugar merchant, and the Russian consignee, who got the lion's share of profits through commissions not only on sales, but upon the heavy import duty, together with fees and tips as varied as the cumshaws of Canton.

In order to absorb to his own profit these heavy charges, William Ropes, of a Salem family long expert in the Russian trade, established himself at St. Petersburg in 1832, and was admitted to the guild of merchants. He gave the Baltic trade a fresh impetus by

---

[1] 1834: Boston–Cuba–St. Petersburg twice, and Boston–Charleston–Marseilles with cotton. 1835–36: Boston–Matanzas–St. Petersburg twice; Boston–Charleston–Rotterdam. 1837: Boston–Rio de Janeiro–Hamburg twice, with coffee, and Boston–Charleston–Amsterdam; etc.

importing Southern cotton in his own ships, to supply the new factories at Narva, Riga, and Reval. Leaving his son William Hooper Ropes in charge of the Russian branch, he returned to Boston, and resumed the active charge of his firm. As soon as mineral illuminating oil began to replace the New Bedford product, William Ropes exported it to Russia, and before his death in 1859 *Ropski kerosin* was known throughout the Empire.

William H. Ropes, attended by his head clerk, and a large dog "Tiger" as protection against bandits, traveled by sleigh thousands of miles in the interior of Russia every winter to buy bolt-rope, crash, and sheet-iron from the local merchants. His hobby was distributing among the peasants religious tracts, translated into Russian by his student brother of the Imperial University; his favorite charity, and his father's, was to give free passage in his ships, and hospitality at his mansion on the English Quay, to overworked New England ministers.

The Ropeses were not the only Russia merchants of Boston. The fortune that built Fenway Court is said to have originated in those northern waters. Enoch Train, the daring and public-spirited founder of the Train packet-line, saw that the Baltic cotton trade would require larger vessels. Waterman & Ewell built for him at Medford in 1839 the ship *St. Petersburg*, which broke all previous records for size in New England shipbuilding; she was 160 feet long, 33 feet broad, and 814 tons burthen. With the painted ports and square stern of a New York packet-ship, she had such beautiful fittings and accommodations as to attract thousands of sight-seers at every port. Richard Trask, of Manchester, her master and part owner, was one of the dandy merchant-captains of his generation. After arranging for the return cargo at St. Petersburg and visiting his friends, he would leave the vessel in charge of the first officer and return *via* London by steamer.

Somewhat akin to the Baltic trade was the coffee carrying-trade from Brazil to Antwerp, Amsterdam, Hamburg, and Königsberg; and the staves and brandy trade between Norfolk and La Rochelle, in which Thomas B. Wales and Nathaniel H. Emmons kept several small vessels employed. But to analyze every minor route of foreign trade that began and ended at Boston would be an endless task. Peruse, if you will, in the Appendix, the list of foreign ports from which vessels cleared for Boston in 1857, for emphatic proof of the variety and interest of her foreign commerce.

*

*   *

Space and time likewise forbid a proper analysis of the North American coasting trade of Massachusetts. In 1831 American tonnage engaged in coasting for the first time exceeded the registered tonnage in foreign trade, and the disproportion grew in spite of the railroads. Coal and cotton explain the change. James Collier, of Cohasset (1813–91), who once won a bet in London for having commanded more vessels and voyages than any shipmaster in port, first won the title of captain at the age of eighteen, by taking the schooner *Profit* from Boston to Norfolk, returning with a cargo of coal for the Ames plow works. It was landed at Weymouth and carted to North Easton. In the forties this trade increased as the use of stoves and furnaces became general, as hardwood disappeared from the Maine coast, and as tidewater textile mills were established at Newburyport, Salem, New Bedford, and Fall River. Until the adoption of steam-towed coal barges, after the Civil War, the freighting of lumber and apples, fish and ice between New England and Philadelphia and Norfolk, to return with coal, employed a great fleet of small sloops and schooners, representing the labor and the savings of seafarers in every village from Eastport to Westport.

The corn and cotton trade with the lower South, which we have already noted in several connections, deserves mention as one of the most lucrative routes for Massachusetts vessels between 1830 and 1860. In part it was a coasting trade; in part, the last sailing-ship phase of a Massachusetts interest two centuries old — the carrying of Southern staples to a market. Year by year the wealthy Cotton Belt wore out more boots and shoes, purchased more cottons for her slaves, used more Quincy granite in her public buildings, and consumed more Fresh Pond ice in her mint juleps. The New England mills, on their part, were calling for more cotton; and every pound of it that they received, before the Civil War, came by sailing vessel from Charleston, Savannah, Mobile, and New Orleans. The factory hands were equally hungry for cheap food. Boston's total imports by sea from New Orleans totaled $3,334,000 in 1839, and steadily rose; in the period from September 1, 1841, to May 1, 1842, one-quarter of the lard, more than one-quarter of the flour, nearly half the pork and more than half the corn shipped out of New Orleans went to Boston.

Sailing packet-lines were insufficient to fill this demand. One hundred and seventy-five vessels cleared from Boston in 1855 for New Orleans alone. But not all of them returned directly to Boston. The typical Massachusetts cotton-carrier, after waiting for a place on the crowded levee of New Orleans, while the air rang with shouts of negro roustabouts and wild chanties of cotton-screwers' gangs, took the best paying freight she could get to any foreign port. In keen competition with the merchant marine of England, France, and Germany, our vessels supplied the cotton-mills of Lancashire, Normandy, Flanders, Alsace, Prussia, Saxony, and the Baltic provinces. When freights were good — and anything above a cent a pound made a 'saving voyage' — a ship would discharge her cargo at Havre or Liverpool, and hasten back in ballast for more cotton.[1] Otherwise she took a European cargo to Boston, or was chartered by a packet-line at Liverpool to relieve the heavy emigrant traffic. Boston's imports from England far exceeded those from any other country, and the freight money on cotton went a long way toward balancing accounts. Cotton, in fact, was the most important medium in our carrying trade, replacing colonial rum and codfish, and the Oriental goods of Federalist days.

Few converts were obtained by the abolitionists in Boston counting-rooms. Society, business, and politics in Massachusetts were dominated by a triple entente between the "Lords of the Lash and the Lords of the Loom" — and the Lords of Long Wharf.

[1] The records of the ship *Rubicon* (Medford built, 490 tons) from 1836 to 1838 show that in two years, on a total investment of $25,094.28 and disbursements of $10,960.40, she made $29,698.43 "cash receipts" for her owners in the New Orleans–Havre cotton trade.

CHAPTER XIX

CAPE COD AND CAPE ANN

1820–1860

CAPE COD was ripening off, as Thoreau walked its
sandy length in 1855. Untouched, through lack of
water-power, by the industrial revolution; neglected
alike by foreign commerce and railroad; producing but
a fraction of its own food; Barnstable County increased in population and in wealth solely by the skill
of its people in farming the sea. The towns and villages of the Cape, from Sandwich to Provincetown,
and down the back side around Chatham to Wood's
Hole, increased their sea-borne tonnage six fold between 1815 and 1850. Not only Barnstable and Provincetown, but every tidal harbor and tiny creek —
Yarmouthport, Sesuet, Namskaket, Herring River,
Rock Harbor, Wellfleet, Pamet, Chatham, Bass River,
Harwichport, Hyannis, Osterville, and Cotuit — had
its fishing fleet, with dependent shipyards, sail-lofts,
stores, and wharves. Coasting vessels plied "down
East" or "out South," and made foreign connections
at Boston, to which every place on the Bay side ran a
sailing packet. Provincetown and Wood's Hole had a
small fleet of whalers, and all parts received an occasional oily bounty from a school of blackfish, driven on
the beach and tried out by the united effort of the
community, with a spirit that would delight Lenin.

Of the minority that did not engage in fishing or
coasting, the more adventurous entered the merchant
marine, the stay-at-homes worked the oyster-beds and
clam-flats, or harnessed wind and sun to extract salt

from the sea.[1] Many young men worked at a trade in
Charleston or some other Southern seaport during
the winter, returning to the Cape by sea in time for
a summer's fishing. Widows and retired captains invested their savings in sixteenth-shares of fishing vessels, or in the stock of a local marine insurance company. Until 1850 almost every one lived in a snug
Cape cottage, built with that nice sense of proportion
that a ship-carpenter instinctively absorbs. The population of thirty-five thousand (1850) was ninety-five
per cent native-born, and in about the same proportion dependent on the sea for a livelihood.

Distinct section that it was, Cape Cod's every town
was distinctive. Chatham had a small fleet of shad-
seiners about 1840. Provincetown, with its capacious
harbor, had the largest fleet of fishermen and whalers,
and the greatest salt-works. Her shores were lined
with picturesque windmills, which pumped sea-water
into pine vats for evaporation; her quaint cottages
emerged from sand and fish-flakes, instead of gardens
and shrubbery. Brewster, having no proper harbor,
was a nursery of sea-captains for the merchant marine,
and snug harbor in their old age. Barnstable, the
county seat, had a native aristocracy of lawyers,
judges, and clipper-ship commanders. Sandwich,
where the Cape begins, capitalized Cape sand. Its
six-acre glass factory was the largest in the country,
and one of the first in New England to use steam
power.

Wellfleet maintained its oyster-breeding reputation.
Seed oysters were obtained in Wareham Harbor, the

[1] The salt industry on the Cape did not entirely close until about
1870, but it was pretty well killed off before the Civil War, through the
import duty being reduced from twenty to two cents per bushel, 1830–46.
In 1837 the Cape had 668 salt-works and produced to the value of
$225,098; in 1855 this had fallen to 181 and $47,657.

Taunton River, and other points in Buzzard's and Narragansett bays. In winter the local mackerel fleet brought bivalves from Chesapeake Bay and bedded them down on the Wellfleet flats, where during the R-less months they grew plump for the Boston market. About 1824 Wellfleet schooners began bringing Virginia oysters directly to Northern markets; but a sojourn behind Billingsgate Island greatly enhanced their value. In the fifties the canning industry extended the market not only for oysters, but for lobster and Penobscot salmon. From colonial times to the present, almost every oyster-dealer in New England has been a Wellfleet man. Isaac Rich climbed on oyster-shells to a fortune, which he left to Boston University.

A regional readjustment in the fishing industry went on between 1835 and 1855.[1] Boston, the second greatest fishing port in 1837, gradually went out of the business, and no other town on Boston Bay but Hingham owned a fishing schooner in 1855. The South Shore and the Merrimac declined; the North Shore remained stationary. The only regions which increased their fleet during these eighteen years were Cape Cod, and her rocky rival Cape Ann. The latter's fishing fleet in 1837 was less than half that of Cape Cod. But in the next twenty years Cape Ann caught up. The population of Gloucester and Rockport (separated in 1840) more than doubled between 1820 and 1855. Sandy Bay Breakwater (hardy perennial of river and harbor bills), which the federal government began to construct about 1836, protected the fishing coves on the exposed side of Cape Ann, and made it possible for the Rockport granite quarries to compete with Quincy. But concentration was the tendency of

[1] See statistics in Appendix.

the age, and "the harbor" (Gloucester) gradually absorbed all Cape Ann fisheries.

Newburyport lost half her fleet in this period, but codfishing remained the typical industry of the smaller ports of Essex County until the Civil War. Swampscott, despite an influx of summer boarders, increased her fleet to thirty-nine small schooners, dried her codfish exceptionally well, and remained the last place where the delectable dunfish was properly cured.[1] It was no uncommon sight to see fifty to one hundred farmers' teams at one time on King's and Blaney's beaches, dickering with the fishermen for a winter's supply.

"Our neighbors of Beverly have dropped quietly back into the fisheries again," writes Dr. Bentley in 1816. "I saw several fields replanted with flakes, which had been divided for house lots. . . . At Beverly they have received half a million of fish in 16 vessels." Her fleet rose from twenty-one sail in 1825 to sixty-four in 1840, when it began to decline: and the Beverly schooners were Grand Bankers, thrice the tonnage of the Swampscott vessels.

Shoemaking brought a great change in the economy of North Shore fishing ports after 1815. The schooners, instead of refitting for a winter's trading voyage, were now hauled out by Thanksgiving Day; the fishermen, instead of idling or shipping abroad, pegged and cut shoes in a neighborly "ten-footer" shop, discussing meanwhile the ways of fish and politicians, ships and women. Many fishermen from 'abroad'

---

[1] Fish for 'dunning' at this period was caught in deep water, preferably off the Isles of Shoals in early spring. It was split and slack salted, piled up for two or three months, covered with salt hay or eel grass in a dark store, uncovered once and restacked under pressure, and by late summer, if nothing went wrong, had acquired the proper ripeness and dun color.

303

(Cape Cod) brought their catch for curing to Beverly,[1] whose rocky shores as far as West Beach were white and odorous every autumn with drying cod. A pleasant, well-balanced life had the North Shore fisherman-farmer-shoemakers, for about two generations. The industrial revolution then made a factory industry of their sociable handicraft; and on the stony acres of their forefathers arose the palaces and Italian gardens of a new feudalism.

Marblehead still had a large fleet of Bankers, and even in its absence the Provincetown mackerel fleet, putting in for shelter, would fill her harbor with sail. Glorious nights there were, when the Cape Codders came ashore, bent on draining every Marblehead grog-shop, kissing every Marblehead girl, and blacking the eyes of every Marblehead boy. Glorious mornings followed, when a clearing northwest breeze sent wavelets slap-slap-slapping on black topsides, while the surf still roared outside; when to the chuckling chorus of halyard blocks, foresails and mainsails arose to catch the dawn; when "Shanandore" or "Lowlands" from five hundred lusty throats, brought up, all standing, such aged natives as had thought it worth while to retire. Glorious days, too, when the Marblehead Banker fleet departed for its summer fare. Church-bells ring, fish-horns blare, and in sight of the whole town each schooner, dressed in all her colors and newest suit, must sail up and down the harbor thrice, and for good luck toss a penny on Halfway Rock.

Plymouth increased her fishing fleet at this period to over fifty sail, and specialized in mackerel; but the smaller South Shore fishing villages allowed their

---

[1] On account of her early railroad facilities, which attracted buyers from the interior. The Eastern Railroad reached Salem in 1838, Marblehead and Beverly in 1839.

fleets to decline in the forties. Probably the active shipyards of Cohasset, Scituate, the North River, and Duxbury were absorbing the slack. West of the Cape there was little codfishing; but the Maine coast was becoming a worthy rival.

Expansion marked the industry as a whole between 1820 and 1860. Mackerel-fishing now for the first time attained the dignity and importance of codfishing. The sportive and elusive mackerel taxed the ingenuity of fishermen far more than the stolid cod, but the amount of him brought into Massachusetts increased from twelve thousand barrels full, the highest for any year before the war, to over three hundred thousand in 1830. Prices rose as well.[1] There followed a lean decade, when the mackerel fled the coast, but in 1840 a series of heavy catches began again. In 1851 the mackerel fleet of Massachusetts numbered eight hundred and fifty sail, of over fifty-three thousand tons burthen.

The same types of vessel were used in mackerel as in codfishing. Chebacco boats and 'heel-tappers' were gradually superseded by pinkies — an enlarged and improved Chebacco boat with bowsprit and jib, measuring twenty to sixty tons.[2] About 1830 a new type of square-sterned schooner, of twenty to ninety tons burthen, came into use. Apple-bowed, barrel-sided, and clumsy craft that they were, these 'new-style bankers' or 'jiggers' had easier lines than the old type, and a flush deck. They were built all along the New

---

[1] The price of No. 1 mackerel rose from $5 per barrel in 1830 to $19 in 1856. Codfish in the same period rose from $2.12 to $3.75 per quintal of 112 pounds.

[2] The measurements of an early pinkie, the "pink-stern schooner *Pink* of Edgartown," in the Plymouth registry for 1810, are 42′ × 12′ 6″ × 5′ 3″, tonnage 24½. One is shown in the engraving of Boston Harbor in chapter XXII.

England shore from Frenchman's Bay to Dartmouth. In accommodations they were no improvement on earlier models. All the cooking, even the tea and coffee, was done in a large iron pot over a brick hearth directly under the fore scuttle, through which the smoke was supposed to find its way out. Halibut's fins and napes, smoked to a pungent flavor on the cabin beams of the pinkies and jiggers, were a favorite delicacy in Massachusetts coast towns.

Swampscott adopted small, fast schooners of improved model about 1840.[1] The launching, at Essex, of the so-called clipper schooner *Romp*, in 1847, extended this principle to the larger vessels. Only two years elapsed before Samuel Hall designed the schooners *Express* and *Telegraph* for the Wellfleet oyster and mackerel fleet. Of clipper model, increased size (one hundred tons or thereabouts), and large sail area, these vessels set the fashion for New England fishing schooners for the next generation. The *Frank Atwood*, designed by Donald McKay in 1868, was the most famous of this class. But the clipper schooners were too shallow and tender for safety; every great storm brought a holocaust of New England fishermen. About 1890 a new, faster, and safer type was evolved through the collaboration of yacht designers with master mariners. To this class belongs the *Esperanto*, champion of the North American fishing fleet in 1920.

In codfishing the ancient method of hand-lining from the vessel's deck, day and night, prevailed until the Civil War. Stories are told of 'high-liners' who fished twenty hours a day, lashed to the rigging lest they fall overboard when they dozed off. Mackerel-fishing was more sporty. The schools were generally found within fifty miles of the New England coast,

[1] See picture of Nahant regatta, above.

and at times they struck into Massachusetts Bay in such numbers that a vessel could make her 'trip o' fish' twixt dawn and dark. But often the mackerel schooners would sail "clear to Scatteree" in search of a fare.

The universal method of catching mackerel was 'jigging.' A mackerel 'jig,' invented about 1812, was simply a hook around the shank of which was cast a plummet of lead or pewter. For bait, herring or small mackerel, or menhaden ('po'gies') were 'slivered' (sliced), and then ground up by the night watch in a bait-mill like a farmer's feed-cutter. A favorite Cape Cod joke was the fisherman whose wife had to grind a bait-mill at home to make him sleep.

A school of mackerel was 'tolled' or attracted to the surface by throwing this chopped bait broadcast while the vessel slowly drifted, hove to. The fish were caught on sliver-baited jigs, each member of the crew handling two or three short lines, and dextrously snapping his mackerel into a barrel with the same motion that jerked him out of water. It was an exciting moment when flashes of silver and drumming of lively fish in empty barrels announced that a 'spurt' had struck the edge of the fleet; and each master, with hair's-breadth handling that a yachtsman would envy, endeavored to dribble his schooner under the lee bow of some vessel with a 'fishy' skipper, like "Osceola Dick" Rich, of Truro, or John Pew, of Gloucester. The sight of such a fleet, two hundred sail, perhaps, engaged in these nervous evolutions; or (as Thoreau saw them) 'pouring around the Cape'; or, winging it for home with a full fare, was one of the many beautiful maritime spectacles of sailing days.

Mackerel were dressed and salted on board the vessel that caught them, culled (graded) on shore under the eye of a deputy-inspector appointed by the commonwealth, and barreled by young boys at three to five cents a barrel. Massachusetts-inspected salt mackerel was distributed all over the country. In 1835 Georgia took thirty-seven thousand barrels, and Philadelphia, one hundred thousand. Toward the end of our period some sharp Yankees who lived in states where there were no inspection laws, began "re-inspecting" Massachusetts mackerel, so that the lower grades could be passed off on inland consumers as number one.

Both mackerel and codfishing were much hampered by the British treaty of 1818, under which the Canadian and Provincial authorities undertook to withdraw our ancient access to the shores and territorial waters of Labrador and the Bay of Chaleur. A revival came in the thirties, when Gloucestermen began to frequent the Georges Bank, only a hundred miles east of Cape Cod. For generations fishermen had visited these dangerous ocean shoals without daring to anchor, for fear of being 'drored under' by the tide; and modern drift-fishing with cusk bait had not been invented. After Captain Samuel Wonson had proved one could anchor in safety, winter-fishing on the Georges became the chief supply for the fresh-fish business.

This important branch of the fisheries, nowadays far more lucrative than the salt-fish business, began its first extension beyond tidewater radius about 1837, when some smart Yankee combined ice, fresh fish, and the railroad. The fish were brought alive in salt-water wells in the vessels' holds [1] to Boston, where they were dressed, iced, and shipped inland by rail. As early as the season of 1843–44, one Boston firm was sending almost half a million pounds of fresh cod, haddock,

[1] Vessels with wells for keeping fish alive were called 'smacks,' the only use of that term in the Massachusetts fisheries.

and halibut to New York, Albany, and Philadelphia. When the railroad reached Gloucester, in 1846, that port began to compete with Boston in fresh-fishing, and two or three years later the Georges Bankers began to carry ice with them, and to chill the fish as soon as caught; a method which enabled even mackerel to be shipped fresh. Haddock and halibut, formerly a drug in the market, now became valuable parts of the catch.

The market for salt codfish changed radically after the Peace of Ghent. Exports to Europe fell off to almost nothing by 1832. The West Indies and Surinam, where Gloucester disposed of her hake and lowest-grade dried fish, took over ninety per cent of our foreign exports; but the amount remained constant to the average of Federalist days. All the increase in production was absorbed by the domestic market, which in 1840 took three-quarters of the fish cured in New England. Yankee pioneers saw to it that a taste for salt-fish dinners kept pace with the westward-striding frontier. Consequently there was an increase in the Grand Banks codfishing fleet, parallel to that of the mackerel fishermen.

Although the fisheries made a smaller contribution than whaling to the production statistics of Massachusetts, the workers got a much larger share of the profits. In cod and mackerel fishing the share system has continued to this day, and has never become the caricature of communism that it did in New Bedford.

At Gloucester, the vessels were owned by a distinct class of merchant-shipowners, who also kept general stores and acted as wholesale distributers. All supplies were furnished by the owners, each fisherman getting half of his catch, and the skipper an additional bonus of six to eight per cent on the gross amount. On Cape Cod and the other fishing sections, the system was more democratic. The vessels were owned generally in sixteenth-shares; sometimes, in part, by their own crews. Every one fished "on his own hook," furnishing his lines and gear and part of his food. The "great general" — essential food such as salt meat and biscuit, and ship chandlery — was furnished by the owners, who deducted the cost from the "whole stock" (gross proceeds) of the trip before a division was made.[1] In some ports there was also a "small general" including firewood, beans, potatoes, and meal, the cost of which was divided among the crew. Prior to the temperance movement rum was considered as necessary for the fisherman as bait for the fish; and every one took from three to six gallons of the liquor to sea with him for a four months' cruise. But "at the present time," writes Dr. Thatcher of Plymouth in 1832, "some vessels go entirely without ardent spirits." Having deducted the "great general," the owners took one-quarter to three-eighths of the net proceeds, and the rest was divided among the crew in proportion to the amount each man caught. In mackerel-fishing it made a great difference from what part of the vessel one fished; hence every man's station was allotted beforehand.

Codfishermen received, in addition, a bonus of eight to ten dollars a year from the federal government. A Gloucester physician stirred up a tempest in 1840, when he exposed methods by which mackerel-fisher-

[1] Illustrated by the "Settlement" of one trip of the Wellfleet mackerel schooner *Boundbrook* in 1843. The "whole stock" was sold for $836.11. Outfitter's bill was $83.92, and the "great general" (food furnished by owners), $87.65. The owners' share — 25 per cent of the "whole stock" after these items were deducted — was $166.13. Eleven members of the crew divided the rest, the lowest share being $18.78. The skipper and two others got $54.09 apiece.

men became codfishermen for bounty-getting purposes. But by constantly reiterating the "nursery of our seamen" and "cradle of the American Navy" argument, Massachusetts congressmen managed to retain the federal bounty until 1866. There is no doubt that the men needed it. The average earnings of a Gloucester fisherman, for the working year of nine months, were estimated at one hundred and fifty-seven dollars in 1850. A fair-sized Cape Cod fisherman's family needed a hundred dollars more than that to carry it through the winter, and the maximum ever made by a lucky fisherman in a banner year was only eight to nine hundred dollars. Their calling was most dangerous. Seventy-eight men of the Cape Cod fleet were drowned in 1837. Truro, Dennis, and Yarmouth lost eighty-seven bread-winners in the October gale of 1841, which swept away the new Pigeon Cove breakwater on Cape Ann, and destroyed fourteen out of sixteen vessels owned at the Cove, representing a lifetime's savings of many hard-working men. Eleven vessels from Marblehead, with sixty-five men and boys, went down in the September gale of 1846; and the "Minot's Light" gale of October, 1851, took a fearful toll from every fishing village in New England. Except in the shoemaking region, a season's gains were generally used up by the spring, and a fisherman's family lived on credit in his absence. Bad luck or misfortune would prolong the debt to the vessel's owner or the local storekeeper (often the same person), indefinitely. But on the whole, especially on the North Shore and Cape Cod, the fishermen seem to have been a much happier and more independent class of seafarers than the whalemen or merchant sailors.

The decade 1850–1860 marks the end of an era in the Massachusetts fisheries. On the cod banks, dory hand-lining and trawling commenced. Mackerel-fishing was revolutionized by the purse seine; and the clipper fishing schooner was perfected. Gloucester initiated and reaped the benefit of these modern improvements. Her branch railroad, connecting her with Boston in 1846, attracted buyers from all parts of the country. Her vessel owners, commanding more capital than the Cape-Codders, and living in one compact community, were better able to survive years of bad luck and disaster, more prompt to scrap obsolete vessels, and to adopt new methods. Isaac Higgins, of Gloucester, invented the modern seine boat, a model which no other builder to this day has been able to improve. The Canadian Reciprocity Treaty of 1854, notwithstanding the competition of Canadian fish, restored access to the inshore "Bay" fisheries, and permitted free import of Newfoundland herring for bait. Foreign immigrants settled in Gloucester in large numbers; and by the close of the Civil War, it was by far the greatest fishing town in America, with a fleet of three hundred and forty-one cod and mackerel schooners, a tonnage greater than Salem's, and an annual catch worth almost three million dollars. Gloucester, too, has been afflicted (or blessed, if you like) with factories and summer visitors; but Gloucester still farms the sea. Her population of twenty-four thousand, in 1920, depends largely on the sacred cod and his humbler cousins.

For Cape Cod, however, the decade 1850–1860 marks a decline both in population and maritime activity. Various are the explanations. Her capitalist class was too small, poor, and conservative to adopt the new methods. Modern purse-seining required strong men, giving no employment to the boys who were useful in jigging. Lack of rail transportation (although the Old Colony Railroad did finally wander into Provincetown in 1873) gave the profits of distribution to Boston wholesalers. After the Civil War the Cape Cod fleet began to concentrate in Wellfleet and Provincetown. Elsewhere wise men imitated Captain Zebina H. Small, of Harwich, who sold his fishing vessel in 1845 and set out a cranberry bog. Others emigrated to Boston, New York, and the West, where the sturdy qualities of their salty upbringing helped many to acquire fortunes, and summer estates on Cape Cod.

CHAPTER XX

THE WHALERS

1815-1860

O the whaleman's joys! O I cruise my old cruise again!
I feel the ship's motion under me, I feel the Atlantic breezes fanning
    me,
I hear the cry again sent down from the mast-head, *There — she*
    blows!
— Again I spring up the rigging to look with the rest — We see —
    we descend, wild with excitement,
I leap in the lower'd boat — We row toward our prey, where he lies,
We approach stealthy and silent — I see the mountainous mass,
    lethargic, basking,
I see the harpooner standing up — I see the weapon dart from his
    vigorous arm:
O swift, again, now, far out in the ocean, the wounded whale, settling,
    running to windward, tows me,
— Again I see him rise to breathe — We row close again,
I see a lance driven through his side, press'd deep, turn'd in the
    wound,
Again we back off — I see him settle again — the life is leaving him
    fast,
As he rises he spouts blood — I see him swim in circles narrower
    and narrower, swiftly cutting the water — I see him die;
He gives one convulsive leap in the centre of the circle, and then
    falls flat and still in the bloody foam.

          — WALT WHITMAN, "Song of Joys"

WHEN Boston absorbed the foreign commerce of Massachusetts, New Bedford became the whaling metropolis of the world. Nantucket, after losing half her fleet of forty-six whalers during the war, began to recover in 1818. By the end of another year she had a fleet of sixty whalers, and fourscore sail in the coasting trade as well. In 1843, the peak year of her population

314

and prosperity, Nantucket had nine thousand souls, seventy-five hundred sheep, eighty-eight whalers, and the largest output of refined oil and sperm candles of any American community. With a high school, an Athenæum, and a Lyceum; Nantucket, for all her pristine simplicity, had caught the cultural waves from 'off-island.' But her whalemen, by following a mistaken policy of sperm or nothing, ran out of luck. Vessels had to be floated over the harbor bar on 'camels,' at great expense. Population and fleet began to taper down. The last forlorn whaling barque sailed from Nantucket in 1870, but in the summer of 1920 the eighty-year-old *Charles W. Morgan* of New Bedford was bravely fitting out for another voyage.

"New Bedford is not nearer to the whales than New London or Portland," wrote Emerson, "yet they have all the equipments for a whaler ready, and they hug an oil-cask like a brother." He guessed the secret of New Bedford's success. Her spacious harbor, in contrast to the bar-blocked entrance to Nantucket; her mainland situation, and her railroad connections counted for much; but her persistent specialization in whaling alone, counted most. Other small seaports of New England hugged the delusion that foreign trade would return; New Bedford hugged her oil-casks. Her Quaker shipowners who had made fortunes by neutral trading before 1812, perceived that the palmy days of the carrying trade were past, refitted their merchantmen as whalers, and went out after oil with a spirit and perseverance that made their town within six years the first whaling port of North America. They were as tight-fisted, cruel and ruthless a set of exploiters as you can find in American history, these oil kings of New Bedford. But they were canny as well. By intelligent specialization they escaped the commercial extinction that overtook the smaller Massachusetts seaports; and instead of awaiting the inevitable decline of whaling, they chose the very height of its prosperity to give a new hostage to fortune — the Wamsutta cotton-mill.

Fairhaven, on the opposite side of New Bedford Harbor, became the third whaling center by 1831, although later passed by New London. Edgartown on the Vineyard had a fleet of ten to twenty whalers in the forties and fifties, and Provincetown at one time had as many as thirty. Every little seaport on Buzzard's Bay — Dartmouth and Mattapoisett and Marion, Wareham and Westport, Wood's Hole and Rochester — entered the game. In fact there were few seaports of Massachusetts and Long Island Sound that did not at one time or another go in for blubber-hunting; but all north of Cape Cod gave it up after a short trial. New Bedford's fleet surpassed all others combined, attaining three hundred and thirty vessels in 1857. The population of four thousand in 1820 had tripled by 1840, and almost doubled again in the next twenty years. With its oil refineries, cooper's shops, tool-works, and the hundred-and-one industries subsidiary to whaling, New Bedford became a hive of industry; it was the fifth port for shipping in the United States, and was pushing Baltimore hard for fourth place.

The historic process of opening new whaling grounds continued. By 1821 there were five recognized grounds in the Pacific Ocean — the 'on-shore' along the coast of Chile, the 'off-shore' between 5° and 10° south latitude and longitude 105°–125° west, discovered by Captain George W. Gardner, of Nantucket, in 1818; the 'country whaling,' among the Pacific reefs and islands; the Indian Ocean; and the coast of Japan, which was first visited in 1820 by Captain Joseph Allen, of Nantucket, following a tip from Jonathan Winship, the Boston Nor'westman. In 1835, when Captain Barzillai T. Folger, of the Nantucket ship *Ganges*, took the first right whale on the Kodiak ground, the vessels extended their cruising grounds to the Northwest Coast and Alaska. Eight years later two New Bedford masters discovered the value of the bowhead whale off the coast of Kamchatka; and by 1851 Melville could write with truth that the oil fleet of Massachusetts was "penetrating even through Bering's Strait, and into the remotest secret drawers and lockers of the world." [1]

A summer's cruise in the Arctic Ocean gave the keenest delight to owners and skippers, as the midnight sun enabled them to work their crews twenty-four hours a day.

When in 1839 sperm-oil rose above a dollar a gallon for the first time since the war, Nantucket increased her fleet from sixty-four to eighty-one vessels, New Bedford and Fairhaven from eighty-nine to two hundred and twenty-one, and others in proportion. Yet the price of oil and bone, after a brief depression, rose to unheard-of figures during this golden age of the industry — $1.77 for sperm and 79 cents for whale-oil in 1855–56, 97 cents a pound for whalebone; although two millions and a half pounds were landed that year as against twenty thousand in 1817, when the price was twelve cents. By 1840 half a million gallons of sperm-oil, four and a half million of whale-oil, and two million pounds of bone were exported from the United States. Whaling and the manufacture of whaling products became the leading industry in Massachu-

---

[1] *Moby Dick*, chap. cv. All other quotations in this chapter are from the same whaling classic.

setts after shoes and cottons, and provided commerce with an important export medium.[1]

Little technical advance seems to have been made at this period. A toggle harpoon that locked the iron in the whale's back came into general use. The barque rig became popular for whaling vessels, which now averaged between three hundred and five hundred tons burthen; but little if any improvement was made in the model. 'Spouters,' or 'blubber-boilers,' as the merchant marine called them, were still broad on the beam, bluff-bowed, and "sailed about as fast as you can whip a toad through tar." Capacity, not speed, was the desired quality; hence many ships which had outlived their usefulness in the merchant service were converted into whalers. The whaleboats (rowboats carried aboard the whalers, and used to chase the quarry) were beautiful craft, perfected by a century of experience. Double-ended, twenty-eight to thirty feet long, six feet broad, and but twenty-six inches deep amidships, with half-inch cedar planking on white-oak frames, propelled by a spritsail or by five stout fourteen- to eighteen-foot oars, "like noiseless nautilus shells their light prows sped through the sea." For a nautical thriller give us a fifteen-knot "Nantucket sleigh-ride" over great Pacific rollers, in a whaleboat fastened onto a gallied whale, steersman straining on his twenty-two-foot oar to prevent an upset, and the line smoking as it whips around the loggerhead. No wonder that Hawaiian royalty, in its pageants, used a New Bedford whaleboat for triumphal car.

[1] A good part, but not all of the oil was handled by Massachusetts merchants. Charles W. Morgan, of New Bedford, sent part of his cargoes to his brother Thomas W. Morgan at Philadelphia, part to Josiah Bradlee, of Boston, and part to Hussey & Macy, a Nantucket firm in New York. He also exported oil in his own vessels to Europe, and imported cargoes of general merchandise.

THE WHALERS

It was a golden age for owners. The ship *Lagoda*, belonging to Jonathan Bourne and others, netted them an average of ninety-eight per cent profit for each of the six voyages she made between 1841 and 1860.[1] Several simple Quaker families of 1815 had become millionaires by 1840. The nucleus of the great Howland and Hetty Green fortunes was gathered in 1824, when Isaac Howland, Jr., died. Stately mansions of granite in the neo-classic style, and elaborate Gothic cottages, arose on the high ground overlooking the harbor, amid ample lawns and luxuriant gardens. New Bedford society combined the grace of provincial Newburyport and the power of Federalist Salem. . . . But it was an iron age for the men who did the work.

Whaling skippers had been proverbial for cruelty and whale-ship owners for extortion, since colonial days; but the generation of 1830–60 surpassed its forbears. The old 'lay' system, it will be remembered, gave each whaleman a fractional share of the proceeds of the voyage. On paper, this sounds so fair and just that a gullible economic historian has called it "the best coöperation of capital, capitalizer, and laborer ever accomplished." Yet by 1830, if not earlier, this coöperation had been perverted into a foul system of exploitation.

In the first place, the dividend of a voyage was usually computed not on what the cargo fetched, but on oil prices fixed by the owner on arrival, at a rate well below the market price, which was constantly

[1] These voyages ranged in length between two and four years. On her next voyages, during the Civil War, the *Lagoda* netted her owners 219 and 363 per cent profit. The average cost of a whaler, fitted for sea, was estimated in 1841 at $20,120, of which about half was the value of the vessel and the other half outfit. The *Lagoda's* cost of fitting out came very close to this average. She measured 107' 6" × 26' 9" × 18' 4", 371 tons.

tending upward. The 'lay' or proportion of the catch granted an able seaman declined to one-seventy-fifth or one-ninety-fifth, and that of a green hand to one-one-hundred-and-fiftieth, one-two-hundredth, or as little as ignorant men could be induced to take. Divide fifty to seventy-five thousand dollars, a high average yield for a voyage at this period, by 175, and you get $285.72 to $428.57; a green hand's gross compensation for three to four years' labor at sea.[1] Even this

[1] The following account of a voyage of the New Bedford whaling ship *Benjamin Tucker* between 1839 and 1843 is fairly typical of a number I have seen in the New Bedford public library. Accounts of men who did not complete the voyage are omitted.

	Lay	Share of proceeds of voyage	Charged for outfit, plus 25 per cent	Captain's bill (slop-chest, and advances of spending money)
Captain.........	1/16	$2358.75	..	..
First Mate.......	1/24	1572.50	..	..
2d "	1/43	1023.95	..	..
3d "	1/65	677.38	..	..
4th "	1/78	564.48	..	..
Boat steerer......	1/87	506.09	..	38.98
Boat steerer......	1/95	463.47	74.36	64.12
" "	"	"	..	82.03
" "	"	"	..	90.68
Cook............	1/150	293.83	90.00	123.48
Seaman	1/170	259.00	21.00	66.02
"	"	"	36.40	52.12
"	1/160	275.12	107.00	76.66
Landsman	1/190	231.73	107.57	63.46
"	"	"	100.70	76.10

In addition, each man had charged against him the above-mentioned fees for fitting out, discharging cargo, and medicine chest; but no insurance. The two landsmen and the last seaman left the ship owing the owners money, at the end of this four-year voyage. After another voyage on the same ship, one green hand was paid off with $1.31. and another with $16.

beggarly sum was begrudged him by the owners, who devised various means to rob him thereof. On many ships ten per cent was deducted for 'leakage,' and three per cent for insurance; yet if the ship and cargo were lost, all the insurance money went to the owners. Certain owners charged against each lay the value of the casks, and a commission for selling the oil, in spite of judicial decisions against the legality of such practice. Each whaleman was charged eight to ten dollars for fitting out, and the same for discharging the vessel; and a dollar and a half for his share of the medicine chest. For his 'expenses' and 'outfit,' some 'land-shark' outfitter at New Bedford was given a good round sum, on which the owners charged the men twenty-five per cent interest; and the 'slop-chest' absorbed a good part of the rest.

This slop-chest was the skipper's store, from which the men replenished their tattered garments and empty tobacco pouches at a high advance on cost.[1] It existed on merchantmen as well. But on many whalers the only way for a man to get spending money at Fayal or Honolulu or Papeete was to buy slops at inflated prices and sell them ashore for a song. Consequently

[1] Oral tradition, and some of the leading authorities on the whaling industry, state that several hundred per cent profit was made by the slop-chest. In the ship's disbursement accounts I have examined, the profits were fairly reasonable, judged by 1921 standards. Here are some extracts from the 'slop-chest invoice' of the *Benjamin Tucker:*

	Cost	Sell at
Monkey jackets............	$6.50	$10.00
Trousers..................	2.40	4.00
Guernsey frocks...........	.87	1.50
Scotch caps	.37	.62
Jack-knives...............	.16–.29	.40–.50
Tobacco, lb...............	.16	.25

The slop-chest was also used in trading with natives for supplies, and contained bolts of cheap cottons, and other merchandise for this especial purpose.

many whaling ships returned to New Bedford after a cruise of several years, with every green hand's 'lay' eaten up by his debts to the ship.

Except for the boat-steerers or harpooners, who lived apart from the common sailors and had a 'lay' that netted them something, whaling vessels did not ship seamen. Neither American seamen nor any other kind would have stood for the extortion and cruelty practiced by owners and skippers. Shipping agents, with offices in New York, Boston, and inland cities like Buffalo, circulated lurid handbills depicting the excitement of the chase and the fat profits of a voyage. Their principal victims were farmer boys from New England and New York, bitten with the lure of the sea. Unemployed immigrants and mill-hands, fugitives from justice, and human derelicts were also drawn in. Many are the stories of old-time whaling agents. If a raw rustic protested against the size of his lay, the agent would magnanimously grant him one-two-hundred-and-seventy-fifth instead of one-hundred-and-seventy-fifth. A well-known Boston agent, after describing to a Maine ploughboy the imaginary joys of this glorious profession, concluded confidentially: "Now, Hiram, I'll be *honest* with yer. When yer out in the boats chasin' whales, yer git yer mince-pie *cold!*"

During the first months of a whaling voyage the green hands were 'learned' the ropes with a rope's end, taught to row the whaleboats, and broken in generally. Their numbers were increased by a few hungry and docile 'Portygees' at Fayal or St. Iago, where the whaling vessels touched to trade liquor for fresh provisions and to ship home the oil obtained on the passage across.[1] This led to an extensive migration from

[1] "We are in advance to all your crew from 70 to 80 dollars, it will therefore be necessary to obtain some oil before going into port as they

322

the Azores and Cape Verde Islands to New Bedford, until to-day the Western Islanders and Bravas are the most numerous alien element in the Old Colony, and in parts of it the sole cultivators of the soil.

Whaling vessels never returned to New Bedford or Nantucket with the same crew that they shipped. Many whalemen deserted their floating hells in the Pacific Islands. Those who kept out of debt to the ship were encouraged to desert, or abandoned on frivolous pretexts, in defiance of the law, that their lays might be forfeited.[1] And once a Pacific beachcomber, a man seldom became anything better. A United States consul in the Pacific estimated in 1859 that three or four thousand young men were annually lost to their country through this channel. To replace them, Kanakas, Tongatabooars, Filipinos, and even Fiji cannibals like Melville's hero Queequeg, were signed on for a nominal wage or microscopic lay. Whaling vessels no longer returned as soon as their holds were full; a cargo would be shipped home by merchant vessels from Honolulu, and the voyage prolonged until the old hooker crawled around the Horn with a yard of weed on her bottom and a crew that looked like shipwrecked mariners.

These three- and four-year voyages,[2] touching at

may be likely to desert — in which case we are losers." (Charles W. Morgan's instructions to Capt. Charles Downs of the barque *President*, "4th mo., 23d, 1830.") The captain of another whaler is instructed not to stop at the Westward Islands, as $100 or more has been expended for each whaleman's 'outfit.'

[1] The most impressive fact in the ship's disbursement accounts I have examined is the large number of men who deserted at outlandish ports, although money was coming to them. If a deserter was apprehended, the local police fees were charged up to him, with 25 per cent interest to boot.

[2] The average voyage of fifty-two sperm whalers and fifty right whalers which returned in 1847, was respectively forty-five months, twelve days, and thirty-one months, seven days.

no civilized port, brought out the worst traits of human nature. Whalers' forecastles were more efficient schools of vice than reformatories. Brutality from officers to men was the rule. Many whaling skippers, who on shore passed as pious friends or church-members, were cold-blooded, heartless fiends on the quarterdeck. Then, having made conditions such that no decent American would knowingly ship on a whaler, the blubber barons used the character of the crews they obtained as an argument for still harsher discipline. Men were hazed until they deserted, became cringing beasts, or mutinied. The ingenuity of whaling skippers in devising devilish punishments surpasses belief. Nor should one forget other ways in which these blackguards degraded the flag and the name of America. "Paying with the foretopsail" (sailing away without paying) was frequently practiced on Pacific islanders who had furnished supplies. The numerous conflicts between whalemen and natives were generally due to the meanness and rascality of skippers. Another practice, by no means uncommon at New Bedford and the Sound ports, was to fit out a whaler for a slaving voyage, unbeknown to the crew. As late as 1861 the owners of two New Bedford barques were condemned to hard labor in jail for slave-trading.

Whaling, after all, was better than most systems of peonage that flourish to-day, for it released its victims after a single voyage. Rarely, if a green hand made good with the skipper, he could be able seaman or boat-steerer (harpooner) on his second voyage; but the good 'short lays' were generally reserved for native Nantucketers, New Bedfordites, and Gay Head Indians. Compensations there were, even in a whaleman's life. If his vessel ran into several 'pods' of whales in succession, he was worked until he dropped, and then kicked to his feet; but ordinarily he had plenty of leisure to play cards and smoke, and to carve sperm whales' teeth into marvelous 'scrimshaw work' and 'jagging wheels.' There was nothing in the merchant marine corresponding to the friendly 'gams' or visits between whalers at sea; half the officers and crew of each vessel spending several hours, even the whole night, aboard the other.[1] But the great redeeming feature of whaling was the sport of it.

"There she blows! — there she breaches!" from the masthead lookout, was a magic formula that exalted this sordid, cruel business to an inspiring game; a game that made the rawest greenie a loyal team-mate of the hardest officer. First there was the bustle of sending away the boats, then the long, hard pull to the quarry, each of the four mates exhorting his crew with picturesque epithets to win the race: "Sing out and say something, my hearties. Roar and pull, my thunder-bolts! Beach me, beach me on their black backs, boys; only do that for me, and I'll sign over to you my Martha's Vineyard plantation, boys; including wife and children, boys! Lay me on — lay me on! O Lord, Lord! but I shall go stark, staring mad! See! See that white water!" The rowers' backs are to the whale, it is bad form to glance around, they know not how near they are until the mate shouts to the bow oar, the harpooner, *"Stand up, and let him have it!"* A shock as bow grounds on blubber, a frantic *"Starn all!"* and the death duel begins.

Anything may happen then. At best, a Nantucket sleighride, waves rushing past the whaleboats with a "surging, hollow roar . . . like gigantic bowls in a

---

[1] "Endeavor to avoid those [ships] that wish to spend much time in gamming — as a lone chance is generally best," writes Charles R. Tucker, owner, to Captain Charles Starbuck in 1836.

boundless bowling-green; the brief suspended agony of the boat, as it would tip for an instant on the knife-like edge of the sharper waves, that almost seemed threatening to cut it in two; the sudden profound dip into the watery glens and hollows; the keen spurrings and goadings to gain the top of the opposite hill; the headlong, sled-like slide down its other side; . . . the cries of the headsmen and harpooners, and the shuddering gasps of the oarsmen, with the wondrous sight of the ivory *Pequod* bearing down upon her boats with outstretched sails, like a wild hen after her screaming brood." Finally the whale slows down, exhausted, and the crew pull up on him, hand over hand on the line, and dispatch him with a few well-timed thrusts; then pull quickly out of his death-flurry. At worst, a canny old 'sparm' sinks out of sight, rises with open jaws, directly under the boat, and shoots with it twenty feet into the air, crushing its sides like an egg-shell, while the crew jump for their lives into seething, blood-streaked foam.

Whalemen enjoyed a variety of adventures such as no other calling approached, such as no millionaire big-game hunter of to-day can command. "Not the raw recruit, marching from the bosom of his wife into the fever heat of his first battle; not the dead man's ghost encountering the first unknown phantom in the other world; — neither of these can feel stranger and stronger emotions than that man does, who for the first time finds himself pulling into the charmed churned circle of the hunted sperm whale." When that moment came, no braver or gamier men could be found on blue water, than the whalemen of New England.

CHAPTER XXI

OH! CALIFORNIA

1844–1850

Oh! Susannah, darling, take your ease,
For we have beat the clipper fleet —
The Sovereign of the Seas.

THUS roared in lusty chorus one hundred seamen on
the Boston clipper ship *Sovereign of the Seas*, as she
sailed through Golden Gate, on November 15, 1852.
Before her, behind a hedge of spars and rigging,
swarmed a hill of human ants, building a great city
where ten years before the only signs of human life
were a mission village, and a Boston hide-drogher.
The refrain of that old popular song, the anthem of
the Argonauts, resounds through the clipper-ship era
of maritime Massachusetts.

Imagine a Yankee Rip van Winkle, who had slept
out his twenty years within hailing distance of the
State House dome. As he looked about him in 1853
the most astonishing sight would be — not the railroad, not the telegraph, not the steamship — but the
clipper ship. During the last half of his sleep there had
taken place the greatest revolution in naval architecture since the days of Hawkins and Drake. Below in
Boston Harbor, and setting sail for a port whose name
he had never heard, were vessels four and five times
as large as any he had ever seen, with canvas five and
six times the utmost area that the old Boston East-
Indiamen dared spread to the lightest air.

Now, before we relate this revolution, a paragraph
of definitions. A *ship*, as old-time sailors use the word,

327

and as I have attempted to use it throughout this book, meant a full-rigged ship, a three-masted vessel with square sails on all three masts. A *clipper ship*, as distinguished from other ships, was built and rigged with a view to speed, rather than carrying capacity or economy. Although larger, in general, than the older sailing vessels, it was the model and the rig of clipper ships that made them such, not their size. They were sharper in the ends, longer in proportion to their breadth, and more heavily sparred than the full-bodied, bluff-bowed ships of previous, and even later generations.[1] For the clipper ship came all at once, and fled as quickly as she came. There had been clipper *schooners* and clipper *brigs* since 1812, the term "clipper" connoting speed and smartness; but only six or eight clipper *ships* had been built before 1850. Then were brought forth, like so many Cythereas arising from the sea, the fairest vessels that ever sailed, to meet a special need — speed to California at any price or risk.

*
* *

About 1840 the rate of increase in the American merchant marine began to accelerate. The basic cause was ability of American shipbuilders and ship-owners to keep pace with the growing wealth, prosperity, and population of America. In 1849 Parliament repealed the Navigation Acts, thereby throwing open the British market to the products of New

[1] Compare in the accompanying illustration the ship *Mary Glover*, a non-clipper built in the clipper-ship era, with the clipper ship *Wild Ranger;* or, better still, visit the Peabody Museum, Salem, and compare the half-models of the *Flying Cloud* and the frigate *Constitution;* or the Marine Museum at the Old State House, Boston, to compare models of different types.

England shipyards. At the same time the China trade was prospering; and competition between the ships of Russell & Co., the New York firms, and the great British houses, to market the new teas, stimulated shipbuilders.

These conditions created a demand for more ships, speedier ships, and bigger ships. Samuel Hall, of East Boston, built for the Forbes's China fleet in 1839 an unusually fast ship *Akbar*, 650 tons, the last word of the Medford type of 1830. New York builders knew how to construct the larger vessels through their experience with the North Atlantic packets; but the merchants wanted something more than size. Baltimore builders had the reputation for speed, through their clipper schooners and brigs of the long, low, rakish type beloved by slavers, pirates, and novelists. Samuel Hall had successfully copied or adapted their lines for pilot schooners, fishing schooners, and small opium clippers. But the Baltimore clipper model was as unsuitable for a vessel of one thousand tons, as would be a cat-boat model for a fishing schooner. For centuries, shipbuilders had maintained that you could have either speed or burthen, not both; but New York and Boston wanted both, and they got it.

Although Boston carried the clipper ship to its ultimate perfection, New York invented the type. John W. Griffeths, chief draughtsman of Smith & Dimon, produced in 1845 the *Rainbow*, 750 tons, the first extreme clipper ship. Her long, fine ends and cross-section like a flattened V, came from the Baltimore clipper; but the concave lines of her bow above the water-line, a characteristic feature of the clipper ships, were suggested by the model of a Singapore sampan which Captain Bob Waterman brought home.

After some remarkable passages to China, the *Rain-bow's* model was imitated in five or six clipper ships of moderate burthen, built at New York between 1844 and 1848. As yet not a single vessel of this type had been launched from a Massachusetts yard. But the way was being prepared.

Donald McKay, born of Scots stock at Shelburne, Nova Scotia, in 1810, played about the local yards as a boy, and built a fishing boat with his brother in their early teens. Stimulated, perhaps, by a wandering Sam Slick, this youthful 'blue-nose' emigrated to New York, obtained employment at the shipyard of Isaac Webb, and quickly mastered the profession. Luckily for Massachusetts, he turned eastward again at the age of thirty, when he was ready to launch out as a master builder. At first working under John Currier, Jr., a leading shipbuilder of Newburyport, he became his partner in 1841, and produced for New York order two ships which proved wonders for finish, appearance, and speed.

In 1843 Enoch Train, a Boston merchant in the South American and Baltic trades, decided that his city must have a line of Liverpool sailing packets. He doubted whether any New England yard were capable of turning one out. Meeting by chance the New York owner of Donald McKay's first ship, he heard such praise of the young master builder of Newburyport as to give him the contract for his first packet. When he saw the *Joshua Bates*, this pioneer ship of his new line, glide gracefully into the Merrimac, Enoch Train recognized the genius of her builder. At his persuasion, and backed by his financial influence, McKay established a new shipyard at East Boston. There he built in rapid succession, the *Ocean Monarch*,[1] *Daniel*

---

[1] *Ocean Monarch*, 178' 6" × 40' × 26' 10", 1301 tons; built 1848.

OH! CALIFORNIA

Webster,[1] and other famous packet-ships for the Train Line, and (in 1846) the *New World*, 1404 tons, a record in size, for a New York firm. These ships were not clippers, but they established the reputation of Donald McKay, and gave him the practice and equipment to astonish the world when another event created a demand for clipper ships of fifteen hundred tons upwards.

*

* *

On January 24, 1848, a workman at Sutter's Mill, California, discovered a gold nugget in the raceway. When the news reached the Atlantic coast, it was received with incredulity, but by the end of the year, when reports were accompanied by actual nuggets, the gold-fever of '49 swept through Massachusetts. Farmers mortgaged their farms, workmen downed tools, clerks left counting-rooms, and even ministers abandoned their pulpits in order to seek wealth in this land of Havilah. Few Yankee Argonauts took the usual overland trail. True to type, they chose the ocean route. But like most of the 'forty-niners,' many of them went organized in semi-communistic brotherhoods. How this idea originated no one seems to know. Whether Fourierism had any influence is doubtful, and the Communist Manifesto could hardly have inspired a movement, the sole object of which was money-getting. A few companies were financed by local capitalists, in return for a guaranteed percentage of the winnings, precisely as the merchant adventurers of Old England 'grub-staked' the Pilgrim fathers. But for the most part the gold-seekers of Massachu-

[1] *Daniel Webster*, 185' × 37' 3" × 24' (unusually long and narrow for a packet ship), 1187 tons; built 1850.

331

setts journeyed West in organized groups, each member of which was pledged to serve his fellows to the best of his particular ability, and entitled to receive an equal share in the common gold production.

These emigrant companies varied in number from ten to one hundred and fifty young men, of all trades and professions. There was the Bunker Hill Mining & Trading Company, composed of thirty mechanics from Charlestown, Cambridge, and Somerville, paying five hundred dollars each; the New Bedford Company, commanded by Rotches and Delanos; the El Dorado Association of Roxbury; the Hampshire & Holyoke Mining & Trading Company; the Sagamore & Sacramento Company of Lynn; the Cotuit Port Association; the Winnigahee Mining Company of Edgartown; the Hyannis Gold Company; the Cape Ann Pioneers; and at least a hundred and fifty others from all parts of the state.

A few of these emigrant companies followed the transcontinental route. The Overland Company, of fifty young Roxbury men, marched in gray-and-gold uniforms, with seven wagons, thirty-one mules, four horses, six dogs, two colored servants, and four musicians. They arrived in Sacramento after intense sufferings, and heavy casualties among the mules. A few took the Panama route, but suffered great hardships crossing the Isthmus, and were charged from two hundred to six hundred dollars each for passage thence to San Francisco. But the great majority took sail around the Horn. Not clipper ships; far from it! There were few companies like the exclusive North Western of Boston, composed of Adamses, Dorrs, and Whipples paying a thousand dollars each, which could afford a crack clipper brig. Few shipowners would charter. The oldest, slowest, and most decrepit ves-

sels were purchased, because they were cheap. Many
companies, especially those recruited on Cape Cod and
Nantucket, handled their own vessels. Twelve out of
one company of sixteen that left the island on February 1, 1849, were whaling captains, as familiar with
the route to 'Frisco as with "Marm Hackett's garden."
The gold-fever drained Nantucket of one-quarter of
its voting population in nine months. In the same
period eight hundred men left New Bedford for the
mines. There were one hundred and fifty clearances
from Boston to California in 1849, one hundred and
sixty-six in 1850, and many more from the smaller
ports.

The Mexican War had hardly disturbed Massachusetts; but all through forty-nine the Bay State
presented the spectacle of a community preparing for
war on a large scale. Prudent companies took two
years' provision, and stories of 'Frisco lawlessness
made every emigrant a walking arsenal. Beef-packing
establishments, ship-biscuit bakeries and firearm man-
ufactories were running full blast; and the Ames plow
works turned from agricultural machinery to picks
and shovels. "The members of a society could be told
by their slouched hats, high boots, careless attire and
general appearance of reckless daring and potential
wealth," writes Dr. Octavius T. Howe. On the Sabbath preceding departure each company marched in a
body to hear a farewell sermon (Genesis II, 12, being
the favorite text), and to receive one or more Bibles
each from sympathetic and envious neighbors. Most
companies took care to admit only men of good character, and their by-laws usually contain prohibitions of
drunkenness, gambling, and swearing, which, like all
their regulations, were well enough observed until
they reached California. The Boston *Journal* pub-

lished a special California edition for circulation on the Coast.

When the Salem barque *Eliza* cast off from Derby Wharf for California, late in '48, one of the passengers sang the following words to the popular tune of "Oh! Susannah":

> I came from Salem City,
>   With my washbowl on my knee.
> I'm going to California,
>   The gold dust for to see.
> It rained all night the day I left,
>   The weather it was dry,
> The sun so hot I froze to death,
>   Oh! brothers, don't you cry.
>   *Oh! California,*
>   *That's the land for me!*
>   *I'm going to Sacramento*
>   *With my washbowl on my knee.*
>
> I jumped aboard the 'Liza ship,
>   And traveled on the sea,
> And every time I thought of home
>   I wished it wasn't me!
>   *Oh! California,*
>   *That's the land for me!*
>   *I'm off for Californi-a*
>   *With my washbowl on my knee.*

This song in countless versions, but with the same washbowl chorus, became the anthem of the forty-niners.

Deep-sea sailormen have always insisted that the discipline and safety of a ship can only be maintained by despotic power in the master. But democracy ruled on the forty-niner vessels. Each company, although composed in good part of master mariners, was a miniature soviet. The captain was elected, and sometimes deposed by majority vote; and the same method

334

OH! CALIFORNIA

determined ports of call, and whether the Straits of Magellan or the Cape Horn were chosen. One night off the River Plate on the little schooner *Roanoke*, belonging to the Boston Marine Mining Company, all the watch were below playing whist with the skipper, except a man at the wheel and another on the lookout. The latter, seeing a squall approach, called repeatedly to his captain to send up the watch, but the game was too interesting to interrupt. Finally he sang out, "Say, Captain, if you don't send that watch up to take in the flying jib, you can take it in yourself, I'll be d—d if I'm going to get wet!"

In spite of these soviet methods (or because of them some will say) it seems that every one of these small and often superannuated vessels arrived safely at San Francisco. But ship fever (typhus) took a heavy toll of their passengers, on the five to eight months' voyage.

On arrival, each member's part was provided in the by-laws. Some were to stick to the ship, guard the stores, or cook; the majority wash for gold; but all share alike what the mining members produced. What actually happened is well told in a doggerel poem by Isaac W. Baker, in his manuscript "Journal of Proceedings on board the barque *San Francisco*, of and from Beverly for California":

> The San Francisco Company, of which I've often told,
> At Sacramento has arrived in search of glittering gold,
> The bark hauled in, the cargo out, and that is not the worst
> The Company, like all the rest, have had a talk and burst.
> *For 't was, talk, talk, growl, growl, talk, talk away,*
> *The devil a bit of comfort's here in Californi-a.*
>
> While on the passage all was well, and every thing was nice,
> And if there was a civil growl, 't was settled in a trice,
> But here example had been set by companies before,
> Who'd all dissolved and nothing less, so we did nothing more
> *But talk, talk,* etc.

335

We'd forty men of forty minds, instead of one alone,
And each wished to convert the rest, but still preferred his own,
Now in some places this might do, but here it won't, you see,
For independence is the word in Californi-e.

At first the price of lumber fell, which made it bad for us,
Some wished to sell and some did not, which made the matter
    worse,
Some longed to start into the mines and let the Barkey stay
While others said it would n't do for all to go away.

Some longed to get their ounce a day, while others knew they
    could n't,
And wished to share and keep all square, but then the workers
    would n't.
A meeting of the whole was called, the question put and tried,
Our Constitution voted down, our Bye Laws null and void.

Now carpenters can take a job and work for what they please,
And those who do not like to work can loaf and take their ease
And squads can form for travelling, or any thing they choose,
And if they don't a fortune make, they 'll not have it to lose.
    And can chat, chat, sing, sing, chat, chat away,
    And take all comfort that they can in Californi-a.

Within three weeks of landing on California soil,
every emigrant company dissolved into its separate,
individual elements. For a treasure-seeking enterprise like that of '49, in a setting of pioneer individual-
ism, communism was about as well suited as to the
New York stock exchange or the Supreme Council of
the League of Nations.

The Massachusetts forty-niners did not go to California to settle. The average man's intention was to
make his pile and return home rich. A few did come
back to dazzle the natives, and a few became California millionaires; but the greater part went broke.
It was not the miners who made the big money in '49–
'50, but the men who exploited the miners.

Of the many stories of fortunes lost and won by

emigrating Yankees, that of Dr. Samuel Merritt, of Plymouth, is typical. Liquidating his property, he purchased a brig and loaded her with merchandise and passengers. At the last moment he decided to invest in tacks for the California market, and started on horseback for the Duxbury tack factory. On the way he was overtaken by a messenger, who recalled him to attend an accident, immediately after which he had to sail, without the tacks. They were selling for five dollars a paper at San Francisco when he arrived. At Valparaiso, on the way, another fortune was missed by failing to fill up a hole in the cargo with potatoes, of which the San Francisco market was totally denuded. But the bottom had fallen out of the market for every other article in his cargo. However, within a year his medical practice at San Francisco brought him forty thousand dollars.

Hoping to become the Frederic Tudor of the coast, Dr. Merritt chartered a Maine brig to load ice at Puget Sound and bring it to San Francisco in time for summer. His captain discovered that Puget Sound was not Maine, but returned with a load of piles in lieu of ice. Piles happened to be much wanted then for wharves, and the venture proved profitable, as did a second of the same nature. Vessels began to flock northward for piles, so the Doctor wisely decided he had had the cream, and would let them take the skim milk. He directed his shipmaster to take Puget Sound timber to Australia, to exchange for coal. Again the captain used good judgment. Instead of coal, he returned with a load of oranges from the Society Islands, and made another killing. Dr. Merritt then closed his office, purchased a large tract of land across the Bay, created the city of Oakland, and in due course became a multi-millionaire, mayor of the city, and owner of the finest yacht on the Coast.

A stranger fate was that of John Higgins, of Brewster, forty-niner who never reached California. Working his way out on a steamer, he was wrecked on the Australian coast, shipped as second mate on a brig, was shipwrecked again, and drifted to the Wellington Islands, where the natives received him with open arms. He married the chief's daughter, established a trading business with the whalers, and left two sons to continue his work of civilization, which even the missionaries acknowledged to be more successful than any black-coated brother possibly could have done.

Many Massachusetts shipowners sent their vessels with full cargoes to San Francisco in time to obtain the prices of '49 that seem fabulous even to-day — forty-four dollars a barrel for flour, sixteen dollars a bushel for potatoes, ten dollars a dozen for eggs that had been around the Horn, one thousand per cent profit on lumber. Freights rose to such figures that the ship *Argonaut*, built at Medford in 1849 for John E. Lodge, paid for herself before casting off her lines for her maiden voyage. When reports of these prices reached the merchant-shipowners, they rushed cargoes of every sort and description around the Horn, until in 1851 the market became glutted and unopened cases of dry goods were used for sidewalks in the muddy streets of San Francisco. Between June 26 and July 28, 1850, there entered the Golden Gate seventeen vessels from New York and sixteen from Boston, whose average passage was one hundred and fifty-nine days. Yet on July 24 there arrived at San Francisco the little New York clipper ship *Sea Witch*, just ninety-seven days out. Every mercantile agency in San Francisco began clamoring for goods to be shipped by clipper, and the shipyards responded to their demand.

CHAPTER XXII

THE CLIPPER SHIP

1850–1854

THE golden sands of California were a quickening force to the shipyards of Massachusetts. For four years they teemed with the noblest fleet of sailing vessels that man has ever seen or is likely to see.

Massachusetts launched her first clipper ships in 1850, from the yard of Samuel Hall; the *Surprise* [1] for the Salem Lows, then of New York; and the *Game-Cock* [2] for Daniel C. Bacon, of Boston.

Samuel Hall, now fifty years old, was the most eminent shipbuilder in the commonwealth. Of an old Marshfield family, he served his apprenticeship on the North River, and at his majority left for Medford with a capital consisting of a broad-axe and twenty-five cents. After pursuing his trade on the Mystic, the Penobscot, and at Duxbury, he became, as we have seen, the pioneer master builder of East Boston. The *Game-Cock* and *Surprise* were designed by a twenty-three-year-old Bostonian named Samuel H. Pook, [3] the first independent architect of merchant vessels in New England.

Well did Sam Hall choose the name of his first

[1] *Surprise*, 183′ 6″ × 38′ 8″ × 22′, 1261 tons.
[2] *Game-Cock*, 190′ 6″× 39′ 10″ × 22′, 1392 tons.
[3] Samuel Hartt Pook (1827–1901) designed three of the eighteen California clippers that made a voyage of less than one hundred days from an Atlantic port to San Francisco before 1861 — the *Surprise*, *Witchcraft*, and *Herald of the Morning*; and the *Northern Light*, which has the record from San Francisco to Boston. An early advocate of iron-clads, he became, like his father, Samuel Moore Pook (1804–78) a naval constructor, U.S.N., and remained in the service until 1889.

clipper ship. One surprise of her launching was a banquet, not for owners and bankers and all bumbledom, but for the mothers, wives, and sweethearts of the workingmen who built the ship. The next sensation came when she was launched fully rigged, with her gear rove off, all three skysail yards crossed, and colors flying. Water-front pessimists expected her to capsize with such heavy top-hamper. Others said she would slide into the harbor mud and stick there. But with half Boston cheering, and the bells of every church and meeting-house jangling out a welcome, the *Surprise* clave the water with her sharp stern, shot out into the harbor, swayed gently to get her balance, and paused, erect, with the air of a young and insolent queen.

She was the first clipper ship commanded by Philip Dumaresq.[1] He came of a long line of merchant-captains. His mother belonged to the Gardiner-Hallowell family, and Philip was born on one of their great Kennebec estates in 1809. But like his only peers on clipper quarterdecks, Captains "Bully" Waterman, of New York, "Nat" Palmer, of Stonington, and "Perk" Cressy, of Marblehead, Captain Dumaresq had followed the sea since his teens, and worked his way up from before the mast. At twenty-two he received his first command, and in Russell & Co.'s China fleet became noted for his expert navigation, for quiet, effective discipline, and for getting the utmost speed out of a vessel. The *Surprise*, under Captain Dumaresq, again fulfilled the promise of her name. On her maiden voyage she knocked a day off the *Sea Witch's* record to San Francisco, which conservatives had ascribed to Waterman's luck. But the new mark of ninety-six days did not last long.

[1] Pronounced "D'merrick."

THE CLIPPER SHIP

On a bitterly cold December afternoon in 1850, Donald McKay launched the *Stag-Hound*, his first clipper. Pioneer of a new fifteen-hundred-ton class, the *Stag-Hound* both by her appearance and her performance [1] placed Donald McKay at the head of his profession. Before many months passed the head of the New York firm of Grinnell, Minturn & Co. visited McKay's yard, and took a fancy to a ship that was being built for Enoch Train. He offered double the contract price to the owner, who could not afford to refuse. It was a good bargain for Grinnell & Minturn; for this was the *Flying Cloud*.

McKay built faster clippers and larger clippers; but for perfection and beauty of design, weatherliness and consistent speed under every condition, neither he nor any one else surpassed the *Flying Cloud*. She was the fastest vessel on long voyages that ever sailed under the American flag.

Her dimensions were 229 feet length on deck, 40 feet, 8 inches breadth, and 21 feet, 6 inches depth; registered tonnage 1783. Her figurehead was a winged angel blowing a trumpet just under the bowsprit. Captain Josiah Perkins Cressy,[2] of Marblehead, thirty-seven years old but fourteen years a shipmaster, was her commander. On her maiden voyage in the summer of 1851 the *Flying Cloud* made a day's run of 374 miles, logged 1256 miles in four consecutive days, and arrived at San Francisco eighty-nine days out of New York. This run was only twice equaled, by herself in 1854, and by the *Andrew Jackson* in 1860. On her

[1] The *Stag-Hound* (209' × 39' 8" × 21', 1534 tons) holds the record of thirteen days from Boston Light to the equator, no other ship having come within three days of it, whether from Boston or Sandy Hook. She has second-best record, eight days, twenty hours, from San Francisco to Honolulu.

[2] Pronounced "Creecy."

return passage, having crossed the Pacific to Canton for a cargo of tea, the *Flying Cloud* made the two thousand miles from that port to Java Head in six days, almost halving the previous record. In addition, she has the best average for three, four, and five voyages from an Atlantic port to San Francisco.

Donald McKay was an unusual combination of artist and scientist, of idealist and practical man of business. With dark hair curling back from a high, intellectual forehead, powerful Roman nose, inscrutable brown eyes, and firm lips, he was as fair to look upon as his ships. His serene and beautiful character won him the respect and the affection of his employees, and made the atmosphere of his shipbuilding yard that of a happy, loyal family. His ships were alive to him, and when permitted to name them himself by a wise owner, he invariably chose something fitting and beautiful. *Stag-Hound* and *Mastiff* for two powerful, determined clippers that could grapple with every element but fire; *Flying Cloud* — her rivals knew what that meant, when she tore by them at sea; *Flying Fish* and *Westward Ho!* — both of the California fleet; *Romance of the Seas* for a ship whose sleek, slender beauty reminded the old salts of their youthful visits to Nukahiva; *Sovereign of the Seas* for a stately clipper that made a marvelous record against head winds and hurricanes; *Great Republic* for the ship of ships; *Lightning* for the fastest sailing vessel ever built, and *Glory of the Seas* for his last, and in some respects his best, creation.

Experience, character, and mathematics self-taught were the firm soil from which the genius of Donald McKay blossomed. He designed every vessel built in his yard, and personally attended to every detail of her construction.

THE CLIPPER SHIP

... First with nicest skill and art,
Perfect and finished in every part,
A little model the Master wrought,
Which should be to the larger plan
What the child is to the man,
Its counterpart in miniature.

From the model the lines were taken off, enlarged to their proper dimensions, and laid down in the mold-loft. When the great frames were in place, Donald McKay would inspect the ship's skeleton from every angle, clothing it in imagination with skin of oak; and if anything looked wrong by perhaps an eighth of an inch, he chalked a frame for shaving off or filling out. By such methods were designed these great clipper ships that moved faster through the water, laden down as they were with heavy cargoes, than any sailing yacht or fancy racing machine designed by the scientific architects of to-day.[1] Eight knots an hour is considered good speed for an *America's* cup race of thirty miles. The *Red Jacket* logged an average of 14.7 for six consecutive days in the Western Ocean; the *Lightning* did 15.5 for ten days, covering 3722 miles, and averaged 11 for an entire passage from Australia to England. A speed of 12.5 knots on a broad reach in smooth waters, by the *Resolute* or *Shamrock*, excites the yachting reporters. The *Lightning* logged 18.2 for twenty-four hours in 1854, and there is a record that the *James Baines* on an Australian voyage in 1856 attained a speed of 21 knots.[2]

[1] No disparagement of modern naval architects is intended; they have progressed far beyond the designs of the fifties in fishing schooners and yachts. Yet, I am informed by one of the most eminent among them, no one to-day could make an essential improvement over the McKay clippers, for a sailing ship of their size.

[2] In justice to the improved full-bodied vessels built at this period, it

343

The records show conclusively Donald McKay's supremacy over any other builder, and the supremacy of Massachusetts builders over those of any other state. Only twenty-two passages from an Atlantic port around Cape Horn to San Francisco, in less than one hundred days, are on record. Of these, seven were made by McKay ships — *Flying Cloud* and *Flying Fish*, two each; *Great Republic*, *Romance of the Seas*, and *Glory of the Seas*. Only two other builders, Samuel Hall, of Boston, with the *John Gilpin* and *Surprise*, and Westervelt, of New York, have even two voyages in this honor list. Including the *Witchcraft*, built by Paul Curtis at Chelsea, and the *Herald of the Morning*, built by Hayden & Cudworth at Medford, we have one-half of these record voyages over the longest race-course in the world, to the credit of Massachusetts-built vessels. Of the rest, four belong to the other New England states, and seven to New York.[1]

There were a dozen or more Massachusetts builders besides Donald McKay and Samuel Hall, who built clipper ships that were a credit to the commonwealth. Edwin and Harrison O. Briggs, of South Boston, grand-

should be remarked that they too made some remarkable passages. In 1854 the barque *Dragon* of Salem, 289 tons, Captain Thomas C. Dunn, built at Newburyport in 1850, made the 16,670-mile run from Salem to the Fiji Islands in eighty-five days; an average of 8.2 knots for the entire voyage. Few tramp steamers to-day could do better.

[1] The list of all California outward passages between 1850 and 1861 made in 110 days or better (in Captain Clark's *Clipper Ship Era*, Appendix II) gives the same result. Nineteen are by McKay ships. His nearest competitor, Webb, of New York, has fifteen. All the other Boston builders together have twenty-two, all the other New York builders, twenty-three. Medford builders have seventeen; other Massachusetts builders, seven. Yet out of 171 California clipper ships and barques listed by Captain Clark, McKay built only ten; Samuel Hall and Briggs Bros., of Boston, and Webb, of New York, each built eleven. In addition, McKay built the great Australian clippers which do not figure in this list, and which no builder, American or foreign, equaled.

sons of the North River builder of the *Columbia*, specialized in medium clipper ships, a class somewhat underbred in appearance compared with the *Flying Cloud* and *Surprise*, but with carefully designed waterlines and small displacement which often produced remarkable speed. Their *Northern Light*,[1] under the command of Captain Hatch, completed a round voyage from Boston to San Francisco in exactly seven months. On the homeward passage, off Cape Horn, she passed the New York clipper ship *Contest*, which had sailed a day earlier; and with skysails, ringtail and studdingsails set on both sides, alow and aloft, she slipped into the Narrows of Boston Harbor on the evening of May 27, 1853, just seventy-six days, five hours, from San Francisco. That record remains good to this day.[2]

Other bright lights of Briggs Brothers were the *Boston Light*, *Starlight*, and the ill-fated *Golden Light*, which, ten days out on her first voyage, was set afire by lightning, and abandoned at sea.

Robert E. Jackson, of East Boston, built the *Winged Racer*, *John Bertram*, *Blue Jacket*, and the *Queen of Clippers*,[3] "one of the finest and largest of these ships," wrote Frank Marryat, the English traveler, from San Francisco. "She is extremely sharp at either end, and, 'bows on,' she has the appearance of a wedge. Her accommodations are as perfect as those of a first-class ocean steamer, and are as handsomely decorated; and,

---

[1] *Northern Light*, 171' 4" × 36' × 21' 9", 1021 tons; built 1851.

[2] In San Francisco voyages the homeward passage was much easier than the outward owing to prevailing westerly winds. Consequently the outward passage is always selected as a test of a vessel's performance, and the *Northern Light's* feat by no means equals the *Flying Cloud's* record of eighty-nine days to San Francisco. But she made Manila in eighty-nine days from Boston in 1856.

[3] *Queen of Clippers*, 248' 6" × 45' × 24', 2360 tons; built in 1853 for Seccomb & Taylor, of Boston, but sold to Zerega & Co., of New York.

as it is worthy of remark that great attention has been paid to the comfort of the crew." Paul Curtis's *Witchcraft* was a fast and handsome clipper, with a grim Salem witch for her figure-head. Medford builders like J. O. Curtis, Hayden & Cudworth, and S. Lapham have more fast California passages to their credit, considering the number they built, than those of any other place. Several smaller clipper ships were built by the Shivericks, at East Dennis, by J. M. Hood & Co. at Somerset, and by the experienced builders of Newburyport, who surpassed all others for careful work and finish. The *Dreadnought*, built by Currier and Townsend, became the most famous Liverpool packet-ship, and was the only clipper to have a chanty composed in her special honor. Captain Samuel Samuels, of New York, unexcelled as a driver of men and vessels, commanded this "saucy, wild packet" for almost seventy passages across the Atlantic, in which she made several eastward runs under fourteen days.[1]

One finds many new names in the list of Massachusetts owners of clipper ships. Their great initial cost and maintenance expense brought about a separation of shipowner and merchant. The clippers were really

[1] *Dreadnought*, 220′ × 39′ × 26′, 1400 tons. Captain Clark (*Clipper Ship Era*, 246), by printing her actual log as given in three Liverpool papers, has definitely exploded the myth of the *Dreadnought's* nine-day seventeen-hour passage, from Sandy Hook to Queenstown in March, 1859, which Captain Samuels never claimed until the twentieth century. For evidence on the other side of this famous controversy, see F. B. C. Bradlee, *The Dreadnought* (2d ed., 1920). Mr. Bradlee has discovered a second "nine-day passage" in the *Illustrated London News*, July 9, 1859, which states that the *Dreadnought* "arrived off Cape Clear on the 27th ult., in nine days from New York." But the *New York Herald* of June 17, p. 8e, reports by telegraph from "Sandy Hook, June 16, sunset, . . . the ship Dreadnaught, for Liverpool, passed the bar at 12½ P.M. Wind SW, light." On July 19, p. 8c, it reports her arrival at Liverpool on July 2.

large packet-ships, whose owners depended for profit on freight and passage money, not on speculative cargoes of their own. And profit they certainly did make, in the flush days of 1850–53, for the glut of 1851 at San Francisco did not last long. Freight ranged as high as sixty dollars per ton, and it was an unlucky ship that did not pay for herself by her first round voyage to California. The *Surprise* did so, and made fifty thousand dollars to boot.

Many of the most famous Massachusetts-built clippers were owned by New York or British firms, and never saw Boston after their first departure. Others, owned by Boston or Salem firms, were operated out of New York. But there were still a goodly number that plied regularly from Boston to San Francisco, and then crossed the Pacific to bring tea, hemp, and sugar to England and America. Several clipper ships were owned on shares, like the old-timers, but operated by regular packet-lines. Such a one was the *Wild Ranger*,[1] built by J. O. Curtis at Medford in 1853 for various Searses and Thachers of Cape Cod, and commanded on two California voyages by one of their number, twenty-four-year-old J. Henry Sears, of Brewster.

In May, 1853, an intending passenger for San Francisco, perusing the shipping columns of the Boston "Daily Advertiser," would be embarrassed to make a choice. Winsor's Regular Line offer the "first-class clipper ships" *Belle of the West* and *Bonita*, and the "half-clipper barque" *Cochituate*. Timothy Davis & Co.'s Line advertise the "half clipper ship *Sabine*"

---

[1] *Wild Ranger*, 180′ × 35′ 4″ × 23′, 1044 tons. She was chartered to Glidden & Williams's Line. The ship *Mary Glover*, here depicted to show the contrast between a clipper and a contemporary full-bodied ship, was 595 tons, built by Briggs Brothers, at South Boston, in 1840. She was a very successful ship. and was reported still alive in 1900.

and the "new and beautiful clipper ship *Juniper*." [1]
Glidden & Williams make the bravest display with
the "magnificent first-class clipper ship *White Swal-
low*," to be followed by the *Wild Ranger* and *John
Bertram;* the "new and beautiful half clipper ship
West Wind" and the "first-class and well-known
packet-ship *Western Star*." This was the greatest of
the Boston firms operating clipper ships. Its San
Francisco line also contained, at one time or another,
the *Witch of the Wave, Golden West, Queen of the Seas,
Westward Ho!, Morning Light,* and *Sierra Nevada.*
Sampson & Tappan owned the *Flying Fish, Winged
Racer,* and *Nightingale,* a supremely beautiful extreme
clipper built in Portsmouth, New Hampshire, and
named for Jenny Lind. George Bruce Upton owned the
Stag-Hound, Reindeer, Bald Eagle, and *Romance of the
Seas.* James Huckins & Sons had most of the Briggs
Brothers' "Lights." Baker & Morrill owned the *Starlight* and *Southern Cross;* and John E. Lodge (father
of Senator Lodge), the *Argonaut, Don Quixote,* and
Storm King; William Lincoln & Co., the *Golden Eagle,
Kingfisher,* and *White Swallow;* Curtis & Peabody, the
Meteor, Cyclone, Saracen, and *Mameluke.* The *Fear-
less, Galatea,* and two named *Golden Fleece,* carried the
black race-horse flag of William F. Weld & Co., a
house which outlasted most of the merchant-shipowners of Boston, and after the Civil War owned the
largest sailing fleet in America.

Two famous Boston firms of Cape Cod origin were

---

[1] One will search in vain for several of these "clippers" in authorita-
tive lists like Captain Clark's and Dr. O. T. Howe's, for when the clipper
ships became popular, every new vessel of a certain size was advertised
at least as "half-clipper." A rigid distinction is made in the early
American Lloyds' Registers between clipper ships, and sharp ships,
medium ships, and full-bodied ships, only the extremest of clippers
falling in the first class.

THE CLIPPER SHIP

Howes & Crowell, who owned the *Climax*, *Ringleader*, and *Robin Hood*, and D. G. & W. B. Bacon, who owned the *Game-Cock*, *Hoogly*, and *Oriental*. Daniel C. Bacon was a link between the Federalist and the clipper periods, having been mate under William Sturgis in the old Northwest fur trade. In 1852 he was elected president of the American Navigation Club, an association of Boston shipowners and merchants, which offered to back an American against a British clipper for a race from England to China and back, £10,000 a side. Although the stakes were subsequently doubled, no acceptance was received.

There was no veneer or sham about the beauty of the Massachusetts clippers. They were all well and solidly built of the best oak, Southern pine, and hackmatack, copper fastened and sheathed with Taunton yellow metal. Scamping or skimping never occurred to a clipper-ship builder, and if it had, no Yankee workman would have stayed in his yard. In finish the clipper ships surpassed anything previously attempted in marine art. Those built in Newburyport, in particular, were noted for the evenness of their seams and the perfection of their joiner-work. The topsides, planed and sandpapered smooth as a mackerel, were painted a dull black that brought out their lines like a black velvet dress on a beautiful woman. The pine decks were holystoned cream-white. Stanchions, fiferails, and houses shone with mahogany, rosewood, and brass. Many had sumptuous staterooms, cabins, and bathrooms for passengers, that put the old-time stuffy Cunarders to shame. The *Mastiff* had a library costing twelve hundred dollars. Constant improvements were made in gear and rigging. Patent blocks, trusses, and steering gear saved time and labor. The Howes double-topsail rig (an improvement on Captain R. B.

Forbes's invention) was generally adopted by the later clippers, spread to the ships of all nations, and is still in use. No detail was omitted that might increase speed, and no expense spared to make the Massachusetts clippers invulnerable to the most critical nautical eye.

Boston Harbor never presented a more animated spectacle than during the clipper-ship era. One April day in 1854, wrote F. O. Dabney, no less than six large new clippers, undergoing the process of rigging, could be seen from his counting-room windows on Central Wharf. Across the harbor, the East Boston shore from Jeffries' Point to Chelsea Bridge was almost a continuous line of vessels in various stages of construction. Twenty ships of eleven hundred tons upward were built there that year. Some idea of the inner harbor and the water-front may be gained from Mottram's engraving, and from the Bradlee photograph, both made at the end of the era, in 1857. In the center of the engraving is the clipper ship *Nightingale*, a marked contrast in size and form to the old-fashioned ship at the left of the picture. At the extreme left is a typical fishing pinkie; and this side of the *Nightingale*, a coasting schooner. The photograph shows Mediterranean fruiters lined up against Central Wharf, a New York packet-schooner at the extreme right, and in the center, conspicuous among the tier of vessels at the end of India Wharf, the clipper ship *Defender*, built by Donald McKay.

*

* *

The men who handled these great vessels were a class by themselves. The officers, mostly of New England stock and many from Cape Cod, had followed

350

the sea since boyhood, and were steeped in experience. No others could be trusted to drive these saucy, wild clippers against Cape Horn howlers, when the slightest misjudgment meant the loss of a spar, or loss of one hour — which was more important. They were devoted to the rigid traditions of the quarterdeck. The captain gave all his orders through the first officer, except for putting the ship about; and lived in a more dignified seclusion than the colonel of a regiment in a frontier garrison. No one spoke to him unless spoken to; the weather side of the quarterdeck was his private walk; whole voyages passed without a scrap of conversation between master and officers, except in line of duty. Men at the head of the profession like Captain Dumaresq were paid three thousand dollars for an outward passage to San Francisco, and five thousand if they made it under a hundred days.

Occasionally, clipper-ship commanders took their wives with them. Mrs. Cressy was the constant companion of her husband on the *Flying Cloud*. The wife of Captain Charles H. Brown gave birth to a son during a North Pacific gale, when the *Black Prince* was flying under close-reefed topsails. Immediately after, a heavy sea burst in the after cabin deadlight, shooting clear over the box in which the new-born babe was lying. But most remarkable of these brave women of the sea was Mrs. Captain Patten, of the *Neptune's Car*. In the midst of a Cape Horn gale Captain Patten came down with brain fever. The first mate was in irons for insubordination; the second mate was ignorant of navigation. But Mrs. Patten had made herself mistress of the art during a previous voyage. Without question, she took command. For fifty-two days this frail little Boston woman of *nineteen years* navigated a great clipper of eighteen hun-

351

dred tons, tending her husband the while; and took
both safely into San Francisco.[1]

*

* *

Yankee workmen built the clipper ships, but they
were not manned by Americans. The Yankee mariner,
with his neat clothes and perfect seamanship, had
passed into history by 1850. Few Americans could
then be found in the forecastles of merchantmen on
deep waters. When did this change take place? Why
did New Englanders abandon the sea?

In part, no doubt, it was a question of status. The
seaman was not as free as other workmen. His personal liberty was suspended until the end of the voyage.
Discipline was more severe, brutality more common,
and redress more difficult to obtain than in other call-
ings. Laws forbidding such practices as flogging, and
humane judges such as Peleg Sprague, of the District
Court at Boston, could do little to alter the tradition
of centuries. In one of his notable decisions,[2] Judge
Sprague remarked:

Seamen, in general, have little confidence in the justice of those
whom circumstances have placed above them, and there is too much
ground for this feeling. If a seaman is wronged by a subordinate
officer, and makes a complaint to the master, it too often happens
that he not only can obtain no hearing or redress, but brings upon
himself further and greater ill treatment; and an appeal to an
American consul against a master is oftentimes no more successful,
pre-occupied, as that officer is likely to be, by the representations and
influence of the master. Upon his return home, he finds those whom
he has served, the owners of the ship, generally take part, at once,

---

[1] Incredible as it may seem, Mrs. Patten's age is confirmed by the
Boston marriage records, which give her age as sixteen when she married
Captain Patten on April 1, 1853. She was Mary A. Brown, daughter of
George Brown, of Boston.

[2] Swain v. Howland (1858), 1 Sprague, 427.

with the officer, in every controversy with the seamen, and not infrequently exerting themselves to intercept that justice which the law would give him. And if to all this be added peculiar severity, even by the law of his country, . . . he may well be excused for feeling little confidence in the justice of superior powers. This feeling enters into his character, adds to his recklessness, weakens the ties that bind him to his country, and tends to make him a vagrant citizen of the world.

Our clipper ships were, in fact, manned by an international proletariat of the sea, vagrants with an attitude curiously similar to that of the casual workers in the West to-day.

Low wages, even more than low status, were responsible for this condition. In Federalist days an able seaman received eighteen dollars a month on Pacific voyages, and even more in neutral trading. In comparison with shore wages, and in lack of other opportunities, this was sufficient to attract Yankee youngsters to sea, though not to keep them there. During the slack period that followed the War of 1812, twelve dollars became the standard wage. An increase of tonnage in the thirties required more seamen. Instead of raising wages, to compete with the machine-shops and railroads and Western pioneering that were attracting young Yankees, the shipowners maintained or even depressed them, until ordinary and able seamen on California clippers received from eight to twelve dollars a month.[1] In the New Orleans cotton trade, and other lines of commerce out of Boston, as high as eighteen dollars was paid for able seamen, and the Liverpool 'packet-rats' got even more for their short and stormy runs. But in a period of rising costs and wages, the seaman's wage remained stationary, or declined. He had "no Sunday off soundings," and his

[1] Yet in 1856 Boston ship-carpenters and caulkers received $3 for a 6¾ hour day; longshoremen, $2 per tide; stevedores, 25 cents per hour.

calling was the most dangerous in the world. It took strength, skill, and courage to furl topsails on a great clipper ship, with its masts and eighty-foot yards bending like whalebone in a River Plate *pampero*, great blocks beating about like flails, and the No. O. Lowell duck sails slatting with enough force to crush a man's ribs.

Americans would not willingly accept such wages for such work. Coasting vessels, paying eighteen dollars a month, absorbed the Yankee boys with a craving for the sea. The shipowners could have obtained American crews had they been willing to pay for them; but they were not. Like the factory owners, they preferred cheap foreign labor.

A law of 1817 required two-thirds of an American crew to be American citizens. But this law was disregarded, as soon as it became the shipowners' interest to do so; and by the clipper period it was a dead letter. Captain Clark once had a Chinese cook who shipped as "George Harrison of Charlestown, Mass." When applicants for foremast berths became fewer, the shipowner had recourse to shipping agencies, which turned to the sailors' boarding-house keepers, making it their interest to rob and drug seamen in order to sign them on, and pocket their three months' advance wages. Thus began the system of crimping or shanghaiing. The percentage of foreigners and incompetents increased. Men of all nations,[1] and of the most depraved

---

[1] A sample crew is that of the ship *Reindeer*, Canton to Boston: 2 Frenchmen, 1 Portuguese, 1 Cape Verde Islander, 1 Azores man, 1 Italian, 1 Dutchman, 1 Mulatto, 2 Kanakas, 1 Welshman, 1 Swede, 2 Chinese, and 2 Americans. (Boston *Atlas*, July 22, 1851.) The *Black Prince* had even foreign officers. Captain Brown was a Portuguese by birth; the chief mate was Danish, the 2d British, the 3d German, and out of 24 able seamen there were but two Americans; one from Newburyport and one from Boston.

and criminal classes, some of them sailors, but many not, were hoisted, literally dead to the world, aboard the clippers. Habitual drunkards formed the only considerable native element in this human hash. "It is perfectly well known that sailors do get intoxicated," said Judge Sprague, when a pious captain discharged a seaman for a drunken frolic. "Masters hire them with this knowledge, . . . owners get their services at a less price for these very habits; year after year they serve at a mere pittance because of them." Many a landsman, as well, imbibed too much liquor on the Boston water-front, and awoke in the forecastle of a clipper ship bound round the world.

Whenever a Yankee boy had the nerve to go to sea under these conditions, and the pluck to stick it out in such company, he was assured of quick promotion. Arthur H. Clark, the historian of the clipper-ship era, was the son of a Boston Mediterranean merchant and yachtsman. Instead of going to Harvard, he went to sea before the mast in the clipper ship *Black Prince*, returned around the globe, over two years later, as her third mate, and then shipped as second mate of the *Northern Light*. A few more voyages, and he became a shipmaster. Henry Jackson Sargent, Jr., of the Gloucester family that has produced such eminent writers and artists, shipped before the mast at the age of seventeen on the *Flying Fish*,[1] the only ship except the *Flying Cloud* which made two California voyages under one hundred days. Within a few years he was not only the youngest, but one of the most accomplished clipper-ship commanders. The Medford-built clipper *Phantom*, under his command but through no fault of his own, ran on the Prates Shoal in thick,

[1] *Flying Fish*, 207' × 39' 6" × 22', 1506 tons; built by Donald McKay in 1851.

355

heavy weather on July 12, 1862. All hands were saved in the boats, although not all escaped a plundering by Chinese pirates. Obtaining another command in China, at the age of twenty-nine, Captain Sargent sailed from Shanghai, and was never heard from again. To this day, the Pacific holds the secret of his fate and that of his vessel.

If a mate found one or two boys such as these, beside the twoscore drugged and drunken bums, loafers, and rare seamen of all nations and colors delivered him by the crimp, he thanked his stars for it, and gave them separate quarters. For this system did not even deliver sailors, except by accident. Of his crew in the *Flying Cloud's* race with the *N. B. Palmer*, Captain Cressy said: "They worked like one man, and that man a hero." But in every crew shipped under the shanghai method there were bound to be men fit only 'to keep the bread from moulding.' Resenting their involuntary servitude, many did their best to 'soger'; to be 'yard-arm furlers' and 'buntline reefers' — in other words, malingerers. Others watched their chance to start a mutiny; and yet others, who tried to do their duty, seemed shirkers because of their ignorance of English. Hence the brutality for which Yankee mates and masters became notorious.[1] There were clipper ships like the *Northern Light*, where no hand was ever raised against the men, but aboard most of them, after Congress forbade sailors to be 'triced up' and 'introduced to the gunner's daughter' or cat o' nine tails,

[1] It is interesting to note that the practical English author of *The Mate and his Duties* (Liverpool, 1855) says: "It is acknowledged by all parties that they have much better discipline in American ships than we have . . . human nature is not allowed to ooze over, being always in check by the fear of immediate chastisement." He deplores the presence of apprentices on English vessels, as they enable Jack to shirk certain duties as "boy's work."

discipline was only kept by heavy and full portions of 'belaying-pin soup' and 'handspike hash.'

As the men were usually stripped of all they had by the crimps, they were forced to buy clothing on board from the slop-chest; and as the crimp had pocketed their three months' advance wages, they usually ended the voyage destitute or in debt. Then began another segment of the vicious circle, Jack pawning his body for food, shelter, and drink, and awakening with an aching head on board another ship, outward bound.

Various were the remedies proposed. A committee of the Boston Marine Society, consisting of Boston's most respected shipowners, petitioned Congress in 1852 to restore flogging — as if the 'cat' would attract Americans to sea! Captains John Codman and R. B. Forbes wanted an apprentice or school-ship system, which the same Marine Society had rejected many years before. Improvements were made in food and housing; the clipper ships had a deckhouse for their foremast hands, instead of the dark, stuffy forecastle of older vessels; and comparatively good food, with hot tea and coffee, was served. But no one suggested the experiment of attracting Americans to sea by decent wages and a freeman's status. New Englanders have more maritime aptitude than other Americans; but they are not a maritime people like the British or Scandinavians or Greeks, content to serve a lifetime before the mast for a mere pittance. The days were long past when Massachusetts boys had to choose between farming at home and seafaring abroad. In 1850 the workshops of New England needed men, and the great West was calling.

* *
*

"The California passage is the longest and most tedious within the domains of Commerce; many are the vicissitudes that attend it," wrote Lieutenant Maury. "It tries the patience of the navigator, and taxes his energies to the very utmost. . . . It is a great race-course, upon which some of the most beautiful trials of speed the world ever saw have come off."

Every passage from New York or Boston to San Francisco was a race against time, on which the builder's and master's reputation depended; and there were some remarkable ship-to-ship contests over this fifteen-thousand-mile course. One of the best took place in 1854, between the *Romance of the Seas*,[1] Captain Dumaresq, and the *David Brown*, Captain George Brewster. The *Romance*, sailing from Boston two days after her New York rival passed Sandy Hook, caught up with her off the coast of Brazil, and kept her in sight a good part of the passage to the Golden Gate, which both entered side-by-side on March 23, respectively ninety-six and ninety-eight days out. After discharging, they passed out in company, set skysails and royal studdingsails, and kept them set for forty-five days, when the *Romance* entered Hong Kong one hour in the lead.

As California afforded no outward lading in the early fifties, the clipper ships generally returned around the world, by way of China. There they came into competition with British vessels, and the result gave John Bull a worse shock than the yacht *America's* victory. So vastly superior was the speed of the American clippers, that British firms in Hong Kong

[1] *Romance of the Seas*, 240′ 8″ × 34′ 6″ × 20′, 1782 tons; built by Donald McKay in 1853 for G. B. Upton. The *David Brown*, 1715 tons, was built the same year by Roosevelt & Joyce, New York, for A. A. Low & Brother.

paid them seventy-five cents per cubic foot freight on teas to London, as against twenty-eight cents to their own ships.

Crack British East-Indiamen humbly awaited a cargo in the treaty-ports for weeks on end, while one American clipper after another sailed proudly in, and secured a return freight almost before her topsails were furled. When the Yankee beauties arrived in the Thames, their decks were thronged with sight-seers, their records were written up in the leading papers, and naval draughtsmen took off their lines while in dry-dock.

By the time the British builders were learning the first rudiments of clipper designing, the Americans had made still further progress. As to a cathedral builder of the thirteenth century, so to Donald McKay came visions transcending human experience, with the power to transmute them into reality. The public believed he had reached perfection with the *Flying Cloud;* but in 1852 he created the *Sovereign of the Seas.*[1] She had the longest and sharpest ends of any vessel yet built. Her widest point was twenty feet forward of amidships, and her figure-head showed a bronze mer-king, blowing a conch shell. No merchant shipowner, even in that era of adventure, dared order such a vessel. Her building was financed by McKay's loyal friends. But so convincing was her appearance, that immediately after launching she was sold for the record price of $150,000, almost all of which she earned in freight on her first round voyage.

Lauchlan McKay, who, thirty-four years before had helped his brother Donald build their first boat

[1] *Sovereign of the Seas,* 258′ 2″ × 44′ 7″ × 23′ 6″, 2421 tons. The *Westward Hol,* 214′ × 40′ 8″ × 23′ 6″, 1650 tons, was built by Donald McKay the same year, for Sampson & Tappan, of Boston.

in Nova Scotia, commanded this great vessel on hei
maiden voyage to San Francisco. Starting in the un-
favorable month of August, the *Sovereign of the Seas*
encountered southwest gales from the Falklands to
Cape Horn. Topmasts bent like whips to the fearful
snow squalls, yet nothing carried away, and the noble
ship never wore nor missed stays once in the long beat
to windward. Around the Horn she found no better
weather, and in the course of a heavy gale, owing to
the main topmast trestle-trees settling, her main topmast, mizzen topgallantmast, and foretopsail yard
went over the side. Luckily, the captain was an expert
rigger, and had an unusually large crew. Within thirty
hours he had the *Sovereign* under jury rig, doing
twelve knots. And in twelve days' time, by working
day and night, she was almost as well rigged as when
she left Boston. In spite of these mishaps she "beat
the clipper fleet" that sailed with her, and entered
San Francisco one hundred and three days out of New
York; the fastest passage ever made by a ship leaving
the Atlantic coast in August.

On the homeward passage from Honolulu, with a
cargo of oil and whalebone, a short crew, a foretopmast
sprung in two places, and a tender maintopmast,
Captain McKay "passed through a part of the Great
South Sea, which has been seldom traversed by traders." In the forties and fifties south latitude, a long,
rolling swell and the northwest tradewinds hurled
the *Sovereign of the Seas* one quarter of the distance
around the world — 5391 nautical miles — in twenty-
two days. One sea day (March 17–18, 1853) was mem-
orable above all others. Sun and moon appeared only
in brief glimpses. Heavy rain squalls tore down the
wind, whipping to a white froth the crests of enormous
seas that went roaring southward — but not much

faster than their *Sovereign*. When struck by a squall she would send spray masthead high, fly up a point or two, and heeling over try to take her helm and shoot along a deep valley between two towering rollers. Brought to her course again, she would righten with the poise of a thoroughbred, and leap forward as if taking a fresh start. On that day the *Sovereign of the Seas* made 411 nautical miles;[1] an average of 17.7 knots, and a day's run surpassed only by the *Red Jacket* and by three later creations of Donald McKay.

For the year 1853, Donald McKay made another sensation with the *Great Republic*. To appreciate her size, recall that any vessel over 130 feet long and 500 tons burthen was considered large before 1840; that the *Stag-Hound*, 1534 tons, was the first sailing ship built over two hundred feet long; that the *Flying Cloud* was 229 feet long and registered 1793 tons, and the *Sovereign of the Seas*, 258 feet and 2421 tons. The *Great Republic* was 334 feet, 6 inches long, and registered 4556 tons. Fifty-three feet, six inches broad, and thirty-eight feet deep, she was as sharp and shapely a clipper ship as any ever built. No vessel, before or since, has had such enormous spars and sail area. Her main yard was 120 feet long; her fore skysail yard, 40 feet. In addition to her three square-rigged masts she carried a spanker-mast with gaff-topsail and gaff-topgallantsail. The leech and bolt-ropes of the topsails were eight-and-a-half-inch, and the fore and

[1] According to the abstract of her log, printed in Maury's *Sailing Directions*, 6th ed., 757. Yet in Lieutenant Maury's letter of May 10, 1853, to the Secretary of the Navy (reprinted in R. B. Forbes, *Ships of the Past*, 27) he states that the greatest day's run of this passage was "362 knots or 419 statute miles." Captain Clark (p. 220) follows the log's record of 411 miles, which, on account of her easting made during the day, is equivalent to 424 nautical miles in twenty-four hours.

main standing rigging, twelve-and-a-half-inch four-
stranded Russia hemp.

The *Great Republic's* sails, which would have covered over one and a half acres if laid out flat,[1] were
never set. She was towed to New York, where, on the
eve of her maiden voyage, she caught fire, and had to
be scuttled to prevent total loss. Salvaged, razeed
to 3357 tons, and under greatly reduced rig, she made
a voyage of ninety-two days to San Francisco. What
wonders of speed might this ship of ships have performed, as Donald McKay built and rigged her!

The *Great Republic* had been destined for the Australian trade, whither British adventure and emigration were now tending, following a discovery of gold.
The *Sovereign of the Seas*, appearing in Liverpool in
July, 1853, was immediately chartered by James
Baines & Co.'s Australian Black Ball Line, which
charged £7 a ton freight in her to Melbourne, and
offered to return £2 of it if she did not beat every
steamer on the route. Baines kept the money. The
White Star Line, not to be outdone, chartered three
great clipper ships — McKay's *Chariot of Fame*,
Jackson's *Blue Jacket*, and the *Red Jacket*, designed
by Samuel H. Pook and built by George Thomas at
Rockland, Maine. On her passage from New York to
Liverpool the *Red Jacket*, Asa Eldridge master, broke
the record for that route, with rain, hail, or snow
falling throughout the entire trip; and made a day's
run of 413 nautical miles. Her first Australian voyage
was so remarkable that she was purchased by her
British charterers for thirty thousand pounds sterling.
James Baines & Co. then went one better, and contracted with Donald McKay for four great clipper
ships over two thousand tons, which he completed

[1] 15,683 running yards.

362

in the year between February, 1854, and February, 1855.

With this group, the *Lightning*,[1] *Champion of the Seas*,[2] *James Baines*,[3] and *Donald McKay*,[4] American shipbuilding reached its apogee. The *James Baines*, on her way across, made the record transatlantic passage for sailing vessels, twelve days, six hours from Boston Light to Rock Light, Liverpool. "She is so strongly built, so finely finished, and is of so beautiful a model," wrote a contemporary from Liverpool, "that even envy cannot prompt a fault against her. On all hands she has been praised as the most perfect sailing ship that ever entered the river Mersey." The portrait shows her powerful hull, with a row of ports along the passenger quarters; and her enormous rig, second only to the *Great Republic's*. In addition to three skysails, she carried skysail studdingsails and a main moonsail.

Owing to Matthew F. Maury's discoveries, vessels *en route* to Australia now made 48° south latitude before running their easting down, and let the brave west winds sweep them around the world. The *James Baines* in 1855 went from Liverpool to Liverpool in 132 days, omitting her stay at Melbourne. No sailing vessel ever equaled this record.

The *Donald McKay*, on her maiden voyage to Liverpool, made a day's run of 421 miles, mostly under topsails and foresail. But this record had already been surpassed by the *Lightning*. Built long and low, with the most daringly fine bow ever constructed, *Lightning*

[1] *Lightning*, 243′ × 42′ 8″ × 23′, 2084 tons.
[2] *Champion of the Seas*, 252′ × 45′ 6″ × 29′, 2448 tons.
[3] *James Baines*, 266′ × 44′ 7″ × 29′, 2515 tons.
[4] *Donald McKay*, 260′ 6″ × 46′ × 29′, 2595 tons.

looked her name. With mingled pride and regret Boston watched her glide down the harbor, making scarce a ripple in the water as her topsails caught a light land-breeze. On her maiden passage to Liverpool on March 1-2, 1854, she made the remarkable day's run of 436 miles, until recently accepted as world's record. Later research has uncovered two better ones. *Marco Polo*, built in 1851 at St. John, New Brunswick, made a day's run of 438 miles in January, 1854, when running her easting down from the Cape of Good Hope to Australia. But, if Donald McKay lost the blue ribbon to that "Queen of the Blue Noses," he won it back before the year was out. His *Champion of the Seas*, a ship that combined the stately port of a frigate with the airy grace of a yacht, on an outward passage from Liverpool to Melbourne, in the roaring forties south latitude, made 465 nautical miles, noon to noon, on December 11-12.

To realize what these records mean, remember that for almost forty years afterward no steamer could make such a day's run, and that only the fastest express steamers equaled it in the early decades of the twentieth century. No run of 400 miles has ever been made by a modern sailing yacht, though they are built for speed and carry no cargo. *Lightning*, when she made her wonderful record, was laden with 2000 tons of cargo and drew 21 feet of water; the other two were less heavily laden, and *Champion*, larger than *Lightning*, was drawing four feet less than her marks, which helped. Both runs, being on easterly courses, were made in about 23½ hours elapsed time, and this means that *Lightning* logged an average of 18.1 knots and *Champion* the amazing average of 19.78 knots. Obviously they must have hit it up to 22 or 23 knots in squalls.

CHAPTER XXIII

CONCLUSION

1857–1860

THE clipper ships, costly to build and to operate for their burthen, proved prodigal ventures on routes that paid normal freights. David Snow, of Boston, tried his clipper ship *Reporter*[1] in the Boston–New Orleans–Liverpool trade in 1853; but as Captain Octavius Howe wrote, she was a "thousand-ton ship in capacity and a two thousand-ton ship to keep in repair." The pleasure of having the smartest vessel on that route did not compensate for losing voyages, and the *Reporter* was shifted to the California trade.

By 1854 that path of riches yielded but normal profits, and 1855 brought the end of the clipper-ship era in shipbuilding; although American thoroughbreds won the sweepstakes in the world's carrying trade until the Civil War. Donald McKay, after completing his Australian Black Ball liners, wisely concluded that the limit had been reached; and the three or four clipper ships that he built in 1855–56 were of the medium class. Nevertheless the era left its impress on naval architecture. No more bluff-bowed vessels of the ancient model were built, except for whaling. A type of full-bodied ship, like McKay's *Glory of the Seas*, was evolved; fuller and beamier than the clipper ship, less boldly rigged, yet with that clean appearance, round stern, and beautiful rake to the bow which make it difficult to distinguish from the genuine clipper.

[1] *Reporter*, 207' 6" × 39' × 24' 6", 1474 tons; built by Paul Curtis at East Boston, 1853, at a cost of $80,750.

365

Throughout the clipper-ship era, nearly all the traditional lines of Massachusetts maritime commerce continued to expand and new ones were created; cod-fishing and whaling attained their apogee, and the commercial prosperity of Boston, in 1857, reached its high-water mark for the ante-bellum period. The coffee trade with South America declined, owing to the establishment of steamship lines between Europe and Brazil; the Russia trade declined, as Russia's staple exports were being produced to a great extent in the United States; the China trade continued its migration to New York; but all others increased greatly, and Boston continued to hold her ancient supremacy in the East-Indian, Smyrna, Mediterranean, and South American wool trades, and in such Russian trade as remained profitable.[1] Her exports of ice more than doubled between 1847 and 1856, rum rose from four hundred thousand to over one million gallons, and three times as many boots and shoes left the port as ten years previously. The Boston dry-goods trade with the West, the bulk of which still went by water, had doubled since 1854, and increased twenty-fold over 1847. Arrivals from foreign ports at Boston increased fifty per cent between 1845 and 1856, and their tonnage a hundred and twenty per cent; even Newburyport and Salem showed an increase, owing to the new Canadian trade.

The Canadian Reciprocity Treaty of 1854 was of more benefit to Massachusetts commerce than any treaty before or since, for it wiped out the artificial barrier which limited her market and source of supply to the northward and eastward. The trade was conducted almost exclusively in Canadian bottoms, which somewhat obscured its benefits, and gave that increase

[1] See statistics of arrivals in the Appendix.

366

to the statistics of foreign sail in our ports, which has been made so much of by ship-subsidy pamphlets masquerading as histories of the American merchant marine. As a matter of fact, if the "Geordies" and "Johnny wood-boats," as the Yankees called the clumsy down-East schooners, had not been permitted free access to our ports, the Canadians would have made Liverpool their *entrepôt* instead of Boston, or developed their own direct export trade — as they afterwards did, when the reciprocity treaty was abrogated. From Nova Scotia and New Brunswick flowed a constant and increasing stream of firewood, coal, fish, flour, provisions, grain, and dairy products to Boston and the Essex County ports, where the 'blue-nose' merchants made their purchases of East- and West-India goods, manufactures, whaling products, and hides.

Boston now had the facilities and the materials for an export trade to the newer countries, to California, Australia, and South Africa. New England manufactures, though less in value, were then much more diversified than nowadays, when lines such as beef-packing, furniture, and vehicles have been forced to move nearer the raw materials. Whatever was lacking came from other parts of the world to Boston wharves. A merchant could make up at short notice, within half a mile of State Street, an export cargo containing the entire apparatus of civilized life, from cradles and teething-rings to coffins and tombstones. Of such nature were the outward ladings to California, Australia, and Cape Town in the eighteen-fifties. Ploughs and printing-presses, picks and shovels, absinthe and rum, house-frames and grindstones, clocks and dictionaries, melodeons and cabinet organs, fancy biscuits and canned salmon, oysters and lobsters; in fact everything one can imagine went through Boston on its way to the miners and ranchers of the white man's new empires. Henry W. Peabody and others operated lines of Australian packets, which brought back wool and hides.[1] Benjamin C. Pray and others kept a fleet of barques plying between Boston and Cape Town, Port Elizabeth and East London, where fifty years before the only American trade had been a little smuggling of East-India goods on homeward passages. From South Africa were brought wool, goatskins, ostrich feathers, and, after 1870, diamonds.[2] The California trade entered a new phase in 1855, when the Somerset-built clipper barque *Greenfield* took the first consignment of grain from San Francisco, and the Newburyport-built clipper ship *Charmer* of Boston took a full cargo of California wheat to New York, receiving twenty-eight dollars a ton freight.

In September, 1857, came a great financial crisis, which, unlike that of twenty years previous, affected Boston most grievously. The East-India merchants, anticipating a stoppage of trade by the Sepoy mutiny, had glutted the Boston market with Calcutta goods. Prices of all sorts of merchandise fell one-quarter to one-half, and freights sunk until it paid a shipowner to let his vessels rot.

For two years ocean freights were dull and business depressed. The Canadian trade alone showed conspicuous progress. By 1860 conditions were getting back to normal. Of the world's fleet *en route* to Australia in January of that year, thirteen ships were

[1] Six different Australian packet-lines, none of them operating clipper ships, announce sailings in the Boston *Daily Advertiser* for March 7, 1853, and Oak Hall advertises "clothing manufactured expressly for the Australian and California markets.'"

[2] It was Benjamin S. Pray who, in coöperation with a Boston jeweler, introduced diamond-cutting into the United States.

from Boston, as against twelve ships and seven barques from New York, and none from any other American port save San Francisco. The merchants, tardily appreciating the importance of steam navigation, built four splendid iron screw steamers over two hundred feet long, for two new lines to Charleston and New Orleans.[1] The sailing fleet found better employment than in any year since 1857. Then came the firing on Fort Sumter; and for four years the best energies of Massachusetts, maritime and interior, were devoted to preserving the Union.

*

*   *

Every great war has brought an upheaval in Massachusetts commerce; some for the better, but the Civil War conspicuously for the worse. Not that the Confederate cruisers were responsible. The American merchant marine had increased and prospered during the earlier wars, in spite of depredations infinitely greater than those of the *Alabama* and her consorts. So prospered, of late, the British marine, despite German under-sea boats. I agree with John R. Spears that the decadence of American shipping " was wholly due to natural causes — to conditions of national development . . . that were unavoidable." The Civil War merely hastened a process that had already begun, the substitution of steam for sail. It was the ostrich-like attitude of maritime Massachusetts toward this process, more than the war, by which she lost her ancient preëminence. Far better had the brains and en-

---

[1] The *Massachusetts, South Carolina, Merrimack*, and *Mississippi*. They were designed by Samuel H. Pook and built by Harrison Loring at South Boston in 1860–61. The Merchants' and Miners' Line to Norfolk and Baltimore, founded a few years previously, acquired two iron side-wheelers in 1860, and the Philadelphia Line was also improved.

369

ergy that produced the clipper ships been put into the iron screw steamer (in the same sense that Phidias had been better employed in sanitation, and Euripides in discovering the printing press). After Appomattox, national expansion and the protective tariff killed or atrophied many lines of commerce in which Massachusetts merchants had specialized; and the transatlantic cable made merchants, in the old sense, anachronisms. Several firms continued the carrying trade profitably in sailing vessels for some years; and many seamen remained faithful to sail for the rest of their lives. But it was Maine rather than Massachusetts that kept the flag afloat at the spanker-gaff of sailing ships. The era of tramp steamers and four or five per cent profit had little attraction for merchants who could gain six to ten per cent by exploiting the great West. Many an old shipowner's ledger, that begins with tea and indigo and sixteenth-shares of the ship *Canton Packet* and brig *Owhyhee*, ends up by recording large blocks of C. B. & Q., and Calumet & Hecla.

*

* *

The maritime history of Massachusetts, then, as distinct from that of America, ends with the passing of the clipper. 'T was a glorious ending! Never, in these United States, has the brain of man conceived, or the hand of man fashioned, so perfect a thing as the clipper ship. In her, the long-suppressed artistic impulse of a practical, hard-worked race burst into flower. The *Flying Cloud* was our Rheims, the *Sovereign of the Seas* our Parthenon, the *Lightning* our Amiens; but they were monuments carved from snow. For a brief moment of time they flashed their splendor around the world, then disappeared with the sudden

370

completeness of the wild pigeon. One by one they sailed out of Boston, to return no more. A tragic or mysterious end was the privilege of many ships favored by the gods. Others, with lofty rig cut down to cautious dimensions, with glistening decks and topsides scarred and neglected, limped about the seas under foreign flags, like faded beauties forced upon the street.

The master builders, reluctant to raise barnyard fowls where once they had reared eagles, dropped off one by one. Donald McKay, dying almost in poverty after a career that should have brought him wealth and honor, sleeps at Newburyport among the comrades of his young manhood. Boston has erected a noble monument to him and his ship, designed by William T. Aldrich and Philip Sears, on Castle Island facing the old ship channel. And in the elm branches over McKay's grave the brave west winds, which he loved so well, murmur soft versions of the tunes they once played on the shrouds of his glorious ships.

Now he has been joined by the last of the men he knew and loved, the shipbuilders and

Sea-captains young or old, and the mates, and ... intrepid sailors
Pick'd sparingly without noise by thee, old ocean, chosen by thee, ...
Suckled by thee, old husky nurse, embodying thee,
Indomitable, untamed as thee.

*

*   *

The seaports of Massachusetts have turned their backs to the element that made them great, save for play and for fishing; Boston alone is still in the deep-sea game. But all her modern docks and terminals and dredged channels will avail nothing, if the spirit perish that led her founders to "trye all ports."

Sicut patribus . . . We can ask no more here. But in that unknown harbor toward which we all are scudding may our eyes behold some vision like that vouchsafed our fathers, when a California clipper ship made port after a voyage around the world.

A summer day with a sea-turn in the wind. The Grand Banks fog, rolling in wave after wave, is dissolved by the perfumed breath of New England hayfields into a gentle haze, that turns the State House dome to old gold, films brick walls with a soft patina, and sifts blue shadows among the foliage of the Common elms. Out of the mist in Massachusetts Bay comes riding a clipper ship, with the effortless speed of an albatross. Her proud commander keeps skysails and studdingsails set past Boston light. After the long voyage she is in the pink of condition. Paintwork is spotless, decks holystoned cream-white, shrouds freshly tarred, ratlines square. Viewed through a powerful glass, her seizings, flemish-eyes, splices, and pointings are the perfection of the old-time art of rigging. The chafing-gear has just been removed, leaving spars and shrouds immaculate. The boys touched up her skysail poles with white paint, as she crossed the Bay. Boom-ending her studdingsails and hauling a few points on the wind to shoot the Narrows, between Georges and Gallups and Lovells Islands, she pays off again through President Road, and comes booming up the stream, a sight so beautiful that even the lounging soldiers at the Castle, persistent baiters of passing crews, are dumb with wonder and admiration.

Colored pennants on Telegraph Hill have announced her coming to all who know the code. Topliff's News Room breaks into a buzz of conversation, comparing records and guessing at freight money;

372

CONCLUSION

owners and agents walk briskly down State Street;
countingroom clerks hang out of windows to watch
her strike skysails and royals; the crimps and hussies
of Ann Street foregather, to offer Jack a few days'
scabrous pleasure before selling him to a new master.
By the time the ship has reached the inner harbor,
thousands of critical eyes are watching her every
movement, quick to note if in any respect the mate has
failed to make sailormen out of her crew of broken
Argonauts, beach-combers, Kanakas, and Lascars.

The 'old man' stalks the quarterdeck in top hat and
frock coat, with the proper air of detachment; but
the first mate is as busy as the devil in a gale of wind.
Off India Wharf the ship rounds into the wind with a
graceful curve, crew leaping into the rigging to furl
topgallant sails as if shot upward by the blast of pro-
fanity from the mate's bull-like throat. With backed
topsails her way is checked, and the cable rattles out
of the chain lockers for the first time since Shanghai.
Sails are clewed up. Yards are braced to a perfect
parallel, and running gear neatly coiled down. A warp
is passed from capstan to stringer, and all hands on
the capstan-bars walk her up to the wharf with the
closing chantey of a deep-sea voyage:

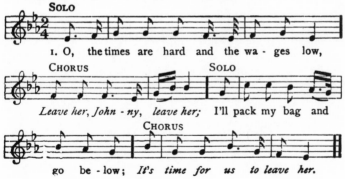

1. O, the times are hard and the wa-ges low,
Leave her, John-ny, leave her; I'll pack my bag and
go be-low; It's time for us to leave her.

SUPPLEMENT OF LETTERS

Following the first publication of this book, the author received a considerable number of letters of correction and supplement, which seem to demand reprinting here as part of the record for *The Maritime History of Massachusetts*.

From Lincoln Colcord, Searsport, Maine,
December 21, 1921

I HAVE received from you a copy of the book, and another from Houghton Mifflin, for which many thanks. You shouldn't have depleted your own stock, however; I merely was growling at the inefficiency of publishers who, because they haven't the ability to develop a proper sales system, must charge twice as much for books as they are worth, in order to make both ends meet.

This enables me to advise you that the Stupendous Error occurs on page 268, second paragraph, fourth line — "and put to sea in a sou'easter." A Puritan and the son of Puritans, inheritor of a quick eye and a ready chuckle for the downfall of others, it gives me a great glee to find this after all; for, to tell the truth, I'd begun to fear that the error might be my own. And that, of course, would have made it an entirely different matter.

Searching through the book — which, let me assure you, makes fine reading wherever you pick it up, so that I was considerably bothered and led astray from my main purpose last evening — I came upon another slip of the tongue, which I had passed in the first reading. This lies on page 82, second paragraph, fifth line

— "Within ten minutes she had made a running moor, *brailed up* her sails, and warped into the best berth."

I think there is no circumstance under which a square-rigged ship could be said to "brail up" her sails. There are so many ways, you know, in which the various sails of a square-rigger are taken from the breeze: the courses are either "hauled up" or "taken in"; the lower topsails are "clewed up," but *never* "hauled up"; the upper topsails are "lowered away"; the topgallantsails, royals, and skysails are "clewed up," but *never* "lowered away" (except in a detail-command to the man who is handling the halyards); the jibs and staysails are "hauled down," but *never*, of course, "clewed up" or "lowered away"; the spanker, however, is "lowered away," and nothing else; and all these sails, irrespectively, can be "taken in": there are so many ways, in fact, that only a most liberally general term could properly be used to cover the whole operation.

All things considered, I would say that "taken in" would be the proper term to use in this case. "Furled" also is properly used to designate the operation of stripping a ship of her sails. "She has made a running moor, *furled* her sails, and warped into the best berth," would be entirely correct; yet "furled" seems to signify a more complete operation than "taken in." At the same time, the word "furled," by professional usage, has considerable poetic latitude. While it specifically defines the completed operation on the sail, it also, correctly used, has a more general application; to the mind of a sailor it does not by any means invariably suggest the actual stowing of the sail, but often signifies merely its "taking in."

"Doused" would be another general term that you

could have used, although I never have liked it. It
suggests to my mind baggy sails and clumsy, wall-
sided hulls, the pompous days of the East India Company; it's a lazy, leisurely word, a romantic, land-
lubberish word, a word for poets and fancy novelists, a
word archaic and unreal. "She doused her sails" —
bah! No spruce ship ever did such a thing, no proper
sailor-man ever wet his lips with such a puling phrase.
The word never was current in the American merchant
marine; I don't remember ever to have heard it. A
word for travellers and lexicographers — and damned
historians.

Strange to say, you also could have said with
propriety, "She made a running moor, *clewed up* her
sails, and warped into the best berth," although the
term specifically cannot be applied to more than half
of the sails in question. Like all such matters of usage
and latitude, there are no rules broad enough to cover
the ground; all is exception.

The point I am coming at is, of course, that "brailing
up," the term you used, is not a general term at all.
On the contrary, it is highly specific. According to
my sense of nautical phraseology, "brailing" defines
the operation of taking in a sail which *travels* on a
horizontal spar; and a "brail" is one of the ropes which
haul it in against the mast. The spanker on an English
bark or ship commonly "brails in"; that is, it travels
by hoops on the boom and gaff, and the gaff is a stationary spar. Square-rigged American ships of my
day often carried a main-spencer or trysail for use in
heaving the ship to in heavy weather; this sail travelled
on a stationary gaff just below the main-top, and
was "brailed in" against the lower mast when not set;
it had no boom. It was the only piece of canvas on an

377

American square-rigged ship to which the term "brail in" could apply; although I have heard of topsail schooners in the old days which carried a lower sail, dropping from the fore yard, used for fair-weather running, that sometimes was "brailed in" and furled against the mast rather than "hauled up" to the yard.

You'll notice, furthermore, that I have been saying "brailed *in*" instead of "brailed *up*." The specific sense of "brailing," that is, the act of hauling in a sail against the mast on a horizontal spar, implied an "*in*wardness" rather than an "*up*wardness." I'm not aware that "brailing *up*" is permissible; that anything *can* be "brailed *up*"; that anything *ever was* "brailed up"; that "brailing up" can be anything more than a misalliance of the sturdy old seaman "brail" with that loose and promiscuous New England "uppishness" which moves unconsciously in our blood and being when we say, "he climbed up out of the boat," "come up here," "run up town," and the like, which runs transcendentally through all our speech, a reflection, perhaps, of uplifted hearts — or maybe of upturned noses — or, even more likely, of upheld palms.

Having now established our thesis, let us bring the good ship to her moorings at the end of Derby Wharf under the critical eye of a town that reared its children on tar and gave them bags of salt to suck for sugartits. It was a pleasant summer morning. Captain Hardtack briskly walked the quarterdeck, concealing his pride and sentimental eagerness beneath a mask of stern dignity and supreme indifference. The mate, Mr. Marlinspike, was able to give vent to his dangerously compressed ego in a whirlwind of activity, seeing

378

that every rope was clear and every man at his post. A fresh southwesterly breeze heeled the tall ship handsomely as she slipped through the still water of the bay. As the houses of the well-remembered town became more distinct, etc., etc.

At length Captain Hardtack stopped at the corner of the after house, scanned for a moment the remaining distance to be traversed, then lifted his voice in a sharp command.

"Haul up the courses, Mr. Marlinspike! Take in the staysails, and let the jibs run down!"

"Aye, aye, sir! Man the jib and staysail downhauls! Let go the halyards when you're ready! Start the weather main sheet, there! Fore and cross-jack the same! Man clew-garnets and buntlines! Spill 'em nicely, there, boys! Starboard clew-garnets, now! Up with 'em! Smartly, my lads!"

"Take in the skysails, royals, and topgallantsails, as fast as you can!" roared Captain Hardtack, when the above operation had been concluded.

At this command the deck became a confusion of men running to new posts, a confusion which marvellously resolved itself to order as the crew anticipated the work that lay before them. Above the excitement the voice of the redoubtable Marlinspike could be heard by watchers on the end of Derby Wharf.

"Skysail sheets and halyards, there! Lower away a little! Now start the sheets! Clewlines and spilling-lines, ready! Let go your halyards! Snatch 'em up, my lads! Now — royal sheets and halyards! Clewlines and spilling-lines! Up with 'em! Let go all! Hold topgallant halyards a minute! Now — let 'em run down! Clewlines and spilling-lines! Lively — up they go!"

For a few minutes the ship forged ahead under topsails, spanker, and foretopmast-staysail. (Forgot that foretopmast-staysail; it should have been left set. Also, she carries single topsails, which would be *clewed up* after the yard had been lowered to the cap of the masthead. With double topsails, the upper topsail would be lowered away till the yard rested on the lower topsail yard; the sail simply would be spilled and furled in this position, without starting the sheets; while the lower topsail, on a stationary yard, would be "taken in" or "clewed up.") She was now approaching the end of Derby Wharf, carrying some three or four knots of headway. On the alert for the next order, Mr. Marlinspike drifted aft along the weather alley, where Captain Hardtack stood closely scanning the shore.

"There's old Nate Ellis on the capstan of the wharf, Captain Hardtack. I recognized that droop to his left shoulder as soon as he came over the horizon." The mate threw out this permissible familiarity over his own shoulder, his attention still riveted on the main deck of the ship.

Captain Hardtack allowed himself a single degree of relaxation, gave a short laugh, and turned his eyes for an instant towards the end of the wharf. "Yes, I saw him. Droops a couple of inches lower than it did two years ago." Changing his voice, and pulling his eyes away from the land — for, indeed, in that brief instant he had seen a great deal more than old Nate Ellis — he wrapped himself again in the mantle of authority. "All ready, Mr. Marlinspike. Take in the fore and mizzen topsails!"

The mate leaped forward like a piece of machinery. "Fore and mizzen topsail halyards! Lower away!"

he shouted. "Steady, steady! Clewlines and spilling-lines! Lively, my lads! They're watching you now — they can count the hairs of your head! Lively, aloft there! Jump out on those topsail yards!" For a crew waiting aloft on each mast had furled every sail as fast as it came in.

The critical moment had now arrived. Captain Hardtack stood motionless at the weather rail, estimating his distances. "Let her luff!" he said in a low voice to the helmsman behind him. "Put your helm down a little. A little more. A little more!" The ship began to swing into the wind along a narrowing arc; the object was to bring her head into the wind exactly off the shoreward end of Derby Wharf, so that the backened main topsail would check her headway in that position and send her gently sternward into a berth at the end of the pier.

"Hard down!" said the captain sharply. The helmsman whirled the spokes, the ship answered the rudder like a yacht, coming into the wind in perfect position. (Might as well make it perfect in a yarn, you know — it's the only chance at perfection you ever get.) For an instant she hung motionless (that is, after she'd quit forging ahead), then slowly gathered sternway — "Put your helm amidships, there!" — and drifted in against the wharf.

"Take in the main topsail, Mr. Marlinspike! Let that foretopmast staysail run down!"

"Aye, aye, sir! Let go the main topsail halyards! Hey, you boys aloft there, look out for that sail against the mast! Clewlines and spilling-lines, now! Pick it up lively, lads!"

"Send a couple of men aft to take in the spanker, Mr. Marlinspike."

"Aye, aye, sir! Long Tom and Charlie, there! Lower away the spanker!"

As the ship settled against the wharf, a quiet voice spoke from the capstan abreast the taffrail, where an elderly and important-looking individual had been standing alone for the past twenty minutes, as if in entire confidence that the ship would come to him. Now and then a man going down the wharf would pass a deferential word with him; and when at length he spoke to the captain, everyone paused to listen.

"How do you do, Captain Hardtack? You made a handy moor, sir."

"Thank you, sir," said the captain to his owner. "We are all well aboard, sir. I have brought you coffee instead of pepper, Captain Martingale."

"I smelled it," said the other dryly. "Well, I think there will be no quarrel over that, Captain Hardtack." Without another word he stalked up the wharf; while Captain Hardtack, having nothing more to do on deck, and under the absolute necessity of preserving his dignity, went solemnly below to collect his papers and other valuables.

(Now, the truth of the matter was, old skinflint Martingale had wanted to yell and fling his old bones into a dance of rejoicing when he smelled that coffee; for pepper had dropped to less than nothing since three shiploads had arrived that same week; while coffee was being clamored for by the markets of Boston and farther west. And Captain Hardtack, the young scapegrace, was in reality on the point of unmanly tears, what with pride at his judgment, excitement over the recent exploit of rounding his ship to so perfectly in the eyes of his little world, and strange emotion when he thought of the girl in town who was shortly to become his bride. In reality, he had to dodge below to pull himself together; and what he did there was not connected with the ship's business. He went to his room, to the starboard wall of his room, put his forehead against the cool paintwork, and stood there in silence for several minutes, adrift and helpless in the sensation of joy.)

Well, anyway, that's how they took in her sails, as far as I can remember. If you were to submit this to Captain Clark, he probably would pick a dozen flaws in it; for I've forgotten the better part, I am afraid. I left the sea at fourteen, you know, and never have been a professional sailor.

From Elizabeth Goodwin Chapin, New York City,
November 26, 1921

I HAVE been having a wonderful time starting in to read *The Maritime History of Massachusetts*, now that the regular trade edition makes it possible for me to acquire a copy. Not the least of my pleasures has been discovering that Monhegan Island is mentioned on page 9. (I might remark in passing that among the "passionate devotees" of the New England coast, the worshippers of Nantucket have nothing *on* the maniacs who summer on Monhegan — it is religion pure and undefiled for them just to say the name!) I know it is pretty cheeky for a citizen to try to offer news to a historian, but I am wondering — in view of your statement that no monument or tablet commemorates Captain John Smith in the region of his choice — if you know of the tercentenary observed August 6, 1914, on Monhegan, under the auspices of the Maine Historical Society? I was not there that summer, but had a program of the affair, and picture of the tablet, a large and dignified bronze, set into a great boulder just where the so-called road forks as it reaches the school-house.

Of course, that was only a local celebration, but the tablet is seen each summer by hundreds of visitors to that incomparable spot, and the Islanders are very proud of having once had the gallant Captain for a neighbor, so to speak.

From Michael J. Canavan, Boston, February 1, 1922

I HAVE just been reading with much pleasure your *Maritime History of Massachusetts*.

Two stories occurred to me, which I should like to have seen in it.

One was of Mr. William Austin. He was talking of luck; and said that after insuring his fleet for years, he figured up and came to the conclusion he had been foolish to do this. He had had no losses, and the insurance money would have paid for another ship or two. He gave orders not to insure.

In the course of the next year there were violent storms, and from that and other causes disaster piled up, and most of his fleet was lost. He believed that he was ruined, and had not enough left to meet his obligations and go on.

"But the insurance will meet most of these losses." — "Insurance! I've got no insurance." — "Why, your ships were all insured." An explanation followed, and the clerk said he had received no orders *not* to insure; and when the proper time came, did as he had always done. Somebody's mistake had saved him.

In regard to Donald McKay, I knew Mrs. McKay, and was a neighbor of Edward P. Bliss who married her daughter. Bliss told me that Mr. McKay had an order for a clipper ship to be delivered at **Liverpool**. The Englishman came over and inspected her **when** she was all ready to sail. The marriage took place, and McKay decided to take his wife to England in her for the wedding trip. The Englishman was invited to make the passage with them, but he had to get back home as quick as possible, and took the Cunarder. Donald McKay saw him off, hurried his bride on board the clipper, and set sail a short time after the Cunarder. Every sail was spread. The west winds were strong. Hatches were battened down, and Mrs. McKay was kept below.

When the Cunarder reached Liverpool, the Englishman saw a ship exactly like the one he had left at **East** Boston; and as he passed her, there stood Donald McKay shouting a greeting to him!

Mr. Bliss always addressed his wife as "*Cressy*," which seemed to me a pet name for Christina until I ran across Captain Cressy in your book.

One time the Lexington D.A.R. met at their house, and they were urging Mrs. Bliss to join; and she replied that she was not eligible. "Oh, yes, you are, Cressy; your great-grandfather was at Bunker Hill." — "Nonsense! Hold your tongue, Ed." Donald McKay's grandfather was at Bunker Hill — but as a lieutenant on H.M.S. *Lively*.

From Edwin Tenney Brewster, Andover, Massachusetts,.
January 30, 1923

I HAVE just finished reading — with the greatest delight — your really thrilling account of Massachusetts shipping. My only regret is that there is not more — to bring the story down to the six-master era,. of which I recall the beginnings.

There is, however, one quite unimportant point on which my own recollection differs a little from your account. I send you, therefore, a note on the item, in case the matter ever becomes worth looking into. Of course, you will not consider this in any wise a letter to be answered.

I used to spend my summers at Pigeon Cove on Cape Ann, from about 1875 onward. Your account (page 311) fits exactly what I have been told about the breakwater which makes Pigeon Cove harbor, a small affair owned locally, like a half-dozen others along that shore.

But the Sandy Bay Breakwater (page 302) was a quite different affair. This was begun by the government sometime — for a guess — in the late '80's, and never carried far enough to "protect" anything but the Member of Congress from the district. The last I heard, in Wilson's first administration, as I recall, the whole project was abandoned about half-completed.

Moreover, in my time there was still a third breakwater — Rockport and Pigeon Cove being the other two — built by the Rockport Granite Company, from which most of the stone was shipped, including that which went into the great Sandy Bay structure. If that breakwater "made it possible ... to compete with Quincy," it must have been only because the government dole helped to take care of the "overhead." At any rate, I wasn't born till '66, and I was in college at least, and I think graduated, before the first stroke of work was done on the great government enterprise which you assign to 1836. But, of course, I may quite misinterpret your text.

SUPPLEMENT OF LETTERS

From A. F. Taylor, London, December 3, 1923

MY FATHER went from Devon with many others in 1854 to the gold diggings near Melbourne (Black-wood) — the following year my mother, myself, and sister went out to him. Very shortly after our arrival my father and mother were both killed together by the falling of a tree behind them at the diggings. I and my sister were sent home in the *James Baines*, I think. I passed my ninth birthday on the voyage in 1856, and my sister was about five — she became ill and died on board and was buried at sea, I think near Cape Horn. I shall never forget the throwing overboard. On that voyage we were raced by the *Lightning* — she left Melbourne seventeen days after us and arrived at Liverpool one day before us. We were said to be very foul with barnacles. I understand the *James Baines* made only one or two more trips, brought home jute, caught fire by spontaneous combustion, and burnt in Liverpool Docks, and from the salvage some part of a pier at Liverpool was built. I remember some incidents of the voyage, as swinging from loose ropes, the singing of the sailors when hauling the ropes, the catching a shark, the lack of wind at the Equator where we lay about for days, the coming up behind of the *Lightning* and her passing us.

I had no idea these ships were built in America until reading your book.

From C. P. Philbrick, Wymore, Nebraska, 1924

IN THE year 1843, my father sailed from San Pedro, California, on a return voyage from Boston two years previous in the ship *Alert*, Captain Faucon (his son was in later years car accountant at Lincoln, Nebraska,

387

for the B. & M.). On the ship was Richard Henry Dana who had gone "round the Horn" as a seaman on the brig *Pilgrim* shortly after having graduated at Harvard College, for the benefit of his health, and who, upon return to Boston wrote *Two Years Before the Mast* which production is read by the cadets at Annapolis as a kind of side issue in their naval curriculum.

Some three months after his return to Boston, Father met Captain Forbes with whom he had sailed a previous voyage to China. The Captain asked him to go over to Donald McKay's shipyard at East Boston and have a look at a ship then on the stocks, that was expected to be one of the fastest clipper ships to sail the ocean. McKay was a noted shipbuilder of the day and had already constructed and launched several fast vessels. Arriving at the yard, the ship was found to be about complete, showing what seamen term "fine lines" of hull construction, and "pierced" for twenty-four guns; that is, having twelve gun portholes on each side, and was to be christened *Antelope* when launched. Forbes said that he was going to sail with a first-class picked crew; men that he knew to be extra able seamen, young and vigorous and ready to fight man or the Devil, and that her complement would be sixty men. At that time, a crew of about fourteen men was a complement for a merchant vessel and Father expressed surprise at the fact that the armament and crew was to approximate that of a man-of-war, and from the fact that the United States was at peace with all nations he knew that no armed vessel could sail from construction at any seaport of this country without "letters of marque," and in the absence of war, would only be rated as an armed pirate if sailing under armament. Captain Forbes gave him a "side-slant look-over" and told him to ask no questions, but "put his John Hancock on shipping articles and be under pay from that moment." The wages offered were much better than commonly paid sailors at that time, and the articles were soon signed. In due time the ship was launched and sailed out of Boston with her guns "stowed" in the hold as *cargo*. Not a man "before the mast" knew its destination and cared less. The vessel was well supplied with "grub" and "grog"; a comfortable clean "foksl" and a couple of "nigger cooks," who were not only artists in the galley, but who also added the accomplishments of fiddle and banjo manipulators of more than ordinary ability, and who promised the crew that with

"Horn-pipes, jigs, strathspeys and reels to
Put life and mettle in their heels."

Such a lovely prospect was all that "Jack" could wish, and the *Antelope* skimmed away on a southeasterly course:

"A Yankee ship and a Yankee crew,
Tally-i-ho-ye-know!
Over the main like a sea-gull flew;
Sing-hey and aloft ye go!"

Down around Cape Town, thence northeasterly up through the Mozambique Channel between Africa and Madagascar, out through the Indian Ocean to the Gulf of Arabia and to Bombay. Here was located the business firm of "Russell, Forbes & Sturgis," dealers, exporters and importers of anything and everything that brought in finally the "Almighty Dollar."

Coolies were soon "toting" little packages of brick size aboard the ship and stowing in the hold, and those of the sailors who ventured to investigate found them to consist of a black, gummy substance that no one of their gang knew what nomenclature to give it until one old wise main-topman whispered, "poppy juice," and then all knew that the ship was taking on a cargo of opium, and gradually it came to be known that each little "brick" was worth about sixteen dollars United States gold. Finally the *Antelope* sailed out of Bombay and, when well at sea, up came the twenty-four twelve-pounder guns from the hold, they were mounted, gun crews told off, and a swivel gun, which under other conditions would have been mounted forward as a "bow-chaser," was located "aft" on the poop deck to *repel chasers*, as the ship was not intended to be a chaser herself, but expected to be "chased," and it was. Malay pirates infested those waters at the time, and it was "every fellow for himself and the Devil for the hindmost."

Down around Ceylon, through the Straits of Sumatra, thence into the South China Sea and up to the mouth of the Canton River, where the real fun commenced. Each night a boat's crew of sixteen oars would go ashore with a load of "poppy juice." China had legislated the importation of opium out of existence, but like our present "18th Amendment," the prospect of financial benefit encouraged a disregard of the mandate, and a boat's crew that could earn extra pay of $15 00 per man per trip were quite willing to chance a death by decapitation if caught by the Mandarin boat's crew that acted as a coast guard; the Yankee Jacks trusting to their prowess as manipulators of a sixteen-foot oar and "shoot to kill" if necessary, whereby they could evade the Mandarin boats and "earn the honest penny."

Another peculiar thing that favored them was that if they succeeded in emptying the boat of its cargo of opium, simply casting it on the beach to be seized by the Chinese smugglers awaiting its reception, before the Mandarin boats reached them, the crew was "immune" and it was up to the "Chinks" ashore to stand for beheading if caught, while the Yankee boys could have reserved seats at the show and "josh" the executioners. The "House" lost nothing even if the Mandarins captured the cargo, because each brick was paid for the moment it was checked "over the side" from the ship by a representative of the Chinese smugglers, they assuming all risk other than the "beheading" of the Americans if caught. Happily none of the sailors was ever caught, but my father carried long knife scars on his body, received in encounters with the Mandarins, notably a bad "bug-a-lug" scrap on the Island of Macao (pronounced "Mack-ow"), where it had been prearranged to make a landing of "poppy juice." This is a Portuguese penal point and the "House" had to settle with the "Porty-gees" for having caused a rumpus in their domain. Portugal could make no demand on the United States for reparation because our people were engaged in unlawful commerce on the high seas; in fact, they were next door to pirates and were subject to punitive treatment by any nation that might capture them. The ship did not fly the United States colors while cruising in the Indian Ocean; only the "House Flag"; but inasmuch as the old *Antelope* was raising "Merry Hell" with every Malay pirate proa that attempted to overhaul it, and helping to rid the Indian Ocean of those vermin, "John Bull," "Musseer Crapaud," and the Spanish Dons all kept hands off. Quite likely, too, there was a "gentlemen's agreement" with a financial clause in it.

The *Antelope* continued in this *missionary* work for about three years and the "House" finally sold the ship to the Chinese Government for a few pennies more than its original cost. The "Chinks" converted it into a naval vessel, but lost it during a hurricane off Formosa.

Captain Forbes and his crew went to Bombay and from there with another "House" ship to Antwerp via Cape of Good Hope. From that port Father returned to the United States and entered the Navy at the outbreak of the Mexican War in 1846.

My father used frequently to calculate about what the earnings of the *Antelope* must have been during its cruises in the "poppy-juice" industry, and it was always two figures followed by three groups of ciphers. He always thought, however, that the "old hooker" deserved all her earnings on account of the pious work it did in practically wiping out the Malay pirates. He insisted that Forbes and his sixty-odd Yankee boys accomplished more than the combined efforts of English, French, and Spanish war vessels, because she could outsail anything in those waters to begin with and could also outshoot, out cut, or out "damn" anything handled by any other set of men.

Perhaps had John M. Forbes been living when the "Burlington" adopted a "trade-mark," he might have suggested a "Poppy."

I regret that I cannot give you the entire song: "A Yankee ship and a Yankee crew," etc. One other verse only can I recall now:

SUPPLEMENT OF LETTERS

"Her sails were set to catch the wind,
    Tally-i-ho-ye-know;
Columbia's shore she left behind,
    Sing-hey and aloft ye go."

Later, the song tells of heavy seas encountered:

"And she buried her lee cat-head."

I have a faint recollection of my father and Captain Jo Nickerson once singing it together over our back-yard fence, with the assistance of one or two more old "Captain Cuttles," who had been (possibly) mildly "splicing the main-brace" together that night. They sang and sang until Father, who was then Captain of that police district, suggested that possibly they were becoming "nuisances" in that neighborhood and should all "turn in."

Another old "chanty" of which I can recall but one verse, commenced:

"I wish I was old Stormy's son;
    Storm-along, storm-along;
I'd give the sailors plenty fun,
    Storm-along Stormy."

APPENDIX

I

COD AND MACKEREL FISHERIES OF MASSACHUSETTS
1837–1865

Fishing ports of	Vessels fitted out			Value of catch		Hands em- ployed
	Year	No.	Tonnage	Cod	Mackerel	
ESSEX COUNTY, N. of Cape Ann	1837	151	8,019	$50,048	$150,647	1,135
	1855	60	4,105	30,000	93,020	705
	1865	83	4,245	42,606	108,988	767
CAPE ANN	1837	221	9,824	186,516	335,566	1,580
	1855	347	21,269	346,850	421,991	3,177
	1865	378	25,836	839,675	2,259,150	4,939
NORTH SHORE	1837	151	10,232	275,799	33,950	1,133
	1855	146	11,184	471,249	193,550	991
	1865	80	5,631	360,508	47,925	643
BOSTON BAY	1837	241	15,281	488,010	478,407	2,572
	1855	109	8,595	4,500	331,364	1,264
	1865	58	2,969	159,900	241,482	471
SOUTH SHORE (Cohasset to Plymouth, incl.)	1837	168	11,302	187,214	148,034	1,418
	1855	100	7,014	120,117	75,698	893
	1865	75	5,360	337,720	127,500	706
CAPE COD	1837	359	21,280	392,772	490,638	3,371
	1855	376	26,757	443,869	450,984	3,389
	1865	314	50,166	976,328	1,169,074	3,832

APPENDIX: STATISTICS

II

ANNUAL AVERAGES OF MASSACHUSETTS WHALING INDUSTRY, AT THREE EARLY PERIODS[1]

Dates	Number of vessels annually fitted out for		Tonnage			Gallons of oil brought in	
	Northern fishery	Southern fishery	Total	Average per vessel		Sperm	Whale
				No.	So.		
1771–75	183	121	27,840	75	115	1,250,785	272,475
1787–89	91	31	10,210	64	142	251,370	413,595
1803–06	30		9,360	312		395,640	677,422 [2]

[1] Tables for the first two periods are compiled from those in Pitkin, *Statistical View* (1816 ed.), 78–79; for 1803–06, the best years of the Federalist period, from the tables in the appendix to W. S. Tower, *History of American Whaling Industry*. The only Massachusetts ports fitting out whalers between 1803 and 1806 were Nantucket and New Bedford, and the only other American whaling ports were Hudson and Sag Harbor, N.Y., and New London, Conn., each of which fitted out an average of one whaler annually.
[2] Average for 1805–06 only.

III

COMPARISON OF ARRIVALS FROM CERTAIN FOREIGN PORTS AT BOSTON, NEW YORK, PHILADELPHIA, BALTIMORE, AND NEW ORLEANS, 1857 [1]

Vessels from	Boston	New York	Philadelphia	Baltimore	New Orleans
British East Indies	98	37	..	..	..
Manila, Batavia, etc.	24	20	..	..	..
China	6	41	..	..	..
Chile	15	2	..	12	..
Buenos Aires	15	26	..	3	..
Brazil	17	151	45	74	83
Porto Rico	7	192	16	56	7
Hayti and St. Domingo	161	174	15	..	..
Cuba	289	967	163	81	311
Russia	23	8	..	..	..
Mediterranean	111	179	48	22	66
Turkey	24	7	..	..	..
British West Indies	29	261	54	90	25
England	110	583	75	30	1136
Canada and Maritime Provinces	1913	342	77	73	..
Total	2842	2990	493	441	1628

[1] Boston Board of Trade, *Fourth Annual Report* (1858), 85.

IV

FOREIGN PLACES WHENCE VESSELS ARRIVED IN PRINCIPAL CUSTOMS DISTRICTS OF MASSACHUSETTS, YEAR ENDING JUNE 30, 1857 [1]

	New-buryport		Glouces-ter		Salem		Boston		New Bedford	
	No.	Tons	No.	Tons	No.	Tons	No.	Tons	No.	Tons
British East Indies	..	..	..	..	1	275	98	80,780	..	..
Philippines	..	..	..	..	1	289	19	14,429	..	..
Dutch East Indies	..	..	..	..	..	..	5	3,390	..	..
China	..	..	..	..	..	..	6	3,368	..	..
Africa	..	..	..	..	32	7,843	15	4,058	..	..
Azores, Cape Verde Islands, Canaries	..	..	..	..	..	..	15	3,835	4	941
Gibraltar & Malta	..	..	..	..	..	..	3	582	..	..
Spanish Mediterranean ports	..	..	..	..	..	..	17	4,879	..	..
French Mediterranean ports	..	..	..	..	1	341	14	5,502	..	..
Sardinia	..	..	..	..	..	..	5	2,466	..	..
Tuscany	..	..	..	..	..	..	10	4,389	..	..
Naples & Sicily	..	..	..	..	..	..	65	22,285	..	..
Smyrna	..	..	..	..	..	..	24	8,026	..	..
Black Sea	..	..	..	..	..	..	1	527	..	..
Portugal	..	..	..	..	..	..	2	771	..	..
Spain, Atlantic ports	1	300	1	492	3	733	17	14,657	..	..
France, " "	..	..	..	..	..	..	5	1,858	..	..
Norway & Sweden	..	..	..	..	..	..	10	5,744	..	..
Russia	..	..	..	..	..	..	22	10,452	..	..
England & Scotland	..	..	4	2,198	2	707	140	143,299	..	..
Belgium & Holland	..	..	..	..	..	..	22	10,380	..	..
Canada	..	..	..	..	8	915	1	156	1	104
Maritime Provinces	29	2,340	183	15,885	290	24,978	1913	235,998	42	5,957
S. Pierre & Miquelon	..	..	..	..	..	..	6	727	..	..
Cuba	..	..	..	..	..	..	289	70,526	1	51
Porto Rico	8	1,120	..	..	..	..	7	1,101	..	..
British W. Indies	..	..	..	..	1	171	29	5,929	..	..
Other W. Indies	..	..	..	..	3	708	12	2,249	..	..
Hayti & San Domingo	..	..	1	194	..	..	161	27,028	..	..
British Honduras	..	..	..	..	..	..	5	1,111	..	..
Mexico & Central America	..	..	..	..	..	..	6	1,124	..	..
New Grenada & Venezuela	..	..	..	..	..	..	3	596	..	..
Surinam & Cayenne	..	..	22	5,206	11	2,095	11	2,113	..	..
Brazil	..	..	..	..	14	2,430	17	3,695	..	..
Argentine Republic	..	..	..	..	4	1,194	15	4,823	..	..
Uruguay	..	..	..	..	1	222	..	..	..	..
Chile	..	..	..	..	..	..	15	7,927	..	..
Peru	..	..	..	..	..	..	3	2,087	..	..
Sandwich Islands	..	..	..	..	..	..	1	1,089	3	2,391
Returned from Whaling	..	..	..	..	3	617	3	845	132	40,565
Total	38	3,760	211	23,975	375	43,488	3012	714,821	183	50,009

[1] From *Commerce and Navigation Reports* of the Secretary of the Treasury, 1857. Vessels are entered only once for a voyage in this table, generally from the last port of call, or from the port where the principal cargo was taken.

TONNAGE OF SHIPPING OWNED IN EACH CUSTOMS DISTRICT OF MASSACHUSETTS, AND IN THE DISTRICT OF NEW YORK CITY. 1798-1860.[1]

DISTRICT[2]	Dec. 31, 1798	Dec. 31, 1800	Dec. 31, 1807	Dec. 31, 1810	Dec. 31, 1820	Dec. 31, 1830	Sept. 30, 1840	June 30, 1850	June 30, 1855	June 30, 1860
Newburyport	19,673	20,615	34,630	39,100	20,441	16,577	23,965	23,261	40,827	31,225
Ipswich	(with	Salem)	1,395	1,277	2,374	2,331	3,739	578	418	976
Gloucester	10,279	9,375	13,052	11,394	11,440	11,741	17,072	22,474	34,237	40,500
Salem	25,646	25,821	41,083	41,463	33,046	28,195	37,020	28,916	30,236	27,538
Beverly								3,173	5,362	6,283
Marblehead	18,829	19,965	21,608	20,922	11,954	6,949	12,478	6,842	8,869	7,906
Boston	80,741	96,312	119,510	149,121	126,323	135,009	220,243	320,687	546,269	464,213
Plymouth	9,798	10,707	20,761	23,028	21,070	19,476	27,504	10,722	10,235	8,210
Fall River	5,468	5,996	6,780	7,126	6,353	3,661	8,815	13,101	20,534	16,128
New Bedford	14,532	16,355	25,222	26,378	32,245	55,256	89,089	127,960	169,986	149,700
Barnstable	16,100	13,707	18,454	16,175	20,810	25,184	56,556	91,102	80,615	63,566
Edgartown	402	645	1,000	1,392	1,500	2,792	8,130	7,609	8,484	8,753
Nantucket	13,709	11,760	17,540	16,777	28,513	22,327	31,915	29,012	23,135	10,437
TOTAL, MASS.	215,177	231,258	321,035	354,153	316,069	329,498	536,526	685,437	979,207	835,435
New York	155,435	146,442	217,381	268,548	231,215	256,557	414,817	835,867	1,288,235	1,464,001

[1] From the *Commerce and Navigation Reports* and *American State Papers Commerce and Navigation*, I and II.

[2] *Newburyport* district included all towns on the lower Merrimac; *Ipswich* included Essex, and until after 1800 both were included in Salem; *Gloucester* included Rockport and Manchester; the district of *Salem and Beverly*, separated after 1840, included Danvers; *Marblehead* included Swampscott and Nahant; *Boston* included Charlestown, Medford, all towns on Boston Bay, and Cohasset. *Plymouth* included Scituate, Duxbury and Kingston; *Barnstable* included the whole of Cape Cod; Fall River (called *Dighton* before 1840), included all ports on the Taunton River; *New Bedford* included Fairhaven, the western side of Buzzards Bay, and Westport; *Edgartown* included Martha's Vineyard and Elizabeth Islands.

BIBLIOGRAPHY OF THE MARITIME
HISTORY OF MASSACHUSETTS
1783–1860

ABBREVIATIONS: E.I. = Essex Institute, Salem; *E.I.H.C.* = *Essex Institute Historical Collections.* H.C.L. = Harvard College Library. M.H.S. = Massachusetts Historical Society; *Proc. M.H.S.* = *Proceedings* of the same. p.p. = privately printed. Works cited are printed at Boston unless otherwise stated.

I wish to acknowledge my indebtedness for information, pictures, and for various facilities and courtesies, to Captain Arthur H. Clark, of Newburyport; Mr. Fred W. Tibbets, of Gloucester; Miss Elsie Heard, of Ipswich; Mrs. A. P. Loring, Jr., Miss Katherine Loring, and Mr. J. A. Marsters, of Beverly; Mrs. George Wheatland and Messrs. Henry W. Belknap, Lawrence W. Jenkins, George R. Putnam, John Robinson, and William J. Sullivan, of Salem; Messrs. F. B. C. Bradlee, Joseph W. Coates, and Benjamin L. Lindsey, of Marblehead; Messrs. Charles K. Bolton, James H. Bowditch, Frederic Cunningham, Henry R. Dalton, George F. Dow, Frederick C. Fletcher, Allan Forbes, Thomas G. Frothingham, Roland Gray, Dr. O. T. Howe, William C. Hunneman, Thomas P. Martin, Dr. Frederick Merk, J. Grafton Minot, Miss Grace Nute, Charles F. Read, André C. Reggio, Robert B. Smith, F. W. Sprague, Rev. John W. Suter, Charles H. Taylor, Jr., William Ropes Trask, Julius H. Tuttle, Perry Walton, and Frederick S. Whitwell, of Boston and Cambridge; Mr. Charles Torrey, of Brookline; Mr. Edward Gray, of Milton; Mrs. F. W. Sargent, of Wellesley; Mrs. Ellen Trask, of Lincoln; Mr. George Shaw, of Concord; Mr. Edmund P. Collier, of Cohasset; Messrs. E. W. Bradford and Arthur Lord, of Plymouth; Dr. William H. Chapman and Mrs. A. S. Cobb, of Brewster; Mr. Everett I. Nye, of Wellfleet; Messrs. George H. Tripp and Frank Wood, of New Bedford; Miss Susan E. Brock, of Nantucket; Captain John W. Pease, of Edgartown; Mr. Charles Lyon Chandler, of Philadelphia; Mr. H. K. Devereux, of Cleveland; Mr. Irving Grinnell. of New Hamburg, New York; and Mr. Samuel Hale Pearson, of Buenos Aires.

BIBLIOGRAPHY

I. GENERAL

1. MANUSCRIPT SOURCES. The Custom House Records of the old customs districts of Massachusetts are invaluable for foreign and coastwise commerce, shipping, and the fisheries. For an account of the present state and location of these records see *Proc. M.H.S.* for 1921. These Customs Records show *what* trade was carried on; but the mercantile and shipping MSS. of individuals and firms, including letter-books, ledgers, account books, log books and sea journals, show better *how* it was carried on. The most important public conlections of this class are in the Beverly Hist. Society, the E.I., the H.C.L., the M.H.S. and the New Bedford Public Library. The bulk of such material is still in private hands, and much of it is destroyed every year by otherwise intelligent people. Although of slight intrinsic value, these MSS. are of immense historic worth; the H.C.L. and the M.H.S. are always glad to store such papers without charge, or to receive them as gifts. Court Records, especially those of the Federal courts in Massachusetts, kept in the Boston Post Office building, are an untouched mine of information on maritime matters; *Sprague's Reports* and the *Digest of Federal Cases* indicate the important cases.

2. NEWSPAPERS. Those of the smaller seaports, excepting New Bedford, afford much less information than do the Customs Records of the general course of commerce; but are valuable for their advertisements and stories of shipwrecks, sea-serpents, etc. But the Boston papers are our sole source for Boston entrances and clearances, as the Boston Customs Records for this period have been destroyed. For the Federalist period the *Columbian Centinel*, and the *Boston Price Current*, beginning 1795 (for the later titles, and check-list, see *Proceedings Am. Antiq. Soc.*, XXV, 278) are best; for the period 1815-1842, *P. P. F. Degrand's Boston Weekly Report* (1819-27, best file in Boston Athenæum), *Boston Commercial Gazette* and *Boston Daily Advertiser;* for the period 1843-60, the *Boston Shipping List and Price Current* (very full information on commerce, and useful yearly summaries, best file at Boston Marine Museum, Old State House); *Boston Atlas* and *Boston Journal.* Hunt's *Merchants' Magazine* (N.Y., 1839-60) is a mine of commercial information.

3. STATISTICS. The *Commerce and Navigation Reports*, annually issued by the Secretary of the Treasury, are to be found in the *American State Papers, Commerce and Navigation* down to 1821; thenceforth issued separately, and also in the regular series of Con-

gressional Documents. For the period 1783–1833, T. Pitkin, *Statistical View* (New Haven, ed. of 1835); Adam Seybert, *Statistical Annals* (Phila. 1818); G. Watterston and N. B. Van Zandt, *Tabular Statistical Views* (Washington, 1828), and *Continuation* of same (1833) will be found more convenient. Many statistics are also given in Hunt's *Merch. Mag.* and in Samuel Hazard (ed.), *Hazard's U.S. Commercial and Statistical Register* (Phila., 1839–42). The State Censuses of *1837* (John P. Bigelow, *Statistical Tables of Certain Branches of Industry*, 1838), *1845* (John G. Palfrey, *Ibid.* 1846), and *1855* contain statistics on shipbuilding, fisheries and whaling only; that of *1865* gives also the coastwise fleet. The best single compilation of Mass. commercial statistics will be found in British Parliamentary Documents, *Accounts and Papers*, XLIX, Part 1, 1846 (part XV of John Macgregor's *Commercial Tariffs*, etc.).

4. GENERAL SECONDARY WORKS. No history of Massachusetts pays the slightest attention to the maritime aspect after the colonial period; but Edward Channing, *History of the U.S.*, vols. III and IV, contains much valuable data on American commerce to 1815. Emory R. Johnson et al., *History of Domestic and Foreign Commerce of the U.S.*, 2 vols. (Washington, 1915), contains a useful digest of federal legislation affecting shipping, fishing, etc. Grace Lee Nute, *American Foreign Commerce 1825–1850* (Radcliffe doctoral dissertation in preparation), aims at completeness for that period. John R. Spears, *The Story of the American Merchant Marine* (N.Y., 1910), is the most honest book on that subject.

5. LOCAL HISTORIES of the maritime towns are usually inadequate or misleading on all maritime activities save privateering; exceptions will be noted below. The "Topographical Descriptions" of various seaport towns in the *Collections of the M.H.S.* 1st ser., vols. I–IX (1792–1804), 2d ser., vols. III, IV, X (1815–23), 3d ser., II (1830), are valuable sources. John W. Barber, *Historical Collections . . . of every Town in Massachusetts* (Worcester, 1839), with woodcuts. There is a useful class of publications on the maritime aspects of certain towns: — Leavitt Sprague, *Barnstable and Yarmouth Sea Captains and Ship Owners* (p.p., 1913). Pamphlets prepared by Walton Adv. Co. for State St. Trust Co.: *Old Shipping Days in Boston* (1918), *Some Merchants and Sea Captains of Old Boston* (1919), *Other Merchants and Sea Captains* (1920). J. Henry Sears, *Brewster Ship Masters* (Yarmouthport, 1906). Edmund P. Collier, *Deep Sea Captains of Cohasset*, (p.p.), Benj. L. Lindsey, *Old Marblehead Sea Captains and the Ships in which They Sailed* (Marblehead Hist.

BIBLIOGRAPHY

Soc., 1915). Ralph D. Paine, *Ships and Sailors of Old Salem* (N.Y., 1908; Chicago, 1912), a topical and comprehensive history of Salem commerce and privateering. *Old Time Ships of Salem* (E. I., Salem, 1917) reproduces several famous Salem vessels in colors, with historical data.

6. BIOGRAPHIES, MEMOIRS, *and* AUTOBIOGRAPHIES OF MERCHANTS, SHIPMASTERS, *etc.* These often contain letters and other source material of great value; many, however, are privately printed and scarce. Several good memoirs of Boston, Salem, and Newburyport merchants will be found in the *E.I.H.C., Proc. M.H.S.*, Freeman Hunt (ed.), *Lives of American Merchants* (N.Y., 1856); Hunt's *Merc. Mag.* (esp. vol. XI); W. H. Bayley & O. O. Jones, *Hist. of the Marine Society of Newburyport* (Nbpt., 1906); J. J. Currier, *History of Newburyport* (Nbpt., 1906) II, chap. XXII. Wm. H. Reed, *Reminiscences of Elisha Atkins* (p.p., 1890). N. I. Bowditch, *Memoir of Nathaniel Bowditch* (3d ed., Cambridge, 1884). [Ann Tracy], *Reminiscences of John Bromfield* (Salem, 1852). H. C. Lodge, *Life and Letters of George Cabot* (1877). Roxana Dabney, *Annals of the Dabney Family at Fayal* (3 vols. p.p., 1892). Wm. T. Davis, *Plymouth Memories of an Octogenarian* (Plymouth, 1906). Anna E. Ticknor, *Memoir of Samuel Eliot* (p.p., 1869). Robert Bennet Forbes, *Personal Reminiscences* (2d. ed., 1882, with additional material; extra-illustrated copy in H.C.L.). Sarah F. Hughes, *Letters and Recollections of John Murray Forbes* (2 vols, 1899). There is also a p.p. 5 vol. edition. *Nathaniel Goddard, Boston Merchant, 1767–1853* (p.p., 1906). Edward Gray, *William Gray of Salem, Merchant* (1914). T. F. Waters, *Augustine Heard and his Friends* (*Publications of the Ipswich Historical Society*, XXI, 1916). T. W. Higginson, *Life and Times of Stephen Higginson* (1907). Osborn Howes, *Autobiographical Sketch, Edited by his children* (p.p., 1894). *The Autobiography of Capt. Zachary G. Lamson 1797–1814, with Introduction and Historical Notes by O. T. Howe* (1908). Martha Nichols (ed.), *George Nichols, Salem Shipmaster and Merchant, An Autobiography* (Salem, 1913). [Lucy W. Peabody], *Henry Wayland Peabody, Merchant* (West Medford, 1909). T. G. Cary, *Memoir of Thomas Handasyd Perkins* (1856). Nathaniel Silsbee, "Biographical Notes," *E.I.H.C.*, XXXV (1899). *Brief Sketch of Capt. Josiah Sturgis* (1844). Julian Sturgis, *From Books and Papers of Russell Sturgis* (p.p., Oxford). J. D. Whidden, *Ocean Life in the old Sailing Ship Days* (1908). Family histories and genealogies, too numerous to mention here, also afforded much information. See also under § 5.

BIBLIOGRAPHY

II. BY SUBJECTS [1]

7. NORTHWEST COAST AND CHINA TRADE.
(a) MANUSCRIPTS (chaps. IV–VI and XVI–XVII). *Bryant & Sturgis MSS., Josiah Marshall MSS., J. P. Cushing MS. letter-book,* Horatio A. Lamb, *Notes on Trade with the Northwest Coast, 1790–1810* (digest of records of J. & T. Lamb), in the H. C. L.; *Boit MSS., Ship Columbia MSS.,* and John Hoskins, *Narrative of the Columbia's Second Voyage,* in M.H.S.; *Solid Men of Boston in the Northwest,* copy in M.H.S. from the Bancroft MSS., Berkeley, California. *Augustine Heard MSS., John Suter MSS.,* and log of ship *Massachusetts,* in private possession. Journals of ships *Concord, Margaret, Hamilton,* and others in E.I., Salem. Reports of Laforêt, Barbé-Marbois, and De Guigne on early American trade with China in Archives des Affaires Etrangères, Paris, "Mémoires et Documents, Etats-Unis," VIII, 207, XIV, 164–69, 369–80; "Asie," XIX, 62, 141, 219.

(b) PRINTED SOURCES. *The Journals of Samuel Shaw, with a life of the Author by Josiah Quincy* (1847). John Boit, Jr., *Remarks on the Ship Columbia's [second] Voyage, Proc. M.H.S.,* LIII (1920). Archibald Cambell, *A Voyage round the World from 1805 to 1812* (N.Y., 1817). Richard J. Cleveland, *Narrative of Voyages and Commercial Enterprises* (2 vols., 1842, and 1 vol., 1850). Amasa Delano, *Narrative of Voyages and Travels* (1817), John D'Wolf, *Voyage to the North Pacific and Journey through Siberia* (Cambridge, 1861). Capt. Eliah Grimes, Letters from N.W. Coast (1822), in *Washington Hist. Quart.,* XI, 174 (1920). Haswell's Journal of the *Columbia's* first Voyage, in appendix to H. H. Bancroft, *Pacific States,* XXII. John R. Jewitt, *Narrative of Adventures* (N.Y., 1816). Bernard Magee, "Observations on the Islands of Juan Fernandez," etc. in *Collections of M.H.S.,* 1st ser., IV, 247. William Moulton, *A Concise Extract from the Sea Journal ... written on board the Onico* (Utica, N.Y., 1804). *The Narrative of David Woodard and four Seamen* (London, 1804). William Sturgis, *The Northwest Fur Trade* (*Old South Leaflets,* no. 219). W. F. Taylor, *Voyage Round the World in the U.S. Frigate Columbia* (New Haven, 1843). William Tufts, "List of American vessels engaged in the Trade of the Northwest Coast, 1787–1809" (incomplete), in James G. Swan, *Northwest Coast* (N.Y., 1837), 423. Charles P. Low, *Some Recollections, 1847–*

---

[1] The general sources and secondary authorities mentioned above have also been drawn upon for these subjects.

BIBLIOGRAPHY

1873 (p.p., 1906). Katherine Hillard, *My Mother's Journal* (1900). William C. Hunter, *The Fan Kwae at Canton before Treaty Days* (London, 1882), and *Bits of Old China* (London, 1885). Robert B. Forbes, *Remarks on China and the China Trade* (1844). *British Parliamentary Papers*, 1830, VI, pp. 350–93.[1] Charles Gützlaff, *Sketch of Chinese History* (London, 1834). John Phipps, *Practical Treatise on China and the Eastern Trade* (Calcutta, 1835).

(c) SECONDARY. For the Northwest Coast and early California trades: — H. H. Bancroft, *History of the Pacific States*, XIV (*California*, II), XXII, and XXIII (*Northwest Coast*, I, II, San Francisco, 1884). For the China trade: — Kenneth S. Latourette, *The History of Early Relations between the United States and China, 1784–1844* (*Trans. Conn. Acad. Arts Sci.*, XX, New Haven, 1917). For sealing: — A. Howard Clark, "The Antarctic Fur-Seal and Sea-Elephant Industry," in G. B. Goode, *Fisheries of the U.S.* (Washington, 1887), VII. Edward G. Porter, "The Ship Columbia and the Discovery of Oregon " with illustrations made on voyage, *N.E. Mag.*, n.s., VI, 472 (1892); reprinted in *Old South Leaflets*, No. 131. Louis Becke and Walter Jeffery, *The Tapu of Banderah* (Phila., 1901). F. W. Howay, "The Voyage of the *Hope*, 1790–92," *Washington Hist. Quart.*, XI (1920). C. G. Loring, "Memoir of William Sturgis," *Proc. M.H.S.*, VII. See also §§ 5 and 6, above.

8. SALEM COMMERCE (chaps. VII, VIII, XIV, and part IV and IX). *The Diary of William Bentley, D.D., 1784–1819* (4 vols., E.I., Salem, 1905–14). Numerous logs, and sea journals and other MSS. in E.I.; *Thorndike MSS.*, Beverly Hist. Soc.; *Cleveland MSS.* and miscellaneous MSS. in Peabody Museum, Salem; *Heard MSS.*, *Silsbee MSS.*, and *Howe MSS.*, in private hands. C. S. Osgood & H. M. Batchelder, *Historical Sketch of Salem* (Salem, 1879) and R. D. Paine, *Ships and Sailors*, are the best secondary accounts; the latter is also a guide to the printed material. Biographies of George Nichols, Edward Gray, Z. G. Lamson, Nathaniel Silsbee (see § 6). Robert E. Peabody, *Merchant Venturers of Old Salem* [the Derbys] (Boston, 1912). Numerous articles and much source material in the *E.I.H.C.* John C. Brent, "Leaves from an African Journal," in *Knickerbocker Mag.*, 1848–50; Montgomery Parker, "Sketches in S. Africa," *Ibid.*, 1850–53. Horatio Bridge, U.S.N., *Journal of an African Cruiser* . . .

---

[1] The title page of this volume is *Reports from Committees, 3, East India Company's Affairs (Lord's Report). Session 5 February—23 July 1830. Vol. VI.* It contains testimony by Joshua Bates and others on the American trade with China.

BIBLIOGRAPHY

edited by *Nathaniel Hawthorne* (N.Y., 1845). *Narrative of the Capture of the brig Mexican by Pirates* (1832, reprinted in *E.I.H.C.*, XXXIII). [J. Oliver and W. S. Dix], *The Wreck of the Glide, with Recollections of the Fijiis*, (N.Y., 1846). J. H. Reynolds, *Voyage of the U.S. Frigate Potomac* (N.Y., 1835).

9. SHIPS AND SHIPBUILDING (chaps. VIII and part of XVI). Henry Hall, *Report on the Shipbuilding Industry* (Washington, 1884) from the 10th Census, is a most unsatisfactory work, but reproduces the lines of some famous vessels. The studies of local shipbuilding seldom give more than the tonnage measurement, and not one discusses the changes in design. A. Vernon Briggs, *History of Shipbuilding on North River, Plymouth County, Mass. . . . 1640–1872* (1887), is most comprehensive and valuable. W. H. Summer, *History of East Boston*, 697, gives a list of vessels there built through 1858. Capt. John Bradford, "Reminiscences of Duxbury Shipbuilding," in L. Bradford, *Hist. of Duxbury*. Charles Brooks, *History of Medford* (1855), pp. 366–79, gives a list of vessels there built between 1803 and 1854; see also *Medford Historical Register*, I, 65, XV, 77. John J. Currier, *Historical Sketch of Ship Building on the Merrimac River* (Nbpt., 1877). Wm. Leavitt, "Materials for the History of Shipbuilding in Salem," in *E.I.H.C.*, VI, VII (1863–65), with full dimensions. A. F. Hitchings & Stephen W. Phillips, *Ship Registers of the District of Salem and Beverly*, 1789–1900 (Salem, 1906, reprinted from *E.I.H.C.*, XXXIX–XLII) is a most useful work of reference; there is great need of a similar one for Boston. H. H. Edes, *Memorial of Josiah Barker* (1891). R. B. Forbes, *Notes on Ships of the Past* (1885), and *A New Rig for Ships* (1849). R. H. Dana, *The Seaman's Friend; containing a Treatise on Practical Seamanship, with Plates; a Dictionary of Sea Terms, Customs and Usages of the Merchant Service; Laws relating to the Practical Duties of Master and Mariner* (1841), is the most useful work of this sort.

10. SHIP PORTRAITS AND MODELS. The best public collections are in the Peabody Museum, Salem; the Boston Marine Museum, Old State House, Boston; the Old Dartmouth Historical Society, New Bedford; the Beverly Historical Society; the Marblehead Historical Society, and the Historical Society of Old Newbury, Newburyport. Private collections to which I have had access, through the kindness of the owners, are those of Charles H. Taylor, Jr., Allan Forbes, and Dr. O. T. Howe, Boston; Frederick C. Fletcher, Herbert Foster Otis, and Charles Torrey, Brookline; F. B. C. Bradlee, Marblehead; and Captain Arthur H. Clark, Newburyport. The East India House,

New York, has a collection of paintings of Massachusetts clipper and packet-ships. Little is known of our ship painters. For Robert Salmon, see *Proceedings Bostonian Society* for Jan. 1895, p. 37. There is a catalogue of his works in the Boston Public Library. Of Bresayant's *Antoine Roux et ses fils* (Marseilles, circ. 1882), I have been unable to find a copy.

11. ARCHITECTURE AND SOCIAL LIFE OF THE MERCHANTS (chaps. IX and XV). Bentley's *Diary* (see § 8); Frank Cousins, *The Colonial Architecture of Salem* (1919); F. Cousins and P. M. Riley, *The Wood-Carver of Salem, Samuel McIntire and his Work* (1916). Mrs. E. Vale Smith, *History of Newburyport* (Nbpt., 1854); Sarah A. Emery, *Reminiscences of a Nonagenarian* (Nbpt., 1879). Albert Hale, *Old Newburyport Houses* (1912). Charles A. Cummings, "Architecture in Boston," in Justin Winsor, *Memorial History of Boston*, IV, chap. VIII. *Bulletin of the Society for the Preservation of New England Antiquities*, and *Old Time New England*, the new monthly magazine of the same Society. Ellen S. Bulfinch, *Life and Letters of Charles Bulfinch* (1896); Ashton R. Willard, "Charles Bulfinch the Architect," in *N.E. Mag.*, n.s., III, 273 (1890). Henry F. Bond, "Old Summer Street, Boston," *Ibid.*, n.s., XIX, 333 (1898). Biographies of merchants (see § 6), esp. of Samuel Eliot and George Nichols. Mary H. Northend, *Memories of Old Salem* (Chicago, 1917). *Act of Incorporation and By-laws of the East India Marine Society* (Salem, 1899). *Catalog of the "Cleopatra's Barge" Exhibition at the Peabody Museum* (with bibliography, Salem, 1916).

12. THE FISHERIES (chaps. X and XIX). There is no wholly satisfactory account of the Massachusetts fisheries, based on original research. The best are Raymond McFarland, *History of the New England Fisheries* (Univ. of Penn., 1911); Lorenzo Sabine, *Report on the Principal Fishermen of the American Seas* (Washington, 1853); G. Brown Goode, *Fisheries ... of the U.S.* (Washington, 1887), VI (Section V, "History and Methods of the Fisheries," vol. I.). Of the local histories, the following are the most useful: Samuel Roads, Jr., *History and Traditions of Marblehead* (1880), (cf. Whidden's *Ocean Life*, cited above, § 6); John J. Babson, *History of Gloucester* (Gloucester, 1860); J. R. Pringle, *History of Gloucester* (*Ibid.*, 1892); [Fred W. Tibbets, ed.], *Memorial of the 250th anniversary of Gloucester* (*Ibid.*, 1901); James Thatcher, *History of Plymouth* (2d ed., 1835); E. V. Bigelow, *History of Cohasset* (1898), Waldo Thompson, *Swampscott* (Lynn, 1885); Shebnah Rich, *Truro — Cape Cod* (Boston, 1883); S. L. Deyo (ed.), *History of Barnstable County* (N.Y.,

BIBLIOGRAPHY

1890); Everett I. Nye, *History of Wellfleet* (Hyannis, 1920). Considerable information and otherwise on the Gloucester fisheries, from various octogenarians' reminiscences, can be found in George H. Procter (compiler), *The Fishermen's Memorial and Record Book* (Glouc., 1873), *The Fisheries of Gloucester, 1623–1876* (*Ibid.*, 1876), *The Fishermen's Own Book* (*Ibid.*, 1882); and Sylvanus Smith, *Fisheries of Cape Ann* (*Ibid.*, 1915). The best description of the life of the fishermen is J. Reynolds, *Peter Gott the Cape Ann Fisherman* (1856). The story of Beverly fisheries is largely in MSS. in the Beverly Hist. Society. For Cape Cod in the Federalist period, the "Topographical Descriptions" in the early volumes of *Collections of the M.H.S.*, are most valuable, as are vol. III of Timothy Dwight, *Travels in New England and New York* (New Haven, 1822), vol. III, and E. A. Kendall, *Travels Through the Northern Parts of the United States in 1807–08* (N.Y., 1809), vol. II. Thoreau's *Cape Cod* is the classic description for about 1850. Albert P. Brigham, *Cape Cod and the Old Colony* (N.Y., 1920) is an admirable study in regional geography. On separate branches: George B. Goode *et al.*, *Materials for a History of the Mackerel Fishery* (from Annual Report of U.S. Commissioner of Fish and Fisheries for 1881), Washington, 1883; Shebnah Rich, *The Mackerel Fishery of North America* (1879). Ernest Ingersoll, *The Oyster Industry* (Washington, 1881, a reprint from Goode's *Fisheries*). Joseph W. Collins, "Evolution of the American Fishing Schooner," *N.E. Mag.*, n.s., XVIII, 336 (1898) is a most valuable article. The models illustrated therein are now mostly in the E.I. and the Annisquam Yacht Club. Pictures of fishing vessels before 1860 are exceedingly rare.

13. FEDERALISM AND NEUTRAL TRADE (chap. XII). *Beverly Shipping MSS.*, Bev. Hist. Soc.; *Boit MSS.* and *William Gray Letter-book* in private hands. G. R. Putnam, *Lighthouses and Lightships of the U.S.* (1917). Capt. Lawrence Furlong, *American Coast Pilot* (Nbpt., 1809). N. Spooner, *Gleanings from Records of Boston Marine Society* (Boston, 1875). Biographies of Bromfield, Forbes, Goddard, Gray, Lamson, Higginson, and Perkins cited in § 6, and S. E. Morison, *H. G. Otis* (1913). Elijah Cobb, *Autobiographical Sketch* (written about 1845, printed in Yarmouth *Register*, photostat copy in M.H.S.). R. E. Peabody, *Merchant Venturers* (§ 8); R. J. Cleveland, *Voyages* (§ 7). For South American Trade: — Charles Lyon Chandler, articles in *Am. Hist. Rev.*, XXIII, 816–26 (1918), *Hisp. Am. Hist. Rev.*, II, 26–54 (1919); III, 159–66 (1920); and *Inter-American Acquaintances* (2d ed., Sewanee, Tenn., 1917).

14. EMBARGO AND WAR OF 1812 (chap. XIII). Biographies cited above. C. F. Adams (ed.), *Memoirs of J. Q. Adams*, II (Phila., 1874); Worthington C. Ford (ed.), *Writings of J. Q. Adams*, III, IV (N.Y., 1914). Histories of maritime towns, especially L. B. Ellis, *History of New Bedford* (Syracuse, N.Y., 1892); Freeman's *Cape Cod* and Swift's *Cape Cod*. Wm. Leavitt, "Private Armed Vessels of Salem," in *E.I.H.C.* for 1860. B. B. Crowninshield, "The Private Armed Ship America," *E.I.H.C.*, XXXVII. Log of *Brutus* in Boston Marine Society; papers of the *Grand Turk* in Beverly Hist. Society. Bentley's *Diary*. David Porter, *Journal of Cruise in U.S. Frigate Essex* (N.Y., 1822). *Autobiography of Elder Joseph Bates* (Battle Creek, 1868); *Report of Committee of House of Representatives on Impressments* (1813); account of Salem impressments in *E.I.H.C.*, XLIX, 321.

15. HAWAIIAN, SOUTH SEA, AND CALIFORNIA HIDE TRADE (chap. XVI). *Bryant & Sturgis, Josiah Marshall*, and *James Hunnewell MSS.*, H.C.L.; S. E. Morison, "Boston Traders in Hawaii, 1789–1823," *Proc. M.H.S.*, LIV, 9 (October, 1920), and authorities therein cited. For California, see Charles E. Chapman, "The Literature of California History," *Southwestern Hist. Quar.*, XXII, 318–52 (1919), and add Lieut. Joseph W. Revere, U.S.N., *A Tour of Duty in California* (N.Y., 1849). The classic narrative of this trade is R. H. Dana, *Two Years before the Mast* (N.Y., 1840, and numerous later editions). R. B. Forbes, *Notes on Navigation* (1884).

16. MARITIME AND COMMERCIAL BOSTON TO 1850 (chap. XV, and parts of others) has received much less adequate treatment than Salem. Hamilton A. Hill, *Trade and Commerce of Boston* (Reprinted from *Professional and Industrial History of Suffolk Co.*, II, 1894) is a mere sketch, but useful as far as it goes. *Bostonian Society Publications*, passim. *Bowen's Picture of Boston* (3d ed., 1838). State St. Trust Co. pamphlets (see § 5). Biographies (§ 6). N. Spooner, *Gleanings* (§ 13). James H. Lanman, "The Commerce of Boston," in Hunt's *Merc. Mag.*, X, 421 (1844) and Charles Hudson "Mass. and her Resources," in *Ibid.*, IX, 426. "Shipping of the Port of Boston," in *Ibid.*, XIV, 83 (1845). E. J. Howard, "Commercial Review of Fifty Years," in Boston Board of Trade, *27th* and *29th Annual Reports* (1880, 1882). *The Life of Father Taylor, the Sailor Preacher* (Boston, 1904), includes an earlier biography by Haven and Russell, and several short sketches. Fitz Henry Smith, Jr., *Storms and Shipwrecks in Boston Bay, and the Record of the Life Savers of Hull* (p.p., 1918, reprinted from *Bostonian Society Publications*).

BIBLIOGRAPHY

R. B. Forbes, *A Discursive Sketch on Yachting* (1888), and *Voyage of the Jamestown* (1847).

17. STEAM NAVIGATION AND SAILING PACKET LINES (chap. xv). F. B. C. Bradlee, *Steam Navigation in New England* (Salem, 1920, reprinted from *E.I.H.C.*) gives a detailed account of the lines north of Boston with illustrations. The same author, in a series of articles in the *International Marine Engineering* between 1910 and 1920, describes the lines south of Boston. His *The Dreadnought of New-buryport* (Salem, 1920, reprinted with additions from *E.I.H.C.*), contains material on the sailing packets. Samuel Samuels, *From the Forecastle to the Cabin* (N.Y., 1887). Moses W. Mann, "Medford Steamboat Days," *Medford Historical Register*, XVII, 92 (1914). Pliny Miles, *Advantages of Ocean Steam Navigation* (1857) contains much data on Southern coasting trade. R. B. Forbes, *The Auxiliary Screw Ship "Massachusetts"* (1853), and *Remarks on Ocean Steam Navigation* (1855).

18. EAST INDIA AND ICE TRADE. *Frederic Tudor MSS.*, in private hands, and Tudor's own story, written in 1849, in *Proc. M.H.S.*, III, 53–60. Boston Board of Trade, *Third Annual Report* (1857).

19. WHALING. There is need of a comprehensive history of this industry, paying due attention to the labor and business aspects, and using the almost untouched mines of information in the New Bedford *Whalemen's Shipping List* (1843–1916), the New Bedford customs records, and the log books and business records at the New Bedford Public Library and elsewhere. The standard histories are Obed Macy, *History of Nantucket* (1835); Alexander Starbuck, *History of the American Whale Fishery* (with complete list of whaling voyages, Waltham, 1878); and Walter S. Tower, *History of the American Whale Fishery* (Pub. of the U. of Penn. No. 20, 1907), with bibliography and statistics. Another whaling bibliography which lists many periodical articles and titles not found in Tower, is [G. H. Tripp], *A Collection of Books, Pamphlets, Log Books, Pictures, etc. Illustrating Whales and the Whale Fishery contained in the Free Public Library, New Bedford, Mass.* (2d ed., April, 1920). The chapter by James T. Brown in G. B. Goode, *Fisheries of the U.S.* (Washington, 1887), VII, 218–93, gives the most detailed account of methods and appliances. Hussey & Robinson, *Catalogue of Nantucket Whalers . . . from 1815 to 1870* (Nantucket, 1876) is a useful check-list. John R. Spears, *The Story of the New England Whalers* (N.Y., 1908), with a chapter on the slavers; and A. Hyatt Verrill, *The Real Story of the Whaler* (N.Y., 1916), are the best popular de-

BIBLIOGRAPHY

scriptions and histories. Herman Melville's classic, *Moby-Dick, or the White Whale* (1st ed., 1851), gives the writer's experiences in the form of a novel. Other whaling novels by whalemen are Joseph C. Hart, *Miriam Coffin* (2 vols, N.Y., 1835, and later editions), and William Hussey Macy, *There She Blows!* (1877) and C. H. Robbins *The Gam* (New Bedford, 1899), a group of short stories. Among the dozens of whaling voyage narratives: J. Ross Browne, *Etchings of a Whaling Cruise* (N.Y., 1846), gives the viewpoint of a green hand; Charles Nordhoff, *Whaling and Fishing* (Cincinnati, 1856) that of an able seaman under a decent skipper. J. N. Reynolds's *Report on Islands discovered by Whalers in the Pacific* (1835) is in *23 Cong., 2d sess., Ho. Exec. Doc.* III, No. 105. Charles Wilkes, U.S.N., in his *Narrative of the U.S. Exploring Expedition*, 1838–42 (London, 1845), v., Chap. XII, gives a list of the whaling grounds and describes certain practices, which are also exposed by F. M. Ringgold (U.S. consul at Puita, P.I.) in an official report summarized in Hunt's *Merch. Mag.*, XLI, 391 (1859); and denounced by the Rev. Francis Wayland in *The Claims of the Whalemen on Christian Benevolence* (New Bedford, 1843). *The Old Dartmouth Historical Sketches* (quarterly of the Old Dartmouth Historical Society), especially nos. 14, 38, 44, and 45, are full of valuable material.

20. THE CLIPPER-SHIP ERA (chaps. XXI–XXIII). Captain Arthur H. Clark's incomparable *Clipper Ship Era* (N.Y., 1911), and Dr. Octavius T. Howe's MS. history of the clipper ships and MS. history of the '49 movement, are the principal authorities on which I have relied. The dimensions of clipper ships given in the footnotes are taken for the most part from the Boston ship registry at the Boston custom house. Henry Blaney, *Journal of Voyage to China and Return*, 1851–53 (p.p., 1913). Lieut. M. F. Maury, *Explanations and Sailing Directions* (6th ed., Phila., 1854). *Percy Chase MSS.*, H.C.L., a compilation of clipper and other ships' records. *Description of the Largest Ship in the World, the New Clipper Great Republic* (1853). R. B. Forbes, *To Merchants, Underwriters and others Interested* (1853), and *An Appeal to Merchants and Ship Owners on the subject of Seamen* (1854). For the commerce of the period 1850–60 the *Boston Board of Trade Reports*, beginning 1854, are most important; those of 1880 and 1882 give additional matter.

INDEX

The Supplement and Appendices are not indexed.

Adams, John, 135, 165, 174–75.
Adams, John Quincy, 194, 197, 278.
Africa, trade with, 33, 220–22; *see* Slave Trade, South Africa, Zanzibar.
Akbar, 329.
Alaska, *see* Northwest Coast.
Albatross, 53, 58.
Alert (1), 70; (2), 77n., 256.
Algiers, trade with, 194.
Allen, Capt. Joseph, 317.
Alsop, Richard, 269n.
America, 93, 100, 201.
American Hero, 203.
American Revolution, 23, 27–30.
Ames plow works, 297, 333.
Amory, Thomas, 21.
Amory, Thomas Jr. & Co., 55, 57n., 205.
Amsterdam, trade with, 177–79, 297.
Andrew Jackson, 233n., 341.
Anjer, 67, 259.
Ann Alexander, 180.
Architecture, chapter ix, 153, 229, 237–38.
Argonaut, 338, 348.
Ariadne, 205.
Astrea (1), 35, 48, 49, 83, 92, 154; (2), 94, 108, 115.
Atahualpa, 69, 72, 112.
Atlantic, 48.
Auction tax, 275.
Austin, J. L. & B., 57n.
Australia, 62; clipper ships, 362–64; trade with, 367–69.
Avon, 248.
Azores, *see* Western Islands.

Bacon, Daniel C., 339, 349.
Bailey, Capt. John, 171.
Baltic trade, origin, 154; Napoleonic period, 139, 155, 179, 189n.,

193–95; later, 216, 289, 294–97, 366; statistics, 397.
Baltimore, clippers, 100, 201, 292, 329; shipping statistics, 396.
Bangor, 236.
Baring Brothers & Co., 168–69, 274.
Barnard, Capt. Moses, 94.
Barnstable, 146, 203, 264n., 301; statistics, 398.
Basey, Capt. Jonathan, 178.
Batavia, trade with, 48, 52, 91, 182–83, 275, 397.
Bates, Joshua, 274.
Becket, 262.
Becket, Retire, 80.
Benjamin, 73.
Bentley, Rev. William, 92, 122, 179; quoted, 24, 33, 89, 98, 111, 123, 137, 142, 149, 153, 191.
Bethel, 20.
Betsey, brig, 155; brigantine, 59n.; ship, 178.
Beverly, 79n., 141; commerce and fishing in 1785–1800, 32, 38, 141–42; War of 1812, 208, 210; after 1815, 294n., 303–304; forty-niners, 335; shipping statistics, 398.
Beverly Farms, 141, 245.
Black Ball Line, 232.
Black Prince, 351, 354n.
Blake, Capt. Charles, 246.
Blessing of the Bay, 14.
Blue Jacket, 345, 362.
Boit, Capt. John, Jr., 73–76, 171; quoted, 50.
Bombay, trade with, 45, 85–87.
Boot and Shoe trade, 21, 267, 288, 298, 366.
Bordman, William, Jr., 57n., 247, 261, his mercantile ventures, 287–90.
Boston, position, 3, 6; colonial, 20;

411

INDEX

INDEX

INDEX

415

416

INDEX

nial prosperity, 23; Federal period, 48, 109, 136–41, 179, 190; War of 1812, 199, 208; period 1815–40, commerce, 216–17; fisheries, 304; shipping, 398.
Margaret (1), 50, 107n.; (2), 183.
Maria, 157n.
Marion, 316.
Marquesas Islands, 54, 203, 265.
Marshall, Chief Justice, 197–98.
Marshall, Josiah, 129, 260–65.
Martinique, *see* West Indies.
Mary Glover, 328, 347.
Massachusetts (1), 52, 107n., 114; (2), 183; steamboat, 235.
Massachusetts Bay, 6.
Massachusetts-Bay, Colony of, 10–18.
Massachusetts-Bay, Province of, 18
Mastiff, 342, 349.
Mattapoisett, 105, 316.
Mauritius, trade with, 73, 75, 86, 170–71.
Maury, Lieut. M. F., 358, 361n., 363.
Mayflower, dimensions, 15n.; voyage, 8, 10.
Mayo, Capt. Jeremiah, 116.
Mayo, Capt. M. H., 208.
Medford, shipbuilding, 14, 102–03, 236, 254–56n., 293n., 296; clipper ships, 344n., 346, 355.
Mediterranean, trade with, colonial, 13–14; Federalist period, 176–77, 194; after 1815, 286–94.
Melville, Herman, quoted, 227, 317, 323, 325–26.
Mentor, 77n., 262.
Merchant, definition, 24; colonial life, 25; of Federalist Salem, 122; of Federalist Boston, 128–32; of later Boston, 239–41, 244, 285, 290.
Mermaid, 247.
Merrill, Orlando B., 102.
Merrimac River, 2, 151; shipbuilding, 101–02, 152, 255, 256n. See Newburyport.
Merrimack, 155.
Merritt, Dr. Samuel, 337.
Merry Quaker, 105.
Mexican, 270.

Middlesex Canal, 216, 236.
Minerva, 104.
Minot's Light, 4, 164, 311.
Mississippi valley, trade with, 252, 298.
Mitter, Rajkissen, 282.
Mocha, trade with, 92, 93, 181.
Morgan, Charles W., 318n., 323n.
Morgan, Junius S., 218.
Mount Vernon, of Salem, 98, 175–77; of New York, 104.

Nahant, 123, 236, 244–48.
Nancy, 155.
Nantucket, description, 5, 15, 159; settlement, 155–56; lighthouses, 168n.; population, 315; steamboats, 236; forty-niners, 333; statistics, 395, 398; War of 1812; 208; whaling, early, 20, 31, 156; of Federalist period, 157–59; after 1815, 314–17.
Nantucket South Shoals, 7, 164.
Natchez, 100.
Naushon, 246.
Nautilus, 242.
Navigation, 113–17; aids to, 161–64.
Neptune, 221.
Neptune's Car, 351.
New Bedford, 6, 156, 314–16; commerce, 179–80, 294n.; during War of 1812, 199, 207; population, 316–17; shipping statistics, 189n., 397–98; society, 319; whaling, 31, 157, chap. xx; forty-niners, 333.
Newburyport, 2, 151–54; fisheries, 152, 303; commerce, in Federalist period, 108, 151–55, 191, 216, 294n.; population, 151, 216; shipbuilding, 101–02, 189, 338, 349; War of 1812, 199, 207; after war, statistics, 397–98.
New Orleans, trade with, 298–99, 365, 369; statistics, 396.
New World, 331.
New York, 44; competition with Massachusetts in China trade, 44, 275–76; in shipping, etc., 188–89, 215–17, 225–27, 252, 291, 369; privateering, 199; comparative statistics, 396–98; clip-

417

INDEX

INDEX

INDEX

Federalist period, 110–11; of 1830, 257: of clipper period, 351–54.
Wagon trade, 206.
Wales, Thomas B., 295, 297.
Wallis, Mrs., 220.
War of 1812, 195–212.
Ward, Capt. William, 86.
Wareham, 105, 207.
Waterman, Capt. Bob, 100, 329, 340.
Waterman & Ewell, 293n., 296.
Water Witch, 292–93.
Wave, 247.
Webster, Daniel, 214, 246, 264n.
Weld, Wm. F. & Co., 348.
Wellfleet, 25, 114n., 148, 149, 301–02, 306, 313.
Wells, 190.
West, Capt. Ebenezer, 45.
Western Islands, colonial trade with, 13; neutral trade, 176, 179, 180, 193; later trade, 293–94; whaling, 321–23.
West India trade, origin, 12, 17, 19; after Revolution, 31, 32, 38; Federalist period, 83, 84, 111, 139, 141, 151–55, 181, 185, 188, 189n., 280; after 1815, 216, 280–81; 293–95, 309; statistics, 396–97.
Weston, Ezra, 104, 290.
Westward Ho! 342, 348.
Whaling, origin, 20; from Cape Cod, 146, 305; from Nantucket, to 1812, 156–59; statistics, 396;

after 1815, chap. xx; crews, 158, 322–24; grounds, 157, 262–64, 316–17· 'lays,' 158, 319–22; length of voyage, 323n.; methods, 318–26; prices, 158, 317.
Whampoa, 64, 205.
Wheelwright, William, 269n.
Whipple, Jonathan, 222.
White, William P., 182.
Whitman, Walt, quoted, 250–52, 314.
Whittier, J. G., quoted, 2, 3, 140· 156.
Wild Ranger, 328, 347, 348.
William and Henry, 82.
Williams family, 176n.
Winde, Louis, 248n.
Winged Racer, 345.
Winship, Jonathan, Jr., 57–59, 204, 317.
Winship family, 58–60.
Winsor, Joshua, 145.
Winthrop, John, 11, 12, 16.
Winthrop and Mary, 142.
Witchcraft, 339n.
Woodbury, Peter, 150.
Wood's Hole, 7, 146, 247, 300.
Wonson, Capt. Samuel, 308.

Yachting, 123, 191, 244–49.
Yankee race, 21, 22.

Zanzibar, trade with, 222–23.
Zephyr, brig, 277; ship, 220, 258.
Zerega & Co., 345n.
Zotoff, 220.